Interpreting as Interact

LANGUAGE IN SOCIAL LIFE SERIES

Series Editor: Professor Christopher N. Candlin

Language and power
Norman Fairclough

Discourse and the translator
Basil Hatim and Ian Mason

Planning language, planning inequality
James W. Tollefson

Language and ideology in children's fiction
John Stephens

Linguistics and aphasia
Ruth Lesser and Lesley Milroy

Language and the law
John Gibbons

The cultural politics of English as an international language
Alastair Pennycook

Literacy practices: investigating literacy in social contexts
Mike Baynham

Critical discourse analysis: the critical study of language
Norman Fairclough

Fictions at work: language and social practice in fiction
Mary Talbot

Knowledge machines: language and information in a technological society
Denise E. Murray

Achieving understanding: discourse in intercultural encounters
Katharina Bremer, Celia Roberts, Marie-Thérèse Vasseur,
Margaret Simonot and Peter Broeder

The construction of professional discourse
Britt-Louise Gunnarsson, Per Linell and Bengt Nordberg

Mediated discourse as social interaction
Ron Scollon

Interpreting as interaction
Cecilia Wadensjö

Interpreting as Interaction

Cecilia Wadensjö

Routledge
Taylor & Francis Group

LONDON AND NEW YORK

First published 1998 by Addison Wesley Longman Limited

Published 2013 by Routledge
2 Park Square, Milton Park, Abingdon, Oxon OX14 4RN
711 Third Avenue, New York, NY 10017, USA

Routledge is an imprint of the Taylor & Francis Group, an informa business

Notices
Knowledge and best practice in this field are constantly changing. As new research and experience broaden our understanding, changes in research methods, professional practices, or medical treatment may become necessary.

Practitioners and researchers must always rely on their own experience and knowledge in evaluating and using any information, methods, compounds, or experiments described herein. In using such information or methods they should be mindful of their own safety and the safety of others, including parties for whom they have a professional responsibility.

To the fullest extent of the law, neither the Publisher nor the authors, contributors, or editors, assume any liability for any injury and/or damage to persons or property as a matter of products liability, negligence or otherwise, or from any use or operation of any methods, products, instructions, or ideas contained in the material herein.

ISBN 13: 978-0-582-28910-9 (pbk)

British Library Cataloguing-in-Publication Data

A catalogue record for this book is
available from the British Library

Library of Congress Cataloging-in-Publication Data

Wadensjö, Cecilia, 1954–
      Interpreting in interaction / Cecilia Wadensjö.
         p.   cm. — (Language in social life series)
      Includes bibliographical references (p.) and index.
      ISBN 0-582-28911-4. — ISBN 0-582-28910-6 (pbk.)
      1. Translating and interpreting.   2. Social interaction.
   I. Title.   II. Series.
   P306.W33   1998
   418'.02—dc21   98-20140
                                                        CIP

Set by 35 in 10/12pt Palatino

Contents

Author's Acknowledgements

This book is about dialogue interpreting, an activity which in various ways has formed a major part of my professional life over the past two decades. Working with interpreting, as a freelance interpreter and as a researcher, I have been lucky to meet many colleagues who have generously shared their insights in the complex and fascinating world of communication in face-to-face interaction. Interpreters are used to not being seen, and sometimes pride themselves on 'disappearing' in the background. I would be happy if this book contributes to making them and their profession more visible.

The studies which form the basis of this book were funded by grants from four Swedish grant-giving bodies, which I most gratefully acknowledge: The Bank of Sweden Tercentenary Foundation (89/44), The Swedish Council for Research in the Humanities and Social Sciences (F 402:87), The Swedish Ministry of Labour (DEIFO 34/89) and the Swedish Council for Social Research (93-2002:1A).

The book develops thoughts and perspectives which I first presented in my Ph.D. thesis (Wadensjö 1992). This early stage of the present book-project benefited enormously from constructive and critical comments from various colleagues, in particular Per Linell, my former advisor, and also from Karin Aronsson, Ann-Carita Evaldsson and Roger Säljö. I am lucky to have been able to profit from the generous and creative atmosphere of the Department of Communication Studies at Linköping University also as a post-graduate. Among the guest-researchers, who have helped made Linköping a rich environment for conducting research, I wish to mention in particular Jörg Bergmann, who read my thesis as a faculty opponent, and encouraged me to see new potentials for development, and David Middleton, who gave constructive feedback to the last chapter of the new manuscript.

Over the years, a number of people – interpreters, instructors, students, researchers and others – have helped me clarify the theoretical, methodological and empirical issues which are explored in this book. I highly appreciate the feedback I have received from participants at various forums where parts of the present work were presented, such as training courses for interpreters, seminars and conferences in pragmatics, sociolinguistics, social anthropology, translation and interpreting. Thanks to those who invited me.

Above all, I wish to thank Chris Candlin, General Editor of the *Language in Social Life* Series, whose guidance and suggestions were most helpful in producing the final version of the manuscript. Special thanks to Graham H. Turner for his critical proofreading of my English.

Last but not least, I owe a considerable debt of gratitude to those whose name I, for reasons of confidentiality, cannot mention – the interpreters and the people who occasionally needed their assistance in communicating – those who volunteered for my data collections. For generously accepting my intrusion in your everyday life, and letting me document and analyse your interaction, sincere thanks to you all.

Cecilia Wadensjö
Linköping 1998

Publisher's Acknowledgements

We are indebted to the following for permission to reproduce copyright material:

David Amzallag for the photograph on page 12 *Helen Saunders, Alexander Kölpin and Caroline Cavallo, The Royal Danish Ballet, in Agon. Ballet for Twelve Dancers.*

General Editor's Preface

There is a sense in which interpreting has always been something of a poor relation to translating, seen as a professional activity. In part this impression may be due to the fact that the terms are frequently coupled, as if the former was naturally locked in with the latter, a sub-class of it, if you like, a natural enough a reaction, perhaps, in that one view would have each activity involved in language transfer in the process of recoding messages. Furthermore, although translating has an extraordinarily extensive and well-documented professional history, one which has touched on many fields and in which it has established itself as a valued activity, say in literary studies, in history, in science and technology, or in politics and diplomacy, this cannot be said to anything like the same degree about interpreting, which seems to have been seen more as a craft, and while increasingly now regarded as a professional activity in its own right, with accreditation, standards and extensive training, still has not, at least until relatively recently, been seen as a subject of much study and research.

Perhaps like translation at one stage, there was and is a resistance among interpreting practitioners to theoretical explanation based on empirical study. If this is the case within interpreting, it is no less true that in sister areas of research and scholarship like applied linguistics, where, although translating has always had a strong profile in conferences and publications, interpreting has hardly featured until quite recently. In the professional literature those references to research studies in interpreting one finds are, with very few exceptions, almost inevitably recent, in the last ten years, and for the most part related to policy and practice issues arising in key professions such as medicine, the law, diplomacy, or to matters concerning accreditation and professional development.

Even within interpreting, as this book makes clear, the reflective emphasis has been on conference or courtroom interpreting rather than more broadly on what has come to be termed community interpreting. Furthermore, only some key figures have seen interpreting as much as a social as a linguistic process. It is significant, for example, that the first international conference on this community interpreting theme, in Canada, was only convened a few years ago.

This separation of interpreting from empirical and theoretical research is hard to understand; after all, a moment's reflection would throw up a host of interesting and researchable questions surrounding the interpreting process. Some of these questions, of course, present themselves equally in the field of translating, for example how important matters of equivalence are to be handled, whether translating is to be seen as a monologic or as an interactive process, or what degrees of creative latitude are to be favoured in relation to given texts, or how, in an increasingly intertextual and interdiscursive world, translators should best deal with issues surrounding the generic integrity of texts. Other questions have a particular significance in the interpreting context, for example those concerning psycholinguistic matters of an individual practitioner's cognitive interpreting capacity, especially the relationship between real time processing and levels of accuracy in simultaneous interpreting, or the linguistic question of the variable demands posed on interpreters by different language systems and codes in the wide range of interpreting contexts that one might identify, or, as here in this innovative and original contribution by Cecilia Wadensjö to the *Language in Social Life Series*, the interactive sociolinguistic and intercultural issues surrounding interpreting in the contexts of interpersonal interaction in these community setting.

As an illustration of the research potential, especially of the latter, a few voices from professional interpreters in such settings (drawn from personal experience of two recent studies in Australia) are suggestive for such a research agenda:

- . . . and a lot of interpreters suffer burn-out, especially full-time freelancers. If you get a series of cases such as child molestation and rape, you have to learn how to manage it. . . .
- . . . a lot of us get caught up with this issue of 'the ethics of confidentiality' thinking you cannot talk about it. But you have to get things off your chest. . . .

- ... you aren't given enough information when walking into an assignment and you can't say no at the time if you think the work is above your capacity ...
- ... I had to go to an assignment that lasted about three hours and it was about a sexual assault case. When I finished I had 5 minutes to get to my next appointment which was a case of psychogeriatrics, and in those 5 minutes I had to clear my mind. Now healthcare professionals can quite often understand this but try to say that to a lawyer or a solicitor and you get a different reaction ...

OR

- ... the use of interpreters is often restricted only to diagnostic interviews and that less than one in six clinical staff in public mental health services speak a second language to a clinically useful level. The critical factor in the use of interpreters is not just proficiency and skill but some degree of specialisation in psychiatric interpreting and availability for regular appointments.

From such voices, the linkages to be made between the study of interpreting practices and the analysis of the multiple and often hybrid discourses characteristic of particular social-institutional practices become sharply clear, but not only these. Issues of ethical behaviour, the social psychological analysis of professional and client attitudes, the study of how matters of personal and professional identity impinge on professional practice, in particular the vexed question in community interpreting of advocacy, and the processes by which interpreters manage their duality of client – those accessing services and those providing them – all suggest a research agenda which is inevitably and characteristically interdisciplinary. As Dr Wadensjö makes very clear, it is an agenda which requires not only an interaction between the study of talk as text and talk as activity but also one which to be explanatorily adequate must presume a grounded analysis of such an interaction, one linked closely with an understanding of the historical, structural and social conditions under which the talk is produced and against which it is interpreted on particular occasions.

To explore and undertake such a research agenda, a particular, complex stance on the part of the researcher is needed; one which from a sociological perspective begins from an 'thick' understanding of the communities of practice in which interpreting takes place, and the roles it plays in participants' lives, in its instances, its critical moments and in its crucial sites. To that is needed a grasp of the professional conditions under which interpreters work, the multiplicity of organizations, institutions and participants with which they necessarily relate and by whom they are always variably positioned. Such a stance towards interpreting is not only dialogic, as the author makes clear in her references to Bakhtin, it is also quite characteristically heteroglossic. From a discursive and linguistic perspective, understanding interpreting practices must presume constant intertextuality and interdiscursivity in the target data, as well as (though this is in itself problematic enough) understanding by the analyst of the effects on interpreting practice of local constraining factors on effective interpreting delivery such as the administrative nightmare in many multilingual communities of matching interpreting resources to client interpreting needs. Matching a Bosnian woman refugee with experiences of torture who is the victim of domestic violence at night and who needs hospital attention, with a trained female interpreter is by no means unusual and tends to concentrate the analyst's mind wonderfully when approaching interactional data from such not at all uncommon encounters.

To give another telling example: no explanatory analysis of interpreting practice in the community field of psychiatric services in multilingual communities can afford to underplay the effect on the interpreting process not just of the technical knowledge and the interpersonal sensitivities of the interpreter that are foregrounded by such interactions, but also the pressure on speedy action and resolution exerted by case management processes driven by exigencies of economic rationalism which seek to regularize, standardize and quantify time-on-task for the treatment of the psychiatrically ill. Interpreters are *always* placed in this contested arena between being providers of a service and being agents of authority and control. The discourses of community interpreting, seen from this perspective, are not merely linguistically and discursively complex, their range and realizations are immediately constrained by circumstances of practice, and, beyond the individual instance, illuminative of much more far-reaching issues of the relationships between client and the instrumentalities of society and the state.

What is of the greatest value in this remarkable book is that the author has succeeded in maintaining and displaying this situated understanding of the mediated practice of interpreting. Interpreting, like the roles of interpreters themselves, is classically mediated; the innovation here is to take up the suggestive groundwork of Goffman, in particular, to link it with contemporary interpretations of Bakhtin drawn from the work of critical discourse analysis, and then apply it to interpreting by focusing on key encounters within a particular community of practice. What then emerges is a book in which the data and the accounts – of which the author provides innumerable and telling examples from her own professional experience – are continually theorized not just in terms of a theory of language but as a theory of discourse. Just as meanings are made in the negotiative interplay of interaction, so their accounting here displays how the descriptive analysis of text as product needs to be linked to ethnomethodological interpretation of the processes of discourse, and enriched by the ethnographic narratives of the participants. So much is in itself refreshingly interdisciplinary in applied linguistics; what makes the book usefully disturbing to the largely secular concerns of applied linguists is the introduction of the moral and ethical dimension. If it is the case that the verbatim accounting axiomatically required of interpreters – especially in the legal context – is regularly unattainable on linguistic grounds and in any case at odds with co-constructive models of the communication process, it is also, as the voices above imply, regularly non-guaranteeable on ethical and moral grounds. Not that this is just a matter of whether an interpreter makes some active choice to use her intermediary position and linguistic skills to advocate for either client, however indirectly, it is simply the case, as Dr Wadensjö points out, that the presence of interpreters changes the nature of the institutional practice. Guaranteeing clients' rights in an interpreter-mediated court process, for example, cannot to taken for granted, especially in systems where two languages are admissible and where which language to choose and when is not merely governed by participants' perceived linguistic expertise, or indeed by personal choice, but influenced by lawyers' strategic sense of which language choice will maximize their likelihood of winning the case. Inferring interpreting processes from the textual products of encounters can be deeply misleading. Expertise and partiality cannot simply be read off the transcript.

I make a reference above to the place of interpreting studies in applied linguistics, and the need for the latter to include more interpreting research within its canon. This book makes the case convincingly. It does so not just by making texts and the process of creating texts central, though it does do that, but also by providing a classic example of how the social practices of an institution can be said and shown to be characterized by its discourses, in particular how its disciplinary contestations and struggles are discursively mediated. In doing so it not only evidences the linguistic turn in sociological analysis but also shows how a discourse analysis cannot usefully operate, or even be carried out, without such institutional grounding. *Interpreting as Interaction* thus, like interpreting itself, mediates between two clients, here the client disciplines of the social and the discoursal. It provides the argument many of us seek for a confluence of such disciplines in both the training of sociologists and that of discourse analysts and applied linguists. It does more, however, since it provides a way in which the history of professions, as here that of interpreting, can be documented by reference to an account of their emergent and changing practices, in particular to those characteristically discourse-mediated, and of the changing and alternating attitudes of their members towards such practices.

Insofar as discourse and professional practice are thus mutually influencing, there is yet another, and potentially extremely powerful and compelling, consequence of the approach taken in this book. I refer to the way in which discursive competence can be measured as an index of professional quality. Interpreters, after all, present a *locus classicus*. They are measured by their discursive skill. How this skill is to be defined directly impinges on their worth in their linguistic marketplace. Accuracy, interpersonal sensitivity, intercultural nuance, generic integrity are as much indices of quality for them as their professional knowledge, indeed with interpreters, in practice more so. Interpreters, in short, constitute emblematically what many other professions also reflect. Indeed it would be hard to find examples of such professions which did not in their articles of membership – their core competencies – highlight communicative ability, whether this be in the worlds of medicine, accountancy, the law, engineering and in a host of others. Indeed in some, like engineering, such communicative competence ranks higher than technical skill and in others, like medicine and nursing, the core defining site of the profession is being redefined as the interaction between professional and client. Now, if this competence is indeed meant to be criterial, a marker of quality, then it needs measuring, it needs benchmarking. The only way in which this quality can be evaluated is through a principled and grounded approach to the analysis of discourse in professional public and social practice. For that to be remotely possible, the type of study articulated with such clarity and imagination in Cecilia Wadensjö's book must be replicated widely.

Interpreted from these perspectives, then, *Interpreting as Interaction*, like all books destined to be landmarks, conveys much more than it initially suggests. Not only does it address a hitherto under-researched community of practice, it shows quite convincingly how the linguistic and discursive interconnect with the social and the social psychological, offering evidence of the need for interdisciplinary research and researcher training. More than this, however, it makes the case to the profession itself that its own expertise can be divulged, analysed, displayed and brought into the arena of the principled and consistent determination of professional ability. As has gradually, and sometimes painfully, been the case with translators, the work of interpreters is defined here not as some craft, achievable however only by a select few, who then guild-like mentored their chosen apprentices, but as an approachable and attainable profession, with standards and training pathways informed and mediated though explicit requirements, social, linguistic and discursive. To have set the scene for that sea-change is the real innovation of this sensitive and masterly book.

Professor Christopher N. Candlin
General Editor
City University of Hong Kong

Transcription Conventions

(Simplified after Sacks *et al.* 1978:731–3.)

[	line brackets indicate that people are speaking simultaneously
,	continuing intonation (usually with rising or sustained tone)
.	terminating intonation (usually with a falling tone)
?	questioning intonation (usually with rising tone)
-	sudden cut-off of the current sound
. . .	open-ended intonation (fading out, ambiguous intonation terminal)
e:::	long vowel (example)
(.)	a short silence (micro-pause)
(1)	one second silence
((looks up))	non-verbal feature (example)
boldface	words spoken with emphasis
° °	part of an utterance framed by these is spoken relatively quietly
(xxx)	inaudible passage
italics	author's "back-translation" (Baker 1992) of Swedish and Russian talk
[ ]	text framed by these constitutes a comment to the English translation
→	line in the transcript is relevant to the point being made in the text

ONE

Just an ordinary hearing

The hearing takes place somewhere in the middle of Sweden, at a police station in the town centre, upstairs on the second floor, in a small office in the immigration department. Four people have gathered for a short encounter, a male officer and his visitors, three women. The window behind the officer's back is slightly open. It is an ordinary, mild, Nordic summer day.

One of the women has been called to the office to be interviewed about an application. She is a stranger to the place and to the people. Her problem is to prove herself suitably qualified to receive permission to stay in Sweden. This conversation, she knows, is crucial. Her problem involves correctly estimating what will get her application looked upon favourably, and to what extent she will be able to influence the authorities' decision about her and her family's future life.

As for the officer on the other side of the desk, he is highly experienced in this type of interview. To him it is just another routine case. This has been his workplace for more than ten years, and he knows perfectly well what information his employers regard as being relevant to obtain from an applicant. His job is to write a report, on the basis of which they will make their decision. He follows a prepared questionnaire, and he knows roughly on what grounds applications are usually refused or approved. His problem is to judge whether or not the person providing the information is trustworthy. Another problem is to give a reliable impression of himself, as a just civil servant of a democratic country. At the point where we enter the encounter, he is making inquiries about the applicant's citizenship:

"And what do you think yourself? You are Greek, I know, you said that you are Greek, but it is one thing to consider . . . according to

1

nationality and another thing to consider yourself to be a citizen of
a certain state, I have in mind – meaning a state"

"I think that I am . . . a citizen of the Soviet Union. because. I was
born there and I have been living there and there are many
nationalities living in the Soviet Union."

"No no she answered that she is a citizen of the USSR."

"And even if I have been living all my life in the Soviet Union,
anyhow I am counted as a Greek and not as a Russian. And in the
passport- in the passport it also says that I am Greek- of Greek
nationality."

"And can you show me where?"

"No not in this one. This is an international passport and I had in
mind a national one . . ."

What appears above is a written English translation of utterances
which were originally voiced in Swedish and Russian. In the real
communication situation the police officer and the applicant were
assisted by an interpreter, translating what they said into their respective languages. Quoted above is the interpreter's speech alone.
Extracted in this way, one of her utterances – *No no she answered
that she is a citizen of the USSR* – seems to be somewhat incongruous
with the rest of the sequence. Who is the "she" referred to? Who is
addressed? On whose behalf?

As it appears, the interpreter here comes in with an initiative
of her own. Evidently, more is going on in the entire interaction
than is reflected in the transcription of her utterances, even if these
indeed do reflect what has been said by the others. It looks as if the
interpreter takes on responsibility for some kind of interactional
problem. What is she doing? Just translating? Interpreting? Mediating? Counteracting misunderstanding? Advocating?

There were four people present in the office on that occasion. I
was the third woman in the room, observing the interview and documenting it on tape. Each of us had different goals in the encounter,
vis-à-vis each other and in relation to the meeting itself, but we all
– the police officer, the applicant, the interpreter and the researcher-
observer – had one thing in common. We all understood and accepted
the conversation as an interpreted one.

This book is about interpreter-mediated conversation as a mode
of communication, about interpreters and their responsibilities, about
what they do, what they think they should do and what others expect
them to do in face-to-face, institutional encounters.

Following a descriptive approach to studies of interpreting, I will take the acting subjects' definition of the situation. Given that people understand the communicative activity they are involved in to be an 'interpreter-mediated encounter' – how do they interact, as interpreters and as primary interlocutors respectively? The book is concerned with what goes on between the participants of this kind of encounter, rather than what goes on between the ears of the interpreters. Communicative conventions are normally shaped in and by monolingual interaction. How does the interpreter-mediated mode of communication affect these conventions? How is feared or suspected miscommunication handled? How, in interpreter-mediated encounters, is responsibility for the substance and the progression of interaction distributed between interlocutors? How can interpreters mark distinction between saying what others mean, on the one hand, and, on the other hand, talking on their own behalf?

1. THE THEMES OF THIS BOOK

The approach in this work could be defined overall as a descriptive one. I will avoid giving oversimplified 'directions for interpreting' and problematize rather than confirm conventional normative thinking. The book aims at providing a set of analytical tools, food for thought and fuel for discussions. The main method is detailed analysis of discourse, documented in authentic encounters between people not able or willing to communicate in a common language. Through analysis of real-life situations I have gained knowledge about the dynamics of interpreter-mediated encounters.

The assistance of interpreters is a usual way to overcome language barriers in the everyday routines of many public institutions. Interpreter-mediated interaction, however, puts specific demands on those interacting; on interpreters, officials and lay people alike. A person involved in this, at one level of meaning, non-standard way of communicating, may experience it as problematic. The directness and transparency of ordinary talk is, by necessity, lacking. Making the dynamics of interpreter-mediated interaction more transparent, this book suggests ways to prepare for work in this mode, for interpreters and for actors dependent on interpreters' assistance.

The aim of this book is also to develop a theoretical model of interpreter-mediated interaction shaped on the relevant practice. Of course, *theoretical models* are substantially different from *actual cases*. A theory of this complex and varying activity applies to cases in general. Actual cases are unique. The general case exists like an idea, while actual cases take place in reality, and each demands unique efforts from their participants, including the interpreter.

Nevertheless, if interpreting is to be acknowledged as a profession also when it occurs outside of international conferences, i.e. in the everyday life of public institutions and organisations, and if those of us who work as interpreters in legal, health, social service and other institutional face-to-face encounters are to gain the confidence and respect of the public, we need to have well-founded and shared ideas about what interpreting in these settings is all about, what interpreters are good for, and about preferred standards to apply in various situations.

1.1 Description before prescription

After reading the introductory vignette, many readers' first reflections might well focus on whether or not the interpreter correctly translated the officer's and the applicant's original utterances (and also, perhaps, whether they were subsequently correctly translated into English). My written quotations of spontaneous speech may indeed *look* a bit odd to a reader's eye. Nevertheless, my informed guess is that the interlocutors themselves did not reflect a lot on correctness in translation – at least, not while they were talking. They were much too occupied with making sense of what they *heard*, and with immediately responding to it.

Traditionally, studies on translation and interpretation are normative in character, either providing directives for correct translation, or building upon (implicit or explicit) ideas of correct language use. Authors' perception of correctness in language use sometimes takes written language standards for granted even if the use of written texts generally differs rather substantially from language use in spontaneous spoken interaction.

Being myself an interpreter, I have felt a lack of theoretical ground for my work in this profession, and this became an important part of the impetus for this book. Through my readings, I have found studies of translation and interpretation to cover three main areas of interest. Many works investigate and evaluate the effectiveness of *didactic strategies* and models for translator and interpreter training.

The normative (prescribing) orientation is often strong, since the adequacy and accuracy of teachers' and students' performances are of central interest. Other authors are primarily concerned with *the quality* (adequacy, correctness etc.) *of translators' and interpreters' work*. Investigations and evaluations are performed through comparisons between original source language texts and translated target language texts. If emphasis is put on the original authors and their intentions the normative interest may focus on whether or not, or to what extent, translations and interpretations succeed or fail in *fulfilling these intentions*. A communicative perspective, in contrast, would mean that imagined readers or listeners and their needs and expectations are brought more into focus. These kinds of studies, promoted in modern translation theory (e.g. Toury 1995) are more concerned with how translations respond to the expectations and *needs of a target culture*.

A third body of literature focuses on the *cognitive processes* involved in translating and interpreting; on what goes on in the minds of translators and interpreters. This approach has been applied particularly to studies of simultaneous interpreting. Scientific investigations concern the performing interpreters' cognitive skills, and the cognitive constraints involved in their working process. Theoretically this approach has close links to psycholinguistics, which often results in the application of a deductive, experimental or quasi-experimental research design. Studies with this orientation may also be normative, involving evaluations of individuals' success or failure in correctly (within certain time-limits etc.) fulfilling given tasks.

This book takes a fourth stance and explores the social order of real-life interpreter-mediated conversations. It tries to detect what people present in these take as the normal, adequate, correct etc. way to act, given the current situation. For whom, when and why are what norms of language use valid? For instance, what communicative conventions are involved when the interpreter in the example above, talking on behalf of another person, suddenly switches from 'I' to an emphasised 'she'?

1.2 Interpreting versus advocacy

In her textbook on translation, Baker (1992) states that "as translators, we are primarily concerned with communicating the overall meaning of a stretch of language" (1992:10). For pedagogical reasons she then follows a bottom-up approach rather that a top-down one, taking words and phrases as starting points when defining units that would carry this "meaning". This choice is somewhat at odds with Baker's own conviction and with current reasoning in linguistics and translation studies. Hatim and Mason (1990) and several others suggest a top-down model, starting analyses of translation problems and strategies from text-type, and from the notion of texts as situated in contexts of culture.

It may be true, as Baker argues, that the bottom-up model is much easier to understand for people who have little training in linguistics (Baker 1992:6). It has a disadvantage though, which in the exploration of interpreter-mediated dialogue must be seen as a major drawback. It may contribute to cementing the position that words in and of themselves carry meaning, a meaning that can be decoded and subsequently re-coded into words belonging to another language.

I have participated in debates focusing on interpreters' rights and obligations where a simplified version of this position is taken as an argument against interpreters' advocacy. This 'can be decoded and re-coded' is, it seems, easily transformed into a 'shall'. In line with this claim, two roles are frequently juxtaposed – 'translator' versus 'mediator', or (as for instance in the public service debate in Australia, United Kingdom and Canada) *interpreting versus advocacy*. 'Advocacy' in this context stands for actively supporting, defending and pleading for one of the parties – the client – while 'interpreting' would mean to avoid any such activity.

This juxtaposition also seems to play a certain role for researchers exploring interpreter-mediated discourse data. For example, Knapp-Potthoff and Knapp (1986) observe a tendency to be a 'true third party', rather than a 'mere medium of transmission', among people acting as interpreters, partly as an outcome of these persons' lack of professionalism. One should note, however, that 'professional interpreting' in their terminology seems to stand for simultaneous conference interpreting, that is interpreting performed by people who are enclosed separately in a booth, effectively removed from face-to-face interaction (Knapp-Potthoff and Knapp 1986:153).

In my view this counter positioning, requiring a strong division between 'translation' and 'mediation' is partly an academic construct, intimately tied to conventional preconceptions of language, mind and communication. Regarding 'interpreter-mediated interaction' as a social phenomenon and the basic unit of investigation I must see 'interpreting' as consisting of both aspects. In theory, translating and mediating may be distinguishable activities, but in practice they are intimately intertwined.

Since I am dealing with spoken interaction, the starting point is not text-types but *speech genres*, situated in their socio-cultural contexts. This concept is borrowed from the Russian language philosopher Mikhail M. Bakhtin (Russian original 1979, translation in English 1986), whose work is an essential source of inspiration for this book. Following his ideas I will problematize the notion of 'word' and 'meaning'. Again I will take the perspective of the acting subjects – the individuals whose interaction I am analysing – and try to find out what meaning *they* attribute to particular words; how phrases and stretches of talk make sense to different actors in situated events. This approach allows me to go beyond the discussion of 'translation' versus 'mediation', to explore instead the *dynamic inter-activity* of interpreter-mediated conversation. I take for granted that individuals, including interpreters, are subjects who make sense in their own subjective ways. Starting from an interactionistic perspective, 'language' or 'languages' as systems of linguistic items are partly of analytical interest, but the focus is on the dynamic processes of individuals' *language use*.

To recast Baker's (1992:10) statement of my aims, applying the alternative point of departure: As interpreters working in face-to-face interaction we are primarily concerned with making sense of what others say, and communicating this in other words in order to enable a conversation between people who cannot or do not wish to speak in a common language.

1.3 The channel metaphor

The present work suggests a new direction for research on interpretation based on a *dialogic*, rather than a *monologic* view on language and language use, following the works of Bakhtin (1979/1986a), Voloshinov (1930/1986) and some of their supporters (Holquist 1990, Wertsch 1991).

The ordinary image of the interpreter is very much influenced by a 'transfer' model of communication. This way of thinking of human interaction, as a *unidirectional process of transfer* from one person to another, is what the philosopher Reddy (1979) called *the conduit model* of communication.

The *normative role* of interpreter, to use a term from Goffman (1961) – that is, what interpreters in principle think they are doing or ought to be doing when they do a good job – is deeply influenced by the conduit model of communication. Metaphors used to describe the function of interpreters are quite revealing on this point. Take, for instance, 'the telephone', 'the echo machine' or 'the mouthpiece' – all instruments conveying information without themselves affecting this information except in a merely technical sense. Interpreters are thought of, and think of themselves as conveyers of others' words and utterances. The interpreter as channel through which prepared messages go back and forth is a model that is perfectly in line with the norm of non-involvement. Roy (1989) discussed this at length in her sociolinguistic analysis of a sign language interpreted encounter.

The conduit model is *monological*. This means that language use is regarded from the perspective of the speaker. The meaning of words and utterances are seen as resulting from the *speaker's intentions or strategies* alone, while co-present people are seen as recipients of the units of information prepared by the speaker. It is as if, while creating meaning, the individual speaker is thought away from her interactional context and thought into *a social vacuum*. The monological view of language and language use links at one point with lexicographic theory, conceptualizing languages in terms of morphemes, words, sentences and other textual structures perceived of as 'carrying' certain meanings. Standardized (and standardizing) grammars and lexica provide a strong support to this model of thought.

The *dialogical* model, in contrast, implies that the meaning conveyed in and by talk is partly a joint product. Sense is made in and by a common activity. Communication, as well as mis-communication, presupposes a certain reciprocity between the people involved. The dialogical model provides a frame for explorations of the multi-directional and multi-layered processes of interaction. It allows me to investigate the *multiple functions of words and utterances in layers of social contexts* (cf. Chapter 2 on the difference between monologism and dialogism).

In research on interpreting, the monological, essentially textual model is frequently used as a resource. People's talk (as well as the interpreter's job) is explored as *text*, or *production of texts*, in the one or the other language. Investigations normally reveal facts about the relationship between a given 'text' and established standards in a given, linguistically and grammatically defined language.

An alternative is to see talk as *activity*, or rather activities, other than text production. This is an essentially different point of departure, which links to sociolinguistics and social psychology. However the one approach does not exclude the other. They correspond to different levels of abstraction.

'Talk as text' and 'talk as activity' are both shorthand for two models of thinking about discourse which I have found existing in parallel in both theory and practice of interpreting. When interpreters and people in general talk about interpreting, they tend to conceive of this as individuals' production of text. When people engage in interpreter-mediated interaction, however, they may be seen – and see themselves – as doing all kinds of things, such as interviewing, joking, arguing, complying, and so forth. This applies to interpreters and to other participants alike. Yet the idea of text-production may still be present. Interpreters may perceive themselves as producers of text(s), since they constantly have to decontextualize others' utterances to provide second versions of them. Furthermore, people in legal settings may understand interpreters as text-producers, since this is what most legal systems reduce them to.

Interpreters constantly use the 'textual' model of thinking, and it is a helpful tool in the process of interpreting. At times, however, it can prevent them from understanding the situation they take part in. The textual view is useful in the research process for structuring empirical data. By necessity, when transcribing discourse data, transforming tape-recorded voices into written words and utterances, I apply a textual view on language. Analysing the dynamics of the interaction represented by these words and utterances, however, I have found the 'talk-as-text' model insufficient, and, if used alone, partly misleading. Looking at talk also as social interaction, as activities other than text-production, allows for a more thorough exploration of interpreter-mediated communication.

1.4 Multilingualism as normality

A frequent image of the interpreter is that of a "necessary evil", to quote the famous English-French conference interpreter Jean Herbert (1952:4). In my view, this metaphor reflects an underlying mistrust and fear of the alien and the deviant. The monolingual situation is taken as the normal case by which the 'abnormal', bilingual case is measured. This view on normality, I would argue, is also the basic logic behind studies of interpreting concentrating on omissions and distortions, asking questions such as: What gets lost? and What gets added? Seen from another perspective, though, the interpreter-mediated encounter implies its own conditions and organizational principles – conditions which are 'normal' or 'natural' *for this kind of talk*. An alternative way to explore it is therefore to ask: What is specific about this mode of communication?

It is practically impossible to disregard the long historical tradition depicting the interpreter as a remedy to an abnormal case. The idea is linked to the dreams of the Enlightenment philosophers (Leibniz, Descartes) about the possibility of unifying the nations and the opposing religious camps in Europe of their time with the help of a common, logic, universal language. It also has connections to nationalistic thinking about one nation meaning one language (and two languages meaning one too many). Monolingualism has indeed been seen as the normal case, at least in most parts of the Western world. It implies, on the one hand, that each language is perceived as a closed entity. On the other hand, an individual is seen as normally identifying with only one of these; one specific 'native' language. And yet simple observation reveals the widespread global phenomenon of individuals speaking more than one language, and/or fundamentally different varieties of the 'same' language. Moreover, migrants, tourists, soldiers, businesspeople and other travellers constantly bring their language(s) into contact with others. The logical conclusion would be that the multilingual society needs to be investigated in its own right.

1.5 A communicative *pas de trois*

Focusing on the mediating function of interpreters I turned to Sociology for inspiration. The German sociologist Georg Simmel, active around the turn of last century, discusses in one of his essays how the number of people in groups and organizations influences the social interaction that takes place in them (Simmel 1964:118ff.).[1] Among other things, he compares the unit of two people (for instance a married couple) and the unit of three (for instance the family with one child). The existence of a dyad as a unit of two, he argues, is based directly on the existence of the individuals involved, while a constellation of three or more persons has an existence as a group even when one person is missing. The individual may feel the group to be present and acting also in his absence. Contrasting the dyad and the triad, Simmel further states that "among three elements, each one operates as an intermediary between the other two". And the twofold function of a mediating person is to unite and to separate (Simmel 1964:135).

Simmel's work was translated into English during his own lifetime, at the beginning of the twentieth century, which made it influential in the development of Anglo-American sociology. His influence can be traced also in the social psychology of Erving Goffman, an author whose work this book draws on quite substantially. Simmel's sociology had a great impact on the intellectual climate at the University of Chicago during Goffman's apprenticeship there between 1945 and 1954.

For instance, Goffman more than once stresses the reciprocal impact of interactional behaviour on the individual actors of a group and on the group as a whole. He applies this idea both to more or less stable social groupings and to situated encounters, where the constancy of the group is of secondary interest, and the focus instead is set on face-to-face interaction as a system of activity.

Goffman's work has in turn had a great impact within diverse, and sometimes overlapping, scientific traditions, such as linguistic anthropology, sociology of language and discourse analysis. For instance, Goffman (1981) sees as a weakness that analysis of authentic discourse is exercised mainly on dyads. Authors such as Duranti (1986), Haviland (1986), Goodwin and Goodwin (1992) have argued against this general tendency and explored empirical data collected in encounters where the conversational exchange involves more than two persons (cf. also Duranti and Goodwin's seminal introduction to their edited book *Rethinking Context* from 1992). Moreover, they point out that conceptual tools for analysis which derive from studies based on conversations between two cannot automatically be applied to studies of triads or larger groups of people.

Indeed, there is reason to believe that interactions involving three or more individuals have a complexity which is not comparable to interaction in dyads. The interpreter-mediated conversation is a special case. It is obvious that the communicative activities involved in this kind of encounter are in some senses dyadic, in other respects triadic, and the active subjects may fluctuate in their attitudes concerning which of these constellations takes priority.

In an interpreter-mediated conversation, the lack of communicative contact between two parties not talking each other's language is

Helen Saunders, Alexander Kölpin and Caroline Cavallo,
The Royal Danish Ballet, in Agon. Ballet for Twelve Dancers.
(Photograph copyright: David Amzallag)

effectively remedied thanks to the interpreter. Yet while their indirect relationship is undoubtedly and considerably *strengthened,* a
potential direct connection between the primary interlocutors may
simultaneously be *disturbed.* My aim is to explore how the interpreter-
mediated conversation is qualitatively *different* from encounters where
the participants communicate directly.

Comparing people taking part in a conversation with dancers,
coordinating their turns on the floor, the interpreter-mediated encounter can be seen as a special kind of dance for two with an additional
third person; a communicative *pas de trois.*

1.6 Interpreters in society – service and control

Traditionally, the training of interpreters is associated with the world
of diplomacy and international conferences. In modern society, however, interpreters are seen in many other settings, such as courts,
hospitals, police-stations, social welfare centres and other public institutions. The verbal exchange taking place is sometimes impossible

without the assistance of people serving as interpreters. These could be, for instance, the participating laypeople's more-or-less bilingual friends or children, or whoever happens to be available at the institutions in question. When communicative problems of this kind become more frequent than public institutions can handle on an *ad hoc* basis, societies tend to start building up structures for providing interpreters to work in public settings.

In recent years, numerous attempts have been made in many countries, at both local and state authority levels, to set up administrative networks, and to build training programmes for interpreters working within social service, legal, health and mental health institutions. A practical need for interpreter assistance, and the necessity of their formal training is often acknowledged. Sometimes this is followed by official legislation or at least by establishing professional rules for interpreting and/or use of interpreters in these settings.

For instance, according to a Swedish law, in force since 1975, persons who do not understand or speak Swedish well enough have the right to an interpreter during court trials and in other encounters with the public. The law states that an interpreter should be called upon if needed, and responsibility for calling in an interpreter lies with the institutions. The law is meant to protect the rights of the non-Swedish-speaking party (Chapter 5, Section 6 of the Code of Judicial Procedure, *rättegångsbalken,* and Section 50 of the Administrative Procedures Act, *förvaltningsprocesslagen).*

In practice, of course, representatives of the majority – that is to say, court officials, the police, people working within social service organizations etc. – are most of the time no less dependent on the assistance of interpreters than are their clients and patients. They need interpreters to be able to carry out their duties. Seen from this perspective, the law thus also protects the social and legal system itself. When interpreters give voice to others and listen on others' behalf they provide a certain service, and simultaneously they also fill a function in the institutional system of control, by seeing to it that interaction continues, that a certain agenda is kept; that the professional party may inform and the layperson gets informed.

Interpreters can be perceived as actors within the *service system* of the society, and at the same time within the public *system of control.* Civil rights and civil responsibilities are two sides of the same coin. This duality in the role of interpreter is made manifest in interpreters' translating and coordinating of others' interaction. What manifests as social order at the micro level, in forms of talk between people involved in face-to-face encounters, reflects a social structure that is present also at the macro level, in the institution, and possibly in the society at large. All the more important then to raise questions about the implications of theoretical insights for practice, and concerning the impact of empirical findings on theory.

Drawing on a growing body of literature within the sociology of language, ethnomethodology, discourse analysis and studies of institutional, interethnic communication, this book describes and explores interpreter-mediated talk as a pervasive activity in modern society, where multilingualism is the norm rather than the exception. Exploring discourse data collected in authentic medical and legal encounters I follow a path established by authors such as Anderson (1976), Harris (1981) and Berk-Seligson (1990), who all focus on interpreting as a matter of both linguistic and social competence.

I will investigate social conventions of language use tied to particular physical surroundings, to constellations of people, to the respective individuals' competence, expectations and goals. In my view, the interpreter's task must be understood as partly dependent on these factors. The individuals whom they assist and these people's relationships with one another form an essential part of the interpreter's working conditions.

2. HOW THIS BOOK IS ORGANIZED

Practically all interpreters that I have met, including those involved in the present study, have their more-or-less euphoric stories about remarkably successful jobs. Less flattering cases have also been mentioned to me in confidence. These are occasions which have raised feelings of awkwardness and guilt. Talking about such instances undoubtedly helps interpreters to build up a professional attitude and to prepare for new answers to the constantly-repeated question: 'How am I to interpret correctly?' All interpreters with some experience could contribute to a list of interesting cases where their professional skill and competence was put to the test. However, if I was to describe and explore only such instances, I would run the risk of taking in too much all at once and losing sight of the fundamental characteristics and mechanisms of 'ordinary', more commonplace situations. The aim of the present book is to approach interpreting from the opposite direction, to problematize the seemingly unproblematic. For instance, it draws upon investigations of mono-lingual discourse carried out by Gumperz and his associates (1982a, b), Erickson and Schultz (1982) and many others, which convincingly describe how laypeople on the one hand, and representatives of various public institutions on the other, who are involved in the same situation and are speaking the same language, may be guided differently by verbal and non-verbal contextualization cues because of diverse linguistic and socio-cultural backgrounds.

With few exceptions, the existing research on interpreting investigates the work of conference interpreters, and particularly those performing in the simultaneous mode. In recent years, court interpreting attracts a growing number of scholars. But interpreting in face-to-face encounters is still an undertheorized field of research. It is a social phenomenon on the whole not much described in the literature. The idea is here to *describe*, rather than *prescribe*, which, as mentioned above, traditionally has been the tendency in much literature on translation and interpretation. Hopefully this book will inspire the collection and exploration of discourse data from a range of different situations, involving diverse constellations of people, various institutional settings and various combinations of languages.

The following will be my main points of departure:

- Interpreters are seen as both translators and mediators,
- Interpreters' and others' contributions in conversation are regarded both as individual actions and as communicative 'inter-actions',
- The interpreter-mediated encounter is seen as a special case of communication, comprising organizational standards from both dyadic and triadic interaction.

In short, this book promotes face-to-face interpreting as a field of research in its own right, and suggests directing investigations within this field on *the dynamics of interpreter-mediated encounters*. In line with current thinking within translation studies (e.g. Snell-Hornby 1988, Toury 1995) it emphasizes the interdisciplinary potential of interpretation studies. Being a hybrid field of study, it has no strong disciplinary fences to protect, which I see as an advantage. Another main aim of this book is that researchers within various scientific traditions looking into *the multiple functions of talk in social interaction* should 'discover' a particular kind of three-party or multi-party communication that can serve as a naturally occurring 'experimental field'.

2.1 Grounding theories

In a literate society, where almost all spheres of life are invaded by texts, it is perhaps not surprising that the notion of 'language' is often equated with the concept of 'text'. In everyday life, and also in linguistics and other sciences the text-metaphor colours our pre-conception of speech (cf. e.g. Linell 1988, Säljö 1988). The point of Chapter 2, following this introduction, is to account for some main theoretical and analytical implications of viewing talk on the one hand as *text* (or text-production), and, on the other hand, as *activity* (other than text-production). This means that the chapter will take a brief look at theories of language use including translation and interpretation, where the opposition between these approaches can be found reflected. Chapter 2 will point out differences between a *monologic* and a *dialogic* view of language and mind, and connect this to Bakhtin's language philosophy. The chapter will also discuss the relevance of the dialogic perspective when investigating the dynamics of interpreter-mediated conversation.

Chapter 3 describes community interpreting in relation to other types of interpreting and as a phenomenon in modern society. Some general information is given on the labour market for interpreters working in health-care, legal and social service settings. One section provides a few examples of pioneering efforts made – in various countries – to professionalize and institutionalize the role of interpreter working in public institutions. Chapter 3 also includes a section on Codes of Conduct for interpreters and guides to best practice for officials working with interpreters.

Chapter 4 explores concepts such as *intermediary, gatekeeper,* and *non-person,* found in the literature within sociology and social anthropology, and their possible relevance to studies concerned with interpreting in face-to-face interaction. It also reviews recent empirical studies of interpreting in face-to-face situations, mostly from legal settings.

Chapter 5 discusses practical and theoretical considerations for research on interpreter-mediated discourse data.

The analytical framework presented draws on the social psychology of Erving Goffman. Following a dialogic view of language and mind (cf. Chapter 2), contributions to discourse (interpreters' and others') are explored as *answers*, partly shaped by the socially and culturally defined roles performed in the situations where they appear. The unit of basic interest is not the individual, but the group of people. Chapter 5 explores Goffman's concepts of role. In his model, what is expressed in official rules, codes and ideas of conduct (*normative role*) is contrasted against how people actually perform while enacting a certain role (*typical role*) (Goffman 1961). 'Normative role' defines the difference between good and bad performance, for instance, between good and bad interpreting. 'Typical role' is to define the limits of a certain role, for instance, between 'interpreter' and 'not interpreter'.

In addition, the chapter outlines Goffman's model of *participation framework* (Goffman 1981). Alternative development of this model is discussed, and an expanded model is suggested, which provides a major tool for the explorations of interactional dynamics carried out in later chapters (especially Chapter 7).

Chapter 5 further discusses methods for data-collection and outlines the method applied in the present work. This includes transcription of authentic speech as analytical method.

The transcriptions subsequently analysed in the empirical chapters involve Russian and Swedish. The choice of these languages is governed first and foremost by my own linguistic competence. This does not exclude, however, that most of the resulting descriptions and findings are, to all appearances, valid for interpreter-mediated interaction involving all kinds of language combinations.

In the analyses, English is utilized as a third language, the main function of which is to guarantee the reader's access to examples. It also serves in part as the researcher's analytic device. Translation forced me to treat Swedish – my first language – and Russian – my second language – as equally foreign. This often functioned as an eye-opener, and helped me put question marks around phenomena that I would otherwise have taken for granted.

2.2 Exploring authentic, non-experimental data

Chapter 6 looks at interpreter-mediated discourse mainly from a *textual* point of view. Utterances voiced by the interlocutors are analysed as one would texts. These are categorized basically as *originals*, i.e. contributions provided by primary interlocutors, and *interpreters' utterances*. The latter are, in turn, regarded, on the one hand, from the point of view of translation, and then distinguished as more or less 'close' or 'divergent' *renditions*. On the other hand, the interpreters' utterances are seen from the point of view of their coordinating function and accordingly classified as more-or-less implicitly or explicitly *coordinating moves*.

Investigations of the relationship between these lead to two complementary and mutually compatible typologies. These correspond to the two intertwined functions interpreters typically carry in interaction, that of *translating* and that of *coordinating* others' talk. In different degrees, one or other of these aspects will come to the fore in interpreters' words and actions.

Chapter 7 explores the interpreter-mediated conversation as a *situated activity*; more precisely, as an instance of a particular kind of three-party interaction. Focusing on talk as activity, it investigates the communicative dynamics and the organization of the joint enterprise – conversation.

The chapter investigates how the interpreter's and the primary parties' words and deeds condition one another, for instance, in terms of how people act from varying stances as participants; how individuals take responsibility for the substance and the progression of talk; how interlocutors in interaction display various modes of speaking and listening, thereby various *participation status* (Goffman 1981). The chapter provides a tentative systematization of different circumstances conditioning the organization of talk in interpreter-mediated interaction. These may be either of a *global* character, i.e. connected to various types of situations (e.g. the police interrogation or the child care interview) or of a more *local* nature, negotiated on a turn-by-turn level.

Interpreters are constantly concerned with norms for good interpreting. This is quite natural for several reasons, one being that their task as it is officially formulated expects them to interpret to the best of their abilities. Another reason is linked to the question which naturally follows when one starts to explore how interpreter-mediated interaction is organized, namely how the responsibility for this organization is distributed and handled. This is, in turn, strongly linked to the goal in any conversation: the achievement, at least at some level, of shared understanding. For interpreters on duty, it is a self-evident goal to promote a certain shared understanding between the primary parties.

Interaction can continue and be developed, however, even when people differ fundamentally in their opinion of what it is all about. In one sense, social interaction is driven by lack of shared understanding. Such a lack can also exist without being detected, let alone counteracted, while interaction is going on. Chapter 8 focuses on *mis-communication events* (Linell 1995), i.e. instances where one or more interlocutors appear to have sensed mis-understanding, and then taken measures to remedy it. It investigates the role and responsibility of interpreters for the primary parties' achieving shared and mutual understanding.

Intimately tied to this issue is the question of how interpreters make themselves accountable as trustworthy professionals. When a primary interlocutor experiences being misunderstood, a shadow may easily fall on the person in the middle. Before suspecting the other party of talking nonsense, or oneself of being unclear, many would rather suspect the interpreter of getting things wrong.

In Chapter 9 the theme of responsibility continues with questions exploring the interpreter's performance as an art of reporting others' words. What do interpreters mean when they say what others mean to say? How do interpreters mark distinction between their own and others' responsibility for the words and utterances they voice? Chapter 9 problematizes the notion of *neutrality*, for instance, by investigating the *commenting aspect* inherent in the reporting of others' speech (Voloshinov 1930). The chapter works with a tentative model of how interpreters relate to others' talk. Two basic approaches to this activity are distinguished, *relaying by displaying* at the one extreme, and, at the other, *relaying by replaying*. The first stands for interpreters' *presenting* the other's words and simultaneously emphasizing personal non-involvement in what they voice, whereas the second would apply to instances in which interpreters strive at *re-presenting* the whole appearance of another person's utterance.

2.3 Drawing conclusions

Chapter 10 sums up the main theoretical and practical implications of dialogism and monologism in the study of interpreting in face-to-face interaction. The picture of the responsibility involved in interpreting, as it is formed by the analyses in the empirical chapters, should provide a frame for further discussions on teaching and training of interpreters and practitioners, nurses, officers and others who are dependent on their assistance.

Interpreters could be perceived as *non-persons*. The concept is borrowed from an essay by Goffman from 1959 (Goffman 1990). As 'non-persons', they enjoy certain unique rights in a conversation. The involvement of interpreters is comparable with the role of photographers. When present at a conversation, they participate in it on their own conditions. They may be included and excluded; include or exclude themselves. Becoming the subject of scientific and professional discussions, the non-person position of interpreters may be changed, for better or worse.

A considerable number of people – immigrants and refugees, and representatives of legal and other societal institutions – are dependent on the services of interpreters. A third issue to be raised concerns interpreters' potential roles as mediators promoting on the one hand, and inhibiting on the other hand, communicative contact between people, some of whom count as members of a majority, while others – for various reasons – stand forth as members of minorities. In practice, people may share membership of both these groups. For instance, some of the Swedish-speaking experts in my examples at one point immigrated to Sweden from other countries, or their parents did, or grandparents. . . .

Chapter 10 also includes some suggestions for future research, in which institutional interpreter-mediated face-to-face interaction could be utilized as an empirical field. A discussion is initiated concerning the definition of key criteria as regards interpreters' professionalism.

NOTE

1. Published in English translation in 1902 in two issues (VIII, No. 1, 1–46, July 1902 and No. 2, 158–196, September 1902) of *The American Journal of Sociology*.

TWO

Talk as text and talk as activity

If I tell you that it is sometimes correct to interpret *da,* 'yes' in Russian, as *nej,* 'no' in Swedish, some of you may think I am joking, talking Orwellian Newspeak, or simply have gone too far into relativistic theories of meaning. Nevertheless, I once, in a case of minor theft, at the beginning of the court proceedings when the judge asked for the suspect's view of the charges against him, and he answered with a simple *da* ('yes'), interpreted this as: *nej* ('no'). I did not think then that I made a mistake, and I have not changed my mind. I will soon explain why. Let me first just mention that this example serves to introduce and illustrate the complementarity of two diametrically different approaches to interpreting – *talk* represented *as text* and *talk* seen *as activity.* The idea is to demonstrate that this theoretical distinction is useful in the exploration of interpreter-mediated discourse.

1. OPPOSING AND INTERDEPENDENT VIEWS

Both in practice, working as interpreters, and when theorizing about interpreting, we tend to apply two general models of talk existing in parallel, and often without making a clear distinction between them. 'Talk as text' and 'talk as activity' are in one sense diametrically opposing conceptualizations, founded as they are in diverse theoretical frameworks. From another point of view they are interdependent. The present section will outline some general ideas about how they can complement one another in practice and in theory.

'Talk as text', in my understanding, connects to a monological view of language and mind, while 'talk as activity' associates with dialogism. At the end of this chapter I will expound further on the difference between monologism and dialogism, following the language philosophy of Mikhail M. Bakhtin and a few of his followers. Before this I will make a short excursion into the field of Translation studies, where the dominant approach has been the textual one.

1.1 Text production vs. situated sense-making

When working with transcriptions of authentic talk, in the process of documentation and systematization, I freeze parts of the data in textual structures. I am then bound to organize and see the interpreter-mediated discourse as a text and to treat its constituents (semantic, phonetic, turn-constructional) in isolation. Acknowledging at the same time the artificiality of this view of language use, I can use the text as a tool for exploring, from the authentic participants' point of view, issues of semantics, phonetics, turn-taking, and so forth. When raising questions about the socio-cultural significance of activities represented by a text, about the actors' situated organization of talk, I look upon talk as activity, as consisting of a range of activities at different levels. This perspective also gives me a chance to reflect upon the transcribing of tape-recorded talk, if you wish, the transcriber's 'text production' (cf. Chapter 5:2.3).

An outline of 'talk-as-text' and 'talk-as-activity' may be phrased in the following way:

Talk as text – text production and text processing

- Language use is explored as speakers' productions of different types of text(s).
- The functions of verbal actions are understood as being tied to meanings inherent in the respective languages in which the texts are produced (vocabulary, syntax, prosodic patterns, etc.).
- Utterances are viewed as units of meaning that consist of smaller units of meaning such as words and morphemes; each of them is equally meaningful.

Talk as activity – interaction and situated sense making

- Language use is explored as an (inter)activity occurring simultaneously with other kinds of human activity.
- The functions of verbal actions are understood as being tied to the actors' understanding of these actions in the situation

at hand. The actors' view, in turn, depends on their expectations and communicative projects.
– Utterances are viewed as activities that are part of situated interactions, and make sense to those involved, depending on the type of situation at hand, on the number of people present, and their mutual alliances and mutual involvement.

1.2 A case in court

To demonstrate how the two approaches – 'talk as text' and 'talk as activity' – can complement one another, I will use the court proceeding example mentioned in the introduction.

Just before the exchange I described above, the judge had asked: "Do you confess the theft?" This is the routine in Swedish court proceedings. When a trial begins, the prosecutor reads the charges and the judge asks for the suspect's point of view. Then the suspect is supposed to plead guilty or not guilty. In Swedish, this is normally phrased as the question "do you confess so-and-so", where so-and-so involves naming the crime (for instance "theft") and the expected answer is simply "yes" or "no". But in this case the judge's inquiry was answered by a lengthy explanation, which I interpreted. The suspect had not understood that the judge needed a straightforward 'yes' or 'no'. To put a close to the routine she reformulated her question:

Judge:	Så du erkänner inte stölden.
	So you don't confess the theft.
Interpreter:	Значит вы не признаётесь в краже.
	That is you don't confess the theft.
Suspect:	Да.
	Yes.
Interpreter:	Nej.
	No.

Applying the text-model I would perhaps start by identifying an *error*: Why is the suspect's "yes" interpreted as "no"? Comparing this pair of utterances in the context of the longer sequence of talk I could claim that the interpreter's "no" is a *compensation for a lack of equivalence* between Swedish and Russian, rather than a 'literal' translation of the preceding "yes". With the interactionistic approach, on the other hand, I would look for other types of explanations. I would not invoke at all any general rules of equivalence, but try to take the perspectives of those acting, to understand what the judge, the suspect and the interpreter were trying to do in relation to each other in the situation at hand.

A descriptive, non-normative, interactionistic approach implies that the participants' contributions are seen as part of concrete conversations, situated in time and space. Moreover, it stipulates that the sense people make out of utterances in conversation depends on social and cultural conventions tied to language use in interaction generally, and language use specifically within one type of activity or the other. It also assumes that an utterance fills certain functions not out of context, but in the context of the given sequence of talk.

Hence, the suspect's "yes" was designed to function as a preliminary statement that the interpreter would repeat in Swedish. Moreover, it was intended as an answer to the judge's question, as a denial of guilt and a confirmation of the correctness of the statement "so you don't confess the theft". In Russian these activities are realized with a *da*, 'yes'. In Swedish, the corresponding actions in this situation are conventionally accomplished with a *nej*, 'no'. The Swedish word *ja* 'yes' would have been quite confusing, since it would remain unclear what it actually was supposed to confirm. This is partly due to the fact that there is another word for 'yes' in Swedish, namely *jo*, which here would have indicated that the suspect indeed *was* admitting guilt. Following upon a *negated* statement or a question, *jo*, 'yes' conventionally states the reversed opinion. In the above sequence it would have meant a denial of the *negation*.

1.3 Alternatives and complements

The above example illustrates in a simple way how an interactionally orientated approach links with a dialogical view of language and mind. According to such a view, meanings are not simply properties of lexical items, or sequences of words, and a speaker cannot independently, for instance by force of her intentions, determine once and for all the meanings of the glosses and expressions she utters. Meanings are continuously established and re-established *between* people in actual social interaction.

The words *da* (yes) and *nyet* (no) are relatively well known, and therefore transparent also to people who do not speak Russian. I remember very vividly from that day in court that one of the Swedish lay assessors looked at me with a questioning expression on his face.

And at this very moment it suddenly struck me that "yes" was the 'source' corresponding to my 'target' "no". In other words, upon second thoughts, I saw "yes" and "no" in terms of 'original' and 'translation' (as texts) but while performing automatically, as it were, in the role of interpreter, I repeated to the best of my ability the activity of denying.

Two languages and a correspondence between units which 'belong' to these languages seem to be the basic preconditions without which there can be no definition and no theory of translation, and also no theory of interpretation, provided interpretation is seen as a kind of translation. Different points of departure, however, lead to significantly different questions about these phenomena. On the one hand, I may use models provided by linguistics and investigate translations in terms of *text units* 'belonging' to one of a pair of *two languages*. 'Two languages' as given facts provide a comparative frame to explore 'originals' and 'translations'. On the other hand, I can raise questions about social and linguistic conventions, communicative projects, sharedness and misfit, starting from concrete events in *situated systems of activity* (Goffman 1981),[1] given that the *language users* involved in these conceive of the events as entailing translation. I would call the first approach 'talk as text' and the latter 'talk as activity'.

2. TRANSLATION STUDIES – AN INTER-DISCIPLINE

'Translation studies' is a young academic discipline. Today, research on all kinds of translating and interpreting is referred to by this term. Toury (1980, 1995), following Holmes (1988), uses the term "inter-discipline". Holmes sees the interdisciplinarity within translation studies as a teamwork between specialists in a variety of fields – text studies, psycho- and socio-linguistics, literary studies, psychology and sociology (Holmes 1988:101).

Interdisciplinarity can also mean a shared subject area. Whether starting from established disciplines, or from fields of study where the shared theoretical and methodological orientation goes across disciplines, interdisciplinarity can optimally lead to fruitful combinations of ideas and scientific traditions. This presupposes, however, an openness to problematize and develop also the most basic theoretical assumptions; an openness to, and insight into, diverse perspectives and research interests.

Translation studies involves several different research approaches, scientific methods and traditions. The area is sometimes organized into translation studies and interpretation studies as a sub-field. Another possibility would be to distinguish between, on the one hand, experimentally designed studies proposing and testing hypotheses, and, on the other hand, studies designed to generate knowledge by applying an inductive research model. In the short history of translation studies, this way of organizing the field has been seen only recently, which relates to the parallel development of two core research trends, two approaches to the role of the translator. Many scholars draw theoretically and methodologically from cognitive psychology and focus on the translator's intra-personal, mental processes. Others work in the traditions of micro sociology, discourse analysis and ethnography of speaking and study inter-personal, social processes between translators and their clients. The distinction between monologism and dialogism has so far been problematized only in the latter of these sub-fields.

2.1 The written language bias

A textual approach to translation (and interpretation) might appear self-evident in view of the fact that translations relate to written originals. In addition to this, written translations can indeed be observed as textual objects. Furthermore, ever since the fifties, when the first attempts were made to establish translation studies among the scientific disciplines, the connection to Linguistics has been close, and from this discipline translation studies inherited a written language bias (for linguistics, cf. discussion by communication theorist Linell, 1982).

Besides, the history of translating (and interpreting) as professions is intimately tied to the diffusion of written documents of legal, religious, cultural, scientific and political importance, and to the spreading of literacy (see Delisle, Woodsworth *et al.* (1995) for an historical overview). It goes without saying that translators of sacred or politically important texts have been 'source text' oriented, and applied a monological view of language (regarding meaning as a property of the text). When the influence of a specific text is linked to divine and/or earthly authorities, this also means that a translation needs divine sanction, or blessings from those who exercise (and monopolize) religious and political power. The practical function of the text makes those using it expect and demand the translators' loyalty as a guarantee against blasphemy and disrespect.

A large proportion of the literature on translation (and interpretation) has been produced explicitly to set standards, sometimes to guarantee a certain style in the translation of particular texts, or types of texts and utterances, sometimes specifically for didactic purposes. When these goals are pursued, a written language bias perhaps also springs naturally from the need for established and shared norms that can easily be related to. The relatively stable linguistic rules described in grammars and lexica would then appear as convenient norms of 'equivalence', 'correctness' and so forth. Translation and interpretation studies have developed as an academic field partly as a result of scholars questioning the practical validity of these norms for 'equivalence' between texts, and norms for professional loyalties.

2.2 Translatability and language metaphors

Historically, the issue of translatability – that is, the question how to determine the *limits* of translation – has been a central issue in translation studies. The two classical preconceptions of translation (and interpretation) as theory and practice are associated with this question. On the one hand, translation is taken to imply a *problem of transferring* a source text to a target text. On the other hand it is viewed as a *problem of finding out the hidden meaning(s)* behind the original; the author's (or speaker's) actual intention(s). In a circular dependence, these theoretical notions of translation in turn motivate the issue of translatability.

This traditional issue – whether or not, or to what extent, texts are translatable – follows theoretically from the kind of linguistic approach applied in studies of translation between the early postwar years and the 1970s. There has been a radical shift within linguistics during that time, directing the focus more towards language in use, as an alternative or a complement to the more traditional preconception of language as an autonomous system, and, as Snell-Hornby (1991) reminds us, this shift is visible also in the field of translation studies.

The shift partly coincided with the spread of audiotaping as a documenting technique, and the resultant opportunities to analyse in detail spontaneous speech. New explorations showing that word order, syntax etc. in spoken interaction often deviate considerably from written language standards, lead to a general reconsideration of what should be counted as 'correct' language use, and likewise how languages generally should be described.

A current trend in translation studies, drawing on insights from pragmatics, discourse analysis and text linguistics, promotes what can be termed a 'top-down' approach, that is, to adopt a textual analysis that proceeds from whole to part, or from text to sign, rather than starting from lexical items or other units taken from grammatical theory. For instance, Reiß and Vermeer (1984) promote a *skopos* theory, Snell-Hornby (1988), advances an *integrated approach*, and Hatim and Mason (1990), propose an analytical model where the starting point is *text-type as situated in its contexts of culture*.

This does not, however, preclude the discussion and description of translation in terms of 'faithful' versus 'free', 'literal' versus 'figurative', 'equivalent' versus 'non-equivalent' etc., that is, discussions presupposing the 'existence' of meaning(s) as properties of linguistic items, or as determined by the speaker alone; the 'existence' of meaning(s) of words towards which actors may relate more or less freely. To some extent we are all fenced in by this conventional metaphorical thinking. These oppositions belong to ideas about the nature of language and of texts which in fact are applied from at least Cicero in the first century BC (Vermeer 1988:93–128). These dichotomies have been dominating in the philosophy of language over the centuries. As Voloshinov (1930/1986) points out in his book *Marxism and the philosophy of language*, their predominance in linguistics and theories of language is much supported by the appearance of standardized (and standardizing!) dictionaries and grammars.

Voloshinov defines two principal, dominating preconceptions of language. On the one hand, language is seen as an abstract stable system, an object as it were, reflecting objects in the world. On the other hand, language is viewed as the creative subject's, i.e. the individual's, tool. Voloshinov discusses this in terms of *individualistic subjectivism* and *abstract objectivism* (1930, Part II, Chapter 1). (This does not mean that he sees one or the other of them as 'false' or as 'true' – they are just two widespread language metaphors.)

In search of a general theory of translation, Toury (1980), himself working mainly with written translation, declares a non-interest in the issue of translatability. He criticizes traditional linguistic approaches for being concerned with hypothetical translations of decontextualized expressions or strips of texts in textbooks, instead of what he calls "existing translations" (Toury 1980:43). In his view, an utterance or a text which is accepted and functions as a translation in a particular community constitutes in itself a solution to a *practical* problem of translatability. Investigations into translating performed as juxtaposition of texts (originals and translations) always imply a comparison of categories selected by the analyst in a hypothetical construct (Toury 1980:112–13). In other words, the question of translatability, as it is traditionally put forward, must, according to Toury, be perceived as a purely academic one: it presupposes a perspective from outside. As such, it essentially misses translatability as a problem lived by the participants who are involved in a here-and-now communicative activity.

2.3 Translational norms

Toury is thus one of the many scholars in the field today who emphasize that translations must be understood and explored in relation to the socio-cultural contexts in which they appear. The conclusion he draws from this, given his research interests, is that translatorship amounts first and foremost to being able to *play a social role*, i.e. to fulfil a function allotted by a community – to the activity, its practitioners and their products – in a way which is deemed appropriate in its own terms of reference (Toury 1995:53).

His proposed programme for "Descriptive Translation Studies" is defined as "target-oriented", and translation as a fact of and a requirement of a "target culture". In short, his research programme is phrased as a search for norms (basically social and cultural ones) that underlie existing translations from different times, countries, areas of the society etc.; what criteria for correctness or readability translators in different times and places have used.

This target-orientation differs from what can be found in earlier literature, for instance, in the works of Eugene Nida. During the sixties and seventies he developed a theory of translation, or, more precisely, a theory of evangelical Bible translation (e.g. 1964, 1976, 1977). His point of departure was that the traditional concentration on the author's intentions and on the linguistic features of the source texts, had led to an underestimation of translation as "an act of communication" (Nida 1977:227). If considered at all, he argued, the translators' audience was idealized in the sense that people's ability to evaluate the difference between source- and target-texts was taken for granted, as if the audience consisted of teachers of translation or fellow-translators.

Nida instead proposed to focus on accomplished communicative results, posing questions like: What is lost in translations? and How can losses in and by translating be minimized? (Nida 1976:63). Thus presupposing a comparison between a given translation and an optimal translation, his programme for translatologists is normative in character.

2.4 Translators as moral human beings or information-processing systems

Hatim and Mason (1990), in a review of tendencies within translation studies, conclude that recent developments such as "context-sensitive linguistics, sociolinguistics, discourse studies and artificial intelligence", provide a new direction for the future. It is one which restores to the translator the central role in a process of cross-cultural communication and ceases to regard equivalence merely as a matter of entities within texts (Hatim and Mason 1990:35). The actual move away from the issue of translatability and towards studies in translational norms has brought the translator more into focus, and the questions that arise include: What is done by translators and interpreters? How is translating and interpreting actually accomplished?

The lion's share of the literature on translation and interpretation topicalizes this issue as a fundamentally *moral* one, a question of how to remain faithful to original speakers and/or stay loyal to professional norms. Many works in the field discuss and define correctness and adequacy, striving to answer to both the scientific need to generate new knowledge, and the professional need for didactic and other advice.

However, a considerable body of literature on translating and interpreting principally banishes moral issues and quality questions from the realm of theory. If it is concerned with norms at all, the concept of 'norm' is taken as referring to internalized semantic norms. The aim of these studies is to learn about translating and interpreting in terms of individuals' cognitive (or even brain) functions, i.e. by looking at these actors as information-processing systems and their translating activity as consisting of specific types of *cognitive processes*, also termed 'decoding' and 'encoding operations' (e.g. Barik 1972). A method developed for empirical studies in this tradition is think-aloud introspection. For instance, Krings (1986) investigates by this method how a group of students arrived at their German translations of a newspaper text written in French.

From a similar perspective, Holz-Mänttäri (1984, 1988) outlines a programme for translation studies, in which she suggests tracing the competence for 'translatorial action' in the "basic biological-social elements of the system 'man'". Translatorial action is defined as "a mental process that can, presumably, be explained by modern neurophysiological knowledge", and the ability to translate as a specific "artificial-professional competence", different from "evolutionary-natural communicative competence" (Holz-Mänttäri 1988:7). Inquiries about translating would therefore include studies of cognitive processes involved in the very translating, and also those involved while signing up for a translating job, and preparing for it. Holz-Mänttäri points to the importance of accounting for the translator's background knowledge concerning the prospective functions and expected audience of a translated text.

Regardless of this interest in the translator's dependence on other people, Mänttäri's as well as Krings' approach implies a more or less isolated focus on translating as the *individual* translator's or interpreter's action, based on an internalized competence. Mänttäri sees translation and interpreting basically as a specific kind of professional action (*translatorisches Handeln*). Yet, as Rommetveit argues, the representational-computational models within mainstream individual cognitive psychology and cognitive science are monologically based and converge in an image of Man as an essentially asocial, but highly complex information-processing device. The alternative, he suggests, is a dialogically based social-cognitive approach to human cognition and communication, and the presupposition underlying this other approach can be converted into statements about the social nature of Man and the embeddedness of the individual mind in a cultural collectivity (Rommetveit 1992).

The above-mentioned notions of 'decoding' and 'encoding' clearly connect with what I here call a 'textual' view of talk. These concepts belong to a model of communication where the original message is identical with the message received. The semiotician Lotman (1992), discussing the notion of 'code', argues that the concepts of 'language' and 'code' are far from compatible, since the latter brings associations to artificial languages, "structures without a memory", created for certain purposes and established once and for all. A language, he argues, is "a code plus its history". If we could transfer information through a structure without a memory, the information would be identical at both ends, but the value of this information would be severely restricted. An established code system can perhaps function sufficiently for giving and taking orders, he suggests, but a structure without a memory cannot fulfil all the diverse functions we conventionally ascribe to language (Lotman 1992:12ff).

3. IN SEARCH OF A THEORY OF SENSE-MAKING

As Keith (1984) points out, most teaching institutions clearly differentiate between translators' and interpreters' skills in training and recruitment practice. When it comes to theory, the distinction between translating and interpreting is not always emphasized, even if a few suggestions to establish research on interpretation as a separate area have appeared during the last few years, including a special issue of *Target* devoted to "Interpretation Research" (Gile 1995). The issue covers a number of approaches and it also shows that research on interpreting is no less an 'inter-discipline' than translation studies generally.

3.1 *La théorie de sens*

From the late sixties onwards the 'Paris School' – Seleskovitch, Lederer and others at the *Ecole Supérieure d'Interprètes et de Traducteurs* (ESIT) – has had a great impact on training and research in the area of interpreting. Seleskovitch (1978) reacts against translation theories based on contrastive linguistics, picks up on trends from current psycholinguistics and proposes an interpretive theory of conference interpreting, *La théorie de sens*. In line with the paradigmatic shift within linguistics, it moves away from studies of the syntactic structure of sentences invented (written) by grammarians, towards investigations of spoken language.

In the tradition of other famous interpreters and teachers, such as Herbert (1952), Ekvall (1960) and Schmidt (1964), Seleskovitch is drawing on personal experiences rather than referring to systematic investigations. Her lack of empirical underpinnings has been criticized in recent works on interpreting, for instance by Gile (1990), Moser-Mercer (1991) and Schjoldager (1994). This critique has given

Seleskovitch's early writings new currency, in relation to which researchers in the rapidly growing field have thought to develop the ideas further.

La théorie de sens partly appears as a juxtaposition of the two conventional views on language and mind mentioned above, what Voloshinov terms *individualistic subjectivism* and *abstract objectivism* (see above, paragraph 2.2). In an article published in English Seleskovitch writes: "The sensing of what is meant as opposed to knowing a language as such is the very foundation of interpretation" (Seleskovitch 1977:28). In *Interpreting for International Conferences*, a translation and adaptation of her doctoral dissertation (in French 1969, in English 1978), latching on to the discussion on translatability, Seleskovitch claims that *"virtually all words are untranslatable*, if we define as translatable words which have an exact equivalent in another language and which retain this exact equivalency regardless of context" (Seleskovitch 1978:85). Throughout her work she points to the insufficiency of looking only for formal textual correspondence between originals and translations. She goes as far as claiming that *"what the interpreter says is, in principle, independent of the source language"* (Seleskovitch 1978:98). Interpretation she defines as "to a great extent, the verbal expression of things and ideas accompanied by the nondeliberate creation of temporary linguistic equivalence" (Seleskovitch 1978:87).

Central to her *théorie de sens* is that interpreters' utterances are (should be) equivalent expressions of others' ideas, rather than repetitions of the all too static linguistic equivalents of others' original utterances. When these are first comprehended, the interpreter, as it were, leaves (should leave) the linguistic forms behind and delivers in the other language only the *sense* of the original. (The concept Seleskovitch uses for this is *deverbalisation*, discussed in French in her and Lederer's joint work from 1984, and in Lederer's more recent book on translation from 1994.)

To understand the idea of 'deverbalization', one additionally needs to know what the *théorie de sens* presupposes about international conferences and the delegates attending them. Seleskovitch problematizes the possible goals speakers may pursue as questions of "conveying messages" and "expressing ideas". Moreover, she seemingly counts on the sharing, between delegates, of a notion of appropriateness and of effectiveness. She treats as a given fact that speakers concentrate on clarifying their ideas and expressing them appropriately. The interpreter, in turn, is supposed to concentrate on expressing these ideas and on choosing the terms which he or she feels will most effectively convey them (Seleskovitch 1978:98).

When the author notes that the aim of her work is to "examine the techniques and mental processes which enable the conference interpreter to successfully play the role of intermediary" (Seleskovitch 1978:10), it is understood that successfulness, to the author, would mean to cope with the interpreter's "sole responsibility", that is *to make sure that his listeners immediately understand what has been said"* (Seleskovitch 1978:111). In essence, Seleskovitch takes speakers' messages as existing facts, for the interpreter to grasp correctly and make others understand (correctly).

Providing the profession with a theoretical base has probably served at one level to improve the interpreter's status; to bring light upon this actor as someone to be reckoned with in international politics, law and business, as an active participant in a social context, in other words, as anything but a passive tool. One must keep in mind though, that Seleskovitch's theory is tailor-made for her own professional field of conference interpreters, and not for the field of interpreting generally. In her approach, 'speakers' equals 'people delivering speeches', that is, prepared monologues which are often read from written scripts. Moreover, the role of conference interpreter is regarded as a role of intermediary between parties who are all specialists and people in power, sharing conditions and interests, including that of arriving, at some level of meaning, at a shared and mutual understanding (cf. Chapter 4 below for a discussion on the concept of intermediary).

Seleskovitch's work consists of descriptions of the role of conference interpreter which simultaneously are designed to work as prescriptions of what interpreters *ought* to do; to set standards and provide a common policy. In her view, the interpreter is (should be) ultimately capable of being "totally faithful to the original meaning" (Seleskovitch 1978:101). This does not mean, however, that she is unaware of speakers' dependence upon listeners' feedback in the process of formulating utterances. The latter would then indicate a dialogical view of language. We could trace some of this in her observation that delegates sometimes develop a shared vocabulary, which is shared only in the new, linguistically and culturally mixed environment. Perhaps this view also lies behind her distinction between the 'primary' or 'lexical' meaning of words on the one hand and, on the other, meaning derived from 'the context', from real life situations (Seleskovitch 1978:86). Again, however, it must be noted that 'context' is not really problematized, and while 'contextual' meaning is taken as *ad hoc*, 'lexical' meaning is perceived of as the basic, predetermined one. Her theoretical approach is, after all, founded in linguistic theory distinguishing between languages (such as French or English) as self-contained, meaningful systems, in a monologistic view of language use as the speaker's creation of a given (linguistically based) meaning, and in an individualistic view of the interpreter as a complex information-processing device.

3.2 Talk as text and translation as equivalent text

Seleskovitch's theory of interpreting thus claims insights in the mental processes taking place in the interpreter's brain. It involves what may be called a mentalistic view of interpreting. A similar view is present in several works in the field. Language use is regularly conceptualized in the literature as 'text processing' and/or 'text production'. And it is as if this idea also colours the view of what primary interlocutors do, namely producing and processing the 'source texts' that correspond to the translator's or interpreter's 'target texts'.

For instance, Kalina (1992), presenting a 'strategic' approach to interpreting didactics, phrases the interpreter's concern as the rule-governed production of texts, corresponding to texts produced by others. In a more recent article, written together with Kohn, the term used is not 'text' but 'discourse' – "source and target discourse" (Kohn and Kalina 1996), but the foregrounding of this one activity remains – the production of source discourse and target discourse respectively – based as it is on a "mental-modelling view of communication and interpreting/translation" (Kohn and Kalina 1996:120). Kalina sees translation as a constant mental reaction. As she puts it: "unlike the text addressee, the interpreter is not at liberty to choose in which way he will react to an utterance. His reaction (i.e. translation) is a constant and has been fixed in advance" (Kalina 1992:253).

In principle, it may be true that interpreters' liberties are in some sense restricted by the ways in which they are expected to take part in a communicative event. Seen from the point of view of concrete individuals involved in interpreter-mediated interaction, however, the quoted statement could be considered to represent wishful thinking. The lack of "liberty to choose" is perhaps understandable as a defining prerequisite when, as in the case of Kohn and Kalina, the object of study is again conference interpreting, and interpreters are by definition people who deliver a second version of others' speeches. It sounds even more like wishful thinking, though, when the authors, just like Seleskovitch before them, take it as given that "speakers/listeners want to understand each other, and they want to achieve this in a correct and appropriate way" (Kohn and Kalina 1996:122–23).

Explorations of authentic face-to-face interpreter-mediated interaction considerably modify such a view of interlocutors' intentions. Interpreters' reactions to primary parties' utterances can there be described as flexible rather than 'fixed in advance'. Furthermore, the co-actors can be described as neither necessarily cooperative in speaking and listening, nor as having a shared understanding of what is correct and appropriate.

Regarding interpreters' activity solely as production of equivalent texts, where equivalent implies correct, appropriate, successful, etc., we end up identifying part of what interpreters in practice do as something else than interpreting. If the text-production view is combined with a monological view of language and language use, this something-else-part will be described as individual deficiencies and failures.

3.3 A matter of semantics and a matter of perspectives

The text metaphor is a powerful one. Harris (1992b) warns that, "in the translation context, 'text' loses important implications if we do not restrict it to texts possessing a high degree of discourse complexity, and which are usually written or, if spoken, prepared in advance" (Harris 1992b:102). This remark is interesting, for *what* it states about discourse complexity, and for the fact *that* it does so. In what sense do written texts possess a higher degree of discourse complexity than spontaneous speech? Why is this noted in a paper which declares primacy of spoken language over written?

The quote is drawn from a paper debating the importance of doing research on 'natural translation',[2] a direction much promoted by Harris (1978 (together with Sherwood), 1990, 1992a), defined as "the translation done by bilinguals in everyday circumstances without special training for it" (Harris 1992a). Prototypical examples of 'natural translation' would be immigrant children assisting their parents as interpreters at the doctor's, or in reading messages from the authorities.

It should not be surprising, Harris argues, if researchers arrive at opposing views when they work with opposing premises; when what one accepts as being 'translation' does not fit with others' definition of the same concept. To illustrate this, Harris contrasts two discrepant definitions of 'translation' and explains the divergence between them by reference to their authors' basically different research interests (1992b:100). One definition is borrowed from Wilss (1981):

> Translation is a series of reformulation processes transposing a source-language text into a target-language text which is as closely equivalent to the former as possible; these processes suppose a syntactic, semantic and pragmatic comprehension of the content of the text (translation of the German original[3] from Harris 1992b:99).

This definition of 'translation' is used by Krings (1986) in a work where he disqualifies as "unreasonable" Harris's proposal for translation studies to give priority to investigations of 'natural translation' (Krings 1986:19).

Harris in turn prefers a definition of 'translation' suggested by Rabin (1958): "Translation is a process by which a spoken or written utterance takes place in one language which is intended and presumed to convey the same meaning as a previously existing utterance in another language" (Rabin 1958:123). In the following discussion, Harris explains the difference between these definitions, which would also explain the lack of shared understanding between himself and Krings.

At first sight this could appear like a clash between a textual and an activity orientated approach. Where Wilss (and Krings) speak of "text", Rabin uses "spoken or written utterance". Harris describes this as a matter of semantic non-conformity. Moreover, he identifies a difference between requirements for equivalence, between Wilss's "very close equivalence at three levels (syntactic, semantic and pragmatic)" and Rabin's equivalence in "meaning". Harris prefers the latter since it is, as he argues, much simpler, and it can be applied to 'natural translation' data.

Harris's and Krings's interests and points of departure may differ in many respects. Yet, to my mind, when Harris interprets Rabin's definition of 'translation' he does this partly according to Krings's conditions. He seems to embrace the idea that definitions of 'translation' (must?) include a quality requirement. Krings argues that the relation between "a source-language text" and "a target-language text" must fulfil certain predefined criteria to make a candidate translation qualify as a "real" translation. In Harris's case, the same would be argued for the relation between two "written or spoken utterances". I see this partly as a result of Harris's project to promote a definition of 'translation' which allows researchers to regard 'natural translation' as 'real' translation.

In my view, the significant difference between the above definitions of 'translation' lies in the implied frames of reference. This is touched upon by Harris, when he mentions that Wilss's definition is very suitable as an instruction to a translation class. Two opposing perspectives are manifest in the fact that Wilss writes *ist* ("is") where Rabin puts "is intended and presumed to". In Rabin's definition, 'translation' is what observed subjects identify as translation, while Wilss's definition relies on researchers' or other observers' understanding of concepts belonging to linguistic theory. In other words, Rabin takes as his point of departure the perspective of those whose talk is being observed (an inside perspective), while Wilss presupposes what might be called a 'perspective from outside'. The latter is *descriptive* while the former, in contrast, is fundamentally *prescriptive*.

4. MONOLOGISM, DIALOGISM AND STUDIES ON INTERPRETING

Central to theories of translation is the notion of how texts, utterances and words interconnect with meaning(s), which in turn links to the notion of what a word *is*. Bakhtin (1979/1986a) in his essay on speech genres, suggests an interesting way to look at how words relate to meanings which escapes traditional oppositions such as 'literal' versus 'contextual' meaning and 'lexical' versus 'pragmatic' meaning. This section is devoted to exploring his view of the nature of words, and the relevance of this view in investigations of interpreter-mediated interaction.

4.1 Bakhtin's theory of the appropriation of others' words

Outlining his interactionistic view of language and mind, Bakhtin (1979/1986a) argues that a word (Ru: *slovo*), exists in *three aspects*.

These aspects are in practice simultaneously and equally relevant, yet, in theory, it is possible and fruitful to distinguish between them.

A word has one existence as a *dictionary* gloss, with a range of potential 'meanings' (*znacheniya*). This aspect of the word lacks both emotional expressiveness and loadedness with values, since we have, theoretically, disconnected it from a living context. It lacks 'sense' (*smysl*).

The second aspect of the word is connected to *others' use* of it. When individuals say or write a word, they, to some extent, reproduce the presuppositions, including values, emotions and contexts, that are associated with others' use of the same word, echoing in turn yet others' applications at different times and places.

The third aspect of the word is connected to a specific utterance, at a particular instance. I attribute sense to a word also in and by *my own use* of this word, in a particular situation, where I have my specific interests and goals. Thus, this third aspect is part and parcel of the actual utterance in which it is spoken.

> The word [. . .] becomes "one's own" only when the speaker populates it with his own intentions, his own accent, when he appropriates the word, adapting it to his own semantic and expressive intention. Prior to this moment of appropriation, the word does not exist in a neutral and impersonal language (it is not, after all, out of the dictionary that the speaker gets his words!), but rather it exists in other people's mouths, in other people's contexts, serving other people's intentions: it is from there that one must take the word, and make it one's own (Bakhtin, 1981:293–94).

Speaking about the individual's *appropriation* of the word, Bakhtin perceives language as something *connecting* individuals with one another, whilst simultaneously being the concrete means by which people can express themselves as individuals.

4.2 Meanings and the dialogic organization of language use

The idea of words existing in different aspects derives from a central notion in the work of Bakhtin, namely that of the *dialogic* organization and life of language. Studying the nature of the novel, Bakhtin observes that what is written by one individual, the author, reflects not just this person's consciousness. It invokes also the perspectives and voices of a diversity of other consciousnesses, from different cultures and times; the voices of the characters described, and also the voice of the current reader of the novel in question. Stories, texts, utterances, etc. reflect, and refract the multiple voices by which languages live and develop (Bakhtin 1984:18).

When one person explicitly quotes another's talk, this is a particularly obvious example of how language is continuously re-used to serve partly new functions. Consequently, if we consider that interpreting is a kind of quoting, interpreter-mediated conversations would provide excellent occasions to explore how the dialogical opposition between the voices involved creates new meanings.

To quote Bakhtin's contemporary and fellow countryman, the philosopher Voloshinov:

> . . . as we know, the real unit of language that is implemented in speech (*Sprache als Rede*) is not the individual, isolated monologic utterance, but the interaction of at least two utterances – in a word, dialogue. The productive study of dialogue presupposes, however, a more profound investigation of the forms used in reported speech, since these forms reflect basic and constant tendencies in the *active reception of other speakers' speech*, and it is this reception, after all, that is fundamental also for dialogue (Voloshinov 1986:117).[4]

According to Bakhtin, an utterance thus has connections backwards in time, but it also links to the future. It is constituted by its *addressivity*. Even if I talk or write only to myself I address an abstract other, and the speech, or the text, is in principle open for a concrete other's *answer*. A word has a sense (*smysl*) only in a social context, and this sense is not constant but changes and multiplies in and by human inter-activity. The typical connections one may experience between the meanings (*znacheniya*) of a word, and a concrete object or reality under typical conditions, may support the idea that a typical expressiveness, as Bakhtin writes, "settles in layers on" or "adheres to" (*naslaivajutsja na*) particular words. However, he continues, "this typical, generic expressiveness, of course, belongs not to the word as an entity of a language, is not included in its meaning, but reflects only the relation of the word and its meanings to a genre, that is to typical utterances" (Bakhtin 1979:282).[5]

When interpreting in everyday life is thought about in terms of possible 'losses of information', this reflects an idea of 'information' as belonging to words, of 'facts' and 'emotions' as properties of speech. Accordingly, the work of interpreters would consist solely of a production of 'texts', possessing the same information, facts and emotions as the original 'texts'/utterances. This represents a monological preconception of language.

4.3 Abstract norms and concrete acts

Bakhtin's theory provides a ground for a distinction between normative activity (activity in principle) and real life activity (the actual cases). Only in theory is the utterance the carrier of specific information, and only theoretically is it an instantiation of linguistic or other rules. Rules belong to an idealized, abstract world. They 'exist' in the minds of people. Utterances, in contrast, belong to the concrete world. In practice, an utterance in the oral or the text-bound mode can be seen as correct, incorrect, equivalent, translatable, adequate, etc. in relation to different, pre-established norms. An individual who is occupied with interpreting *relates* to linguistic, social, and other cultural norms, but interpreting as activity can never be a simple application of norms of grammar, generic style, politeness, and so forth. Such a view would presuppose the denial of personal responsibility. As Bakhtin puts it elsewhere: "The [human] will is indeed creatively active in the act, but does in no way generate a norm, a general proposition" (Bakhtin 1986b:101).[6] An act of translating is in practice performed by a specific 'I', speaking, or writing on behalf of a substantial other. As Bakhtin argues, "there is no person in general, there is me, there is a definite concrete other: my close friend, my contemporary (social humanity), the past and future of real people (of real historical humanity)" (Bakhtin 1986b:117).[7]

Bakhtin's view of the nature of discourse has far-reaching theoretical implications when applied to studies of interpreting in face-to-face interaction. In sum, it implies that language is viewed and explored as a *historical and social phenomenon,* continuously reproduced and recreated by being used. The use of language is regarded as *social activities*, connected to different genres and layers of contexts.

In contrast to the monological *conduit model* (cf. above Chapter 1, section 1:3 "The channel metaphor"), the Bakhtinian interactionistic model is *dialogical*. Meanings conveyed by language use are conceptualized as co-constructed *between* speaker and hearer(s) *in interaction* (cf. also Goodwin and Duranti 1992). Meaning cannot be described entirely in terms of individuals' intentions, nor as properties of languages or words. The meaning(s) individuals ascribe to words and phrases is matched against time, place, social situations and thereby associated communicative genres. Talk provides in itself a social context to ongoing talk.

The different epistemologies, monologism and dialogism, imply different units of analysis. As Linell (1996:14) puts it: "Whilst monologism assumes individuals and societies (cultures) to be analytical primes, dialogism takes *actions and interactions*, e.g. the discursive practices, *in their contexts* as basic units" (cf. also Holquist 1990, Marková and Foppa 1990).

Interpreters on duty understand themselves not only to be translating between two languages, but also to be performing on others' behalf various activities, such as persuading, agreeing, lying, questioning, claiming, explaining, comforting, accusing, denying, co-ordinating interaction, and so forth. This links more to a dialogical view of language and mind.

4.4 Equivalence between texts and/or focal events in a field of action

Exploring authentic cases of interpreting, and starting out from the 'textual' view of languages, i.e. languages as stable, 'meaningful' systems – for instance, English and Mandarin, Swedish and Russian, American English and American Sign Language – I apply a perspective which in principle is independent of what those present at actual utterances in these languages experience there-and-then. Most of the time this outside perspective will function when organizing data, but I will also come across utterances consisting of words which according to linguistic theory do not 'belong' to any language, and words which look the same in many languages and therefore could 'belong' to both languages used in an interpreter-mediated encounter. For instance, how do I know in which language someone says "mhm"?

Nevertheless, having established utterances in the one or the other language as research units for the exploration of interpreter-mediated talk, I may go ahead to examine the utterances as one would texts. At this point I also need criteria by which the relationship between the 'texts' can be explored and evaluated. Traditionally this relationship is expressed in terms of equivalence. Recent literature within Translation studies distinguishes between different types of equivalence – grammatical, lexical and pragmatic (e.g. Hatim and Mason 1990, Baker 1992). Accordingly, grammar, lexical choice and pragmatic function(s) would be possible measures by which I could classify relationships of equivalence between originals and translations.

These criteria for equivalence I would associate with a monological view of language, and a model of communication in which speakers are understood to match their intentions with the respective (national) language's ready-made structures of meanings, and where the communicative process is taken as a unidirectional process of transfer.

A dialogical point of view, in contrast, implies that an utterance is seen as a link in a chain of utterances, as a thread in a net of intertwined communicative behaviour. Meanings conveyed are seen as resulting from joint efforts between the people involved. Hence, the meanings of an original utterance will depend on how it is reacted to by people present at it (the other interlocutor(s) and the interpreter), on preceding and following sequences of talk, on non-verbal communicative behaviour and extra linguistic features defined by and defining the speech situation. The meanings of an utterance depend on participants' mutual expectations, physical circumstances and artefacts, and on whether the utterance is part of a focused event or disattended by those present at it. Following Duranti and Goodwin (1992) the notion of context can be understood as involving a *figure-ground* relationship "a fundamental juxtaposition of two entities: (1) a focal event; and (2) a field of action within which that event is embedded" (Duranti and Goodwin 1992:3).

4.5 Conceptual traps

Listening to tape-recorded talk and reading the transcriptions of it as separate utterances, I may imagine the speaker's intentions for a particular utterance on the basis of my general knowledge about linguistic and social conventions. Given certain conditions – what Austin (1962)[8] when developing his theory of communicative actions termed "felicity conditions" – people can be seen typically to be accomplishing certain actions by using certain words in a specific, conventional order. He points to the necessity of paying attention to the contexts in which words occur, in order to understand how they get to be meaningful to people.

Hence, when analysing equivalence between utterances (i.e. comparing originals and translations) on the basis of the function(s) they are designed to perform, I am more or less consciously taking into consideration contextual aspects manifest in the situation. In fact, it is hard to *avoid* perceiving talk as activity when examining pragmatic functions. It can also be hard to keep away from drawing conclusions about speakers' intentions. When applying a textual approach, I have reason to consider what may be called its inherent conceptual traps. Analysing transcribed interpreter-mediated talk, I have found the following three to be the major traps:

First, when regarding talk as text and interpreting as text-producing, I tend to *downplay the importance of all of the other activities* identifiable in interaction, performed by the interpreter and by other interlocutors. Related to this, the text model may lead me to ascribe to language users, interpreters as well as primary interlocutors, *the intention* to produce text, as it were, for its own sake.

Secondly, I may tend to *focus on discourse details which in practice were not part of a focal event,* partly because the textual representation allows it – and invites it – and partly because the text model presupposes all parts of discourse to be operationalized as either 'source-text' or 'target-text'.

Thirdly, the text-orientated approach implies a tendency to metaphorically picture languages as subjects. Some languages 'lack' certain concepts while others 'have' them, some 'make' certain distinctions and others do not. As a logical consequence of this, language users in turn tend to be objectified, and *responsibility for verbal activities tends to be partly de-personified.*

If applied to interpreting in face-to-face interaction, *monologism* would thus include the idea of *two languages and two cultures* ('source' and 'target') as existing, and existing separately from one another, while *dialogism* would foreground *actions and interactions* taking place in *a concrete situation* which represents a mixture of linguistic and social conventions and personal preferences.

4.6   Implications for research on institutional discourse

Having identified the opposition between monologism and dialogism I may move on to explore actual interpreter-mediated conversations, both as 'text' and as social (inter)activity. Both approaches are valid in their own ways. In my view, a *combination* of the two models is needed in research on face-to-face interpreting, simply because the complex interconnections and divergences between these theoretical positions are highly relevant in the reality I want to explore. The occasional conflicts between seeing talk as text and talk as activities (other than 'text-production') are part of interpreters' everyday practice.

Being trained as an interpreter, the talk-as-text model is part of how I understand and define what I am doing. For instance, when

I sense or fear misunderstandings, I often seek errors and solutions with the help of the talk-as-text model. Taking a descriptive approach to face-to-face interpreting, a combination of the two models is implied already in the fact that I use a subject's definition of an event as a definition of the object of research. I take as 'interpreting' what people in practice understand as 'interpreting'. Normally 'interpreting' is understood as an activity involving translation, and whether shared or not by all people involved in the actual case, this understanding will have a certain impact on the activities subsequently taking place. Nevertheless, however, words and utterances achieve their meanings primarily in the framework of a particular activity, which in turn associates with a particular speech genre. Individuals' work as interpreters is dialogically organized in accordance with the overarching type of activity in which it takes place (e.g. a medical encounter, a police interrogation).

Secondly, and also regardless of whether or not the subjects have any theoretic or pre-theoretic model of interpreting as involving translation, my way of organizing empirical material when doing research implies that I identify translation as an aspect of what I analyse, even if it is not the *only* aspect, and I always understand it in relation to parallel and overarching activities of which it is a part.

Thirdly, face-to-face interpreting regularly takes place in institutional contexts, in medical and mental health care, in legal and other public settings. As Foucault (1971) and many others after him have shown, institutions live partly by their routines, including their ways of naming and talking about people and events. To some, for instance legal institutions, the use of language is its very foundation, the essence of its work in society.

The legal responsibility of interpreters presupposes a textual model of talk. As Ruth Morris (1993, 1995) concludes from her extensive survey of juridical documents – and what many active interpreters can conclude from their own experience – court interpreters are supposed to perform 'just translation', or 'verbatim translation' and *not* interpretation. As Morris notes, the image is at odds with modern insights about language and communication. This means that more realistic descriptions of interpreter-mediated interaction are urgently needed; empirically founded accounts of this activity, as it happens in legal as well as other institutional settings.

The fact that the very presence of interpreters in various ways transforms judicial proceedings is perhaps understood by many, but in practice it is far from acknowledged. This leaves us with an open question about how to secure individuals' legal rights in situations involving interpreter-mediated interaction.

The discrepancy between ideas and reality will be illustrated in the empirical chapters of this book. It regularly confronts interpreters with practical dilemmas of contradicting demands and expectations. This discrepancy must be seen as also the legal institutions' problem, which boils down to the question how to secure their credibility in situations involving interpreter-mediated interaction. This problem I would call a fundamental one, in a world where multilingualism is the norm rather than the exception.

NOTES

1. See Chapter 5:1.1 for a definition.
2. 'Natural translation' denotes a specialized human predisposition to speak, and to learn how to speak, observed among children growing up as bilinguals. Harris sees links between the translation performed by such children and translation as it is carried out in professional practice. This is taken to support an argument for a re-orientation regarding the choice of material for investigations on "the translation process", aimed at finding out about human cognitive functions (Harris 1992a).
3. Die Übersetzung ist eine Folge von Formulierungsprozessen, die von einem ausgangssprachlichen Text zu einem möglichst äquivalenten zielsprachlichen Text hinüberführen und das syntaktische, semantische und pragmatische Verständnis der Textvorlage voraussetzen (Wilss 1981:460).
4. . . . реальною единицею языка речи (Sprache als Rede), как мы уже знаем, является не изолированное единичное монологическое высказывание, а взаимодействие, по крайней мере, двух высказываний, т.е. диалог. Но продуктивное изучение диалога предполагает более глубокое исследование форм передачи чужой речи, ибо в них отражаются основные и константные тенденции *активного восприятия чужой речи* а ведь это восприятие является основопологающим и для диалоги (Voloshinov 1930:114–15).
5. Author's translation from Russian. The sentence is not included in the English translation (Bakhtin 1986a:87).
6. Author's translation from Russian.
7. Translation taken from an article on Bakhtin's work by Morson and Emerson (1989:20).
8. Austin's theory developed as a reaction against the theory of generative grammar dominating linguistics in the sixties, which emphasizes

internalized knowledge and the idea of biologically based structures of grammar and lexica as part of human nature. But as Duranti and Goodwin remark (1992:17), Austin's philosophy of language is later taken over by authors (for instance, by Searle 1969) who are influenced by what they term the 'cognitive turn' of linguistic studies. This implies a shift of focus, from speakers' activities in context, to their intentions and inner states of mind. We may here note that the 'cognitive turn' coincides with the advance of (conference) interpreting as an academic field.

THREE

Community interpreting: going professional

Partly due to increased mobility of migrants and refugees, the linguistically homogeneous nation hardly exists any longer (if it ever did). People who are supposed to communicate in legal, health and other public settings are sometimes unable to do this in a language in common. A general aim of this book is to elucidate how this fact influences the activities and routines carried out in these institutions. The present chapter provides a brief description of ideas of best practice of interpreters in some countries where interpreting in legal, health, educational and social service settings is relatively well established as a profession. These ideas are generally similar between the countries, to judge from official Codes of Conduct. Outlining these, I will indicate what many professional interpreters principally think they are doing – or should be doing – when acting in the role of interpreter (in Goffman's (1990) terms, these shared ideas would be called the interpreter's *normative role*, cf. Chapter 5:1). The chapter can be read as a background to the investigations performed in Chapters 6 to 9 below.

Interpreters' professional ethics may be similar between various countries, but the practical organization of language services (including those provided by interpreters) varies considerably from country to country, and sometimes within countries. At present, committed individual interpreters, professional associations and interpreter trainers are slowly developing national and international networks (Carr *et al.* 1997). Little by little, awareness is raised among lawyers, health care providers and others about the fact that interpreting regularly occurs and will continue to occur at their work places on an everyday basis. Simultaneously, professionally trained interpreters have gained ground from what have been described as "good but unskilful Samaritans, self-appointed experts and unscrupulous fixers who, often for a fat fee, 'helped' their less linguistically gifted compatriots" (Niska 1991:8).

1. DEFINING COMMUNITY INTERPRETING

Interpreting carried out in face-to-face encounters between officials and laypeople, meeting for a particular purpose at a public institution is (in English-speaking countries) often termed *community interpreting* (cf. e.g. Shackman 1984, Niska 1991, Downing and Swabey 1992, Downing and Helms Tillery 1992, Tebble 1992, Sanders 1992, Solomou 1993, Harris 1994, Kasanji 1995, Schweda Nicholson 1994, Carr *et al.* 1997). Sometimes *liaison interpreting* is used as a synonymous term (e.g. Lang 1978, Keith 1984, Hatim and Mason 1990, Gentile *et al.* 1996). It is probably the kind of interpreting undertaken most frequently in the world at large. Once performed only by volunteers, *ad hoc* bilinguals, friends, and relatives (even children) this type of interpreting has, during the last few decades, been developing into a profession. The professionalization process manifests itself in the emergence of interpreters' associations, educational programmes and certification examinations.

Community interpreting is typically bi-directional, that is, the same interpreter works in the two languages in question. As a rule, it is carried out consecutively upon the original speakers' talk, sequence by sequence. The concept covers both interpreting in face-to-face situations and interpreting provided over the telephone. Health care, mental health, educational, social service and legal interpreting are frequently given as sub-categories, and community interpreting as a more general concept.

In many countries, sign language interpreting, which includes a large proportion of bi-directional interpreting in institutional face-to-face interaction, enjoys public recognition and support as a branch of its own. There are professional associations for sign language interpreters, which, as a rule, are associated with societies for the Deaf. Some countries have educational programmes for sign language interpreters at university level. This is the case, for instance, in the US, where, moreover, the nationwide Registry of Interpreters for the Deaf publishes textbooks and has its own legally enforced certification programme (Frishberg 1986).

1.1 A profession in its infancy

It is perhaps characteristic of a profession in the process of establishing itself that the terminology around it is not settled but overlapping and partly competing. Each qualifier is bound to emphasize a certain perspective. Grounds for classification are, for instance:

- the form of interplay between primary parties' and interpreters' **utterances** (consecutive or simultaneous interpreting; summarizing interpreting; pilot-interpreting or 'relaying', that is when interpreting is made not from an original speech, but from a simultaneously delivered interpreted version, which sometimes happens at conferences);
- the **acoustic quality** of interpreters' utterances (interpreting by whispering = *chuchotage*);
- the social **relation** between interpreters and those whom they are to primarily assist, or who give the assignments (escort or liaison interpreting);
- the social **status** of interpreters (e.g. professional, non-professional, native, non-native, and *ad hoc* interpreter);
- the **setting** where the interpreters work (conference, community, public service, court, medical, social service, dialogue, face-to-face interpreting etc.)

My use of 'dialogue interpreting' (Wadensjö 1992, 1995) has indeed been to stress the defining primacy of the *setting* (the communicative exchange) in which the interpreting under investigation takes place. Also, 'community interpreting' foregrounds, if you wish, the setting (the community at large), rather than single individuals.

The position of interpreters working in spoken interaction is by necessity pivotal. While interpreters working among business people and diplomats self-evidently are expected to side with those by whom they are hired, however, the users' expectancy as regards community interpreters may be somewhat contradictory. Officials may count on the interpreter's loyalty, since the interpreter's salary is paid, as a rule, by the public organization. At the same time lay people may expect the interpreter to side with them. After all, language services belong to the individual layperson's public rights. As interpreter, I may often be confronted with the practical dilemma of being simultaneously seen as the layperson's advocate and as the official's helping hand, a dilemma which at times can be further emphasized by existing social antagonism, ethnic tensions and racial prejudice.

The professionalization and institutionalization of interpreting in the public service sphere reflects, on the one hand, an official concern for the legal and social security of minority, migrant and refugee populations. Professional community interpreting is supposed to enable those who lack fluency in the majority language(s) to get full and equal public service from society at large. On the other hand, the organized approach reflects a concern for the authorities' ability to carry out their duties, when dealing with people who are unable or unwilling to communicate in an official language. An interpreter's factual task consists in enabling communication to occur, but not just any communication. An important objective for the professional training of community interpreters is of course to avert errors. Misunderstandings can be both fatal for individuals, and costly to the public purse. For instance, it goes without saying that practitioners can hardly provide adequate health-care if they are unable to communicate (if they do not understand their patients' problems correctly, and if they cannot make themselves adequately understood).

Court interpreting is the kind of 'community interpreting' (in the broad sense) which is so far most described and explored in scholarly literature (cf. Chapter 4). The legal sphere is also where community interpreters' professionalism is most developed as yet. Court interpreters are beginning to write their history. A report by Roberts *et al.* (1981) bears witness to this development in the officially bilingual Canada. González, Vásques and Mikkelson (1991) in their 600-plus page *Fundamentals of Court Interpretation* provide detailed information about the US court system and the history of interpretation services within this system along with recommendations for how to prepare to become a good interpreter and how to behave professionally in and outside court. US court interpreters are provided with certification in special order, by The Administrative Office of the United States Courts. More information of this kind is collected, for instance, in books by de Jongh (1992) and Edwards (1995). A recent book by Colin and Morris (1996) focuses on practice and standards of legal interpreting in England and Wales.

The relatively higher degree of professionalization of court interpreters can partly be explained by internationally established conventions on human rights, and, occasionally, corresponding national laws concerning the individual's right to free assistance of an interpreter when called for to a court of law, the language of which he

or she cannot understand or speak. Most literature on court interpreting communicates that the performance of poorly trained interpreters may lead to unjust convictions and damage the credibility
of the legal system in question. The argument is that adequately
trained interpreters are needed to guarantee that suspects and
witnesses have their say and are correctly heard. It goes without
saying that incompetently performed interpreting can influence negatively how defendants and witnesses are presented in court. As Berk-
Seligson (1990) puts it: "No amount of oath-swearing can guarantee
high quality interpreting from an interpreter who does not have the
necessary competency" (Berk-Seligson 1990:204). In other words, the
quality of interpreting is not a question of interpreters' intentions,
but of their proficiency in the two languages and of their interpreting skill. Yet it remains to be explored how interpreter-training – of
various orientations – correlates with improved chances for just
convictions. Furthermore, the organization of court proceedings
provides a context to interpreting which is regardless of individual interpreters' proficiency. There is a certain risk in directing
attention too much at the interpreter. As Dunnigan and Downing
(1995:108–10) conclude in their case study of legal interpreting on
trial, it is crucial that the courts do not apply a mechanical model of
the role of interpreters and that the officers of the court receive
instruction on what can and what cannot be expected of them.

1.2 A few notes on the labour market

The professionalization process of community interpreters has fluc-
tuated considerably not only from country to country and within
countries but also over time. The instability and stress of the labour
market has sometimes made community interpreters refrain from
putting effort and time into achieving professional qualification,
that is, when and if professional training is available, and afford-
able. And lack of professional training, of course, diminishes one's
preparedness to cope with the difficulties of the job, the psychosocial
ones, concerning status and role performance, as well as those depending on language proficiency.

   Interpreters are more often recruited from a minority than from
the majority population. The individual interpreter's relatively greater
linguistic and cultural competence normally adds to his or her social
status from the point of view of those who experience a lack of such

competence. Simultaneously, association with a minority might lower a person's social status in the eyes of certain members of a majority. A person who does not feel comfortable in a mediating, middle position – and sometimes a genuinely outside one – should probably look for another career.

Some interpreters see community interpreting as a temporary occupation, practised while awaiting an opportunity to start a 'real' job, in particular people who have a background of other professional work which turns out to be difficult to establish in the new country. This expression of interpreters' low self-estimation is a direct reflection of the attitudes met in encounters with others. An interpreter in my interview data (Wadensjö 1987) expressed the expectations she had met quite negatively, which were basically of two kinds: some people believe that anyone who can talk a certain language also can be an interpreter. They simply do not see the efforts put into interpreting and treat interpreters without respect and understanding. Others treat interpreters with an exaggerated respect, as if they were some kind of supernatural beings. According to this interpreter, people's estimation is partly related to the languages spoken. Being from Finland, and having Finnish as her first language, she sometimes experienced her highly qualified work between Swedish (her second language) and Finnish to be much less appreciated than her less qualified interpreting between Swedish and Russian (her third language). This left her with mixed feelings, since it was as if her admirers considered Russian hard to learn but worth learning, while Finnish was something that only Finns know. It is a fact that the value of language knowledge is never constant; that language hierarchies of various kinds may exist within a society, between majority and minority, as well as between minority groups, and attitudes towards interpreters may be affected by attitudes towards the language(s) they speak.

Judging from the relatively low wages, public service interpreting is generally a low status branch, compared with interpreting at conferences and other more glamorous areas of social life. Small wonder then, if people want to switch to something more profitable, for the same or less effort. Some interpreters do not stay in the job simply for reasons of diminishing opportunities to work. Little by little, when a language minority has learnt the majority language, their demand for interpreter-assistance of course disappears correspondingly. It may reappear, however, with new migrants speaking this language.

Fluctuations in the labour market may also be due to more un-predictable factors. New waves of refugees, fleeing wars or political and religious persecution, mean more or less sudden new demands for interpreters. When there are changes in the political climate in the receiving countries concerning asylum and migration, this may also change the need for interpreters. Furthermore, the labour market in a certain area self-evidently increases and decreases with migrants' opportunities to live and work there.

Community interpreters may specialize and work only in a certain sphere, but with a broad profile and flexibility one may improve one's job opportunities. Interpreting in various parts of society can be a very dynamic and rewarding job. One learns about these various spheres and meets a variety of people. Interpreters are often present at particularly dramatic moments in individuals' lives, and get to know both the joyful and the less pleasant sides of society. There is often no doubt that one's assistance is urgently needed. Many inter-preters work on a freelance basis and the assignments may be given at very short notice. This flexible form of organizing work suits some people very well, while others find it too stressful at times. Only in some larger cities' social service agencies, hospitals and similar big institutions, can staff positions sometimes be available for community interpreters.

Some interpreters suffer burn-out from working intensively with cases involving victims of horrors like torture, rape and child molesta-tion. Working alone, a community interpreter may have few (if any) opportunities to get a supervisor's advice, or simply to offload anxi-eties in confidence. The ethics of confidentiality put restrictions upon what may be talked about. Some interpreters feel that they cannot say anything to anyone about what they experience on duty. In these situations, a freelancer's outsider status can be particularly hard to manage. In my interviews with interpreters, their courses of profes-sional training are often mentioned for the reason that they made them feel more self-secure as interpreters, and therefore helped improve their performance on duty.

2. EDUCATION AND CERTIFICATION

Professional training for community interpreters is comparatively well established in countries where the need for reliable interpret-ing is recognized as a concern of society at large (and not a concern for the language minorities primarily or exclusively). For instance, in Australia, in Canada (not least in its Northwest territories) and in the Scandinavian countries, the training of broad profile community interpreters has been supported by national governments since the 1970s (González *et al.* 1991, Niska 1991, Plimer and Candlin 1996).

The education generally has a practical orientation. Courses which are specifically designed for community interpreting tend to be run by colleges rather than by universities, and the body of theoretical knowledge is relatively little in the field. The general goal of these educational programmes is of course to improve interpreting accuracy. The training includes working knowledge of terminology in the language combinations in question, and of procedures and particularities relating to the areas in which the candidate interpreters aim to work (health care, social and legal services and so forth). Interpretation classes may involve language laboratory work, role-playing exercises, training in note-taking techniques, sight translation, written translation, and other didactic techniques applied also in the teaching of conference interpreters. Most programmes are furthermore designed to develop awareness of cultural differences between majorities and minorities. The content of training programmes may vary in scope. Regardless of level of ambition, however, a certain emphasis is put on the ethics of community interpreting. As a rule, courses aim at obtaining the candidate interpreters' commitment to a professional Code of Ethics, and giving guidance in good practice. Interpreters' associations have in many cases played a certain role in the formulation of Codes. At least, associations are crucial when it comes to making sure that norms are officially shared. They may also be involved in certification programmes, which, of course, constitute an important stage in the professionalization process. To my knowledge, the documentation of this process so far mostly covers English-speaking countries, and, consequently, is written mostly in English.

2.1 Pioneering efforts – a few examples

In Australia, the Department of Immigration initiated in 1973 the establishment of a pool for the Emergency Telephone Interpreting Service. This service now (as the Translating and Interpreting Service) provides on-site and 24-hour telephone interpreting in over 100 languages across Australia for the cost of a local call. There are also other, more locally working services. In Australia, hospitals, child-care and social welfare centres, schools, police-stations and courts etc., are obliged by law to call for (and pay for) an interpreter's assistance when the need arises. In practice, however, the provision, training, budget and availability of translation and interpreting services vary greatly in different parts of the country (Plimer and Candlin 1996).

Accreditation of community interpreters has existed since 1977. It is provided by the National Accreditation Authority for Translators and Interpreters, NAATI, in at least 20 different languages (in combination with English). Another important institution is the Australian Institute of Interpreters and Translators (AUSIT) (AUSIT 1992). These and other organizations have made considerable efforts through the years to instruct users of interpretation services. The School of Languages, Interpreting and Translating at Deakin University has run courses in the field of interpreting. From the end of the 1980s until recently (1997) these also included community interpreting. A Masters programme in Translation and Interpretation which centres on issues connected to public service interpreting is being developed at Macquarie University, Sydney.

In New Zealand, the Auckland Institute of Technology in Wellington has run courses in community interpreting between English and some six Asian and Pacific languages. The first professional training programme for Maori interpreters was organized in 1994, but accreditation has been available for English-Maori since 1987. For other languages, interpreters can get accreditation through the NAATI of Australia. Although this organization has no official status in New Zealand, it is widely used as providing a *de facto* standard (Kasanji 1995).

Due to the ethnic structure of the population, the need for and the education of community interpreters in Canada differs between the provinces. The Arctic College in the Northwest Territories has trained interpreters and translators between English and different aboriginal languages since the 1970s. In the state of Alberta, in contrast, the Alberta Vocational College trains interpreters in Eastern European, Latin American, South East Asian and African languages. Moreover, Vancouver Community College, in Vancouver, British Columbia, has offered a certificate programme for court interpreters in different minority languages since 1979.

In the United States too, different states have different policies. The Monterey Institute of International Studies (MIIS) was one of the first institutions in the US to offer courses in court interpreting. Later they started also with medical interpreting. The University of Arizona at Tucson, Arizona, has run courses in court interpreting since the 1980s. The language combination most frequently trained for in the US has long been English–Spanish, but the large increase during the 1980s of immigrants and refugees from Asian, Pacific, Middle East and East European countries is due to augment the number of training programmes for the languages in question (Downing and Helms Tillery 1992).

Many countries in Europe – including Austria, Belgium, France, Germany, Holland, Hungary, Italy, Russia, Spain, Switzerland and the Czech Republic – have well established schools for conference interpreters and translators of diverse profiles, but relatively few efforts have been made to formalize education and tests for public service interpreting. Nevertheless, just as in other parts of the world, court interpreting is comparatively more institutionalized than social service, health and mental health interpreting. Training of court interpreters has started partly thanks to translators' and interpreters' professional associations. For instance, the German national professional association for interpreters and translators, BDÜ (*Bund der Dolmetscher und Übersetzer*) organizes short-term training in court interpreting. The Dutch Translators' Society formulated a Professional Code and a Code of Honour for court interpreters in 1979 (Jansen forthcoming). One may note in this connection that in Spain, as well as in Latin America, court interpreting is less established as a profession compared to legal translation, partly due to the fact that the court system in Spanish-speaking countries has traditionally put a strong emphasis on written statements, and relied relatively less on live witness testimony (Mikkelson 1996).

In the United Kingdom, the Community Interpreter Project, which includes training programmes, was set up in 1983 by The Institute of Linguists in London. The institute is today the examination board providing 'Diplomas in Public Service Interpreting' (DPSI) in some 25 languages. Different colleges all over the UK run short-term courses leading up to the DPSI exams, which take place once a year. Interpreters can specialize in either Local Government, Health or Law. Since 1994, the holder of a DPSI has been entitled to apply for membership of the National Register of Public Service Interpreters.

Among the Scandinavian countries, Sweden pioneered professional training for community interpreters in 1968, at a time when a lot of migrant workers (largely from Finland, but also from the

Mediterranean region) were recruited by Swedish companies. Since the latter part of the 1970s, however, and during the 1980s and 1990s, the stream of migrants to Sweden – as well as to many other receiving countries – has been dominated by refugees and so-called family reunion migrants. Since 1986, the responsibility for providing university-level training in public service interpreting and translation (Diploma courses of one and a half to two years) lies with the Institute for Interpretation and Translation Studies at Stockholm University. A system for community interpreter accreditation valid on a national level has existed in Sweden since 1976. Swedish community interpreters are licensed by a separate state authority, and certification, which in 1998 is available in 30 language combinations (Swedish plus another one), must be renewed every five years.

2.2 Professionalism, Codes of Conduct and users' guides

In locally produced guidelines one may find rules, recommendations and specific requirements for interpreting in health care and mental health care, but 'official' Codes of Ethics often seem to be produced first and foremost with legal settings in mind. In conclusion this section will summarize the main content of these Codes. They are largely similar from one state, province and country to another, and we may recognize in them what, according to the sociologist Parsons (1964), defines 'professionalism'. In his view, 'professionalism' implies the existence of officially *shared ethical norms* for the maintenance of proper conduct. It is further characterized by emotional *neutrality*. Professionals treat all clients equally (universalism). Moreover, in Parsons' view, the individual gains professionality through personal *training* (and not through heritage). Another point concerns the professional's services, which are defined as provided for the collective good, and restricted to a specifically defined *factual task* (functional specificity). By no means all of those acting in the role of interpreter in institutional encounters would identify with these criteria. Applying these criteria to the documented data, however, I have no doubt that those acting as interpreters are involved in a professionalization process.

Where community interpreting is regulated by an official Code of Ethics, it often entails an obligation to avoid siding with any of the parties. The principle of *neutrality and detachment,* taken for granted perhaps first of all for court interpreting, is a major issue of debate among professional community interpreters and interpreter trainers. This principle obliges interpreters not to let personal attitudes colour their interpreting work. It also implies that interpreters must disclose any real or apparent *conflict of interest* (e.g. close relationship with one of the parties in a legal case). Interpreters must not accept assignments where such conflicts are known, and should they come to light in the course of work the interpreter is obliged to unveil the nature of the conflict.

Community interpreting is normally covered by an *Official Secrets Act*. Interpreters must observe strict confidentiality and not disclose any information gained from the assignment to outside parties. Interpreters must interpret *fully and faithfully* everything said by the primary parties, and *keep strictly to the task of interpreting*. This also implies that interpreters must decline assignments which are beyond their capability.

Since the 1970s laws have been in place that anyone living in Sweden who does not speak Swedish or who is severely impaired in speech or hearing enjoys a right to an interpreter when communicating with public institutions. These laws are associated with an official Good Interpreting Practice, *God tolksed* (Kammarkollegiet (Legal, Financial and Administrative Services Agency) 1996). This Swedish Code of Conduct (which is of particular relevance here since it is known and pertinent to the interpreters appearing in the data in later chapters) compares the interpreter's duty to the obligation of a witness under oath: to hide nothing, to add nothing and to change nothing. (In contrast to Anglo-Saxon legal tradition it does not mention 'the whole truth and nothing but the truth'.) The interpreter is described as a kind of witness, but not for a particular side. The interpreter's allegiance is to both parties, or to the person whose utterance he or she is in the process of translating.

The court interpreter's position in relation to the court may vary. As was mentioned above, US certified court interpreters (except those working between American Sign Language and spoken English) are formally recognized as officers of the legal institution. This does not mean that the stipulated ethical rules differ much, but there may be differences in levels of detail. For instance, the New Jersey Supreme Court Task Force on Interpreters and Translation Services (cited by Berk-Seligson 1990:234–8) explicitly advises interpreters on how to dress in court, and debars engaging in behaviour that would draw attention to themselves in court, including imitating gestures or emotions, pointing, or engaging in other paralinguistic conduct (Berk-Seligson 1990:236). This is a point where, for instance, the Swedish Code is not explicit. Here the opposite could be taken as implicitly understood. It is stated that any nuance, including the emotional subtleties in what primary parties say, must be relayed by the interpreter. Just like, for instance, Colin and Morris (1996:146), the Swedish Guide to Good Practice is explicit on the point that interpreting should be performed not in the third person, but in the first person, 'I'-form, in order to promote the primary interlocutors to address one another, and not the interpreter; to say, for example, "I lost my job two weeks ago" and not "(He says that) he lost his job two weeks ago" or "I would like you to tell the court what happened" and not "(She says that) she would like you to tell the court what happened".

Ethical codes become shared not only among interpreters. Interpreters' associations and occasionally legal institutions and scholars of Law are also active in describing and spreading information about the preferred modes of working when instructing and advising public service officials. Guidelines on how to work with interpreters have been provided by institutions such as the NAATI of Australia (see above), the Law Society of New South Wales, Sydney, Australia (1996), and the Ethnic Affairs Service (Department of Internal Affairs) in Auckland, New Zealand (Kasanji 1995).

Guidelines to interpreter users may involve recommendations concerning both how to prepare for an interpreter-mediated encounter, and how to behave while involved in it. For instance, people are advised to allow extra time for an interview when the assistance of an interpreter is planned and, if possible, to hire accredited interpreters. Working with an interpreter, officials are recommended to pause frequently so that the interpreter can remember and interpret what is being said, to avoid separate discussions with the interpreter that leaves the client out, and to speak directly to their counterpart rather than addressing the interpreter (i.e. not "tell him to . . ." etc.; cf. above).

The appropriate degree of interpreters' involvement (or non-involvement) in the primary interlocutors' affairs should in my view be constantly raised as an issue, and thoroughly discussed in every branch and institution where interpreters' assistance is needed. The implication of guidelines to primary parties and interpreters alike demands a basic understanding of the impact an interpreter and third party may have on the ordinary institutional routines and activities.

FOUR

Interpreters and other intermediaries

INTERPRETATION. From Lat. *interpretari,* to expound, explain, *interpres,* an agent, go-between, interpreter; *inter,* between, and the root *pret-,* possibly connected with that seen either in Greek φραζειν, to speak, or πραττειν, to do, in general, the action of explaining, or rendering the sense of an obscure form of words or an unknown tongue into a language comprehended by the person addressed (*Encyclopaedia Britannica* 1910–11, Vol.14:710).

Wherever two persons or parties wish to have some kind of exchange, and direct contact is obstructed by a lack of knowledge, social mobility, mutual interest or language proficiency, there may be an apparent need for an intermediary, a need that can be satisfied given the parties' mutual acceptance of such an actor to assist them. Concurrently with the compartmentalization and diversification of a society, the intermediary's role is routinized and subsequently professionalized. People who are specifically trained and appointed to collect information on others' account and to speak on others' behalf have their given place in a number of social activities, from commercial, political and diplomatic encounters to court proceedings, counselling interviews and family therapy sessions.

This chapter will concentrate on concepts like *intermediary, mediator, gatekeeper* and *non-person.* Exploring how these notions are applied in a variety of scholarly literature, I will show that they have bearing on investigations of interpreter-mediated encounters. Some of the works discussed below deal with interpreting in face-to-face interaction specifically. In this literature, interpreters' 'mediation' is not necessarily presented as a phenomenon to be explored and described, but more often as something that must be prohibited; as 'unprofessional' behaviour; as the individual interpreter's wilful distortion or amateurish shortcomings. In these studies the individual interpreter is the basic unit of study, rather than the interpreter-mediated encounter.

As I discussed in Chapter 2 above, the view of interpreters' 'mediation' as 'something wrong' partly reflects myths about interpreting, founded in a monological preconception of language and mind. The image of the interpreter as a neutral channel and the idea of interpreting as a transfer of texts from one language to another belong in a monological theoretical frame. Consequently, the monological view of language and language use is occasionally present in literature on face-to-face interpreting. This becomes evident, for instance, when an 'erroneous' reality is 'corrected' against implicit or explicit norms.

1. IT TAKES THREE TO MAKE AN INTERMEDIARY

Goffman (1990), in an essay on *discrepant roles* (first published in 1959), draws attention to the fact that a person who mediates between two parties who are in one another's presence, displays behaviour which would have appeared rather strange if one of the two had been absent. The organization of a situation is dependent on all parties involved in it and on how they relate to one another.

Considering this fact, it seems natural to follow Goffman's suggestion concerning the basic analytical unit when investigating a social role, namely the *group and its members* (Goffman 1990:149). In the present case, this implies not the individual interpreter but the interpreter-mediated encounter. It takes a relevant audience to attribute someone a particular social role, and a certain mutuality in the interaction among members of this audience. The relevant audience of a performing interpreter are two or more persons who interact with one another in various languages with the assistance of the interpreter.

1.1 Intermediaries between majority and minority

Bailey (1969), building on a number of anthropological studies, discusses intermediaries' or 'middlemen's' functions in societies with at least two political structures existing in parallel. These are, on a general level, characterized as a more dominant A-structure – as a rule the structure of the state or the majority culture – and a B-structure – a weaker enclave within the domains of this first A-structure. According to Bailey, intermediaries in these contexts can essentially be categorized by two different principles. On the one hand, one can distinguish between those who get their position from the stronger structure, who would be installed to guarantee its normative system, and those whose role is the result of initiatives taken by the weaker one.

On the other hand, Bailey discusses 'middlemen's' function from the point of view of their degree of independence in relation to the primary parties. Thus, the 'pure messenger' would stand for the type of intermediary who is most dependent on primary parties and their actions, while the 'broker' is an actor with a stronger mandate, filling a more complex function with both an overview of, and influence over, the processes by which minority and majority groups intermingle.

Differences in norms and basic values in the separate groups to a great extent condition the intermediary's activity. This also implies, as Bailey points out, that where negotiation is perceived to go wrong, parties tend to direct suspicion at the middleman. Intermediaries of the first category, appointed by the majority group, run the risk of being regarded as spies or traitors, and those appointed by the minority group risk being seen as renegades.

Paine (1971), another anthropologist, doing fieldwork in the Canadian Arctic, distinguishes, like Bailey, between 'brokers' and 'go-betweens'. To him, they signify intermediaries of different social status and influence. To act as a 'broker' would be to take more independent measures to initiate or promote negotiation, while a 'go-between' would only carry out initiatives generated by the primary parties. The role of 'broker', it is said, is often combined with the role of 'patron', i.e. the spokesman, or 'big man' in a minority-group. The spokesman, acting as the connecting link between the Inuit minority society and the Canadian majority society and its institutions, is delegated responsibility and power from both sides. Like Goffman (1990), Paine observes that the position in between is exceptional and potentially a powerful one for the person in the middle.

1.2 Myths about mediators' roles

Gulliver (1979) investigates the mediating process as such, related to a general theory of conflict and negotiation. He starts by remarking that the mediator's role(s) and function(s) have been largely ignored in sociology, as well as in psychology, game theory, or for that matter, his own discipline, anthropology. He is critical of what he sees as stereotyped and ethnocentric images of the mediator.

Among other things, he dismisses as a myth the idea that mediators are merely catalysts or that they, by definition as it were, act impartially (Gulliver 1979:211). In his view, this is more a belief, existing in relatively homogeneous Western societies, than a fact.

Another simplified presupposition is that a mediator's activity would consist just in making the parties collaborate towards a common goal instead of competing. In practice, Gulliver argues, intermediary roles vary a lot. Moreover, there are variations not only in terms of the mediator's strategies and mandates. The situations where the intermediary third party would be expected and accepted also vary between cultures. Likewise, there are variations as to what determines his or her authority.

Gulliver describes mediators' strategic roles on a continuum, representing the range of strengths of interventions. In general, it is stated, a third party who is present at a negotiation will always exert some influence on the process. Gulliver suggests evaluating the status and role of the mediator firstly by reference to his or her possible personal interests in the issue at stake, and secondly, with regard to how, in that case, he or she would be an interested party. Gulliver emphasizes that in the evaluation of intermediaries one should count on the fact that their self-interest sometimes takes over the interest of one or both disputants (Gulliver 1979:217–20).

There are at least two points in Gulliver's investigation that could be significant for descriptions and explorations of institutional interpreter-mediated interaction. The presence of interpreters affects in certain ways – expected and unexpected – the communication between the expert and the layperson. As is well known to experienced interpreters, this kind of conversation implies potentially conflicting viewpoints between the primary parties and thus often gives currency to the question of how to avoid siding with one or the other party. It is in the self-interest of interpreters to be impartial. In taking initiatives to defend their own interests, interpreters will necessarily influence the progression and the content of the current exchange. Does it happen at the expense of (one or both of) the primary parties?

1.3 Formalized and spontaneous intermediaries

Discrepant roles, as defined in Goffman's (1990) essay mentioned above, are roles taken by and given to persons who control the validity of information in a given situation, or, more precisely, the kind of information by which a particular situation is defined by those present as being of a certain kind (e.g. a professional or private conversation, an informal chat or a formal interrogation). Hence control also applies to the kind of talk that would be counted as appropriate and 'belonging' in the situation.

A general theme in Goffman's essay is that individuals are included or excluded in different situations through their social roles. These, in turn, are connected to the actors' presumed or actual access to each other's 'secrets'. This presupposes a fairly broad definition of secret. Almost all information in a social establishment, he argues, has something of an *excluding* function. In other words, what to someone is relevant information, is almost always none of somebody else's business. The moral foundation for the intermediary's position is the very fact that they know 'secrets' of two separate groups (1990:141ff.).

In Goffman's definition, the 'go-between' or 'mediator' is a 'discrepant role' existing in a couple of quite different forms. For instance, he mentions the foreman. As foreman, a person carries out an intermediary function between the workers and the management. This brings to mind what Giles and colleagues show about the non-institutionalized – but nevertheless fairly stable – intermediary roles that are taken by or given to nurses and other members of hospital staff in communication between doctors and patients (Giles *et al.* 1986). The chairperson of formally conducted meetings is another of Goffman's examples. Being in this role one has a responsibility to regulate interaction between those present, and in this way fill a mediator's function. The chairperson in fact serves as a visible model for those taking part in the encounter of how to attend to it.

The role of mediator is especially significant in multi-party interaction. Informal interaction, Goffman argues, can be seen as the formation and re-formation of teams, and the creation and re-creation of go-betweens. Those present will, in varying degree, show a concerned attention to the person speaking. From time to time, different persons will take responsibility for interpreting (in a broad sense) what is said, so that it will be included as a relevant contribution to common talk (Goffman 1990:150).

This phenomenon is perhaps particularly evident when someone is introduced into a situation where others present are already acquainted with one another, or when persons are treated as not fully competent to speak for themselves. An intermediary function is typically taken by or given to parents bringing a child to an expert, say a doctor, and speaking on the child's behalf, even when he or she is explicitly addressed.

1.4 Non-persons – people present but treated as absent

A discrepant role discussed at some length by Goffman (1990) is that of *non-person*. In his definition, actors who play the role of 'non-person' are present during an encounter but in some respect do not take the role either of performer or of audience, nor do they pretend to be what they are not (as informers, decoys, and sometimes detectives would do). A classic type of 'non-person' is the servant. This is an individual who, on the one hand, is expected to be present at particular occasions, and, on the other, is defined in certain ways as someone who is not there (1990:150). Other examples would be the very young, the very old, the sick and, sometimes, the foreigner, who is believed not to understand, at some level, talk among people who share the same presuppositions, insights or means of communication. Participants can, from time to time, regard one another as sufficiently or non-sufficiently competent interlocutors.

As Aronsson (1991) demonstrates – drawing upon Goffman's sociopsychology and with the help of a paediatric case study – what a child says in a paediatric interview will be taken as a contribution to it by the adults, depending on whether the child is treated as fully present at the conversation or not. In other words, negotiations in multi-party talk concern not only the meanings of utterances but, directly or indirectly, also personhood or non-personhood (Aronsson 1991:73). This is the role of 'non-person' regarded from the others' perspective. But, as Goffman points out, one should not underestimate the degree to which the role of 'non-person' can be used as a defence. For instance, in a paediatric situation, this would imply that the child could choose to ignore others' talk and, when he or she felt like it, speak about whatever comes to mind, even at times when the adults expect the child to participate as a competent interlocutor. A 'non-person' enjoys the privileges of being able to address anyone or to ignore being addressed without causing a redefinition of the situation. Broadcasting technicians and photographers typically act as 'non-persons' in this respect, during public ceremonies like concerts and debates, when they take liberties to move about while the audience is supposed to take their seats, and to address anyone as though they were in charge of the event. They are present neither as audience nor as performers, but primarily as mediators, acting on behalf of a non-present audience.

In many respects, the concept of 'non-person' applies to the interpreter in face-to-face interaction. Interpreters play a kind of technical role and are counted as not fully present; there is an expectation that they will contribute nothing to the substance of the current conversation. But there are aspects of this profession that do not fit the description; most significantly, interpreters are indeed supposed to talk publicly. In addition, the interpreter's talk conditions the talk of others (and vice versa).

1.5 Gatekeepers – intermediaries between lay people and institutions

A considerable body of literature has been exploring what Erickson and Schultz (1982) term society's 'gatekeepers', that is, officials working within local bureaucracies that handle and distribute public resources. In their book *The Counsellor as Gatekeeper*, they investigate student counselling interviews. Other encounters of this kind might include job interviews (e.g. Adelswärd 1988) and interviews between social workers and their clients (e.g. Cedersund 1992, Sarangi and Slembrouck 1996). Court trials, too, are a kind of gatekeeping encounter, as are in fact most meetings between lay people and administrators in charge of public goods, services and control functions.

Following Agar (1985) one may identify this kind of encounter as *institutional discourse* and observe in them three constituting phases, namely *diagnosis, report and directive*. 'Diagnosis' is the first, 'fact-finding' part, in which the client's problem(s) is identified and he or she is categorized in institutional terms by the professional party. In parallel, or as a conclusion, the professional compiles a 'report' which belongs to the body of documentation held by the institution. 'Directive', finally, concerns the measures recommended and decisions taken by the professional party. As Agar points out, the established institutional frames allow the professionals to make a limited number of diagnoses, report in certain established ways, and prepare for a circumscribed set of directives. This means that they will control the flow of information by introducing, reinforcing and excluding topics according to the rationalities of the institution.

These are not always plain to see, and often enough not of primary interest to lay people, who therefore have comparatively less scope for controlling the situation (Agar 1985:150–2). The outcome of institutional encounters depends on the intermediary's ability, time and willingness to see the others' perspectives.

To understand gatekeeping and gatekeepers in modern society it is necessary to study its inter-cultural, inter-ethnic and inter-lingual dimensions. Modern society bears the stamp of ongoing international migration, where the inclusion and exclusion of newcomers seems to be an everyday matter. The work of Gumperz and his associates (1982a; 1982b) significantly advanced the academic study of ethnically and culturally mixed institutional discourse. The importance and fruitfulness of an inter-cultural approach has since repeatedly been shown, for instance in a recent work by Bremer and others (1996) reporting from a large European project on second language acquisition among minority workers. It is demonstrated that workers who otherwise spoke quite fluently had difficulties when they had to manage bureaucratic encounters, simply because they were unsure what information would be counted as relevant or irrelevant. From a wide variety of studies it is concluded that the outcome of encounters largely depends on how the minority clients (as patients, applicants, etc.) master what have become the bureaucratically acceptable and expected modes of communication (cf. Bremer *et al.* 1996). Even if the migrants had enough knowledge in the new language to lead a conversation, they had difficulties in deciphering the situations and their *frames*, to use a notion first developed by the US social psychologist Bateson (1972) and subsequently utilized by Goffman (1974) and many of their followers.

Since meetings between lay people and representatives of public institutions follow a routinized pattern, explorations of daily encounters give information about how potential conflict of interest is handled on a daily basis. Investigating these encounters is thus a way to shed light on the effects of public policy. Reading official documents, legal codes and job descriptions is one way to get information about the ideas behind the work of a bureaucracy and professional actors within it. Another way is to explore how official plans become routinized and rationalized in concrete encounters, how political meaning is interpreted and reproduced in practice.

As do all professionalized intermediaries, interpreters work at providing a particular *service*. Simultaneously, they – of necessity – exercise a certain *control*. Obviously, there is a potential conflict between the service and the control aspects, which sometimes surfaces in dilemmas reported in the literature on institutional communication. It largely remains to be investigated how this conflict is handled in institutional interpreter-mediated talk, where the gatekeeping is, in effect, doubled.

2. INTERPRETERS IN FACE-TO-FACE INTERACTION

Interpreting in face-to-face interaction is gradually becoming recognized as a part of the everyday life of public institutions. As was discussed in Chapter 3, the awareness of the phenomenon seems to be growing among officials within the legal sphere, within medical and mental health care, and within social welfare and education. The interpreting taking place there is also slowly becoming established as a subject of empirical research. The number of research projects devoted specifically to this kind of interpreting is, however, still very small. It will probably take some time, but I can foresee interesting ethnographic and biographic works reflecting the function of interpreters in the shaping of modern society, just as one can today read historical literature and interpreters' biographies describing the role of the interpreter in political history at state level.[1]

2.1 Interpreters in fieldwork

In scholarly literature, interpreter-mediated interviews appear first as methodological problems. For instance, Phillips (1960), Hymes (1964) and Crapanzano (1980) all discuss the question of how to evaluate 'facts' collected in fieldwork with the assistance of interpreters.

Recently, Blomqvist (1996) has discussed this issue in connection with her study of water resources and local economy in southern India. Most of her informants spoke only Tamil, a language of which she had hardly any knowledge. Her general impression was that the interpreters, working between English and Tamil, made a highly qualified job, and, as she observes, the interpreters did much more than just translate. It was obvious that they acted in the role of social intermediary. Being unable to initiate a conversation, both because she lacked linguistic knowledge and simply by virtue of being female (her informants were mainly male, as also were her two interpreters), Blomqvist needed assistance to establish the first contact and to introduce herself and her purpose. Accordingly, the interpreters sometimes also covered up for her lack of social competence as defined locally (thereby also covering up for themselves, being associated with a foreign woman).

Problematizing the method of data collection, Blomqvist asked an independent Tamil- and English-speaking person to transcribe one of her many tape-recorded interviews, a particularly long and informative one, and translate the parts spoken in Tamil. Subsequently she investigated the whole transcription, focusing upon how interaction took place in the three-party constellation, and observed that the interpreter sometimes corrected the informant's statements, added complementary information or omitted details. At one point the interpreter retells in a somewhat dramatized fashion a story told by the informant. This, Blomqvist argues, generally seems to serve the goal of making information more coherent and accessible, of facilitating her understanding. By double checking the interview like this, the researcher is given a new and more nuanced picture of her assistant, of his perspectives and motives in his role of intermediary. Thus she is also provided with an instrument that helps her to evaluate both the interviews as data and the 'facts' established in them.

2.2 Colonial and post-colonial interpreting

In anthropological literature from the seventies one finds studies focusing on court interpreting insofar as it provides circumstances in which potential conflicts between minority populations and a colonial administration are made visible (cf. above 4:1.1). For instance, Lang (1976, 1978) reports on case-studies documented in a local court in Papua New Guinea.

In the earlier paper, he gives a short account of the status and the development of local interpreting services. Apart from English, the dominant administrative language, about 700 different vernacular languages are spoken in the country. Lang indirectly criticizes government officials and people working in the judicial sphere for lacking insight when it comes to problems arising through court interpreting. His main goal in this article is to point out the need for formal training of court interpreters; its absence may partly explain why the problems traced are ascribed to the interpreters' lack of proper schooling.

Lang defines as a problem the non-transparent relationship between the (native) interpreters and the (native) clients. From the point of view of court officials, it is impossible to assess the loyalties and/or antagonisms between others present, which of course could be of crucial importance during court trials. Moreover, the paper discusses what is seen as possible "reasons for misinterpretation", namely the interpreter's carelessness, his wilful distortion, his mishearing, and the interpreter's perception of himself as "intermediary" rather than "interpreter proper" (Lang 1976:337). The author does not describe in any detail, let alone problematize, the idealistic nature of the legal image of interpreter that he in fact reproduces. Yet Lang notes a certain interdependence between the actors in court, at least between the interpreter and the client, who is observed to occasionally facilitate the interpretation process, and, at times, make the interpreter's job almost impossible (Lang 1976:357).

The issue of interpreters' conflicting loyalties is described as a basic problem to be handled by medical staff and health care institutions in papers by Kaufert and Koolage (1984) and Kaufert *et al.* (1985), who report on a Canadian project involving anthropological and medical experts. This was designed to elaborate methods for improving biomedical care among Inuit populations, and it was found that the interpreters played a central role in the project. But while these interpreters are expected to act essentially towards one goal – the promotion of biomedical care in place of traditional Inuit health care – court interpreters are generally expected to avoid siding with any party and avoid revealing their own attitudes or interests.

Elsewhere, Lang (1978) investigates a two and a half hour long film-documentation of another trial in Papua New Guinea. Interpreting is carried out between a local vernacular (Enga) and Tok Pisin, a Creole language. From this material he extracts a small segment, about five minutes long, for a detailed moment-by-moment analysis. Lang observes that the interpreter performs a constant visual monitoring of his clients. For instance, he notes that the interpreter seeks to convey his status as a neutral rather than an active initiating party to the proceedings by directing his attention not to any one of the people talking through him, but just to his own hands (Lang 1978:235). The author underlines the significance of what is communicated non-verbally, by gestures, postures and gazes, and concludes that the interpreter's behaviour depends on "the active co-operation of his clients" (Lang 1978:241) (as in the earlier paper, meaning whether the suspects respect the interpreter's role as a neutral party or not). Lang thus concentrates on the interaction between two parties present, leaving the behaviour of court officials unexplored.

2.3 The bilingual courtroom

The Bilingual Courtroom, a book by the US scholar in Hispanic languages Berk-Seligson (1990),[2] is to my knowledge the first comprehensive empirical study of its kind, exploring authentic court interpreting as a social and a linguistic phenomenon. This book demonstrates in several ways how the courtroom is transformed in the presence of the court interpreter. Berk-Seligson states that this is an insight of which those involved are largely unaware. She reports on findings based on seven months of ethnographic observation and tape-recordings in three tiers of the US court system: federal, state and municipal. Theoretically, the author ties in with the *ethnography of speaking* tradition (Hymes, 1962; 1972). Analyses are made of tape-recorded and transcribed trials where the languages spoken were English and Spanish.

Berk-Seligson observes that the image of the court interpreter – prevailing among judges and attorneys as well as among active interpreters – is idealistic rather than realistic. The interpreter, she argues, is no "unobtrusive figure", as the official Code of Ethics anticipates, but brings about key changes in judicial proceedings and affects whatever power an interrogating attorney may have over a testifying witness or defendant. Interpreters exert control in various ways over attorneys' questioning routines, and their activity may work in consonance with the examiner's efforts, but occasionally also against them.

One chapter reports on a study comparing original answers, provided in Spanish by 27 witnesses, and the interpreted versions of these answers in English. There appears to be a general tendency for these interpreters to, as Berk-Seligson puts it, "convert 'fragmented' speech style into a more narrative testimony style". The extension into narrative is accomplished by the introduction of elements that are characteristic of 'powerless' style (Berk-Seligson 1990:119). The terminology as regards different testimony styles is drawn from works by O'Barr and colleagues (e.g. 1980).

Another chapter reports on a set of experimental studies which also borrow ideas of research design from O'Barr's studies. Berk-Seligson examines 551 listeners' reactions to two recordings of actors playing the roles of a Spanish-speaking witness, an English-speaking lawyer and a professional court interpreter. In one recording the interpreter systematically relayed the witness's speech, including the words marking politeness. In the other, these words were systematically omitted. The participants in the test were asked to pretend to be members of a jury and as such to evaluate the witness's testimony. Results from the studies show that the interpreters' speech performances had a great impact in shaping the mock jurors' impressions both of the testifying witnesses and of the examining attorneys. This was true of both monolingual (English-speaking) and bilingual (English- and Spanish-speaking) subjects. Comparing the evaluations of the two versions, it was demonstrated that the difference had affected how participants perceived the witnesses' convincingness, truthfulness, intelligence and competence.

Despite Berk-Seligson's critique against idealistic thinking, one could note a certain bias towards this in her own work. Analysing people's behaviour in court by contrasting it to official ideal preconceptions of court interpreting, some of her conclusions amount to ascribing deficiencies to different actors. For instance, she states that all participants in the courtroom in some way "misconstrue" the interpreter's role (*ibid.*:11). A particular judge's way of addressing the interpreter is described as "abandoning the norms" (*ibid.*:65). A certain witness's behaviour vis-à-vis the interpreter is presented as a "failure" (*ibid.*:151).

2.4 The interpreter – a challenge to the legal world

Berk-Seligson finds that interpreters and interpreter trainers are "overwhelmingly concerned with vocabulary, very little concerned with grammar, and almost completely unaware of pragmatic aspects of speech" (Berk-Seligson 1990:53). This may be true at one level, however, my data indicates that individual interpreters who in some situations express these attitudes towards the profession are, nevertheless, and in other situations, indeed aware of pragmatic aspects of speech, such as style, politeness, ambiguities of situated meanings.

Furthermore, since interpreting in legal, medical and social settings is only beginning to become established as a profession, there is, in my experience, a considerable openness among interpreters to discussing the acceptability and validity of existing or suggested standards. This openness must be related to the relatively foreclosed position found among other practitioners involved, not least in the legal sphere. Morris (1993) in her Ph.D. thesis, and later in a paper in *The Translator* (1995), examines the attitude of members of the legal community to the activities and the status of court interpreters. Her discussions are based on an extensive survey of both historical and recent legal documents, mostly from the English-speaking world. The predominant view on court interpreting, among judges, lawyers, attorneys and so forth, is what she terms a "legal fiction", namely "that L2 = L1, and that the instrument of this equation [i.e. the court interpreter] uses no discretion or freedom of will whatsoever in achieving the goal set by the law" (Morris 1993:136). What court interpreters are supposed to perform is translation, in contrast to interpretation, an activity expected by and acceptable to members of the legal community, but completely forbidden for court interpreters. As was noted in Chapter 2 above, this image fits in with a monological, 'talk-as-text' model of communication.

The verbatim re-performance which lawyers call 'translation' is by numerous real-life examples demonstrated to be an unrealistic, theoretical construct. But, for a variety of reasons, established legal systems show little or no readiness to acknowledge the interpreter-mediated situation as essentially different from the ordinary, monolingual one, and the court interpreter's task as truly interpretative. Instead, the court interpreter is defined as a disembodied, mechanical device, and the court can proceed as if it had been monolingual, and the interpreter's statements can be taken to be just as valid in law as if they had been first-hand utterances. Fenton (1997), however, from her New Zealand perspective, sees a shift beginning to take place in thinking among legal professionals. Quoting Laster and Taylor (1994), two scholars of Law, she notes that the traditional role prescription of the court interpreter is being questioned, and that awareness is being raised among legal professionals about the nature of interpreting as a kind of 'expert opinion'. Hence, she argues, their understanding of the work of the interpreter in court is going away from the conduit model to that of the expert witness (Fenton 1997:33).

Certification of court interpreters is being introduced in many countries to guarantee a certain quality of work. There is no guarantee, however, that interpreters used are indeed certified. Whether or not interpreters are acknowledged as free and wilful agents, the quality of the individual interpreter's performance is not undergoing any systematic control during court proceedings. Hence, lawyers have a space in which they can exploit monolinguals' potential suspicion of faulty or poor interpretation, using a variety of tactical manoeuvres. The quality of a certain piece of interpreting can be estimated, however, if it is documented on tape. When this is the case, interpreters may occasionally be asked to testify to the accuracy of other interpreters whose work is being questioned.

Nevertheless, as most judicial systems are structured today, the legal community cannot afford to have interpreters officially doing more than 'just translating'. Where defendants' and witnesses' speech during the very court procedure is attributed specific proof value (in accordance with the principle of orality), it would obviously be a challenge to the court if interpreters were, for instance, allowed to clarify an attorney's deliberately ambiguous question. It would be a threat to the system if interpreters were allowed to improve the image of witnesses and suspects by rendering eloquently and precisely statements which were originally voiced carelessly and imprecisely. Nevertheless, the law's insistence on interpreters' verbatim 'translation' is a paradoxical defence of the legal system and its language use. To challenge this, as Morris puts it, "the 'languaging' – which is the very essence of law – can shake its foundations" (Morris 1993:32).

Barsky (1994), in his book *Constructing a Productive Other*, which from a range of perspectives thoroughly scrutinizes the recorded and transcribed text of two interpreter-mediated refugee hearings, claims that interpreters working in the type of situation investigated cannot avoid functioning as intercultural mediators, although this function is officially banned rather than recognized.

The contradictions inbuilt in legal systems are also described in an interview study carried out by Falck (1987), a Norwegian scholar of Law. Falck investigates how the legal rights of the individual layperson are defended when he or she does not speak the language of the court, and the role conflicts inherent in interpreters' work in the context of their various loyalties in society. The study seeks to present the perspectives of all parties involved in court interpreting – active interpreters, lawyers, judges, police officers as well as immigrant suspects, witnesses and claimants. A main point in Falck's work is that society's one-sided focus on the *interpreters* and thereby on the problematizing of *these* actors' professional competence and status, may, in practice, lead to a situation in which the structural conditions for the work of interpreters are underestimated as factors possibly jeopardizing the citizen's legal rights. In a recent volume on *Translation and the Law* (Morris *et al.* 1995) nineteen scholars

of law, linguistics, anthropology, languages, translation and interpretation highlight the exposed position of individuals who appear
under the scrutiny of a court without having access to the language
in which justice is administered. Little by little, the shortcomings of
judicial systems – in various parts of the world – in coping with the
consequences of linguistic and cultural diversity is achieving broader
attention.

2.5   On naturalness in conversation and 'natural translation'

Jönsson (1990), in a paper on court interpreting, drawing upon literature within the tradition of conversation analysis, concentrates on
the court personnel. She investigates the verbal back-channelling
behaviour during thirteen interpreter-mediated court trials. These
were documented on audiotape in Swedish courtrooms. Jönsson
evaluates the respective participants' involvement in joint interaction as indicated by the amount of words and feedback tokens they
provide. She observes that the content of what is said is conveyed
between the attorneys and lawyers on the one hand and the layperson on the other, yet more or less *without* the back-channelling
signals. These signals, according to research on conversation in general, are essential for interlocutors' understanding of how to act.
Jönsson concludes that interpreter-mediated interaction in court could
– in part – be described as two simultaneously ongoing dialogues
between the interpreter and the respective parties (Jönsson 1990:84).
   A similar theoretical frame is utilized by other authors, including Linell and colleagues (1992) and Englund Dimitrova (1991,
1997). Englund Dimitrova explores two video-taped and transcribed
interpreter-mediated encounters between Spanish-speaking patients
and Swedish-speaking doctors. The author investigates the 'naturalness' of the conversations taking place, particularly focusing on
participants' – including the interpreter's – turn-taking and back-
channelling behaviour. The interpreters were in both cases qualified and experienced. It is concluded that the interpreter-mediated
meetings did not differ much, as regards an overarching structure,
from what would be expected in monolingual health-care encounters of a similar kind. But the only feedback provided is between
the interpreter and the respective parties, and it is first and foremost non-verbal. Similar findings are presented by Kulick (1982) in

a discourse-analytical study based on data collected on three different occasions: at a dentist's office, a child health-care clinic and a social welfare office. The languages spoken were Swedish and Kurdish.

Knapp-Potthoff and Knapp too apply a discourse-analytical approach when exploring (1986 and 1987) the performance of individuals who act in the role of interpreter, having no special training for this but being fluent in the languages in question. In German the authors used the term *Sprachmittler*; in English 'linguistic mediator' (or simply mediator). Knapp-Potthoff and Knapp (as well as Müller (1989) referred to below), envisage a 'professional' interpreter first and foremost as someone who is physically absent, providing simultaneous or consecutive interpretation as a "voice *ex-machina* from behind the scene" (Müller 1989:714), "giving a more or less literal translation of what is said in language A in language B" (Knapp-Potthoff and Knapp 1986:152). They tend to treat what is thus termed 'professional' interpreting as an actual form of translation activity, rather than as an abstract norm.

In the first paper (Knapp-Potthoff and Knapp 1986) the idea is to contrast the interpreter's performance in a court setting with that in an informal legal advice settings. The degree of formality is presumed to be decisive for how the interpreter performs. The more formal the situation, the more the interpreter is expected to act as a "mere medium of transmission", and less as a "true third party". The role of interpreter is envisaged as a "role continuum", where these would be the polarities (Knapp-Potthoff and Knapp 1986:153).

In the analysis, the authors compare the role performance in the informal encounter – where a German-speaking legal adviser and a Turkish-speaking client interacts with the assistance of a bilingual student – not with the interpreting actually performed in court, but rather with the imagined performance a "mere medium of transmission" would have accomplished. Characteristics of the student's style of interpreting, performing as a "true third party", were summarized in four points. He is said to have had a tendency to, firstly, summarize and rearrange the primary interlocutors' contributions, secondly, engage in negotiating solutions for the client's problems together with the adviser, thirdly, at times act himself as an adviser, and fourthly, permit the primary interlocutors to hold the floor by very long turns at talk. The authors conclude that the student by choosing this extreme mediator's style got himself into a number of difficulties, which in turn, they argue, made the primary interlocutors misunderstand one another.

In the later study, Knapp-Potthoff and Knapp (1987), drawing upon the work of Brown and Levinson (1978) focus on 'politeness-strategies' in what they here term "non-professional interpreting". Their data consists of seven tape-recorded conversations, arranged between Korean-speaking and German-speaking students not sharing a language in common. In each encounter three persons took part, and the *Sprachmittler's* role was in all of them carried out by a certain young Korean student, fluent in both languages.

The authors claim that active face-work of two kinds is inherent in the *Sprachmittler's* role. They discuss face-threats which are linked to the requirements and expectations of the primary parties that they will be adequately presented and get adequate access to conversation. The woman in the middle is said to have a face to protect in her role as interlocutor. The analysis keeps the reader in suspense, however, as to whether or not the primary interlocutors' expectations were actually met. We are again faced with a comparison between interpreting in practice and interpreting in (normative) theory. Another kind of threat is identified as concerning primary interlocutors' face. Knapp-Potthoff and Knapp argue that, depending on the degree to which the mediator identifies with one or the other party, a threat to this party will also be felt as a threat to the *Sprachmittler's* face. However, the analysis gives us no access to information regarding whether, and in that case how, the student, in effect, identified with other participants in the seven encounters. I would see this reasoning as an outcome of what could be termed a 'cognitive' bias. (cf. note p. 47)

Müller (1989) takes on a rather different task, exploring a corpus of five recorded and transcribed interviews, each about an hour long, where there were two interviewers (one with more fluency in German and less in Italian, and the other with the opposite ratio of knowledge in these languages) and two or more adult members of Italian immigrant families (more or less fluent in German). Müller wishes to alert researchers within translation studies to use authentic translating done in everyday circumstances by people who have had no special training for it, to investigate interpreting. This kind of interpreting is what Harris (1992) terms 'natural translation' and promotes as an empirical base for investigations into intra-personal cognitive processes (cf. Chapter 2:3.3). Müller, in contrast, suggests investigating it as an inter-personal activity; how 'natural translation' is introduced, organized and handled by those involved in a multi-party conversation. However, he sides with Knapp-Potthoff and Knapp in his presentation of the non-professional interpreter in contrast to a professional who, by virtue of his or her professionality, would take every second turn at talk and translate everything said by a primary interlocutor as closely as possible. Müller too assumes the non-professional's tendency to be negotiating, or 'mediating', rather than translating 'professionally' to partly derive from the informality of the situations.

2.6 Hidden norms in research on interpreting

The above reviewed cross-disciplinary work on interpreting in face-to-face interaction indicates that studies in interpreting may have a relevance for researchers and students within, for instance, sociology, languages, pragmatics, jurisprudence, and ethnography. The studies made on real-life data have demonstrated the great exploratory potentials of discourse-analytical methods. In most of the studies performed, however, I have found a bias towards normative thinking, more precisely, that norms of interpreting and language use are taken for granted rather than problematized and investigated in their own right.

The normative thinking I have in mind partly results from an underlying preconception of language use as monological. When the 'naturalness' of interpreter-mediated conversation is investigated, the monolingual conversation is sometimes taken not just as a 'norm' by which differences can be made visible, but implicitly as a norm against which the efficiency of an interpreter-mediated talk can be measured and evaluated. For instance, Müller argues that translations are clumsy and costly devices, that retard the flow and progress of conversation (Müller 1989:736). Whether his understood comparison is relevant and justified is not problematized.

Partly, normative thinking results from an underlying monologic preconception of language (what was discussed more generally in Chapter 2). This may explain why it is that, whilst taking communicative aspects of interpreting into account, research in this field nevertheless tends to conceive of it as consisting essentially of one activity – that of providing translations to given originals. There is a strong tendency in the literature towards exploring interpreting as if this was a matter of text production only. This 'talk-as-text' approach to interpreting is frequently combined with established norms and conventions applying not to spoken interaction but to written language use.

In conclusion, applying the dialogic, interactionistic perspective when reconsidering studies carried out, I would argue that what constitutes 'normality' in interpreter-mediated interaction is not something once and for all given, but a task for empirical research to determine by exploring real-life encounters. A main ambition of this book is to show ways to do this, ways which involve a dialogical view of language and mind, and avoids normative thinking of the kinds discussed above. In Chapter 5 I will present some analytical and conceptual tools which can be used for this purpose.

NOTES

1. For a comprehensive overview of this kind of interpreting see the final chapter of the edited volume *Translators Through History* (Delisle and Woodsworth 1995), written by Margareta Bowen in collaboration with David Bowen, Francine Kaufmann and Ingrid Kurz.
2. I reviewed this book in *The Translator* Vol.2/1 1996.

FIVE

Discourse studies – on method and analytical framework

'Interpreting' as object under investigation can be approached from a variety of angles, and analyses carried out may focus on a range of aspects. As Wodak (1996) argues, promoting a "multi-method approach" for the social sciences, qualitative and quantitative methods do not exclude, but, on the contrary, complement each other (Wodak 1996:23). Naturally, the methods used for gaining knowledge about a phenomenon – interviews, statistical calculations, experiments, tests, ethnographic fieldwork, micro-analysis of discourse, and so forth – will partly determine the research findings. For instance, investigations designed to check whether a certain interpreting behaviour correlates with certain circumstances, or whether or not it represents a typical pattern would demand some sort of quantitative approach. Qualitative methods are needed, however, to describe and explore the dynamics of interpreters' communicative behaviour; how and why the interaction order in an interpreter-mediated encounter depends on primary interlocutors' communicative activities, contextual factors, and so forth.

The terminology available to account for the somewhat fuzzy phenomena we call 'dynamics' and 'interaction order' is under constant development. It is in the nature of a dynamic process that the units at work are not self-evident and given. A new way to describe and classify the constituting units of a communicative process may in itself make up the result of an investigation, applying qualitative method.

This chapter suggests some basic terminology which I have found suitable for non-experimentally designed research of interpreter-mediated interaction. The first section will give a background to why this book promotes 'the interpreter-mediated encounter', and not, say, 'interpreting' or 'the interpreter' as the basic unit of research, and discuss the analytical implications of this choice.

The second part of the chapter deals with methodological issues connected to the collection of authentic discourse data, including questions concerning scientific validity and the limits of relevant 'context'. An instance of interpreter-mediated interaction is always part of various social, cultural and subcultural 'contexts'. Which layers of what 'context' are significant to the analysis one intends to undertake?

Moreover, there is a range of practical problems with setting up research projects on authentic interpreter-mediated interaction. One needs access to institutional settings where such encounters normally take place. Lay people, institutional professionals and interpreters, i.e. the prospective research subjects, must give their acceptance before one intrudes into their private and/or working life. There are methodological and analytical implications of the language combinations selected for a study. The forms in which discourse data is collected, and, subsequently, transcribed, also have implications for the kind of analyses that can be performed.

1. SOCIAL ROLE – NORMATIVE, TYPICAL AND PERSONAL STANDARDS

The analytical framework outlined in this section draws heavily on the social psychology of Erving Goffman. Taking 'interpreter-mediated interaction' as the object of exploration I looked for a theoretical model of social interaction and found the work of Goffman to be applicable. I found it fruitful to think, as he argued, that people display different social identities by their mere appearance, and additional social identities are displayed through language use (native language, dialect, sociolect). In conversation, an individual's social identities are brought to the fore in different proportions as interaction progresses. In Goffman's terms, co-interlocutors understand each other as *multiple-role-performers* rather than as persons with one single all-dominating identity (Goffman 1961:142).

Exploring further the concept of 'role', Goffman (1961) links to the anthropological tradition, principally to a classic work by Linton (1936, here:1964). Linton described *status* as a position in a given social system, while *role* in his work stands for the activities holders would engage in, were they to act only in terms of the normative demands upon people in their position. Goffman (1961) starts from this distinction and further problematizes the notion of 'role' as in itself consisting of three different aspects, namely *normative role*, *typical role* and *role performance*.

My point of departure was that the literature on interpreting was dominatingly normative in character and that ideas of how interpreters 'should' perform partly blocked the sight in investigations of actual cases of interpreting. Hence Goffman's distinctions appeared fruitful for the investigation of the role of interpreter.

In his model, 'normative role' would be defined by the commonly shared ideas about a certain activity, what people in general think they are or should be doing when acting in a certain role. The 'normative role' of interpreter is thus what interpreters think they do when they perform well, or at least appropriately as interpreter. Norms become shared through official Codes of Conduct, rules and regulations and through educational programmes.

The notion of 'typical role' takes into account that the conditions for performing a certain role typically fluctuate from time to time and place to place. This means that individuals develop routines to handle typical situations *not* foreseen by shared established norms.

Moreover, in any specific case, there are aspects of the individual's behaviour which stem neither from normative nor from typical standards, but must be explained by circumstances in the situation (e.g. other people present, light, noise, physical objects) and by the performer's personal style while on duty. This is what Goffman identifies for exploration as the individual's 'role performance'.

In taking on a social role, such as interpreter, the individual performers must see to it that they make a credible impression on the *role others*, i.e. the relevant audience with whom they interact in the role in question (Goffman 1961:85). For instance, the typial 'role other' of a doctor is a patient, and for an interpreter it is the two or more primary interlocutors speaking various languages. Interpreters must see to it that the impressions they make on the 'role others' are compatible with role-appropriate personal qualities these ascribe to them. The moral aspect of role, i.e. ideas about rights and wrongs, is what makes the performing individual identify and become identified as a holder of a certain role. An individual's 'role performance' reciprocally becomes identity-providing for the relevant others too, and thus has implications of a sociopsychological kind.

1.1 Role analysis and situated systems of activity

Role analysis may be concerned with the range of activities in different social settings in which a certain actor is typically involved (e.g. at work, at trade union meetings, at holiday resorts). It may also concern the range of activities the actor engages in within the walls of certain establishments (e.g. what nurses do when at the hospital). Alternatively, the study of a particular role may be limited to a particular type of situation (e.g. the role of nurse in the nursing staff conference). Roles pertaining to such activities can be called *activity roles*, and they are part of what Goffman (1961) terms a *situated activity system*, "a face-to-face interaction with others for the performance of a single joint activity, a somewhat closed, self-compensating, self-terminating circuit of interdependent actions" (Goffman 1961:96).

An important analytical implication of role in Goffman's definition is that the elementary unit – in fact the basic concern of role analysis – is not the individual, but the individual acting in a obligatory fashion within a 'system of activity'. To explore a social role he suggests that one start by distinguishing what activity is uniquely performed by individuals acting in this role, compared to the activities performed by the 'role others'.

A situated system of activity thus engages only a part of the individual, and what she does or is at other times and places is not given specific attention. The 'role others' similarly perform other roles at other times and places not necessarily relevant at all other moments. Of basic interest is how the role-holder's and the 'role other's' respective actions, differentiated and interdependent, fit together into patterns defining a situated activity system.

1.1.1 Role distance

Norms of social behaviour are typically brought to attention when people experience them to be transgressed by someone. Garfinkel (1967) effectively demonstrated this through his 'candid camera' type of experiments. In a situation where one individual breaks a shared social norm, for instance ignores the order of a queue, other participants may redefine the event as a non-queue situation, alternatively, may try to make the norm breaker understand the established queue order. Transgressions of norms can also be understood as made 'off-the-record', however, and the definition of the situation remains the same without being pointed out explicitly.

The concept of *role distance* provides a sociological means of dealing with one type in divergence between obligation and actual 'role performance'. In brief, it applies to the case when a conflicting discrepancy occurs between, on the one hand, the self generated in actual social interaction, and, on the other, the self associated with a formal status and identity.

A general point about 'role distance', as well as any aspect of 'role performance', is that the individual's display of it presupposes his or her action and the immediate audience's reaction; i.e. mutual confirmation between co-present people (Goffman 1961:108).

> By introducing an unserious style, the individual can project the claim that nothing happening at the moment to him or through him should be taken as a direct reflection of him, but rather of the person-in-situation that he is mimicking. [. . .] Explanation, apologies, and jokes are all ways in which the individual makes a plea for disqualifying some of the expressive features of the situation as sources of definitions of himself (Goffman 1961:105).

'Role distance' implies that the individual, while deviating from what is regularly seen as typical performance, still acknowledge a certain typical performance as the typical one. In other words, the individual seeks to maintain, on a global level, a particular definition of the situation (as situation-type), while simultaneously devoting a certain effort to expressing the separateness between what a serious performer would do and what he or she is currently doing unseriously, that is, acting not as all accepting performers of the role would normally act. For instance, a professional on duty, say, a police officer, may occasionally address a 'role other', say, a suspect *not* as a typical suspect, but, as e.g. a New Yorker or as a mother, and this may be done without being perceived as contrary to the professional norms of police officer. Such addresses can thus be termed 'role distance' with regard to the occupational role. Conversely, the 'role other' may show 'role distance' in relation to the institutionally defined role (as suspect) and agree to establish an alliance based on shared interests, gender, age, ethnicity, religion, and so forth. 'Role distance', Goffman emphasizes, "is a part (but, of course, only one part) of *typical* role, and this routinized sociological feature should not escape us merely because 'role distance' is not part of the normative framework of role." (Goffman 1961:115).

If a certain kind of 'role distance' is systematically utilized by professionals, this can ultimately lead to a redefinition of their professional role.

1.1.2 Activity role vs. status of participation

Primary parties can expect interpreters to act in certain ways, and interpreters may be more or less willing to meet different expectations. How interpreters must treat their occupational role so as not to jeopardize others' reliance on their professional expertise is a question of balancing contradictory expectations. It remains to be systematically explored how, when, which and why socially and culturally established power relations, inherent in the different situations where interpreters appear, affect the work of interpreter. For this purpose, empirically useful analytical units are needed to distinguish between different dimensions of participation.

Goffman suggests we explore individuals' involvement in social interaction, applying a model he terms *participation framework* (Goffman 1981). The basic idea is that the organization of spoken interaction ultimately results from participants' continuous evaluations and re-evaluations of speaker-hearers' roles or *status of participation*, at the turn-by-turn-level. The substance and the progression of interaction, and subsequently individuals' 'role performance', depend on how interlocutors relate to one another at an utterance-to-utterance level, through potentially changing alignments in the ongoing flow of discourse.

In the literature on how individuals take part in face-to-face interaction the different dimensions of participation (activity role and status of participation) are not always kept apart. Distinguishing between them can help to shed light on the interaction order and the distribution of responsibility in spoken interaction, which is of central interest in my explorations of the role of interpreter.

The potential for change implied by this interactionistic view of social interaction brings to mind what Giddens calls "dialectic of control" (1981:63). Criticizing deterministic tendencies in social theory, he focuses on the connection between agency and power, and argues that the human ability to engage in choice, however restricted the conditions for this may be, means that there is a potential transformative capacity inherent in institutional practices. Social actors are not totally subject to the culturally and socially established structures of power and domination.

1.2 Participation and interaction order

In problematizing the organization of social interaction, one could start by pointing to apparent shortcomings in traditional models of analysing 'speaking' and 'listening'. These activities are traditionally seen as opposite and even as mutually exclusive activities. This fits in with a common-sense idea of communication as a unidirectional transfer from one individual, the speaker, to another, the listener, by means of coded signals carrying meaning(s) through a channel or a medium. The "conduit metaphor" has been suggested by Reddy (1979) as characteristic of this way of conceptualizing linguistic communication. The general epistemology behind the conduit model of communication is that of *monologism* (Marková and Foppa 1990, cf. also Chapter 2:4).

However, as has been demonstrated in numerous analyses of discourse (e.g. Edelsky 1981, Tannen 1984, Goodwin and Goodwin 1992), the activity of talk is carried out simultaneously with listening, and listening may include overt verbal activities, i.e. talk (back-channelling). These two deeply intertwined activities are what constitutes conversation. Moreover, overlaps in conversation are not always brief, and they do not necessarily imply communicative breakdown. Seen from a non-normative, interactionistic perspective, simultaneous talk takes on communicative meaning when it appears, and this in turn is dependent on the situation and those involved. When I argue that meaning is established in interaction, and that interaction is constituted by interlocutors' active speaking and listening, this reflects a *dialogical* view on language and mind (cf. Chapter 2:4).

1.2.1 Listening, speaking and aspects of self

In the introduction to his book *Forms of Talk*, Goffman explains the notion of 'participation framework' in the following way: "When a word is spoken, all those who happen to be in perceptual range of the event will have some sort of participation status relative to it" (1981:3). Depending on how people understand their own and others' involvement in a particular encounter, they will adapt their way of interacting, including their ways of speaking and listening. Focusing at the level of utterances, a person's alignment (as speaker *and* hearer) to a particular utterance can be referred to as his or her *footing*.

'Hearer' is in Goffman's writings not a primitive and indivisible notion. He distinguishes first between the listening of *ratified* and *unratified* recipients. Among the latter one would find, for instance, overhearers and eavesdroppers. Among the former, Goffman distinguished between the *addressed*, the *unaddressed*, and the *bystander's* position in interaction.

The notion of 'speaker' is developed in a different way. Goffman dissects analytically three modes of speaking, i.e. ways of displaying, through talk, aspects of self. The analytical set of positions an individual, while speaking, may take to his or her utterance is referred to as *production format*.

According to the model of 'production format', an individual can relate solely as *animator*, and take responsibility as nothing more than "a sounding box from which utterances come". Alternatively, one can take responsibility as 'animator' and *author*, but not as *principal*. As 'author' one stands as "the agent who puts together, composes, or scripts the lines that are uttered". Speaking without ascribing to someone else the responsibility for what one says, one is simultaneously the 'animator', 'author' and 'principal' of one's utterance. As Goffman puts it, speaking as *principal*, an individual makes himself understood as "the party to whose position, stand and belief the words attest" (1981:226).

As I understand this analytical cluster, it highlights the dialogical relations in spoken interaction. I will briefly compare my interpretation with alternative understandings of the model, developed within pragmatics and research on interpreting.

1.2.2 A proper 'footing'?

Following Goffman, Levinson (1988) in his paper 'Putting Linguistics on a Proper Footing: Explorations in Goffman's concepts of participation', problematizes the traditional concentration on dyads in studies of social interaction, and the tendency to extend a dyadic model of analysis to multiparty interaction. In contrast to Goffman, however, Levinson understands and goes on to explore 'participation' as individuals' presumed or actual attentiveness as 'speaker' *or* 'hearer'. Unlike Goffman, he takes 'speaker' and 'hearer' as separate, social identities. While existing as 'speaker' an individual does not exist, as it were, as 'hearer'.

Levinson borrows Goffman's concepts of 'participation framework' and 'production format' to label two comparable classificatory systems. The former he takes to stand for addressees' or recipients' identities and the latter for speakers' identities. In place of Goffman's concepts, however, Levinson introduces "reception roles" and "production roles" (Levinson 1988:168–9). Subsequently, he lists a number of 'reception roles' and 'production roles' and comes up with two extensive typologies, which he connects to one another in a system of mutually exclusive empirical categories under the heading of "participant roles" (Levinson 1988:172–3). (Levinson talks about participant status and participant roles while Goffman speaks about participation status.)

Levinson's paper is based on three central points of critique of Goffman's model. In his view, it, firstly, does not provide sufficient empirically useful distinctions, secondly, explicates the given categories in too vague a manner, and, thirdly, lacks a distinction between "utterance-event" and "speech-event" (Levinson 1988:169). "Speech-event" is used in Hymes's sense (1964), i.e. as a situation defined by the speech occurring in it, e.g. a conference. "Utterance-event" in Levinson's definition is "that stretch of a turn at talk over which there is a constant set of individuals – i.e. that unit within which the function from the set of participant roles to the set of individuals is held constant" (Levinson 1988:168).

This implies that Levinson's goals and motives differ quite considerably from Goffman's. His project is not to explore the dynamics of social encounters or the interaction order. Levinson's programme is instead basically of a Linnean kind, more precisely that of categorizing individuals' 'participation' in terms of stable, controllable, universally existing, distinct states of mind. He is decomposing into subcategories what *he* understands as "the prototype social roles *par excellence*" – 'speaker' and 'hearer' (Levinson 1988:164). Levinson thus assumes not the fluctuating and multiple subjects' perspectives, but an 'objective' observer's outside perspective. In the end, he seems to fall back on *monologistic* assumptions of language and mind (cf. Chapter 2:4).

1.3 'Participation' in studies on interpreting

Among researchers within translation studies I have found participation being problematized in similar ways in a few cases. For instance, Mason (1990) follows Levinson precisely in categorizing individuals involved in interaction (i.e. not distinguishing between individuals' aspects of self, but between individuals in different 'participant roles').

Edmondson (1986) revises Goffman's model, outlining some pre-liminaries for a theory of mental processes in conference interpreting. He decomposes the notions of 'speaker' and 'hearer' into different sub-roles associated with different responsibilities, for instance, on the one hand, responsibility for "the sounds", "the formulation", "the speaker-meaning", and, on the other, for "uptaking", for "getting the message" and for "responding to the communication" (Edmondson 1986:132). In a monolingual conversation, he argues, an interlocutor normally takes either all speaker- or all hearer-roles. The interpreter, however, Edmondson states, is for at least some of the time of execution, *both* hearer and speaker. Yet interpreters have a limited number of speaker/hearer sub-roles, since being a "Meaner" and a "Responder" do not belong in their responsibilities. Hence, Edmondson concludes, the speaking and hearing of inter-preters is essentially different from that of monolinguals (Edmondson 1986:135–8).

Keith (1984) takes quite another point of departure, discussing what he terms liaison interpreting. He distinguishes in this kind of interpreting two distinct 'footings', namely one where interpreters are, as it were, macro-conversationally orientated, and another where they are text-orientated, translating and dealing with matters of clari-fication, explanation, repetition etc., related to one of the interlocutors' utterances. Liaison interpreting, in Keith's view, thus consists of both translating texts and organizing discourse, which is reminiscent of the general theoretical standpoint in the present work.

1.3.1 Analysing recipientship

When speaking, people normally expect a certain attention from potential recipients present, but not necessarily the same kind of attention from each of them. When listening, in turn, people make accountable what responsibility they take for what happens in interaction, and also what responsibility they wish to ascribe to co-interlocutors. This is displayed through signs of listening and through verbalized responses. The point is that interlocutors regu-larly distinguish not only between different modes of speaking, but also between modes of listening and that these distinctions may be useful in the exploration of social interaction order.

For the purpose of clarification, I will provide three cases, in each of which one mode of listening would be recognized as the dominant one.

Firstly, suppose you are attending a foreign language lesson and the teacher asks you to "please, say after me". In order to be able to repeat exactly, you will adjust your ears so as to memorize the exact words spoken, and you will subsequently repeat them with or without reflecting upon whether you intend something by uttering these specific words.

Secondly, you participate in a small group. Wishing to take part in talk, you will strive to adopt a mode of listening which makes it possible for you to put relevant questions, give relevant answers and comments, to laugh, nod, and so forth on appropriate occasions. This is perhaps the most ordinary way of listening in informal conversation.

Thirdly, you are appointed secretary in a working group, the discussion of which you have to sum up at a later stage. At times you will feel the need to take notes. Ideally, for this purpose you will apply what could be seen as yet another mode of listening.

One listening mode does in principle not exclude the other, but the recipient's focus in the first case is, in a sense, directed backwards; in the second it centres on here and now; and in the third it is orientated forwards, to what may be necessary and useful at a later stage. The analytical distinction connected to recipientship, suggested by Goffman, does not take into account these diverse aspects of listening (cf. above).

1.3.2 Alter-casting and modes of listening

In my view, the analytical cluster of 'participation framework' needs to be complemented for the analysis of listenership. For this purpose I have developed a notion corresponding to 'production format' on the speaking side, namely *reception format*, comprising three different *modes of listening* (and subsequently reacting), that is, analytical roles describing diverse ways to relate to others' utterances while being exposed to them.

Distinguishing between 'production roles' is a way of making explicit in what sense speakers display their own or others' opinions and attitudes. The analytical gain with distinguishing different modes of listening would be to more thoroughly elucidate how individuals demonstrate their own opinions and attitudes concerning rights and responsibilities in interaction.

One mode of listening would be as *reporter*. A 'reporter's' role is seldom explicitly given to a person addressed (except in highly formalized situations, such as the say-after-me language lesson mentioned above). Nevertheless, a reporter's recipientship is not unusual in conversation. As listeners we can have a number of reasons to memorize for repetition words just uttered by another speaker.

A second mode would be as *responder*. Taking/being given a 'responder's' role, persons addressed would anticipate/be expected either to take discourse further by introducing content of their own, or at least – by back-channelling, gazing, etc. – to make salient that they accept being so addressed.

Being addressed, finally, as *recapitulator*, one would be expected to take over the floor, and then, when subsequently speaking, to recapitulate what was said, giving an authorized voice to a prior speaker or group of prior speakers.

When it comes to speaking, the three concepts constituting the 'reception format' – 'reporter', 'responder' and 'recapitulator' – would relate to production format in the following way.

Taking/being given the 'reporter's' role, one would prepare to/ be expected to subsequently relate to one's utterances as 'animator' but not as 'author' nor as 'principal'.

Taking/being given a 'responder's' role, one would be prepared/ expected to relate to one's own talk as 'animator', 'author' and, in principle, as 'principal', i.e. without referring to someone else as the authority behind it.

Taking/being given a 'recapitulator's' role, one would assign to oneself/be assigned the role of 'animator' and 'author', while the role of 'principal' would stay with the person(s) whose talk is being recapitulated.

Participation framework is constantly negotiated in interaction. Therefore, a person's participation status at a particular moment and from a particular individual's point of view can be ascertained only in retrospect. Yet participation status is an analytical resource available not only to researchers, but to interlocutors engaged in spoken interaction too. To interact means to continuously evaluate others' and one's own relation to a focused discourse.

The taking of an oath is a special case where the 'reporter's' listenership combines with the 'principal's' speakership. Oathtakers' listenership is dominatingly the 'reporter's', since they are supposed to repeat exactly the words of, say, a judge. But starting by ritually mentioning themselves – "I, NN, swear . . ." – they also take on the role of 'principal' in relation to what they subsequently say. Swearing implies a ritual spreading of responsibility. The judge, by speaking ceremonially, and by ritually mentioning the oathtaker's name, marks a distinction between his own self ('I' – the one who is swearing a person in) and the other's self ('I' – the one who the oath belongs to). Goffman's ideas concerning speakers' communicative means of marking distinction between self and other, which is part of his 'participation framework' model, will be separately discussed and analytically applied in Chapter 9 below.

1.3.3 Exploring the dynamics of interpreter-mediated encounters

Applying the models of 'reception format' and 'production format', one could think of the interpreter's listening and speaking in the following way. Relating as 'reporter' to an utterance, an interpreter would subsequently speak only in the restricted sense of 'animator' of someone else's speech. This might be how many like to think of the interpreter's function – as someone solely animating others' utterances. Yet, by necessity, interpreters always function also in the role of 'author'.

Having the mandate and the responsibility to compose new versions of utterances, interpreters systematically take the role of 'recapitulator', which means that they relate to their following utterance as 'author' and 'animator', but not as 'principal', a role which is normally occupied by the immediately preceding speaker.

Theoretically, the primary interlocutors are the 'principals', the ultimate sources, of everything said. Reality is more complex.

Taking and/or being ascribed the role of 'responder', interpreters relate to ongoing utterances as ultimate addressees. For instance, when dealing with clarification, in the preparation of a subsequent rendition, interpreters relate to the immediately preceding utterance as would a direct addressee.

Participating in face-to-face interaction interpreters can be, and regularly are, flexible in modes of speaking and listening, and thus relate to what others utter in ways that display different aspects of self.

The individual's participation status is partly a question of her own choice, partly a matter of how co-present people relate to her and to others present.

Largely due to the partial suspension of people's understanding of each other, the interpreter-mediated conversation offers unique opportunities for researchers to trace how participation status is marked and confirmed in and by interaction. Through detailed analysis it should be possible to uncover how interlocutors understand the interaction order as interaction proceeds, how interpreters assist primary interlocutors to orientate themselves within the current framework of participation and how participants perceive the distribution of responsibility for the substance and the progression of current talk.

2. COLLECTING DATA – RECORDING AND TRANSCRIBING

There are many ways to generate knowledge from discourse data. Chapters 6 to 9 in this book demonstrate exploratory and descriptive approaches. Audio recordings of institutional, interpreter-mediated encounters are explored as primary data. Complementary background information was obtained through interviews, participant observation, fieldnotes, and written sources produced by interpreters, institutions and others. This section reports on questions which need careful weighing up while collecting discourse data.

Setting up non-experimental research projects on interpreter-mediated interaction, I have started from an open question, *how* interpreting happens. I did not ask *whether or not* interpreting happens in certain ways, proceeding from a hypothesis which was to be verified or falsified. My collection of data has been organized to include a certain set of institutions, actors, and languages, but these features were not expected to be controllable or stable variables. This analytic terminology belongs to an experimental research design. Exploring the nature of interpreter-mediated interaction, I have rather been asking, as part of my analyses, how interpreters exercise control between participants and how they, in turn, are controlled by 'role others'. And neither the interpreter, nor any other individual actor, is automatically taken to be in all respects representative of a certain social category. In the transcriptions, people are called by real (fictive) names, and not just mentioned as category members.

In non-experimentally designed discourse studies, comparability between each instance of data assembly, i.e. each recorded encounter, is not automatically possible, and not always of interest. Data is not considered valid on the condition that it should involve features which are kept constant between instances. Instead, a central methodological issue concerns how the situations when data is gathered represent what ordinarily happens in the activity the study is designed to explore, what can be thematized as the 'naturalness' of the documented occasions of authentic interaction. The question is then how researchers affect their objects of study.

2.1 On the 'naturalness' of recorded data

It is sometimes argued that people simply forget very quickly the fact that they are being recorded and observed. This may partly be true, but documented subjects probably find it difficult from time to time *not* to pay attention to the fact that they are under surveillance. There is a difference, however, between institutional and informal talk in this regard. Institutional talk is by definition controlled and agenda-bound, and at least lay people involved may experience being objectified and observed in this kind of encounter. The presence of an interpreter in a sense adds to the perception of surveillance, for the lay persons and the professionals alike.

Nevertheless, in authentic institutional encounters people have their own reasons for being involved. Regardless of whether a researcher is present, having as such a certain interest in freezing moments of other individuals' existence, life cannot be suspended. The professionals are doing their ordinary job, and the lay persons are handling their private affairs. And people's understanding of being at a certain institution and being involved in an interpreter-mediated conversation cannot, as it were, be neutralized. The conception of encounters as institutional and/or interpreter-mediated can, in a sense, be reinforced by a researcher's interest in them, precisely for being institutional and/or interpreter-mediated.

Moreover, researchers and recording equipment can mean different things to different actors. As a Spanish–Swedish interpreter in one of my post-interviews expressed it: "The doctor was a much better interpreter-user today than he usually is, but, well, he was being researched." Occasionally, subjects may feel as if they are in something like an examination situation. In that case, it should perhaps be expected that they are trying to do what they understand to be best.

For interpreters, being recorded on duty might be experienced as a great deviation from regularity. Incidentally, they might pay strong attention to the tape-recorder when being subject to this kind of documentation. For instance, in one of my encounters, an interpreter was addressed by a client with a private question, but instead of answering him, she put a finger to her lips and pointed to the tape-recorder.

Nowadays, in England and Wales, police interviews are invariably tape-recorded (Colin and Morris 1996:35), but this has not been the routine at the Swedish police stations where I have done my recordings. In most other public institutions, encounters are seldom or never tape-recorded. Normally, interpreters are alone in the position of being able to control how they manage at work, because of their unique insights into two languages, and of the impermanent nature of speech.

Collecting data, I have normally informed all subjects about my background as Swedish/Russian interpreter. And it can be seen that this and other social roles attributed to me (e.g. researcher, foreigner, fellow country woman) occasionally had an impact on how my subjects perceived the encounters in which they were involved. This was made evident by non-verbal means (e.g. finger to the lips), or by contributions to discourse. For instance, during one of my recordings a Russian–Swedish interpreter searching for a key term in Swedish suddenly turned to me and asked: *ah . . . Cecilia "zhëlchnyj" ty pomnish* ("ah . . . Cecilia 'gall-?' you remember?").

2.1.1 Notions of context

The discussion on 'naturalness' connects to another methodological issue which is familiar in the discourse analytical literature, namely the question of what counts as relevant context in a study of language use in social interaction. Ethnographic methodology is sometimes set against the conversational analysis (CA) approach, which only considers the context created by the discourse itself (Drew and Heritage 1992:16 ff., Silverman 1993:120ff.). Studies within the conversational analysis tradition have shown how participants organize their communicative conduct so as to display and realize their subjective experience of the current social activity, and how they perceive their own and others' roles in it. This is done by reference only to what is explicit in the data. Ethnographically orientated studies, on the other hand, take an interest in language use as part of, or as resulting from, other patterns of social organization. In a study of institutional discourse, this means that the researcher has reasons to obtain a thorough insight into people's long-term or short-term relations and social networks, and into the rules and customs of the institutions where data is collected. Researchers within this tradition also emphasize the necessity of describing the circumstances in which recordings take place, and the researcher's role in creating these circumstances.

Cicourel proposes something of a midway stance. His claim is that *both a broad and a local sense of context* is needed for studies of language use (Cicourel 1992:295 ff.). He thus distinguishes between a locally organized and negotiated context, and a broader sense of context, referring to cultural and social background knowledge, deeply embedded in language use. In this broader sense, context would include participants' and researchers' organizational and interpersonal relationships.

On the one hand, much information is obtained through ethnographic study, and, on the other, spoken interaction always involves markers of different linguistic character (e.g. specific lexical items, syntactical and prosodic pattern, gestures), what Gumperz calls *contextualization cues*.[1] These are observable in discourse itself, and they can be seen as manifestations of the speaker's definition of the situation and his or her current perception of it (Gumperz 1982a:162).

As Bergmann points out, 'local' in this connection can include not only verbal activity, but also matters outside of the verbal flow itself – objects at hand (e.g. a tape recorder) and situated events – which can in themselves constitute a separate local context for subsequent action (e.g. finger to the lips) (Bergmann 1990:206).

The significance of people's attention or inattention to certain objects at hand, to situated events, and to particular verbal activities, occasionally needs to be explained by factors not explicitly manifest in discourse, but taken for granted by the people present in the encounter where the talk took place.

I would principally like to subscribe to Cicourel's proposal, and to his concluding request when discussing how to define the limits of relevant contextual data, namely that the observer is obligated to justify what has been included and what excluded as a result of theoretical goals, methodologies employed and the consistency and convincingness of an argument or analysis (Cicourel 1992:309).

2.2 Subjects and confidentiality

Collecting institutional discourse data as a rule involves, at an initial stage, securing general permission from the institution(s) of current interest, and personal permission from individual representatives willing to be part of the project. These might be the same persons who can provide information about when and where encounters with a suitable profile are to take place. Suitability of course depends on the current focus and research issue. In my selection of encounters, I have generally looked for what – at least from the point of view of the institutions and the interpreters – are considered to be routinely handled, everyday type of cases.

Having the approval of the institution and one or two officials, I went on to seek permission from the lay people and from the interpreters. These should, for ethical reasons, preferably be contacted well in advance. In my studies, I have normally asked permission from the lay people through a letter which was distributed via the institution. Interpreters have been contacted in advance via telephone and often we have met and talked before the recordings took place. All participants have been guaranteed the option, at any moment, to suspend being observed and recorded, and all have been guaranteed anonymity. As indicated above in the section on 'naturalness' (5:2.1), one should be particularly careful not to make the interpreters feel stressed about being observed and recorded; not to make them experience this as a collection of 'the interpreter's errors'.

At all stages of exploration, from organizing recordings to conducting post-encounter interviews, I think it is important to take into consideration that the professionals are in charge of the situations I wish to enter as researcher. The lay persons are visitors and relative newcomers there, and the interpreters are something in between. In my experience, one should be careful not to ask interpreters to secure permission from others. Bearing in mind that a person in an intermediary position is sensitive to accusations of being obtrusive, delegating to an interpreter to suggest what would be a certain intrusion is perhaps not a very good idea. This is one of the reasons why I see an advantage in working with languages in which I am fluent myself.

2.2.1 *Methodological implications of language choice*

The selection of languages is an important issue with methodological and analytical implications. It must, of course, primarily depend upon current research interests. However, there are a few constraints and possibilities inherent in the choice of languages which are worth considering. For instance, if the main focus is linguistic or cultural variation, this could imply a research design involving as many language combinations as possible (or perhaps languages as diverse as possible in structural terms, in the encounters collected).

To gain insight into processes of face-to-face interpreting, and the peculiarities and particularities of this mode of communication, regardless of language combinations, my choice of languages naturally falls on those in which I have linguistic and cultural competence. In this book, Swedish and Russian are therefore the languages represented in the empirical analyses. Similar investigations can be carried out on data involving all possible combinations of languages, provided people who speak these languages are involved in the investigations. For the design applied, a corpus of twenty or even ten short encounters can be considered quite large. A case study can, in principle, be done on a single case. In an investigation of linguistic and/or cultural variation, a larger number of recorded encounters would be needed.

The selection of languages also has methodological implications regarding the post-interviews. To get background information on people's attitudes, expectations and goals, I have tried, after documenting each encounter, to interview, one by one, the people involved. These interviews also provided an opportunity for participants to ask questions, and the researcher to explain.

The interviews I conducted with people in languages which we both spoke (Swedish or Russian) generally gave more spontaneous and substantial information than those made with the assistance of interpreters. It is easy to see that questioning, or just discussing the work of interpreters in the presence of an interpreter, can be taken as face threatening. When using interpreters I tried to minimize this aspect by avoiding the use for interview purposes of interpreters from the recorded encounter. But it is a fact, at least in smaller societies and cities, like the Swedish ones, that immigrant communities are small worlds, and interpreters are well known to all. Confidentiality can be a sensitive issue. Therefore, careful thought must be given to whether and how people are to be interviewed – through interpreters or by bilinguals, through people associated with the language minority, or by bilingual representatives of the language majority (cf. Candlin and Plimer 1996).

To my mind, the relatively modest development of empirical studies in the field of face-to-face interpreting is partly due to the paucity of researchers who are both interested and sufficiently competent in two or more languages. Transcription of interpreter-mediated interaction demands that you are able not only to speak, but also read and write in the two languages in question.

2.3 Transcriptions[2] – an analytic and a didactic tool

My first experience in transcribing spontaneous spoken interaction was eye-opening in many respects. I transcribed my own talk recorded in a situation where I had acted as interpreter. At first it felt embarrassing to discover what looked like errors. I found my interpretations clumsy and imprecise but I consoled myself with the fact that the primary interlocutors spoke 'erroneously'. Transcribing made me realize, for one thing, how significantly written language norms differ from spoken language conventions, and secondly, how strongly I had internalized written language norms into my preconception of interpreting. By forcing myself to write down exactly what people said, and not what they 'should' have said, had they spoken 'correctly', I learned to listen more carefully.

In my view, transcribing recorded data is actually an efficient means for sharpening one's ear and sense of detail, and moreover, for promoting a general understanding of what spontaneous spoken interaction is all about – in other words, this is an exercise that can indeed be utilized in the training of interpreters. Add to this the exercise of translating transcriptions into a third language, and students will gain further insights into both working languages, being forced to distance themselves equally from both of them.

Transcribers sometimes discuss whether variants of pronunciations, emphasis, pitch and so forth should be reflected in text. My position has been to mark these features only at points when they are of importance in the current analysis. One reason is that transcriptions are hard enough to read anyhow, since the orthography usually derives from normal written language. For instance, punctuation symbols are used to mark communicatively relevant prosodic (intonation) terminals, rather than grammatical boundaries as in conventional writing. Also spelling may be non-conventional, to reflect varieties of pronunciation. Moreover, transcribing is extremely time consuming, so sticking to conventional writing when possible is a way to gain time and readability.

Transcription as method and theory has been prospering since the seventies. Papers discussing the analytical effects of transcriptions as texts, and transcribing as an interpreting process have, for example, been written by Jefferson (1973), Ochs (1979), Edelsky (1981), and Erickson (1982). For instance, it is repeatedly argued that, when analysing discourse data, the transcript must be used in close combination with the recordings.

Documenting authentic encounters, some prefer to use audio, others video. There are advantages and disadvantages to both techniques. My choice must depend on what kind of issues I wish to focus on, and what kind of information I need for this purpose. Not least important, it is dependent on my informants' opinion about being documented. Video-recordings, on the one hand, give more information, and information of a more detailed kind. Social interaction consists of much more than verbal activities, hence transcribing talk can catch a great deal, but far from all communication exchanged in and by a given encounter. On the other hand, audio-recording can be seen to be less intrusive, partly because of the less bulky shape of a tape-recorder as compared to a video-camera. It is also considered by many to be less threatening to people's integrity. One should bear in mind that the practice of many institutions is subject to the Official Secrets Act.

In my studies I have so far only used audio recordings. However, normally I have been allowed to be present in the rooms where the encounters have taken place. This has meant that I was able to register details such as gestures, the handling of artefacts and subtleties like embarrassment, mutual concentration and relief, which may otherwise have been lost, even on videotape.

NOTES

1. Before Gumperz, Bateson (1972) in his essay 'The message "This is play"', discussing animal behaviour, introduces the idea that the behaviour in itself contains signals that implicitly point to the currently valid frame of interpretation of the communicative meaning of this behaviour.

2. **Transcription conventions** (simplified after Sacks *et al.* 1978:731–3).

[	line brackets indicate that people are speaking simultaneously
,	continuing intonation (usually with rising or sustained tone)
.	terminating intonation (usually with a falling tone)
?	questioning intonation (usually with rising tone)
-	sudden cut-off of the current sound
. . .	open-ended intonation (fading out, ambiguous intonation terminal)
e:::	long vowel (example)
(.)	a short silence (micro-pause)
(1)	one second silence
((looks up))	non-verbal feature (example)
boldface	words spoken with emphasis
° °	part of an utterance framed by these is spoken relatively quietly
(xxx)	inaudible passage
italics	author's "back-translation" (Baker 1992) of Swedish and Russian talk
[ ]	text framed by these constitutes a comment to the English translation
→	line in the transcript is relevant to the point being made in the text

SIX

Ideal interpreting and actual performance

> . . . as we know, the real unit of language that is implemented in
> speech (*Sprache als Rede*) is not the individual, isolated monologic
> utterance, but the interaction of at least two utterances – in a word,
> dialogue (Voloshinov 1986:117, Russian original from 1930, footnote 4,
> Chapter 2).

This chapter takes as its point of departure the assumption that
interpreters typically tend to lean on a textual model of thinking,
and typically strive to translate primary parties' original utterances
as 'closely' as possible. At least, this is how we often explain to non-
interpreters what we are doing. Given that this is a self-evident
ambition for the interpreter, explorations of authentic interpreter-
mediated interaction show that interpreters in practice may work
with two or more concurrent sets of criteria for 'closeness' (or, if
you wish, 'equivalence') in translation.

In the literature on translation and interpretation, the notion of
'equivalence' is a constant concern. Few, if any, would think of
equivalence as a simple translating word for word, or sentence for
sentence. Such a 'literal' model has long been rejected in the literature. Nevertheless, this notion is strongly associated with a textual model of language; with the idea of translators/interpreters as
basically being occupied with establishing correspondence between
'source texts' and 'target texts'. These are the two fundamental units
in most models of interpreting and translating, and studies in this
field may often be referred to as 'source text' orientated or 'target
text' orientated. The first mentioned normally focus on how the individual translator's or interpreter's work depends on and reflects
the content and intention of 'source' texts. Studies of the latter kind
investigate how interpretations depend on (or may affect) recipients
in the 'target' culture.

In this chapter, I will utilize the established dichotomy, but be neither 'source' nor 'target' orientated, but rather explore the interdependence between various kinds of 'texts', as they manifest themselves in transcribed sequences of interpreter-mediated encounters. I will use a simple model of interpreter-mediated interaction as consisting of basically *two types of utterances,* namely *originals* (i.e. all utterances voiced by primary interlocutors) and *interpreters' utterances* (i.e. all utterances voiced by interpreters).

1. TEXTUAL STRUCTURES IN INTERPRETER-MEDIATED TALK

An institutional conversation in which a professional (P) and a lay person (L) talk with the assistance of a dialogue interpreter (DI)[1] could schematically be presented as follows:

P: Utterance 1 (in the majority (P's) language)
DI: Utterance 1' (= translation of U1 in the minority (L's) language)
L: Utterance 2 (in L's language)
DI: Utterance 2' (= translation of U2 in P's language)
P: Utterance 3 (in P's language)
DI: Utterance 3' (= translation of U3 in L's language)
etc.

The above schema is similar to what Knapp-Potthoff and Knapp term *Normalform der Mittlerdiskursstruktur* ("normal format of [language] mediator's discourse structure" (1985:457). It seems that many of the widespread and shared norms for interpreting presuppose an underlying view of people talking as people producing texts. Essentially, every second utterance is (should be) voiced by the interpreter, immediately at the end of each and every utterance by a primary party. The interpreter's utterances are (should be) second versions of the preceding utterances, recoded in another language. All information explicitly expressed in the first version, the 'original' utterance, including the style and form in which it is voiced, is (should be) relayed as closely as possible.

Applying a textual approach, I regard each speaker's utterance as a separate unit, and from an outside observer's position. The sense which I then may make of a certain utterance is not necessarily obvious for the speaker, or the listeners exposed to this, when it first occurs.

In the sections that follow, I will explore authentic interpreter-mediated interaction. I will compare 'originals' with the subsequent 'interpreter utterances' – as one would 'source texts' with 'target texts' – and identify 'closeness' and 'divergence' between them. The purpose is not primarily to explore reasons *why* the later 'diverge' from – or are 'close' to – the former. The idea is rather to detect potential interactional *functions* of different kinds of utterances.

Moreover, looking at interpreters' utterances not just in relation to immediately preceding primary interlocutors' talk, but in the context of longer stretches of transcribed discourse, will make it possible to explore the coordinating work of these utterances in interaction. I will consider both the translating aspect and the co-ordinating aspect, and explore the diversity of interdependencies between primary interlocutors and interpreters' utterances, starting by making a tentative classification of interpreters' utterances as types of short texts.

Interpreters' utterances can be seen as realizing in interaction two central functions, namely *translating* and *coordinating* the prim-ary parties' utterances. Interpreters take part in situations where they have a unique opportunity to understand everything said and therefore a unique position from which to exercise a certain control. Self-evidently, when people are assisted by interpreters, this fact to some extent will characterize the communicative situation in which they take part. The coordinating work of interpreters' utterances I would claim, indeed makes the interpreter's task a delicate one.

In interaction, interpreters' utterances can function:

- to influence the progress of interaction,
- to influence the substance of interaction,
- to regulate interaction (distribution of turns at talk; speed),
- to determine the on-the-record versus off-the-record distribu-tion of talk,
- to remind parties, implicitly or explicitly, of the interpreter's preferred mode of working,
- to generate a shared discourse and, at some level, a common focus of interaction,
- to sustain a certain definition of the encounter, for instance, as being a medical consultation or a police interrogation,
- to sustain the definition of the encounter as being an interpreter-mediated one.

In dialogue interpreting, the translating and coordinating aspects are *simultaneously present*, and the one does not exclude the other. As a matter of fact, these aspects condition each other. Seen like this, it is not an empirical question *whether* interpreters are translators or mediators – they cannot avoid being both. However, the coordinating and the translating functions are foregrounded at particular moments, sometimes supporting and sometimes disturbing one another.

The two aspects of interpreting – translation and coordination – are in practice inseparable, but it is possible and indeed fruitful theoretically to distinguish between them, and use them as analytical concepts. A detailed analysis of interpreter-mediated discourse will help to sort out how the two functions can fluctuate, and possibly also to see why this happens at particular points.

Focusing on *interpreters' utterances*, I will classify these according to a simple model of *mutually compatible types of short texts*. On the one hand, I will regard them from the point of view of *translating*, and, on the other hand, as resulting from the interpreters' *coordinating* task. These typologies are an outcome of explorations of authentic interpreter-mediated interaction.

1.1 Interpreting as translating: 'close' and 'divergent' renditions

Most interpreters' utterances are analysable as reformulations of prior 'original' utterances and can therefore be termed *renditions*. A 'rendition' is a stretch of text corresponding to an utterance voiced by an interpreter. It relates in some way to an immediately preceding *original*. 'Renditions' can relate to 'originals' in a range of different ways, which may form a basis for classification of 'renditions' into sub-categories. All utterances voiced by primary interactants are counted as 'originals'. Seen in a transcription, an 'original' starts where a primary interlocutor starts to talk and stops where he or she stops talking, that is, when leaving the floor open to someone else, when appointing someone else as the next speaker, when being interrupted by someone starting to talk (including providing supportive feedback) or, when there is a significant silence indicating the end of an utterance.

In interaction, 'originals' serve on the one hand as *'source texts' which are to be followed by corresponding 'target texts'*. On the other hand, they serve as *context(s) in a chain of utterances*, conditioning and shaping further discoursal and contextual development. And even if 'original' utterances in practice are by necessity heard in the context of a particular situation, and in the context of other utterances, the interpreter is to a certain extent forced to de-contextualize each 'original' as a separate unit, and re-contextualize a *new version* of it in the flow of talk.

Regarding the translation aspect of interpreting, recursively comparing 'interpreter utterances' and 'originals', I have arrived at the following taxonomy of 'renditions':

'Close renditions'.   In principle, to qualify as a 'close rendition', the propositional content found explicitly expressed in the 'rendition' must be equally found in the preceding 'original', and the style of the two utterances should be approximately the same.

By definition a 'rendition' is a second, and thus, in at least some respect, a new version of an 'original'. Differences between them can be related to textual and interactional aspects. Comparing 'renditions' with preceding 'originals' as isolated texts, one can find, on the one hand, differences which are best described in terms of lexicon, grammar, syntax, and other 'linguistic' matters. The comparison can, on the other hand, focus on the place of the texts in a given sequential context. Differences and similarities between 'renditions' and preceding 'originals' may then be described also in pragmatic, or functional terms. (For discussion of the theoretical basis for the whole idea of 'renditions' as 'close' or 'divergent', see Chapter 2:4.)

'Expanded renditions'.   An 'expanded rendition' includes more explicitly expressed information than the preceding 'original' utterance.

'Reduced renditions'.   A 'reduced rendition' includes less explicitly expressed information than the preceding 'original' utterance.

'Substituted renditions'.   A 'substituted rendition' consists of a combination of an 'expanded' and a 'reduced' one.

In the above four cases, the 'renditions' correspond to one (usually the immediately prior) 'original' utterance only. I have further distinguished cases where 'renditions' relate to 'originals' in other than a one-to-one correlation, namely:

'Summarized renditions'.   A 'summarized rendition' is a text that corresponds to two or more prior 'originals'. In some cases, it may consist of constituents related to two or more 'originals' provided by one and the same interlocutor. In other cases, the 'summarized

rendition' corresponds to two or more utterances voiced by different individuals. Sometimes an interpreter's utterance and an 'original' can together provide the information summarized in a succeeding 'rendition'.

'Two-part' or 'multi-part renditions'.   The text of a 'two-part rendition' consists of two interpreter's utterances corresponding to one 'original', which is split into parts by another interjected 'original' utterance, the propositional content of which is not reflected in the 'rendition'.

'Non-renditions'.   A 'non-rendition' is a 'text' which is analysable as an interpreter's initiative or response which does not correspond (as translation) to a prior 'original' utterance.

'Zero renditions'.   When comparison starts out not from the 'renditions' but from the 'originals', looking for correspondences among interpreters' utterances may result in cases of 'zero rendition', that is, cases when 'originals' are left untranslated.

The above taxonomy is a fairly straightforward system for classifying 'renditions' in relation to 'originals' at an utterance-to-utterance level. Given these broad and general definitions, one category does not always automatically exclude another. As will be seen, 'renditions' can at times be classified as, for instance, both 'close' and 'substituting'. This would of course make their validity for quantitative investigations quite restricted, but they serve well enough the purpose of demonstrating an elementary variety of textual structures that are represented in transcriptions of interpreter-mediated talk, and of exploring the functions of this variability.

1.2 Interpreting as coordinating: textual vs. interactional orientation

When it comes to categorizing types of interpreters' utterances related to their organizational, coordinating function in interaction, there is no such straightforward comparative approach available as in the case of translating.

Given that I regard 'originals' and 'interpreter utterances' as one would 'source texts' and 'target texts', I can state that the latter normally are designed to solve a problem of translation and a problem of communication. 'Interpreter utterances' are provided in order to bridge a linguistic gap (between two languages in use) and a social gap (between two or more language users). In transcribed discourse it is possible to trace indications of 'interpreter utterances' being designed to match both these tasks. Occasionally the one demands more efforts than the other. One dimension of classification would therefore be whether utterances show evidence of the translating aspect or the coordinating aspect being foregrounded; whether interpreters are *text orientated* or *interactionally orientated.*

The one or the other orientation may be more or less visibly marked in discourse. For example, utterances made by the interpreter which have no counterpart in a preceding 'original' (i.e. those that, seen from the point of view of translation, would count as 'non-renditions') would all indicate a certain 'interactional orientation'. This classifying principle of 'interpreter utterances' could also be phrased as concerning the speaker's explicitness or implicitness as regards the coordinating function of their talk. Cross-classifying types of 'renditions' from the point of view of coordination, 'interpreter utterances' could thus be seen as *implicitly coordinating* and *explicitly coordinating* ones.

Implicitly coordinating 'interpreter utterances'.   Interpreters are implicitly coordinating a conversation simply by talking every now and then. Everything an interpreter says, represents a typical way of handling the coordinating task. 'Interpreter utterances' are normally designed to make the addressed party prepared to receive more talk from the other, or elicit talk from him or her, in other words, to select next speaker. The substance and the progression of talk will be partly determined by whatever the interpreter contributes, or restrains from contributing.

Explicitly coordinating 'interpreters' utterances'.   In transcriptions of interpreter-mediated interaction, some 'interpreter utterances' are particularly visibly designed to do coordinating work. I have in mind those which have no corresponding counterpart in preceding 'originals'.

They can be more or less designed to bridge between the two languages in use. The interpreter may occasionally treat a language and words and utterances 'belonging' to this language in isolation, objectifying, as it were, sequences of talk (seeing talk as 'text'). I will consider this approach as *text orientated.*

Text orientated initiatives would be, for instance:

- requests for clarification,
- requests for time to translate; requests to stop talking,
- comments on translations.

Alternatively, interpreters can be more focused on bridging between the others' respective perspectives. Efforts designed first and foremost towards providing or sustaining the conditions for a shared communicative activity between the primary parties would indicate an *interaction orientated* approach (seeing talk as activity).

Interaction orientated initiatives would be, for instance:

- requests to observe the turntaking order,
- invitations to start or continue talking; requests to stop talking,
- requests for solicited but not yet provided information.

1.3 The relativity of closeness

In the following sections I will explore transcribed excerpts drawn from interpreter-mediated encounters, examining the different grounds on which 'closeness' and 'divergence' between 'texts' may be judged. Identifying various types of 'renditions' and of coordinating 'interpreter utterances', the analysis will highlight basic functions connected to 'expanding', 'reducing', 'substituting', and so on, and elucidate the communicative work accomplished through 'explicit' and 'implicit' coordinating.

The interpreters represented in the present chapter, Ilona, Ivana and Irma, are all experienced with work as community interpreters in the medical and legal spheres. Ilona and Ivana are also formally trained in this kind of interpreting. Ilona has attended some short term courses and Ivana has had three terms of university level training. All three of them acknowledge the Swedish Code of Ethics for interpreters working in the public sphere (see Chapter 3:2.2).

2. "AND CAN YOU SHOW WHERE?"

The excerpts below are drawn from the encounter mentioned in the introduction of this book, a hearing that takes place at the immigration department of a local police-station. It involves a police officer,

Peter, an applicant for Swedish residence permit, Alisa, and an interpreter, Ilona. In reality Russian and Swedish were the languages used.
In the transcript, for the purpose of facilitating readers' understanding, all utterances are also translated into English (see Chapter 5 for
transcription conventions).

Alisa meets the police officer for the first time, and is asked to
identify herself. She does so by showing her Soviet passport. Yet
the officer is not clear about her present status in relation to (what
was at the time) the Soviet Union. When questioned about citizenship the applicant claims that she is Greek. Does she have dual
citizenship? Has she applied for a Greek one? Or is she planning
to? In that case, why then apply for a Swedish residence permit?
From the point of view of the police officer, and the immigration
authorities he represents, citizenship status is of course an issue of
central importance. This is something the interpreter is well aware of.

2.1 Implicit coordination at the expense of closeness

The quoted sequence starts with the officer bringing up the issue of
citizenship by contrasting this notion to the concept of nationality.
At the same time, he gives expression to his doubts about whether
the distinction between these two notions is clear to the applicant.

(1) (G22:9)
1 Peter: ((types)) mm. betraktar du dig **själv** som- ja som grek,
   mm. do you consider yourself as- well as Greek,
2   det har du sagt, men betraktar du dig själv som grekisk
   this you have said, but do you consider yourself as a Greek
3   **medborgare** också? jag vet inte om du förstår
   citizen as well? I don't know if you understand
4   skillnaden mellan att vara- ha en viss nationalitet och
   the difference between being- having a certain nationality
5   att va medborgare?
   and being a citizen?
6 Ilona: а как вы считаете вы сами. вы гречанка, я знаю,
   and what do you think yourself. you are Greek, I know,
7   вы сказали что вы гречанка, но одно дело
   you said that you are Greek, but it's one thing
8   считать ... по национальностям а другое дело
   to count ... in nationalities and another thing
9   считать себя гражданином какого-либо
   to count yourself as citizen of a

10		государства, я имею в виду. в смысле государства.
		state, I have in mind. in the sense of state.
	Alisa:	ну я считаю что я
		well I think that I
11		всё-таки гражданка СССР, раз я там родилась,
		in any case am a citizen of the USSR, since I was born there,
12		это моя родина. (.) там же у нас много
		it is my fatherland. (.) and we have many
13		национальностей живут.
		nationalities living there.
14	Ilona:	ja jag tycker att jag är:::
		well I think I am:::
15	Alisa:	вот,
		so,
16	Ilona:	medborgare i Sovjet. för att. jag är född där och jag har
		citizen of the USSR. because. I was born there and I have been
17		bott där och det är många nationaliteter som bor i
		living there and there are many nationalities living in
18		Sovjet.
		the USSR.
19	Peter:	ja e m nu- nu pratar jag om Grekland. sa jag Sovjet?
		yes er m now- now I'm talking about Greece. did I say the USSR?
20		°idag är det bara ... °
		°today it's just ... °
→ 21	Ilona:	nej nej **hon** svara att
		*no no **she** answered that*
22	Peter:	ja
		yes
→ 23	Ilona:	hon är medborgare i Sovjet.
		she is a citizen of the USSR.

Looking at the first pair of utterances as separate texts – as 'original' and 'rendition' – the interpreter's utterance (1:6–10), compared to the police officer's (1:1–5), involves at least two different kinds of 'substitutions'. To start with, the interrupted onset is 'substituted' by (or 'expanded' into) a question. The officer drops his first line of thought, "do you consider your*self* as-" (1:1). Ilona, in turn, picks up on his emphasized "self". In the 'rendition' it stands out as a salient part of his message, when the word is re-phrased within the full-sentence, coherent question: "and what do you think yourself" (1:6).

But the word stressed by the officer in his second and completed attempt to formulate the question: "do you consider yourself as a Greek *citizen* as well?" (1:2–3) has no correspondence in the 'rendition'. This includes, as did the officer's utterance, a back-grounding statement, confirming that he registered that she is speaking of herself as Greek. It does not include, however, the following question, his wondering about whether the applicant will be able to reply adequately. We may note its potentially face-threatening character. In the 'rendition', this last part of the 'original', phrased as a question (1:3–5), is 'substituted' by a claim. The interpreter partly explains for the applicant in response to the officer's suggestion that she might lack sufficient knowledge (1:7–10).

Comparing this pair of 'original' and 'rendition' would thus indicate that the interpreter's work on establishing necessary conditions for a shared and mutual exchange here clashes with the task of translating as 'closely' as possible the police officer's utterance. Ilona performs implicit coordinating at the cost of 'closeness' in translation. Responding to the officer's doubts, the interpreter restrains from memorizing and translating his exact wordings.

Looking further into the transcription, I can observe that the turntaking pattern derives from the 'normal format'. Seen from the point of view of translation, the two utterances (1:21) and (1:23) (marked with arrows), constitute a 'two-part rendition', summarizing what the applicant meant to say about her citizenship. But if I compare them with the immediately preceding 'original' (1:19–20), they appear to be 'non-renditions'. Regarded from the point of view of coordination, they can be labelled 'explicitly coordinating initiatives'. They respond directly to the police officer's request, and are designed to solve a problem of divergent perspectives. The police officer's one-word-utterance *ja* ("yes") (1:22) in between functions as supportive feedback, confirming his attentive listening.

In interaction, feedback tokens normally signify something like 'I am with you, go on talking'. And this is indeed what Ilona does, completing the statement she just started, "no no *she* answered that she is a citizen of the USSR." (1:21 and 1:23). Ilona apparently feels personally addressed by Peter's question: "yes er m now- now I'm talking about Greece. did I say the USSR? °today it's just . . . °" (1:19–20).

When the interpreter has specified (in 1:21 and 1:23) the applicant's answer, the interaction continues, as we will see below, not with the police officer raising another issue, but by Alisa's further specification on the issue of nationality. Talk has touched upon something which in the Soviet context was of crucial importance, in particular in connection with opportunities for migration.

The following sequence will further illustrate the balance the interpreter seeks to achieve between translation and coordination – bridging differences between languages and between perspectives. The emphasis on one or the other aspect depends largely, it seems, on the situation, as it unfolds utterance by utterance. The example raises the question of possible conditions for the appearance of explicit rather than implicit coordination on the part of the interpreter.

(2) (G22:9–10)

```
24   Alisa:    и всё равно что- даже если в Советском Союзе
               and anyhow if- even if I live in the USSR,
25             живу, я всё равно считаю что я не русская я
               to my mind I am anyhow not Russian I am
26  ⌈         гречанка, всё равно. так официально я гречанка.
   |           Greek, anyhow. so officially I am Greek.
   |Ilona:                      om- än om jag har bott hela mitt liv i Sovjet
   |                            if- even if I have been living all of my life in the USSR
27  ⌈         ändå räknas jag som en grekiska. och inte som en ryska.
   |           I am anyhow counted as a Greek. and not as a Russian.
   |Alisa:                            там у меня в
   ⌊                                  there in my
28  ⌈         паспорте стояло что я гречанка и:::
   |           passport it said that I am Greek and:::
   |Ilona:                            å i passet-
   ⌊                                  and in the passport-
29   Alisa:    вот
               so
30   Ilona:    i passet står det också att jag är grek- av grekisk
               in the passport too it says that I am Greek- of Greek
31             nationalitet.
               nationality.
32   Alisa:    да
               yes
→ 33  Peter:    °kan du visa mig var?°
                °can you show me where?°
→ 34  Ilona:    а вы можете показать где?
                a[nd] can you show where?
35   Alisa:    а нет. не в ЭТОМ. не в ЭТОМ.
               oh no. not in this one. not in this one.
36  ⌈Ilona:    näe inte i den här.
   |           no not in this one.
   |Alisa:                     это вот в советском паспорте. это же
   ⌊                           that is in the Soviet passport. that one is a
```

37	общегражданский. даётся которым-
	union passport given to those-
Ilona:	det här är ett internationellt pass
	this is an international passport
38	och jag menade inrikes . . .
	and I had in mind a national one . . .

The analysis will start from the top of this sequence by comparing Alisa's 'original' (2:24–26) and the following 'rendition' (2:26–27). Ilona's utterance states that Alisa is "counted as a Greek", while the 'original' firstly gives an indication of Alisa's opinion about being Greek or Russian, secondly, acknowledges her officially Greek nationality. The interpreter focuses on Alisa's reformulation and condenses the information. Out of two communicative goals indicated in the 'original', this 'reduced rendition' puts emphasis on the most recently voiced. This part of the information fits the typical needs of a police officer, to record quickly and unambiguously the facts of the case (rather than, for instance, his possible wish to understand the ways in which the applicant in front of him is reasoning).

Further down in the transcription, the applicant comes in with her next contribution (2:27–28) while Ilona is still translating. Before Ilona has finished this next part, Alisa adds a confirming: "so" (2:29). This make (2:28) and (2:30–31) stand out as a 'two-part rendition', while (2:29) as well as the subsequent 'original', *da* ("yes") (2:32), manifest cases of 'zero rendition'.

In a talk-as-text-model a 'zero rendition' would indicate a certain deficiency. Alisa's utterances (in 2:29 and 2:32), as well as the officer's "ja" (1:22) commented upon above, *lack* corresponding translations. Yet this results from my transformation of talk into text. Giving back-channelling tokens the status of separate utterances, the transcription leads me to regard them as 'originals', i.e. texts which ought to be translated. This is not necessarily how they are perceived in interaction. Looking at talk as activity, and at these tokens as parts of a larger sequence, it is evident that they – in the actual situation – are heard as insubstantial, subordinate and supporting feedback.

The function of feedback tokens is intimately linked to their position in the sequence of talk, to the immediacy of their appearance in interaction. Here, Alisa's supportive back-channelling during the 'turn' of the interpreter helps the applicant to communicate (particularly to the police officer) an image of herself as a person who is eager to speak, in a situation where she is dependent upon someone else's assistance for talking.

'Interpreter utterances' sometimes promote one communicative function identified in the 'original' at the expense of another function which this utterance was designed to carry. The interpreter's understanding of the situation as a whole is evidently decisive in this respect. Comparing the 'original' (2:24–26) and the following 'rendition' (2:26–27) again, one can observe grammatical differences. The applicant uses the present tense in the conditional phrase "even if I live in the USSR" (2:25). Ilona, knowing that the person in front of her at present does not live in the USSR, interprets this as a general statement and puts it as: "even if I have been living all my life in the USSR" (2:26–27). The 'rendition' states something about the question of nationality for those living in the USSR. The subsequent 'two-part rendition' (2:28, 2:30) follows the same logic. The interpreter disambiguates and specifies the applicant's message according to the same general conditionality. This means that she uses present tense "in the passport too it says that I am Greek-..." (2:30). In the corresponding 'original', however, the applicant had used past tense: "there in my passport it said ..." (2:27–28), which could indicate that she is speaking only about herself, and about herself as someone who has left the USSR. "There" in Alisa's utterance would then be referring to the former homeland, that is, "there" in the USSR. But the police officer understands the applicant to be talking about "there" in the passport which he at present has in his hand, and when he asks back about "where" in the passport (in 2:33), Ilona must have seen that she had misled him a moment ago. In other words, she urgently needs to put him right again, and at the same time to re-establish a common focus between the primary interlocutors. This is what is accomplished in the last part of the quoted sequence.

2.2   Close translation and implicit coordination

The final sequence, from (2:33) and onwards, involves neither 'non-renditions' nor 'zero renditions'. 'Originals' and 'renditions' correspond one to one, and the correspondence is fairly 'close'. Ilona's utterance in (2:34) compared with Peter's (2:33), seems to be a case of lexically and functionally 'close rendition'. The English translation does not reveal, however, a difference in grammar. The police officer uses *du*, second person <u>singular</u> – the standard and polite pronoun of address in Swedish. Ilona uses *vy*, second person <u>plural</u> – the conventional, polite pronoun of address in Russian. In English both pronouns correspond to "you". Applying grammatical criteria, Ilona's utterance would thus be 'divergent'. More precisely, it could also count as a 'substituting rendition'.

Ilona's next utterance (2:36) looks fairly 'close' as well, in particular if we understand the original's (2:35) repetitiveness as redundant. The number of lexical items is 'reduced', but Alisa's message gets through. On the other hand, to repeat often means to emphasize. Alisa's repeating twice "not in *this one*" (2:35) could be understood as a way of stressing her disagreement. In this case, the 'rendition' (2:36) must be seen as both lexically and functionally 'reduced'.

Comparing the following pair of utterances (2:36–37 and 2:37–38), the 'closeness' is somewhat hidden behind a reversed word order, an added personal pronoun, "I" (2:38), and the interrupted ending "given to those-" (2:37) which is 'reduced'. Alisa says "Soviet" and "union" passport, and from her point of view it is self-evidently how one must classify the passport which the officer is looking at. It is also a given fact that this one is valid internationally and functions only outside the Soviet Union. Ilona, in turn, explicitly mentions "international" and puts it as the opposite of "national". The 'rendition' in this way reminds the officer of the Soviet passport system, which involved two types (a passport valid as a document of identity inside the USSR, and an international passport, which the holder received only when he or she was allowed to travel abroad).

Ilona's utterance (2:37–38) could also be seen as a 'substituting rendition'. The 'original' utterance (2:36–37) may to a reader's eye look rather fragmented, but the interpreter's understanding of it follows logically upon and rounds up the longer sequence of talk, connecting to the issue of citizenship versus nationality which has been under discussion. In other words, the interpretation provided at this particular point in time is partly based on what has been said before in the encounter as a whole.

Regarded from the point of view of coordinating, Ilona's interpretation, it can be seen, is very much geared towards bridging the gap between the primary parties' divergent perspectives, towards assuring a shared focus on the issue of citizenship, and also towards supporting the exchange as such. One of Ilona's utterances is particularly interesting from the point of view of coordinating. As I noted above, comparing the interpreter's utterance (2:34) with the preceding 'original' (2:33), the correspondence between them could be classified as fairly 'close'. Nevertheless, in and by this pair of utterances, the interpreter firmly redirects the interaction order. This is not visible in the transcription, but evident indeed in the here-and-now situation. At the same time as Ilona repeats (2:34) the officer's words (2:33), she also repeats his gesture of handing over the document. But where he had been offering the passport to Ilona, making a quiet request to *her*, as if 'off-the-record', she takes the passport and hands it over to *the applicant*, translating the officer's utterance as she does so. The interpreter in this way signals to the preceding speaker that she does not acknowledge herself as being addressed. She also establishes the status of the preceding utterance as part of on-the-record talk and thereby also re-establishes herself in the middle position of interaction. Simultaneously, the predefined interaction order (original–translation–original, etc.) is put into action. The 'rendition' thus gained an additional function as a means for the interpreter to demonstrate her preferred mode of working and mark her status as *non-person* (Goffman 1990:150, cf. Chapter 4:1.4).

2.3 On the conditions for explicit coordination

Comparing Peter's request discussed above, "can you show me where?" (2:33), with his utterance in (1:19–20) which was followed by an explicitly coordinating utterance, could give us some hints about circumstances that may provoke explicit coordination on the part of the interpreter. A first observation will be that (1:19–20) is much more complex in character than (2:33). The latter consists of a straightforward question explicitly directed to someone addressed as "you"; fairly easy to memorize and to repeat in another language. The former, in contrast, consists of an interrupted onset "yes er m now-" (1:19); a statement "now I'm talking about Greece." (1:19); a question which addresses all present and nobody in particular and may even be rhetorical, "did I say the USSR?" (1:19); and finally a quiet comment, something Peter says as if to himself, "°today it's just . . . °" (1:20). An utterance of this kind is more of a challenge to the interpreter's memory capacity. (The officer's utterance also involves a diversity of something I will, in Chapter 7, discuss as 'footing'.)

Moreover, comparing the propositional content of (1:19–20) and (2:33), the first 'original' concerns 'who said what?', an area (i.e.

talking) where Ilona has expert knowledge as interpreter. The latter, on the other hand, concerns an artefact, the passport, which is observable to all in the room and is at the centre of the action.

A third observation concerns sequentiality. Given Ilona is striving at sticking as 'closely' as possible to the substance of the preceding 'originals' and to the 'normal format' of interaction, the explicit coordinating utterances (1:21 and 1:23) create a context for those that follow in the sense that the interpreter – being 'caught' once by a direct address from the police officer (1:19–20) – may be more on her guard the next time she is directly addressed.

The interpreter partly creates the current working conditions. What Ilona said above in interaction continually had an impact on discourse as a whole; on the situated exchange. Sometimes, concentrating on translating a stretch of lexical items 'as closely as possible' seemingly blocks her ability to see other dimensions of the context as a whole and to take in what was subsequently being done in and by talk. Nevertheless, it is obviously possible at times to combine a strong textual focus with an awareness of the diverse functions inherent in spoken 'texts'.

It should be clear by now that when we look at the coordinating aspect of interpreting, further dimensions of the context in which talk takes place, and which talk in itself forms, have to be fed into the analysis. When talking about the interactional functions of utterances, it is almost impossible to *avoid* conceiving of talk as activity. As the analysis shows, interpreting is much more than something preserved, something lost and/or something added. For analytical purposes, throughout this chapter, talk is perceived first and foremost as types of 'texts'.

3. "SHE COUGHS IN THIS WAY (.) AND IT IS A DRY COUGH"

The following four excerpts are drawn from two medical encounters. They illustrate that the fluency of an interpreter-mediated exchange is dependent on the rapport established between the co-actors, just as is the smoothness of a monolingual conversation. Moreover, fluency depends on the primary parties' image of the interpreter, and on the interpreter's self image.

The first and the two last sequences are drawn from a very animated conversation between a nurse, Nancy, and Maria, a mother of a recently born child. They are assisted by the interpreter Ivana. The present excerpt starts at the point where the Russian-speaking woman raises a new issue, one of several which she had noted in advance on a piece of paper. The woman told me that she did this to gain maximum benefit from the opportunity of receiving language assistance. On other occasions, she and the nurse had tried to communicate in broken English (a language of which practically all Swedes have an elementary school knowledge). Maria looks at the paper and says:

```
(3) (G42:2)
   1  Maria:    и вот (.) например это- я как-то раньше не
                and so (.) for instance this- before I somehow didn't
   2            обращала внимания сейчас обращала. начала
                pay attention now I did pay. she has started
   3            по ночам она у меня так ((coughs))
                at night my [baby] like this
   4 ⌈Ivana:   och. det var något jag inte la märke förut till a- alltså att
   │            and. that was something I didn't pay attention to before tha- that is
     │
     ⌊Maria:                                      насморка нету.
                                                  no cold.
   5 ⌈Ivana:   där att hon ((coughs)) hostar, hostar
   │            that the fact that she (.) coughs, coughs
→    ⌊Nancy:                      hon hostar.
                                  she coughs.
   6 ⌈Ivana:   men nu märker jag de alltså och ho-
   │            but now I notice it and sh-
   │
   ⌊Maria:                        сухой такой вот.
                                  dry like this.
   7  Ivana:    hon hostar på det här sättet ((points with her hand in
                she coughs in this way
   8            Maria's direction)) och det är torrhosta.
                                      and it is a dry cough.
→  9  Nancy:    a ... torrhosta.
                a ... dry cough.
  10  Ivana:    men hon har ingen snuva.
                but she has no cold.
→ 11  Nancy:    ingen snuva.
                no cold.
  12  Ivana:    насморка нет?
                no cold?
```

In this excerpt, Ivana's fastly delivered 'renditions' correspond to the preceding 'originals' not as one-to-one, but in a more complex way. The Russian mother continuously provides information (3:1–3, 3:4, 3:6), and the interpreter rapidly feeds this into the 'rendition', which then, seen as 'text', consists of several parts (3:4, 3:5, 3:6, 3:7–8, 3:10). When listening to the tape and transcribing the conversation, I was immediately struck by the speed of the exchange. The excerpt exemplifies the kinds of 'texts' that result from a mixture of simultaneous and consecutive interpreting. The 'rendition' is also split into what look like separate parts by the nurse's back-channelling contributions. Three times, Nancy repeats single glosses from what the interpreter says (3:5, 3:9, 3:11). Two of them (3:5, 3:9) are not translated into Russian. One of them (3:11), however, becomes part of common discourse when translated with a lexically 'close' – though prosodically, and thereby pragmatically 'divergent' ('substituted') – 'rendition'. Ivana echoes (in 3:12) the nurse's fact-establishing "no cold" (3:11) with a rising, questioning intonation. This 'rendition' therefore did not add a lot of substance to the talk, but in interaction it served to stimulate the progression of the exchange.

Regarded from the point of view of coordination, this is another example of implicit coordination being accomplished through a retrospective transformation of the interactional status of the preceding 'original' (cf. the case of "and can you show where?" above). Nancy's preceding statement (3:11) sounds on the tape as quite a weak initiative, something added primarily to confirm that she keeps listening attentively. In contrast, the interpreter's subsequent version of it becomes a relatively stronger initiative. It is a question, selecting the other primary party as the next speaker.

Interlocutors' small words of back-channelling are rarely translated. It is as if the relative 'transparency' (Müller 1993) of this communicative activity reduces the relevance of translating. As was noted above, the interactive function of feedback in face-to-face interaction automatically challenges the idea of 'close' translations. However 'closely' the interpreter strives to translate, the interpreter-mediated conversation in itself transforms the interactional significance of back-channelling.

Providing 'close renditions' of back-channelling tokens, the interpreter can demonstrate, as it were, her image as a 'close-texts-producer'. It can, at times, be a way to show that one is working extra-hard on living up to predefined norms, including translating everything said by the parties as 'closely' as possible. Simultaneously this may play down the uniqueness of the interpreter's position in interaction, since interpreting odd words of this kind points at the possibility of interpretation being superfluous. In interpreter-mediated encounters, a kind of joyful relief can sometimes be observed when primary parties suddenly find themselves understanding one another directly, and they can laugh at the interpreter being excessively helpful.

3.1 Close and expanding translating

In situations such as this, where the exchange is rapid and interpreters therefore are confronted with extremely tight time-limits, one would normally think that they would display a certain tendency to drop information. The above excerpts, however, do not involve many 'reduced renditions'. Most of what Maria and Nancy explicitly express is integrated in the 'renditions'. In Excerpt 3, there are two pieces of 'text' found in 'originals', that are not reflected in any of the interpreter's utterances. One is the interrupted onset "for instance this-" (3:1). In my data, such parts of 'originals' are, as a rule, not translated. (This instance thus confirms a general observation.) If they are translated, as we saw in Excerpt 1 ("and what do you think yourself", 1:6), they are normally translated in expanded, full sentence versions, rather than as 'false starts'. Another small detail found in the 'original', but not in the nearby 'texts' from the interpreter, is the specification concerning the time when Maria's baby coughs, namely "at night" (3:3).

Apart from these 'reductions', a detailed comparison between 'originals' and 'interpreter's utterances' also shows 'expansions'. Characteristic in these is that they hardly add any substance to the discourse. One could say that they first and foremost put emphasized focus on a central point in Maria's question. Ivana imitates the mother's demonstration of the coughing sound (3:5), then twice names the child's activity, "coughs" (3:5). She repeats it again "she coughs" (3:7) and, moreover, makes a gesture towards the mother, as if pointing retrospectively to *her* coughing sound. Thus 'expanded' the 'rendition' prompts the interlocutors to concentrate on this particular issue of the baby's coughing, and to pay attention to one another. An additional function possibly resulting from this 'expansion' is that the speed of the exchange is somewhat calmed down. In this way the interlocutors, including the interpreter, are given more time to think about what to say.

Finally, Maria provides an 'original' which consists of an elliptic expression "no cold" (3:4). This utterance was reflected in a subsequent 'expanded rendition': "but she has no cold" (3:10). The 'rendition' thus includes a specification of the person who is referred to, namely "she", that is the baby, and a "but", which indicates a comparison. In many instances, 'renditions' are 'expanded' to specify referential and/or interactional meaning of an utterance, in order to rule out possible misunderstanding.

At times the opposite, de-specification, is accomplished through 'expansion'. The following excerpt exemplifies this and yet other functions of 'expanded renditions'. It is drawn from an interview at a health-care clinic. Dora, a Swedish-speaking doctor, meets Paula, a Russian-speaking patient and, as before, Ivana is the interpreter on duty. The excerpt starts at a point where the patient disagrees with the doctor. She had just asked for medicine to help her relax, but the doctor explains that this hardly would be helpful to her, and that she must see her worriedness and distress as quite normal for people in her situation. Paula had just arrived from the USSR to Sweden as a refugee. Having got the doctor's message Paula replies:

(4) (G35:5)

1 Paula: у меня совсем наоборот, я здесь **очень**
to me it is entirely the opposite. I have become very

2 успокоилась. я чувствую что (.) я совершенно не
calm here. I feel that.(.) I am not at all on

3 на пределе и::: абсолютно расслаблена вот (.) у
edge and . . . completely relaxed so . . . I

4 меня- такого не было в Союзе. у меня появилась
have- this didn't happen in the USSR. I have become

5 какая-то плаксивость.
so prone to tears.

6 Ivana: m. m.
m. m.

7 Paula: чего- чего- (мне не свойственно было)
which- which- (was not my typical style)

→ Ivana: näe det är sna- snarare tvärtom alltså, jag vill
no it is rath- rather the opposite that is, I don't want

Dora: mhm
mhm

→ 8 Ivana: inte hålla med dig utan det är snarare tvärtom jag
to agree with you but it is rather the opposite I

9 känner mig lugnare här än i Sovjet. och jag känner
feel calmer here than in the USSR. and I feel

Dora: mhm
mhm

→ 10 ⎡ Ivana: mig mycket avslappnad. och ... liksom de- allting är som
      ⎢   *very relaxed and ... that is it- everything is as it's supposed*
      ⎣ Dora: mhm
                                           mhm
→ 11 ⎡ Ivana: det ska **men** ett- en sak som inte ... har hänt mig i Sovjet
      ⎢   *to be **but** one- one thing that did not ... happen to me in the USSR*
      ⎣ Dora: mm
                                           mm
→ 12   Ivana: att jag har blivit så gråtfärdig- gråtmild. ibland.
                 is that I have become so ready to cry- tearful. sometimes.

In reality, the exchange transcribed above runs very rapidly. Ivana's
'multi-party rendition' (4:6–12) of Paula's disagreement, intersected
with the doctor's feedback "mhm"s, took about as long as the preceding 'original' (4:1–5). Classified in terms of 'closeness' and 'divergence', the 'rendition' would be an 'expanded' one.

Ivana starts by rendering quite closely Paula's expression "no it
is rath- rather the opposite that is" (4:7). The rising intonation in
alltså ("that is") indicates that she intends to continue. Moreover,
expressed in this way, *alltså* conventionally establishes a certain
semantic relationship between the two stretches of talk it connects
(Apfelbaum and Wadensjö 1997). It announces a clarification of the
first part and a second part is consequently added. The 'rendition'
comes to relate to the patient's utterance as 'expanded' in two ways.
First, Ivana emphasizes the disagreement by simply repeating "it is
rather the opposite" (4:7 and 4:8) (answering to Paula's "entirely the
opposite" (4:1) uttered once). Secondly, she specifies by naming explicitly the speaker's, that is Paula's, communicative activity: "I don't
want to agree with you" (4:7–8).

Before Ivana starts to talk, Paula inserts, somewhat hesitantly,
"which- which- was not my typical style" (4:7). In the 'rendition'
this is matched by "*but* one- one thing that did not ... happen to
me in the USSR" (4:11). The 'rendition' is thus 'expanded' to specify
a location ("in the USSR"). This underlines the counterposition
between the patient's actual and former (Swedish and Soviet-time)
states of mind, at the same time as it disqualifies the comparison
phrased by the practitioner, the one between Paula and other people
in her situation as a refugee. The interpreter's version in a sense puts
more energy into Paula's argument.

The contrast between Petra's present and past mental condition
is further emphasized by Ivana's adding of a stressed "but" in this
utterance (4:11). The emphasis on "but" here additionally fills the
function of securing space for the interpreter to continue.

As mentioned above, 'expansion' can also work in an opposite direction, to de-specify what the 'original' is referring to. This happens here at the end of the sequence, when Ivana is to translate the word *plaksivost'* ("tearfulness"/"being prone to tears") uttered by the patient (in 4:5). When interpreting into Swedish (or English for that matter), this typically Russian noun construction challenges the interpreter's inventiveness. Instead of one corresponding word Ivana simply gives two alternative translations of it in Swedish: "ready to cry- tearful" (in 4:12). In conclusion I would argue that this very plain example of an 'expanded' 'rendition' that becomes less precise than the prior 'original' functions interactionally in line with the other 'expanded renditions' analysed in this excerpt, namely to support Paula's argument for getting medical care. They are designed to bridge equally a social gap between different perspectives *and* a linguistic gap between different languages.

3.2 Close and substituting translating

Closing up this section I will go back to the first cited encounter (Excerpt 3), where Nancy and Maria meet at the child care centre. It is further on in the exchange and the mother has just brought up her worries about the redness of the baby's skin. She fears that the little girl has the same problems as her elder sister, and the talk goes on about possible symptoms of allergy. Nancy argues that what the baby has is normal with small children.

(5) (G42:6)
1 Nancy: det kan vara- (.) det kan vara en överkänslighet i deras
it can be- (.) it can be an oversensitivity in their
2 **hud** som gör att dom reagerar.
skin that makes them react.
3 Ivana: может быть, просто у неё **кожечка** немножко
perhaps, simply her baby skin is a little
4 чувствительная.
sensitive.
5 Maria: mhm,
mhm.

It is normal that babies get irritated and their skin is reddened when wearing diapers, and before they get used to new kinds of food. What Maria fears to be an allergic reaction might just be normal. This is something the nurse develops in a longer sequence as her expert opinion, part of which is presented above. Comparing one of the 'originals' (5:1–2) with the subsequent 'rendition' (5:3–4), we can observe that Nancy talks about babies in general, while Ivana's version of it concerns Maria's baby specifically. The pronoun "her" (5:3) corresponds to the 'original' "their" (5:1).

Ivana's translation functionally answers quite closely to the nurse's statement, while textually it answers more directly to the mother's formulation of the issue. Referring specifically to the baby who is focused by both interlocutors, Ivana's 'substituted rendition' bridges the gap between their perspectives. Of the two basic functions inherent in the interpreter's work, coordination of interaction is momentarily the superordinate one, the one that leads the progression of discourse.

The character of this initiative can be further elucidated if we compare it with another one found a moment later in the same encounter. Maria mentions that her baby cries for food every third hour, while she thinks it is enough to satisfy her hunger less frequently.

(6) (G42:6)

26	Maria:	а кормлю только пять раз, что для меня-
		and I feed only five times, what for me-
→ 27	Ivana:	men jag ammar ju henne- кормишь грудью?
		but I breastfeed her- do you breastfeed her?
28	Maria:	нет, всё.
		no, finished.
29	Ivana:	aha, nej, inte ammar uta:::n
		aha, no, not breastfeed bu:::t
30	Nancy:	näe
		no
31	Ivana:	ger henne mat var eh.. femte timme.
		feed her every eh:: fifth hour.
32	Nancy:	jaa
		yeah
33	Ivana:	eller- jag- inte var femte timme. fem gånger om.
		or- I- not every fifth hour. five times in.
34		dygnet,
		twenty-four hours,

The interpreter's contributions (6:27, 6:29, 6:31, 6:33–34) can from the point of view of translation be seen as involving both 'expansion', 'substitution' and, what is most important here, 'summarizing'. Ivana's 'multi-part rendition' summarizes not only what the mother says, but also the part of the exchange that she contributes herself, an exchange which moreover is elicited by the interpreter. The 'rendition' answers to the primary parties' need for translation, and to her own need to correct, clarify and summarize.

Seen from the point of view of coordination, (6:27) involves a request for clarification addressed to the prior speaker. The initiative is designed to disambiguate the intended meaning of the Russian verb *kormit'*. This is necessary when translation into Swedish is requested, since a situation involving a baby child opens up various interpretations. This occurs to Ivana when she has already started to translate. To ensure a correct translation the interpreter has to find out whether Maria means *breastfeed*, which in Swedish is expressed by one specific word *amma*, or simply *feed*, which in Swedish must be expressed with a completely different verb, *mata* ("feed") or the expression *ge mat* ("give food"). Ivana engages in a sequence of clarification, basically to bridge a gap between the two languages. Of the two basic functions inherent in the interpreter's work, the momentarily principal one, by which the discourse progresses, would therefore here be translation.

4. "JUST A SECOND"

In this section the focus will be on functions attained by interpreters' utterances that do not, either in parts or as wholes, have a direct correlate in primary interlocutors' utterances. When analysing transcribed discourse these utterances make the interpreters particularly visible as independent actors. This does not necessarily mean that the primary parties experience them as such. In practice, this category of interpreters' utterances fills a number of functions, more or less explicitly, and more or less firmly coordinating and monitoring interaction. The forms these utterances take are in turn dependent on the primary parties' communicative style, on their respective communicative goals and on how they adapt to one another. The result in terms of 'text' is also dependent on how interpreters understand their professional task and how they manage it in practice.

Seen from the point of view of translation, the utterances in question would count as 'non-renditions'. As will be seen in the analyses, one of the main functions of 'non-renditions' is ultimately to guarantee the primary interlocutors' continued exchange on a mutually focused issue, which simultaneously means that the interpreter also facilitates her job as language mediator in between.

4.1 Explicit coordination and reducing translating

In Excerpt 7 we are back at the immigration department. Anton, an
applicant for a residence permit, meets the police officer Peter. They
are assisted by the interpreter Ilona. The excerpt begins where Anton
is about to explain why he has decided to leave his home country,
the USSR, for good. The applicant starts explaining and mentions
that his mother has lived in Sweden for many years.

(7) (G21:4)

1 Anton: а причина- у меня мать старая . . . ей 75 лет, она
and the reason – my mother is old . . . she is 75 years old, she

2 попала в аварию, я два года назад был здесь, как
had an accident. I was here two years ago, I had

3 раз я приехал второго июля, а двадцать-пятого
just arrived on July second, and on the twenty-fifth

4 у неё случилось. а::: хорошо.
it happened to her. er::: okay.

→ Ilona: секундочку ((taps on Anton's arm))
just a second

5 jo saken är den . . . min mor hon är gammal, hon är 75 år
well the thing is that . . . my mother is old, she is 75 years

6 gammal. hon har varit med om en . . . aa::: krasch eller
old. she has had a . . . er::: crash or

7 katas-
catas-

Anton: она попала в автомобильную катастрофу.
she was in a car crash.

8 Ilona: det var en bil (.) olycka och (.) hon är gammal. ((laughs))
it was a car (.) accident and (.) she is old.

9 Anton: а:::
a:::nd

→ 10 Ilona: °забыла° ((smiles at Anton))
°forgot°

Comparing Anton's 'original' (7:1–4) with what follows in the interpreter's turns (7:4–7, 7:8, 7:10) I can note that the two dates mentioned by Anton were absent in the 'renditions'. From the point of
view of the police officer, these dates, the applicant's first arrival
in Sweden and the date his mother had his accident, were quite
irrelevant. In view of the predefined institutional goal of interaction,
the 'reduced' and 'multi-part rendition' thus accomplishes a concentration on the standard issue in question – reasons for leaving the
home country. In other words, a 'reduced rendition' may potentially

have a time-economizing effect. Given that we assume interpreters to be orientated towards 'close renditions', 'reducing' would be explained as a 'strategy' for getting more rapidly to a particular point which is requested by a primary interlocutor. In this case, however, the interpreter takes time for her own needs, rather than 'saving' time for the primary parties.

It goes without saying that the richer the vocabulary in both languages, the more likely interpreters will find the right word at the right time. Yet of course, cognitive constraints and cognitive resources also have a role to play. With intensive training interpreters can learn to memorize longer and longer sequences of talk. This is not the only capacity that needs to be trained though. Interpreters' preparation must also include reading of special literature on the subjects in question; on immigration legislation, other judicial matters, medicine, nutrition, etc. The better I understand a concept or a phrase and the point of it in the context at hand, the more likely it is that I will be able to memorize and repeat it. Sometimes memorizing depends on note-taking. Many active interpreters witness that dates and other figures are particularly hard to memorize without note-taking, one reason probably being that the exact figures mentioned often do not follow logically from the surrounding discoursal context.

The above excerpt shows an instance where the interpreter for a moment has lost track. The applicant has mentioned the age of his mother and two dates when Ilona interrupts him and urges him explicitly to leave her space: "just a second" (7:4). So he does, but Ilona subsequently leaves the floor after delivering a 'reduced', even fragmented 'rendition' (7:5–7). She seemingly has difficulty in finding an appropriate word in Swedish for "accident". The applicant must have realized that this is the kind of problem she has, since he reformulates himself, using another and more precise term in Russian for "car crash" (7:7). In an 'ordinary' conversation this would constitute an "other-initiated self-repair" (Schegloff, Jefferson and Sacks 1977). In interpreter-mediated talk it may imply the same, but also something else. When the 'repair' is done, the interpreter no longer remembers the dates just mentioned.

The interpreter's complex activity of speaking and listening at the same time demands a specific kind of concentration. Anton's utterance (in 7:7) to Ilona meant an additional strain on her already distracted attention. Most people will recognize the frustration of feeling a word on the tip of your tongue and not being able to pronounce it. A search for the word can absorb your full attention. As interpreter I can seldom afford to fasten on a single gloss, but if I occasionally do, I need to inform co-actors very distinctly, by means of words or gestures, that they have to wait.

Ilona's "just a moment" (7:4) is designed to stop the flow of talk. If her initiative is thus principally interactionally orientated, and secondarily textually orientated (it is, after all, to secure a correct translation, even if Ilona subsequently gives up without producing one), it is the other way around with her utterance that comes shortly afterwards in Russian: "°forgot°" (7:10). This utterance comments on her inability to translate and is primarily designed to inform the applicant (and possibly the researcher) about her troubles. It simultaneously functions as a way to give him back the turn at talk, which is thus the interpreter's means of counteracting a communication breakdown.

Regardless of training, interpreters sometimes need to ask for clarification, or for time to search for words. Being self-assured enough to mark such needs distinctively – without occupying too much communicative space – is a way to demonstrate professionality. Inexperienced interpreters sometimes hesitate to show these kinds of needs, being afraid of showing themselves as lacking competence and trustworthiness; of reminding people of the interpreter's human imperfectness, and of both their own dependence upon this imperfect person's assistance and their own lack of linguistic competence. Frequent pauses in the regular on-the-record exchange between the primary interlocutors can indeed cast doubt on the interpreter's proficiency. The reasons for the pauses also play a role. At times it will give credit to ask questions of clarification. It can strengthen an image of scrupulous, conscientious and careful professional. The more of the others' attention interpreters demand for their own needs, however, the greater the risk that the co-actors will lose patience. What is more, primary interlocutors are often more prepared to engage in talking to the interpreter, than to simply give the interpreter time to think.

4.2 On conventional means of communicative coordination

The following exchange occurs later in the interview at the police station. It is towards the end, and the officer asks about the applicant's possible connections with Germany. He refers to a letter he had just been reading, from the Swedish embassy in Moscow, which says that the applicant has plans to move to Germany. Was he correctly informed? The applicant starts to explain:

(8) (G21:17)

1 Anton: я ехал к матери, но у меня есть подданство
           I went to [my] mother, but I have a German

2   немецкое, во время войны я- мы были в
           citizenship/origin, during the war I- we were in

3   Германии, у меня есть подданство. понимаете?
           Germany, I have a citizenship/origin, understand?

     Ilona: men jag har tyskt medborgarskap, under
                            but I have German citizenship, during

4   kriget hade jag . . .
           the war I had . . .

5 Anton: a?
           what?

→ 6 Ilona: °продолжайте°
           °*carry on.*°
           (0.5)

7 Peter: m . . . ja. °det där blev jag inte klokare på.° det- det- det
           m . . . yes. °that did not make me any the wiser.° there- there- there

8   finns alltså en **uppgift** om att- att man **från** Sverige ska
           *is that is **information** about that- that you **from** Sweden will*

9   resa till Västtyskland för **bosättning** e:::h
           *go to West Germany for **settlement** [there] e:::r*

Excerpt 8 includes two interpreter's utterances. The first of these is, compared to the preceding 'original' (8:1–3), a 'reduced rendition' (8:3–4). It is designed to communicate that the applicant has not yet finished; that the 'original' has stopped in mid-sentence, that the applicant is in the process of completing his line of thought. Ilona signals this in her corresponding utterance by prosodic and linguistic means.

The interpreter apparently does not really make sense of what the applicant says. Ordinarily, an interlocutor can avoid showing lack of knowledge and understanding by staying silent. Interpreters cannot. As a matter of fact, it is not clear at all that the applicant himself knows what he is talking about.

The background here is the following: Traditionally, there are two main principles for how individuals obtain their citizenship at birth. One is the principle of descent (*lat. jus sanguinis*), which means that people's civil rights are connected to the group of people they come from. The other is the territorial principle (*lat. jus soli*), which implies that people's civil rights derive from the place in which they were born. In principle, *poddanstvo,* the concept used by the applicant, matches the first, that is the principle of descent (which is the one adopted in Germany). Within the Soviet Union, both principles existed. People had a Soviet citizenship based on their country of birth, the USSR (normally expressed as *grazhdanstvo*). Additionally, in official documents (such as the internal passport mentioned in the first example in this chapter, cf. Excerpt 2), an individual was also identified as the descendant of a certain ethnic group. The latter could be expressed as *poddanstvo.* In reality, the concept sometimes was (is) used also to signify citizenship when based on place of birth. In Sweden, where the territorial principle is applied, it makes no sense in legal terms to distinguish between *poddanstvo* and *grazhdanstvo.*

Apparently it does not occur to Ilona that this distinction is actualized in Anton's utterance (8:1–3). Moreover, when comparing Anton's (8:1–3) and Ilona's (8:3–4) utterances, we may note that the tag-question "understand?" (in 8:3), inserted by the applicant, belongs to the 'reduced' parts of the 'original'. Reducing it from focused discourse is a way to avoid making explicit the issue of lacking understanding, which naturally is a sensitive one for interpreters. Besides, it might have been that Ilona heard it as a question directed to her, rather than to the police officer. Reducing it additionally functions to avoid letting it show that she was made a direct addressee.

In a monolingual conversation, an utterance like the one in 8:3–4 would normally serve as an attempt to elicit more information, or perhaps a 'repair' (Schegloff, Jefferson and Sacks 1977) from the prior speaker. In this talk it functions in the same way in one direction, as it were. The police officer understands the words in Swedish and also understands that their nature is such that they constitute a partially completed utterance. Hence, he leaves the floor open. But the effect it would conventionally have on the prior speaker here fails to come off. Anton apparently does not accept being appointed to provide something like a 'repair' (8:5). From what comes next – Ilona's explicit "°carry on°" in Russian (8:6) – we understand that this is what she wants him to do. Instead, after 0.5 seconds of silence – which is quite a long period in conversation – the police officer comes in, muttering as if to himself: "m . . . yes. °that did not make me any the wiser.°" (8:7) before he starts anew, requesting information. In Ilona's subsequent 'rendition' this comment is 'reduced'.

Apart from being ironic, the officer's silent introduction (8:7) also topicalizes his lack of understanding. In various ways it involves threats to the participants' faces. The personal style of this interpreter means at times downplaying face-threatening talk and putting blame on herself rather than risking conflict or hostile talk between the primary interlocutors or between them and herself. As a result, the more potential conflict there is in interaction, the more she gets involved in activities designed to 'protect' relations. This 'strategy' is not unusual among interpreters. A simple example which could be seen as deriving from this wish to soften the tone in interaction is found in practically all Russian–Swedish encounters documented, namely the 'substitution' of pronouns of address. Where the standard polite form of address in Russian is second person plural (the *vous* form in French), the corresponding form in Swedish is second person singular (the *tu* form in French). In translations the one is routinely swapped for the other.

An interpreter can sometimes see that the primary interlocutors have different norms or attitudes, and suspect that shared and mutual knowledge about these differences could cause disturbance in interaction. Not letting information about this surface is then a way to avoid provocation, and, in consequence, to simplify the interpreter's own control over ongoing talk. In my experience, the more trained and secure I am as interpreter, the more I will be able to let the primary parties be confronted with and take care of possible conflicts. In 'protecting' interaction from potential 'disturbance', you also prevent people from expressing their frustration, irritation and anger, and you 'protect' their counterparts from learning about what others expect and take for granted. *Face work* (Goffman 1967) in interpreter-mediated interaction will be dealt with in more detail in Chapter 7 below.

4.3 Explicit coordination and summarizing translating

Evidently, the interpreter in Excerpt 8 above lets institutional routines influence her work. In the following example the established routines become quite decisive for the acting interpreter, who here is another person, Irma. In a post interview she spontaneously mentions the Interpreters' Code of Ethics, to which she declares loyalty, even though she is not herself certified. Whatever her principal attitude and normal style of working is, however, in this encounter her efforts are first and foremost directed towards asserting the fulfilment of the institutionally defined routine – serving the suspect with the charges held against him and informing him about how his case is going to be further handled by the Swedish judicial system. The producing of 'close renditions' of everything said by the primary interlocutor is in practice subordinated to these goals.

Irma, the interpreter, is physically not present in the room, but works via an amplified telephone. This explains some of her working style. Present at the police station are the Swedish police officer, Petra, and Stephan, the Russian-speaking suspect. The main interrogation, which was conducted by the same police officer with the assistance of the same interpreter, took place earlier that day. The encounter from which the excerpts are drawn takes all in all about five minutes. It is arranged specifically to notify the detained person about the prosecutor's decisions concerning charges held against him, and about his entitlement to legal counselling.

The interaction is from the beginning established as if separated into two exchanges – one between the officer and Irma and one between her and the suspect. The transcription starts where the tape-recorder was switched on, in the middle of the police officer's introducing utterance.

(9) (P11:1)

1	Petra:	att e::: ja försökte förklara då att han ville erkänna
		that e::: I tried to explain then that he wanted to confess
2		bara försök till stöld. men som sagt det hade ju varit
		only attempted theft. but as [I] said it would have been
3		fullbordat då. om inte larmbågarna hade ljudit.
		fulfilled then. if the alarm hadn't gone off.
4	Irma:	mhm,
		mhm,
→ 5	Petra:	om du förklarar det för honom.
		if you explain that to him.
6	Irma:	ja just det. (.) e:: значит так. вы слышите меня
		yes right. (.) e:: so well. do you hear me
7	Stephan:	да::
		yeah::
	Irma:	скажите, это опять переводчица.
		tell me, this is again the interpreter.
8	Stephan:	хорошо. слушаю.
		okay. I hear.
9	Irma:	мм. инспектор позвонила прокурору и:::
		mm. the inspector phoned the prosecutor a:::nd

10		прокурор решил что вы задержанный. е:::
		the prosecutor decided that you must be taken into custody. e:::
11		посколько есть опасность что вы будете
		since there is a risk that you will
12		укрываться. (.) е::: инспектор постаралась
		hide away. (.) e::: the inspector tried to
13	Stephan:	и:::
		a:::nd
	Irma:	обьяснить что у вас была только попытка к
		explain that you had only attempted
14		воровству и прочее. но (xxx)
		theft and so forth. but (xxx)
	Stephan:	простите, а:: укрыва-
		excuse me er:: hide aw-
15		укрываться в каком смысле?
		hide away in what sense?
16	Irma:	мм (.) но вы в данном случае вы не на свободе.
		mm (.) well at present you are not free.
17		вы задержанный.
		you have been taken into custody.
18	Stephan:	а::: нет. я укрываться не буду. тем более у меня
		er::: no. I don't intend to hide away. all the more since I have
19		семья и::: ребёнок. я не думаю что::: ну ясно.
		a family a:::nd a child. I don't think that ::: well clear.
	Irma:	да ну:::
		yes but:::
20	Stephan:	ответ есть ответ.
		an answer is an answer.
21	Irma:	okej han (.) har det klart för sig.
		okay he (.) has got it clear.

In terms of 'texts', this excerpt – as well as the whole encounter which it is taken from – contains several instances of 'zero rendition', 'summarized rendition' and 'non-rendition'. The police officer asks Irma to "explain" (9:5) to the suspect, and rather than producing 'close renditions', explaining is the task she appears to take on. This implies, on the one hand, that she expands upon the police officer's 'original' utterance. She repeatedly provides details that are normally included in the standard information for those taken into custody. On the other hand, it implies that she answers to initiatives from the suspect directly. He was caught redhanded just outside a shop and when this happened he gave back the goods he had stolen. In his opinion he should therefore be accused only of attempted theft, but "theft" is the charge declared by the prosecutor. This is what the police officer has told the interpreter on the phone, and now counts on her assistance to explain to the suspect. So she leaves it to the interpreter to introduce both herself and this information.

As we note, while explaining to the suspect, Irma does not take in all of what he says as 'originals' to be translated for the officer. Instead she gets back to Petra only with a confirmation that what had to be done has been done: "okay he (.) has got it clear" (9:21). And yet, she never did come to the explanation of why the charge was set as "theft" (because he had been outside the shop and the alarm had gone off) (9:1–3). This information is lost when the suspect raises another issue, latching on to the interpreter's expression *ukryvat'sja* ("hide away") (9:12). The ensuing discussion actually concerns not the charges, but the prosecutor's other decision – that the suspect must be kept in custody. This is the topic which Stephan closes with "well clear. an answer is an answer" (9:19, 9:20). The definition of the charge, as becomes evident later, remains unclear from his point of view.

The police officer goes on to ask a couple of routine questions. After a while comes the one concerning legal counselling during court proceedings. These will take place on the next day, for the issue of a warrant of arrest:

(10) (P11:3)
51   Petra: e re nån speciell advokat han vill ha i morron?
is there a lawyer in particular that he wants to have tomorrow?

52   eller ha- nöjer han me sig
or he- agrees does he to

Irma: скажите пожалуйста ((hawks)) у вас
tell [me/us] please   you have

53   есть право на адвоката у вас какой-нибудь
the right to a lawyer do you have a lawyer of

54   свой адвокат знакомый или имя какое-то
your own acquaintance or someone whose name

55   которое вы хотели бы, предьявить, или же вы
you would like to mention, or do you just

56   согласны на адвоката которого вам просто
agree to the lawyer that they simply

57   дадут.
will give you.

→ 58   Stephan: я отвечаю по-философски. мать мой адвокат.
I answer in a philosophical way. my mother is my lawyer.

59	Irma:	я понимаю. но мать в данный момент не может
		I understand. but your mother at the moment can not
60		вас защитить. так что вы согласны на
		defend you. so do you agree to
61		адвоката которого вам дадут?
		the lawyer they give you?
62	Stephan:	вы знаете, я. считаю что я. (0.1) я считаю что я прав.
		you know, in my opinion I. in my opinion I am right.
		(.)
63	Irma:	скажите. вы согласны на адвоката или есть у
		tell [me/us]. do you agree to the lawyer or do you have
64		вас своё. имя.
		one of your own. a name.
65	Stephan:	нет нет.
		no no.
66	Irma:	согласны?
		you agree?
67	Stephan:	согласен на любого конечно.
		I agree to anyone of course.
→ 68	Irma:	han var lite filosofisk och sa att hans mor är advokat.
		he was a little philosophical and said that his mother is a lawyer.
69		och eh då sa jag att tyvärr kan hon inte vara din biträde.
		and er then I said that unfortunately she can not be your
		defence counsel.
70		ditt biträde och då upprepade frågan och då sa han att
		your defending counsel and then repeated the question and
		then he said
71		han går med på den biträden som (.) han får.
		that he agrees to the defence counsel that (.) he gets.

The suspect, before going to court, is supposed to get the chance to express any preferences regarding legal defence and counselling. The officer's brief mentioning of this issue (10:51) triggers an 'expanded', explaining 'rendition' from the interpreter (10:52–57). After years of work with the police, Irma knows the routine, and she knows how Petra usually does it. In a post interview, the officer mentions that she finds it more natural to talk directly to the interpreter than addressing the suspect. In this particular encounter this is evident. She not only counts the interpreter as her co-interlocutor, but throughout the encounter she trusts Irma to explain for the suspect (whenever Irma finds it necessary), seeing to it that he gets to know what he can expect and what is expected from him. And indeed, Irma's utterances (in 10:52–57, 59–61, 63–64 and 66) are designed so as to mediate what the suspect must know in order to answer in accordance with institutional needs. More precisely, before Stephan's answer is translated back to the officer, he has learned that he should answer only what he is asked about – i.e. either confirm or not confirm – and avoid developing any topics of his own.

Irma's 'summarized rendition' (10:68–71) recapitulates her and the suspect's exchange. Looking more closely, one may observe that the suspect's first answer, mentioning his mother (10:58), is relayed together with the interpreter's own counter argument, but what he says about being right (10:62) is 'reduced' altogether in the 'rendition', as it is ignored in the exchange. In other words, what fits the institutional need for confirmation is translated while the issue where the parties diverge in opinions (what charge should be made against him – theft or attempted theft) is kept off-the-record.

In other words, the 'summarized rendition' (10:68–71) potentially bridges the gap between the interlocutors' different points of view, but one-sidedly on the conditions predefined by the institution. This is accomplished partly by Irma's conceiving of the suspect's utterances as being in the process of developing into an 'original', and that she sees it as her task to monitor the development of this 'original'. As a result, she keeps off-the-record not only doubts about shared understanding, but also signs indicating divergent understandings. Irma works on satisfying as soon as possible the police officer's need for the suspect's "yes" or "no" by making the suspect see what kind of answer the institution counts as appropriate. She firmly directs the layman to take the professional's perspective and sees to it that it is kept in mind until the completion of what from the institution's point of view must be done. In this sense her interpreting is interactionally orientated, and very much so. At the same time, from the point of view of the suspect, her interpreting of his utterances is on the contrary text orientated. A qualified guess would be that he is speaking metaphorically about his mother as his defender (10:58), but Irma relays his statement as if his mother in actual fact was a lawyer, and it had been a serious suggestion (10:68).

When I have presented this material to groups of students and asked what they think is happening, some argue that the interpreter apparently acts as the police officer's helping hand, and others that she helps the suspect understand the foreign routines. I can agree with both of these descriptions. The police officer does not have to get involved in a discussion on something upon which she no longer has an influence, namely the prosecutor's phrasing of the charge. Simultaneously, however, she is prevented from learning what is clear and what is not clear to the suspect. The suspect in turn is 'saved' from arguing something in vain. In principle, when he talks without being translated he is also 'saved' from officially having said things that could be held against him. Only what is voiced by the interpreter may end up in the record as his words.

My additional comment is that Irma's style of interpreting restricts the opportunities for *both* the suspect and the police officer to accomplish something the *interpreter* does not foresee. Moreover, responsibility that normally lies with the police officer and the suspect is here transferred to the woman in the middle.

It must be underlined that the 'texts' interpreters produce, as we have seen in many examples already, are highly dependent on the primary interlocutors' style of interacting. This in turn results not least from the professionals' manner of performing their job, conducting the institutional encounter. It should be plain to see that the style of using an interpreter (and acting as interpreter) which is exemplified here, if it were to be broadly applied in, for instance, police interrogations, would be a real threat to the legal rights of suspects, besides jeopardising the professional honour of the police. Also in medical settings – for instance when the doctor is taking the anamnesis and needs maximal information about the patient – putting a non-medical expert in charge of the encounter seems like taking a great risk.

In the sequence following immediately upon Irma's 'summarized rendition' above (10:68–71), there is another example of the interpreter's firm and momentarily one-sided concentration on textual aspects, this time when translating for the officer.

(11) (P11:3)
72 Petra: mhm. och rysk tolk då.
               mhm. and Russian interpreter then.
→ 73 Irma: и русская переводчица или русский переводчик.
               and Russian (female) interpreter or Russian (male) interpreter.
               (0.2)
74 Irma: hallå
               hello
75 Petra: ja
               yes

76	Irma:	вы слышали меня?
		did you hear me?
77	Stephan:	да.
		yes.
78	Irma:	вы получите переводчика тоже.
		you will get an interpreter as well.
79	Stephan:	хорошо.
		okay.
80	Irma:	okej. han vill ha tolk.
		okay. he wants to have an interpreter.

Telephone interpreting on the whole implies certain specific conditions that are not present in face-to-face interpreting. An important one is that Irma has no immediate access to participants' gaze and body movements, hence she cannot follow how people interact nonverbally. Her 'divergent' utterances: "hello" (11:74) and "did you hear me?" (11:76) clearly bear witness to this. Another difference is that she has no access to the documents and other artefacts that the interacting parties handle. The interpreter and her co-actors are highly dependent on the acoustic quality of the telephone equipment.

When it is clear that the suspect does not have any specific wishes regarding counsel in court, the police officer mentions the issue of interpreting: "mhm. and Russian interpreter then." (11:72). It seems most plausible that this is intended as a request for a similar kind of confirmation. She might take it as self evident that the suspect wants a Russian interpreter, and mention it as a formality, whilst making a note for the secretary about ordering one for tomorrow. The utterance is prosodically more like a statement of fact than a question.

However, if it is intended as a question about whether or not the suspect wishes to have a Russian interpreter in court, a grammatically, and functionally 'closer' 'rendition' (in 11:73) would have included the same words "Russian interpreter" but provided for the feminine form in the accusative (*russkuju perevodchitsu*) and for the masculine in the genitive (*russkogo perevodchika*) (since these cases conventionally follow verbs like "wish" and "want"). The present nominative case endings are conventionally followed by a nominative clause. When the nouns here are left alone, with no predicate to follow, the utterance does not, it seems, make sense to the suspect as a request in his address. Decontextualizing the officer's elliptic utterance, Irma seems to have lost track of the activities just being performed and prepared for in the interaction as a whole. In other words, Irma bridges a linguistic gap, between Swedish and Russian, providing a principally 'close rendition', but simultaneously misses an important contextual link, and, as a result, the message first misses the target. Only when Irma interprets the officer's "mhm. and Russian interpreter then" (11:72) a second time, this time as a statement of fact: "you will get an interpreter as well." (11:78) does the suspect react to it. His short "okay" (11:79) is subsequently interpreted as an answer to an offer to choose: "okay. he wants to have an interpreter." (11:80).

The officer finds no reason to clarify this reply, and yet there might have been one. Since the suspect comes not from Russia, but from another part of the USSR, the officer might indeed have seen the need to find out not just whether he wants an interpreter or not, but if he agrees to have a Russian interpreter or wishes to claim one who speaks his native language. In that case, it would have been more relevant to give an alternative to "Russian" instead of the different gender forms of the noun "interpreter" (*russkaja perevodchitsa, russkij perevodchik*) (11:73), but this never becomes an issue. After an instance of minor confusion, the interaction again runs in accordance with the established routines.

4.4 Explicit coordination and the bridging of perspectives

I will now look at some other occasions involving 'explicit coordinating' and compare the functions of the interpreter's own initiatives with those discussed above. If Irma's 'strategy' was to bridge perspectives mainly on the conditions given by the institution, other examples show how coordinating moves may function to create sharedness on more equal terms between the perspectives of the primary parties two-sidedly.

The examples that follow are from a healthcare clinic, documented in an hour-long encounter in which a practitioner meets a Russian-speaking family who are newly arrived in Sweden as refugees. They have come to the clinic on a second call, to meet the doctor who is supposed to do a general check-up and tell them the results of tests taken last time. People present are Dan, the doctor, a young couple, Vera and Maxim and their five-year-old daughter. The interpreter on duty is Ivana.

We come in when the doctor asks Vera about the treatment she has had for her asthma.

(12) (G32:6)

1   Dan: e::: är det något som har opererats? eller.
             er::: is this something that has been operated on? or.

2   Ivana: вы::: вам дел- проводили? операцию про этому.
             you::: were you ma- operated? on for this.

3   Vera: нет операции не было, катетеризацию
             no there was no operation. they did a

4   проводили.
             catheterization.

→ 5 Ivana: катетеризация?
             catheterization?

6   Maxim: да.
             yes.

7   Ivana: a näe ingen operation men dom förde in en- en kateter.
             yeah no no operation but they inserted a- a catheter.

The interpreter's initiative "catheterization?" (12:5), is a request for clarification, partly in her own interests, so as to check her perception and guarantee a correct translation, which of course ultimately is in the interests of the primary parties. Ivana's request is accomplished by the repetition of a single gloss from the immediately preceding 'original' (12:3–4). It is possible that Ivana also wishes to elicit some further explanation of what this special medical term stands for. Simultaneously, asking back functions so as to gain some time (in this case, very little time, however). The preceding speaker's co-present husband quickly replies "yes", without further explanation, confirming, as it were, the term to be the correct one, or confirming the fact that catheterization indeed took place. Ivana then provides a lexically 'close rendition' of the woman's 'original' utterance, re-using a related medical term "catheter" (12:7).

When addressing a medical practitioner the interpreter's need to reassure herself that she understands the professional language would seem less acute than when she is addressing lay people. Moreover, since the professional party by definition is in charge of an institutional encounter, this person will be expected to ask if he or she does not understand a visitor, even if this, in practice, does not always happen. In the talk from which the preceding excerpts (9, 10 and 11) were drawn, the police officer requires from the suspect only information which she can predict and understand, and hands over to the interpreter (Irma) the responsibility to see to it that the suspect provides this information. Irma is put in charge of the encounter much more than Ivana is in the context of the present encounter.

At a later instance Ivana monitors the exchange more actively. Just like Irma (in Excerpt 10) she repeats a question from the doctor, but the function of Ivana's repetition becomes quite different. Continuing to check up on Vera's asthma, the doctor asks for the year when she became ill:

(13) (G32:7)

1   Dan: mm ((reads)) har du haft astma sen e . . . e . . . sjuttinio?
             mm   have you had asthma since er . . . er . . . seventy-nine?

2 ⌈ Ivana: у вас астма возникла ((knock on door)) в семьдесят-
             your asthma started   in seventy-
  ⌊ Dan: kom in
                                          come in

3   Ivana: девятом году?
             nine?

4   Vera: да.
             yes.

5   Nina: ((nurse enters)) skulle bara behöva lite journaler för efter-
                           just need a few [patient's] notes for the

6 ⌈   middan, det kommer nämligen ingen tolk ((walks out))
             afternoon, the thing is that there won't be an interpreter
→ ⌊ Ivana: (xxx переводчика xxx) в семьдесят девятом да?
             (xxx interpreter xxx)   in seventy-nine, yes?

7   Vera: да
             yes

8   Ivana: ja det var sjuttionio.
             yes it was in seventy-nine.

Excerpt 13 illustrates a case where the bilingual exchange and the 'normal format' is challenged by a new contextual circumstance. The medical consultation is suddenly interrupted when a nurse enters the room and starts talking to the doctor. As can be seen in the transcription, the interpreter in parallel silently (the words are hard to distinguish on the tape) translates for the family. In other words, she treats what the nurse says as 'original', too.

While the nurse is leaving, the interpreter repeats a brief version (13:6) of the practitioner's question (13:1). She had just translated it (13:2–3), and the patient had already confirmed once (13:4) that the year when she got ill was correctly understood. This is exactly when the nurse enters, however, and the conversation is interrupted. Hence, repeating the doctor's question is a way for Ivana to make the patient repeat an answer that has not yet been translated.

Analysing the interactional functions of Ivana's initiative, we may note the following. Promoting a repetition, the interpreter makes sure that the doctor realizes that it is the patient (and not the interpreter) who confirms the year as correct. Moreover, it shows for the interlocutors that Ivana is keeping track of what had been said so far, and demonstrates, as it were, that she works on translating everything said, for all participants to hear. Of course, the second translation of the practitioner's question about what year the asthma started, simultaneously becomes an efficient way to lead the exchange back to where it had been at the time of the interruption. Ivana's new translation (in 13:8) of the patient's confirmation of the year seventy-nine, prompts the practitioner to go back to where he left off. In this way she re-establishes the medical encounter, at the same time as the 'normal format' of interpreter-mediated interaction is reset, both without the interpreter or anyone else being explicit about this.

A moment later, Ivana initiates a dialogue with the professional party and subsequently provides a 'summarized rendition' for the family. The doctor has finished with the mother's case and just started to read the test-results for the little girl. Among other things he states:

(14) (G32:12–13)
```
   1  Dan:    e . . . vad man såg i avföringsprovet var förekomst av
                giardia.
                er . . . what you saw in the stool-test was the presence of giardia.
→  2  Ivana:  säg det på svenska.
                say it in Swedish.
   3  Dan:    a det heter giardia.
                oh it's called giardia.
   4  Ivana:  är det mask?
                is it worms?
   5  Dan:    nej, det är en e . . . ingen mask, men det är en protozo.
                no, it is a er . . . not a worm, but it is a protozoön.
   6  Ivana:  mhm, aha. e . . .
                mhm, aha. e . . .
   7  Dan:    tarminfektion.
                intestinal infection.
→  8  Ivana:  мм. в анализе кала у неё нашли гиардия. я у
                mhm. in her stool-test they found giardia. I
   9          врача спрашивала что это такое, думала что это
                asked the doctor what it is, I thought it was
  10          глисты, но это не глисты это какой-то тип
                worms, but it is not worms it's a kind
  11          простейших.
                of protozoön.
```

Whereas in the earlier example with Irma (Excerpt 10) the exchange which became 'reduced' in a 'summarized' 'rendition', was a request from a primary party (the suspect), here the information that is 'reduced' answers to a request from the interpreter, but it answered in a way which did not fit the current needs of the interpreter.

Comparing the interpreter's 'summarized rendition' arrowed above (14:8–11) with what is said in the preceding seven turns, we find that the content of one exchange of turns (14:2 and 14:3) is 'substituted', and the content of another one (14:6 and 14:7) is 'reduced'. Ivana's initiative to secure a correct translation "say it in Swedish." (14:2), comes back as "I asked the doctor what it is" (14:9). In other words, she explains that the doctor's use of a specific medical term, which she had only a vague idea about, had made her check back. Mentioning how she prepares for the translation Ivana explicitly recalls her translating task.

The latter exchange (14:6 and 14:7), in contrast, has no correspondence in the 'summarized' 'rendition'. The interpreter's part of it (14:6) contains little or no substance, which may explain why it is 'reduced', but what about the doctor's "intestinal infection" (14:7)? To the doctor it may seem as if the problem concerns not only translating between languages, but also between the language of the lay person and that of the professional. He at one point adds this elliptic mentioning of what can be caused by the kind of single-celled organism in question, namely "intestinal infection" (14:7). However, Ivana, in the 'rendition', only uses information concerning "her" translation problem.

5. TRANSLATING AND COORDINATING – TWO ACTIVITIES IN ONE

This chapter has tried to demonstrate that interpreting in face-to-face interaction is constituted by two intimately interdependent activities – translation and coordination. My starting point was to look at interpreter-mediated talk as 'text'. As we have seen, the types of 'texts' distinguishable in transcriptions of spontaneous spoken interaction are not comparable to texts ordinarily created in the written mode. After establishing two types of 'texts' – 'originals' and 'interpreter utterances' – I have compared these as one would 'source texts' and 'target texts'. The contrastive analyses have shown that interpreter-mediated interaction is driven forward in equal proportion by interpreters' translating (production of 'texts') and coordinating of others' talk, and by the balancing between these two aspects. Co-ordinating talk implies coordinating the activities performed in and by talk, including the joint spoken interaction in itself. Interpreters are alternately orientated towards emphasizing the translating aspect (text orientation) and the coordination aspect (interactional orientation).

5.1 The work of 'divergent renditions'

Looking at interpreters' utterances from the point of view of translating, I noted the following functions achieved in interaction:

- 'Renditions' may be 'expanded' or 'substituted' to specify, for instance, the interactional significance of what was said in the 'original', and also persons, times, objects and places indicated by words like "it", "then" and "there".
- 'Renditions' may be 'expanded' to prevent primary inter-locutors' producing new 'originals' while the interpreter needs to concentrate on the search for a word, or needs to calm down the speed of an intensive exchange.
- 'Renditions' may be 'expanded' to name, and thereby specify, a primary interlocutor's dominant communicative activity, as for instance in Excerpt 4 where the 'rendition' was 'expanded' with "I don't want to agree with you" (4:6).
- 'Renditions' may be 'divergent' to specify a certain addressee (for example, "him" may be 'substituted' by "you" and words of explicit address to the interpreter may be omitted).
- In some cases, 'renditions' may also be 'expanded' and 'sub-stituted' to avoid specification of what is talked about, making them more vague than the 'original' utterances (for instance, when this refers to expressions or phenomena that have no direct correspondence in the 'target-culture').
- A 'substituted' 'rendition' could match recipients' expectations of, for example, kind treatment in the case when a speaker appears (deliberately or non-deliberately) impolite.
- 'Renditions' are 'expanded', 'reduced' and/or 'substituted' to mitigate potential threats to mutual confidence. This includes the interlocutors' confidence in each other's good will to under-stand what the respective other wants to say, at least their reliance on each other's interest in taking active part in com-mon interaction.
- As participants in spoken interaction, we tend to perceive some parts of utterances as redundant, while others catch attention. Even if trained interpreters are particularly used to

attentive listening, 'divergent renditions' give evidence of a certain normal selectivity in listening. Typical features of spoken interaction, when found in 'originals' (such as interrupted onsets, elliptic style and repetitive paraphrases within the same utterance), tend to be followed by either 'reduced', 'expanded' or 'substituted renditions', which then become comparatively less fragmented and more written-language-like in style.

- At times 'renditions' may also appear *more* fragmented in style than the corresponding 'originals', or fragmented in a different way, as a result of the interpreter searching (aloud) for a word or a formulation.
- At times I found 'substituted renditions' as a result of interpreters' mediation between, for instance, more formal and less formal styles, or between everyday lay language and professional jargon.
- 'Renditions' may be 'reduced' to concentrate and direct the potential illocutionary force of an 'original' utterance. For instance, when 'originals' start with feedback tokens, rhetorical comments or other short statements that are followed by a stronger initiative, a question or a somewhat opposing (second thoughts) argument, these first parts of the 'originals' are often dropped.
- 'Renditions' are also 'reduced' to minimize the time and space taken by the interpreter's turn, principally to minimize the potential disturbance of the non-standard communicator.
- When primary interlocutors mutually acknowledge competence in the other's language, the interpreter may occasionally experience a reduced relevance in providing 'renditions'. Interpreters sometimes avoid translating at times when the transparency of talk seems obvious, to soothe primary parties' presumed irritation. Sometimes interpreters profit from such occasions to strengthen their identity as 'close-text-producers'.
- 'Renditions' can be 'reduced' to withhold information, for instance about lack of shared understanding, knowledge and confidence, about divergent attitudes and norms, about the other's efforts to take the interpreter as an ally instead of treating her or him as impartial and so forth.
- The most important thing accomplished by 'summarized renditions' and 'zero renditions' is probably an economy of time, for the benefit of what at least one of the co-actors sees as the purpose of the encounter. A time-economizing tendency is

particularly evident when lengthy and inconsistent 'original' utterances are compared with their subsequent short and consistent 'reduced' and 'summarized renditions'. Yet time is sometimes gained at the cost of individuals' anticipated goals being omitted from the agenda. In other words, economizing time at one end may be at the cost of time at the other. And conversely, letting something or someone take time may pay off by saving time for something or someone else.

5.2 The coordinating work of 'interpreters' utterances'

Looking at interpreter-mediated discourse from the point of view of coordination, I saw that exchanges pursue a variety of goals and subgoals other than the production of more or less equivalent 'texts'. As a rule, 'interpreter utterances' function to promote a certain verbal exchange. They can additionally be geared primarily towards generating common focus and mutual attention between the primary interlocutors. They can alternatively be designed to accomplish first and foremost one or other party's performance of a specific activity, for instance to comply or to agree (cf. Excerpt 10).

The coordinating aspect of the role of interpreter derives from the interpreters' unique middle-position. Interpreters are establishing, promoting and controlling connections between primary parties in conversation. These are normally deaf and blind, as it were, to parts of the interaction in which they participate, whereas interpreters have unique, immediate access to almost everything available to ears and eyes.

Primary interlocutors will partly rely on the interpreter to mediate turn-organizational cues signalled in and by talk. Understanding your co-interlocutors only through the interpreter's talk, you will have restricted opportunities to catch signs of their eagerness to talk, to finish talking, to change topic, and so on. And the same would apply to understanding the emotional character of co-interlocutors' talk. Embarrassment, sadness, sincerity and seriousness are feelings you understand not only from the words people use but, perhaps even more, from *how* they use them; from what is expressed with the voice, the face and by body language. A primary party's need for the interpreter's assistance in understanding these kinds of cues may vary. The interpreter is dependent on the interlocutors' interest in each other's emotions.

Conditions under which the coordination aspect tends to dominate before the translating aspect include the following:

- When a correct 'rendition' is jeopardized for perceptual reasons, or because of flaws in the interpreter's productive competence.
- When primary interlocutors' opposing perspectives are suspected or obvious to the interpreter.
- When a primary party displays that what the other said is understood without the interpreter's assistance, and this is transparent in interaction (an occasion that may be used to demonstrate the image of 'close-text-producer').
- When interpreters are 'caught' by the illocutionary force of a primary interlocutor's initiative (e.g. they answer directly to a question or respond directly to an appeal for support).
- When there are parallel discourses, interpreters may feel forced either to focus upon and relay only one of them, thus ignoring the other, or to implicitly or explicitly urge the interlocutors to be more co-ordinated, for instance by prompting someone to repeat an utterance.
- When there is a shift in the frame of common activity, for instance when the professional party goes from interviewing to attending to other matters, from interrogating to checking a written document, or, in a medical context, from interviewing to performing physical examination.

5.3 The speaking side of interpreting

Classifying transcribed utterances as 'close' or 'divergent renditions', I saw that 'closeness' can be understood in a variety of ways. It could also be seen that there is no straight and simple connection between 'close' renditions and mutual understanding, or 'divergent renditions' and lack of shared understanding between the primary parties, a theme which will be further developed in Chapter 8 below.

Given that we think of 'renditions' in terms of 'close' to and 'divergent' from the 'original', it can be seen that the same 'rendition' can be lexically 'close' and functionally 'divergent' or the other way around. And any evaluation of the actual pragmatic functions of utterances must partly be connected to the evaluation of communicative accomplishments.

Realization in practice of 'close' and 'divergent renditions', regardless of how we classify them, is a relational matter. It will depend on the interpreters *and* their co-actors *and* the contextual circumstances.

It goes without saying that how interpreters cope with their job is dependent on their command of the working languages, their knowledge about subject matters, their cognitive competence, their form on the day, their experience and training: but it also depends on their co-actors' interactive styles, expectations and goals. When individuals entertain similar expectations as regards, for instance, what should be accomplished in and by the encounter they are involved in, or what count as relevant facts and appropriate behaviour, the interpreter's task is relatively easy compared to the case where the primary parties' understandings of the situation and each other's obligations and options differ, let alone clash. In a similar way, it makes a difference whether the primary interlocutors' respective views of the interpreter's role coincide or differ: for instance, if one or both interlocutors see the interpreter as linked to their counterpart, if one or both see her or him as their own ally, or if people involved in interaction regard the interpreter as someone associated with neither side.

It is evident that interpreter-mediated interaction is also structured in part by the kind of situation in which it takes place. In the following chapters, examples will show differences in the organization of talk which partly can be explained by the impact of institutional schemata and by the primary parties' goals and expectations connected to these. Moreover, individual interpreters develop their personal styles, more or less utilizing the image of 'text-producer'.

The present analyses have shown that interpreters' impact on the substance and the progression of conversation can be accomplished equally by 'implicit coordination' and 'explicit coordination'. What makes a significant difference is the interpreter's ability to balance 'text orientation' and 'interactional orientation'. To my mind, the potential for developing as an interpreter very much lies in the development of simultaneous attentiveness. This can also be expressed as training one's ability to focus at the same time on a pragmatic level (talk as activity, including the coordination-of-multi-party-interaction-activity), on a linguistic level (talk as text) and on the balance between these two aspects, constantly present in interpreter-mediated interaction. As interpreter I must be sensitive to details, but not fasten on them to the extent that I lose track of the diversity of functions for which any utterance may be interactionally primed.

The present chapter has basically paid attention to the speaking aspect of interpreting. The listening aspect is often neglected in the literature. Yet one's speaking in interaction is conditioned by others' listening, and vice versa. In Chapter 7, I will focus equally on the speaking and the listening part of the interpreter's task and explore interpreter-mediated talk as social interaction. Accordingly, I will investigate how people relate to one another as co-interlocutors through the way they display aspects of self as speakers and as listeners.

Finally, it must be firmly underlined that regarding interpreters as 'text-producers' can lead to a tendency to see their talk (and at times even the primary parties' talk) as the result of conscious 'strategies' in a goal-orientated activity where the goal is simply the production of text. Exploring authentic data, the text-production metaphor has proved useful. It has also been demonstrated, however, that it is far from sufficient when it comes to describing and understanding the nature of interpreter-mediated interaction.

NOTE

1. 'Dialogue interpreter' should here be understood as a technical term, foregrounding the situation of current interest, the situated encounter.

SEVEN

In a communicative pas de trois

> The productive study of dialogue presupposes, however, a more profound investigation of the forms used in reported speech, since these forms reflect basic and constant tendencies in the *active reception of other speakers' speech*, and it is this reception, after all, that is fundamental also for dialogue (Voloshinov 1986:117, cf. Russian original from 1930, footnote 4, Chapter 2).

There is reason to believe that interlocutors in interpreter-mediated conversations systematically differ in their active reception of others' speech, since one of them – the interpreter – has a unique mandate precisely when it comes to listening and speaking. In order to sort out different modes of speaking and hearing and explore the turn-by-turn organization of interpreter-mediated encounters, the present chapter will apply the analytical model of *participation framework* (Goffman 1981) outlined above (Chapter 5).

In four examples I will explore institutional interpreter-mediated encounters as *situated systems of activity* (Goffman 1961), and investigate in detail the interdependence between primary interlocutors' talk and interpreters' role performance. The excerpts are drawn from instances where the coordinating function of the interpreter should stand out particularly clearly to the reader. These instances, it seems, appear not by chance but in combination with certain activities (verbal and other) performed by the primary parties, and in certain constellations of people.

1. EXPLORING INTERPRETER-MEDIATED INTERACTION ORDER

To engage in spoken interaction means to coordinate one's talk with someone else's, and, as a rule, to be alive to others' listening and speaking. In a communicative *pas de trois*, the interpreter's task is to do a certain part of others' sense-making, which includes the task of coordinating their communicative activities. Regarding talk within an interactionist theoretical frame, I will take into account that interlocutors rely on a multitude of sources of information when making sense of words and utterances. Chapter 8 offers a more detailed exploration of 'understanding' at various levels in interpreter-mediated interaction. For present purposes, it is enough to distinguish between three aspects of the way in which interlocutors make sense in and of communicative interaction.

First, interlocutors orientate themselves in talk on the basis of the conventionalized *propositional meanings* of the spoken words and expressions used. Secondly, talk is understood as part of a certain situation. The contextual or *situated meanings* of words are drawn from the type of encounter, from the constellation of people present, from time and place, other activities accompanying talk, from voice characteristics and so forth. Thirdly, in a conversation involving three or more persons, sense is arguably made also on the basis of the *participation framework,* continuously negotiated in and by talk, in other words, on the basis of how interlocutors position themselves in relation to each other; who is understood to be addressed, by whom and how, and, thus, who is obligated to respond, and how.

As Goffman (1990) argues, a conversation between two individuals stands and falls according to their mutual attention. The appearance of a third party means that one individual may be either included or excluded in the union of the two. If included, this individual can him- or herself carry out a mediating function between the others. In an 'ordinary' (non-institutional) monolingual conversation between three or more persons, in principle anyone can take on the role of mediator, seeing to it that a speaker is attended to and included in – or alternatively, excluded from – focused interaction. Moreover, in the course of a single conversation, this function may be carried out by different people (Goffman 1990:141 ff.). In some types of institutional conversation, the responsibility for including (and excluding) participants may be institutionalized too, and lie on a particular role-holder. Obvious examples are the chairperson at a formal meeting and the therapist in a family therapy session. In interpreter-mediated institutional talk, a similar function is inherent in the role of interpreter. In an interpreter-mediated encounter, one actor – the interpreter – is expected to actively, immediately and constantly engage in various aspects of sense making, while the primary interlocutors' understanding of interaction is assumed to be achieved with a certain delay and always via the mediating third party.

1.1 Functions of talk – globally and locally situated

In interpreter-mediated interaction, most of what is said by primary parties is designed to have at least *two functions* – on the one hand, to be *preliminary responses* for the interpreter to respond to by translating into the language of the counterpart; and on the other, to work as *given responses* to the other primary interlocutor questions or propositions.

Other functions of talk, and thereby the dynamics of interpreter-mediated encounters, are dependent on the interpreters and the other interlocutors; on their respective background knowledge, linguistic competence, overall aims and wish to communicate. The dynamics of interaction will largely depend on the socio-cultural conventions associated with the type of situation (in institutional terms) in which the interpreting occurs, and on participants' respective understanding of what it means to speak via an interpreter. These *global* aspects of interaction (as they might be described) comprise a multitude of circumstances. The presence and the use of artefacts, such as protocols and syringes, when focused upon in interaction and used in certain ways, help establishing the transformation of the situation into, for instance, a police interrogation or a doctor–patient encounter. Thus, they are in a way globally present. If we take abstract objects, such as fear and embarrassment, when these dominate in an encounter, then they can also be said to have a global presence in the situation.

What appears within a particular activity type (a police interrogation, a visit at the doctor's) tends reflexively to confirm and reproduce the present situation as being an activity of this particular type. It will normally be taken for granted that the discourse created in the situation will reflect an associated conventional *speech genre* (Bakhtin 1979/86a).[1]

Yet, on the other hand, participants in an encounter have a certain potential capacity to initiate a redefinition of the encounter and ultimately re-evaluate ongoing talk; for instance, they can switch from talking seriously to joking or talking ironically, from being supportive to staying indifferent. Like other encounters, interpreter-mediated ones are conditioned by *local* communicative events, occurring on a turn-by-turn level. Interlocutors continuously relate to each other via words and physical movements; they interact, locally coordinating their deeds and words within the common activity of talk. Unlike monolingual meetings, the local management of interaction here partly lies in the hands of the interpreter.

1.2 On the distribution of responsibility

Before starting with the main analyses, let us take a brief look back. The introductory example in the preceding Chapter 6, basically exploring *talk as text*, was drawn from an interview at a police station. Alisa, an applicant for residence permit in Sweden, claimed that she was Greek and the officer, Peter, tried to find evidence for this in her passport. The sequence where this was done we identified as a pair of 'original' and 'interpreter's utterance'. Seen from the point of view of translation, the latter was categorized as 'close' or 'substituting' 'rendition'.

(G22:10)
Peter: 18.   °kan du visa mig var?°
                °*can you show me where?*°
Ilona: 19.   а вы можете показать где?
                a[nd] can you show where?

We saw in this case, that Ilona's "and can you show me where", apart from constituting a new version in Russian of something said in Swedish, served as an interpreter's stipulated turn, following upon the primary interlocutor's turn at talk. Moreover, we noted a couple of other important functions this utterance was designed to fulfil.

My presence when this exchange took place gave me an important advantage in the analysis. I could see the police officer sitting at his desk, and in front of him a typewriter into which he had fed in a blank report sheet. A standard piece of information which has to be entered onto this form concerns nationality. Peter had no previous information that the woman in front of him was Greek, and when she claimed this he looked at the applicant's passport for confirmation, folded it back and forth and then handed it over to the interpreter, saying, in Swedish, "can you show me where?". The interpreter took the passport, gave it to Alisa, and repeated the officer's words, in Russian. She thus forwarded to Alisa not only the passport but also, in a very concrete way, the question. Her action, accompanying the words, brought in a new referent to the pronoun "you". Ilona's translation, furthermore, served as a comment on the current interaction order, and, simultaneously, promoted a return to the standard organization of the police-interrogation. In and by these actions, a redefinition of the current distribution of responsibility for the substance and the progression of talk was accomplished.

The present chapter will explore in greater detail interpreters' means of managing interaction order and how the efficiency of these means depends on the primary interlocutors' activity.

2. "I HAVE TO RETRAIN MYSELF"

The cases explored in the present chapter are all drawn from encounters at which I was actually present. The first excerpt is taken from the meeting quoted above, recorded at the immigration department of a local Swedish police station. The persons involved are thus Peter, a police officer, Alisa, an applicant for residence permit in Sweden, and the interpreter, Ilona.

The present interest in this particular piece of discourse was originally raised by Ilona. On that day at the police station, when the interview had ended, the applicant left together with the officer while Ilona and I stayed in the room, waiting for the next person to be interviewed. When the others were no longer within hearing distance, Ilona commented in a low voice: *Äsch! pereuchitsja det är väl omskola, skola om sig?* ("Pooh! *pereuchitsja* ["to retrain oneself"] – it *is* retrain, to retrain oneself, isn't it?"). "Yes, but you can take it in different ways" I suggested. "Yes, but you see how fast I am backing out" – 'Yes, yes, it's my fault'" Ilona says, quoting herself. "It wasn't my fault!", she goes on. "It's so typical you know. I get *so* irritated."

Ilona during the encounter seems to take on a responsibility for the interaction, and admits a guilt in a way that she afterwards regrets. She had not made any mistake; or had she? Was her self-criticism misplaced? The present sequence will explore how interpreters' self-blame may serve as a means of managing interaction order.

In interviews of this kind, applicants are requested to provide information on a range of questions. For instance, why they want to stay in the new country, what connection they have to it, the reasons why they have left the former home country, and so forth. Police officers routinely put together reports on the basis of which officers higher up in the bureaucratic hierarchy take decisions concerning applicants' further stay.

In this encounter, the police officer types down the applicant's answer in the process of the hearing. We come in where he starts on a new topic. He urges Alisa to account for how she foresees the possibilities of using her Soviet education in Sweden, given that she is permitted to stay. In reply, the applicant starts by launching the idea of retraining herself.

(1) (G22:4)

1	Peter:	((types for 15 s.)) mm. jag vill att du . . . eem . . . spekulerar
		mm. I want you to . . . erm . . . speculate
2		litegrann. om . . . hur (.) hur du kan använda din
		a little. if . . . how (.) how you can use your
3		utbildning- ditt yrke i Sverige. vet du
		education- your profession in Sweden. do you know
4		nå't sånt? o- **om** du får tillstånd i Sverige. ((starts typing))
		anything about that? i- if you get a permit in Sweden.
5	Ilona:	я хочу чтобы вы::: подумали вслух о том. как вы
		I want you to::: think aloud about. how you
6		сможете использовать свою про- профессию в
		can use your pro- profession in
7		Швеции здесь. **если** вы получите
		Sweden here. if you get
8		разрешение на постоянное жительство.
		a permanent residence permit.
→ 9	Alisa:	ну . . . я думаю что . . . мне надо переучиться.
		well . . . I think that . . . I have to retrain myself.
10	Ilona:	jag tror att jag måste skola om mig.
		I think that I have to retrain myself.
11	Alisa:	ну в смысле того что я во-первых не знаю
		well in the sense that I for one thing don't know the
12		шведского языка,
		Swedish language,
13	Ilona:	med tanke på att jag inte kan svenska.
		bearing in mind that I don't know Swedish.
14	Alisa:	ну и наверно здесь медицина всё-таки не **так**
		well and probably here Medicine after all is not so
15		развита как у нас в Советском Союзе. поэтому . . .
		developed as ours, in the Soviet Union. that's why . . .
	Ilona:	å . . . med tanke
		and . . . bearing in

16   på att . . . e::: medicinsk utveckling är
                mind that . . . er::: medical development
17   inte på samma nivå som i Sovjet.
                isn't at the same level as in the USSR.
18   Alisa: нет. ну в смысле- поэтому- а по специальности
                no. well in the sense- that's why- and my specialty is
19   акушерка-гинеколог, я думаю что и здесь они
                midwife gynaecologist, I think that here these are also
20   требуются. врачи.
                needed. doctors.
21   Ilona: och e::: mitt yrke är . . . barnmorska gynekolog och
                and er::: my profession is . . . midwife gynaecologist and
22   det tror jag nog man behöver såna här med.
                I would think that here these are needed as well.
23   Peter: jaha. skola om sig. ja ja. okej. du- du menar att skaffa
                aha. retrain oneself. yes yes. okay. you- you mean to get
24   dig kunskaper i svenska eller . . . komplettera?
                some knowledge in Swedish or . . . do a refresher course?
25   eller . . . e::: jag hänger upp mig på uttrycket skola om sig.
                or . . . er::: I have problems with the expression retrain oneself.
26   då tänker jag på nåt helt **annat** yrke.
                *then I think about an entirely **different** profession.*
27   °kan vi utreda det. (.) bara lite.°
                °can we clear this up. (.) just a little.°
→ 28   Ilona: a näe det- det var . . . mitt fel.
                a no it- it was . . . my fault.
29   Peter: mm,
                mm,
30   Ilona: de- det var just det hon tänkte på.
                thi- this was exactly what she had in mind.

Ilona's regretful comment after the interview suggests that she had believed her choice of expression in Swedish, *skola om mig* ("retrain myself") (1:10) was faulty; that it does not correspond to the Russian expression Alisa had used. However, she began to doubt that she was wrong, and finally thought that she indeed had interpreted correctly. The standard expressions for 'to retrain (oneself)' in Swedish and Russian respectively, *skola om sig* and *pereuchitsja*, have overlapping, even if not entirely the same meanings in the different languages and cultural spheres. When Ilona realizes this, her grounds for self-blame, as it were, disappear.

It should be noted that when Ilona herself looks back at the situation, she focuses on the expression *pereuchitsja* taken out of context. In other words, she applies a textual perspective when trying to explain that something went 'wrong'. Her comparison of the two expressions as 'texts', however, did not satisfy her as an explanation. Going stepwise through the excerpt I will investigate what led up to the situation where the interpreter pleaded guilty, detect functions of this and other moves in the process of interaction and examine how they interconnect. It will be seen that vagueness occasionally is a challenge in interpreter-mediated interaction. Sometimes interpreters draw conclusions prematurely about what primary parties mean to say, simply because they are expected to translate when the speaker is in the middle of developing a thought.

2.1 Negotiating appropriate talk – negotiating word meaning

From the applicant's first answer (in 1:9), one could get the impression that she thinks of her professional experience as insufficient and perhaps even useless in the Swedish context. Her suggestion of retraining herself could be a way to display interest in and openness for trying something new. Subsequently Alisa specifies her answer (in 1:11–12), however, and does so in a direction that was only vaguely – if at all – reflected in the first reply. She mentions her lack of knowledge of Swedish as one reason why she needs to retrain herself. By using a list-reading intonation and the expression "for one thing" (1:11), the applicant indicates that there is more information to come on the same issue. The list-reading is not signalled in Ilona's utterance following next (1:13), and the officer most probably is not made aware of it. This does not exclude that the *interpreter* expects a continuation however. But meanwhile, thinking twice upon how to continue, Alisa comes up with something that makes her opening statement sound as if totally reconsidered: "well and probably here Medicine after all is not *so* developed as ours, in the Soviet Union. that's why ..." (1:14–15).

At this point one may get the impression that the applicant means to say that medical progress in the USSR must be more advanced than in Sweden. Such a statement does not quite fit with the idea she started out with – her need for retraining. Having many years of experience in a Soviet medical institution, Alisa, in the light of what she argues here, ought to be counted as already very attractive to the Swedish labour market. Does this, in fact, mean that her opening statement is to be seen rather as an unfortunate formulation, that what she really meant to say was just that she has to learn Swedish?

As far as Ilona is concerned, she has her frame of interpretation ready. She is indeed prepared to continue something of a list-reading account, further specifying what the applicant had in mind by *pereuchitsja* ("retraining"; "retrain oneself"). The way Ilona begins to talk: "and ... bearing in mind that ..." (1:15–16), repeating the expression from the preceding turn signals this also to the officer. The interpreter, so it seems, reads in a consistency in the preceding discourse where the grounds for it, from our present point of view, in fact seem quite scarce. Moreover, the somewhat challenging message in Alisa's contribution (in 1:14–15) is moderated. As regards which country has reached the highest level of Medicine, Ilona's version stands out as rather diplomatic: "and ... bearing in mind that ... er::: medical development is not at the same level as in the USSR" (1:15–17).

Whatever consistency there has been so far, Alisa, in her next contribution (1:18), follows through with presenting herself as a well-educated, potentially valuable labour-force resource to Swedish society. Nevertheless, as before, her way of talking reveals a degree of uncertainty. In monolingual talk, interrupted onsets of the kind that can be seen at the beginning of Alisa's utterance ("no. well in the sense- that's why-") (1:18) would most probably make an interlocutor alive to the fact that the speaker has some difficulty in finding the right words. However, in the interpreter-mediated encounter, the interrogator's options are restricted on this point. As was noted above (Chapter 6), these parts of original utterances are typically not textually represented in subsequent translations. Perhaps Peter here does not register at all that Alisa is struggling with her specification of what she in fact means to say on the issue of her education. And indeed, Ilona's utterance corresponding to the one in which Alisa identifies herself professionally, has more of a written-language style ("and er::: my profession is ... midwife gynaecologist and I would think that here these are needed as well.") (1:21–22). It not only starts differently, but also ends in a way which departs from the original.

The applicant underlines obstetrics as being her professional specialization by referring to it in more than one way, a stylistic device often used in spoken interaction. She mentions "midwife gynaecologist" and then finally adds "doctors": ("no. well in the sense- that's why- and my speciality is midwife gynaecologist, I think that here these are also needed. doctors") (1:18–20). The rephrasing has no counterpart in the second version. Whether or not the applicant is aware of this, it could have a specific significance to stress one's status as a doctor in a Swedish context. In this country, midwives function relatively independently from other medical experts in handling mothers during pregnancy and childbirth (Oakley and Houd 1990:42). If the interpreter lacks this contextual information it is probably quite hard for her to anticipate this as a reason for Alisa adding the word 'doctors' (thus seeking to underline and claim a higher level of qualification than is required for midwives in Sweden). If the interpreter indeed knows about the difference, her simplified version somewhat diminishes the potential provocation this statement implies.

At this point Peter reacts to what to him must seem to be something of an inconsistency. He initiates a negotiation of the meaning of *skola om sig* ("retrain oneself"). Looking more closely at his utterance we may note that he starts out with "aha. retrain oneself. yes yes. okay." (1:23) which prosodically is cued as a confirmation, indicating that the prior utterance is understood. Then he draws attention back to the repeated words: "you- you mean to get some knowledge of Swedish or ... do a refresher course? or ... er::: I have problems with the expression retrain oneself. then I think about an entirely *different* profession. °can we clear this up. (.) just a little.°" (1:23–27).

Regardless of what the police officer here wanted to clear up, and who he thought should do this, there was no further clarification on the issue of retraining. The short exchange concerning Alisa's ideas about future use of her Soviet education ended without any more involvement on the part of the applicant. It was cut off when Ilona said: *a näe det- det var ... mitt fel.* ("a no it- it was ... my fault.") (1:28). The interpreter covered up for the expression *skola om sig* ("retrain oneself"), relating to it as something she herself was responsible for, rather than ascribing to the Russian-speaking woman both responsibility for first mentioning it and obligation to explain what she meant.

In terms of participation framework, Ilona in 1:28 related to what she said as 'animator' and 'author'. Moreover, prosodically marking the pronoun *my*, she also appeared as her own 'principal'. She contextualized the mistake as having been an initiative of her own and thereby attention was drawn to herself and away from the applicant. This put a new topic on the agenda. The police officer indicated that he had registered the information but left the initiative with Ilona, contributing only a silent feedback *mm* (1:29). The interpreter responded by concluding (even if quite vaguely) what Alisa had meant by the discussed expression: "thi-this was exactly what she had in mind." (1:30). She thus quickly retreated to the position where Alisa appeared as the ultimate source of her words, and this brought an end to the retrain-oneself topic. The interview continued with the officer bringing up a new, unrelated issue. Via the self-blame sequence an identified threat is warded off and the interaction order re-established.

One may possibly wonder how the police officer finally understood the expression "retrain oneself". The closest I can get to an answer, having no direct access to his record of the interview, is to use the interpreter's translation of the record. It comes at the end of the interview, during which applicants are routinely given the opportunity to check, correct or confirm what has been written about them. From the last part of the present recording I could see that the exchange presented as Example (1) resulted in one single sentence in the officer's notes. In (my translation of) Ilona's translated version it says: "About the future in Sweden: She thinks that she can work as a gynaecologist in the future in Sweden." In other words, even if we can see from the dialogue (in 1:23–27) that the officer is aware of the possibility of changing profession, it is clear that this leaves no trace in his written report. Similarly absent is what appeared in the interview as the applicant's slight inconsistency. Furthermore, the applicant had no objections to the statement when it was read out loud. Of course no analysis ever could determine whether or not (or to what extent) this text actually corresponds to what Alisa had in mind at any particular point in time. What can be further clarified, however, is the connection between what talk is about and how talk is organized.

2.2 Mitigation and discourse control

Goffman (1971) in his book *Relations in Public* identifies a social activity he calls *remedial work*. In his definition, the function of 'remedial work' is to change the meaning that otherwise might be given to an act, transforming what could be seen as offensive into what can be seen as acceptable. This change seems to be accomplished by striking in some way at the moral responsibility otherwise imputed to the offender. This in turn seems to be accomplished by three main devices, namely accounts, apologies, and requests

(Goffman 1971:109). The exchange cited above clearly illustrates that interpreting in face-to-face interaction sometimes involves role-conflicts between demands connected to local turn-by-turn management of interaction, and global demands, linked to principal expectations of interpreters and their recognized functions. Exploring more closely the conflicting demands in this case, I would like to point to the 'remedial work' initiated by the applicant, and the police officer's negotiation of word-meaning.

It appears that 'remedial work' does not necessarily serve in interpreter-mediated encounters the same functions as it does in monolingual ones. For the applicant, a general dilemma in the described situation is that she does not really know what the interrogator expects from her. She can only guess about the motives underlying his questions. At the same time, she is anxious to be cooperative and to make a good impression as an applicant, which includes, if possible, avoiding saying anything that could put her in a bad position (for instance, contradicting herself). Given the socio-cultural conventions attached to police interrogations this could appear to be gravely compromising behaviour. It is not surprising then that the applicant tries to remedy the impression the first utterance may have brought about. To begin with it seems as if she is displaying a wish, a preparedness or a willingness to change professions and then, upon second thoughts, she revises this. It may have come to Alisa's mind that presenting herself as a person with insufficient professional qualifications would perhaps harm her chances of being granted a Swedish residence permit. It could be added here that according to traditional Soviet law, a person's right to settle in a particular place was intimately connected to her enrolment with an employer.

Exploring the interpreter's treatment of the information conveyed, it appears very plausible that she senses this contradiction in Alisa's contributions. Ilona infers from what Alisa says that she thinks her Soviet professional education should be mentioned in positive terms and that the issue of taking up a new profession is in fact irrelevant to the matter and must be downplayed.

As was mentioned above, the interpreter softens Alisa's statement about the superiority of Soviet Medicine (1:14–15). Perhaps Alisa's statement makes no sense at all to Ilona, in particular if she is not aware of the different roles during pregnancy and childbirth of midwives and doctors in Swedish and Soviet health care respectively. No doubt, however, the interpreter is acquainted with the practical realities of public health care in both Sweden and the former USSR and is aware of the comparatively low material standard in Soviet health care of the time. She might even guess that the applicant is well aware of this too, and therefore find her statement quite provocative (close to lying to make a better impression, as it were). She also might think that if the police officer has any insight into Soviet public health-care standards, he will immediately think that Alisa is trying to improve her position on false grounds.

An applicant's ambition to make a good impression is quite understandable, not least for an interpreter on duty. Likewise, Ilona is aware of the fact that police officers need to collect straightforward, truthful answers rather than made-up stories. In order to get them, they are supposed to conduct interviews in a way which supports an atmosphere of trust and cooperation. These are the potentially contradictory unwritten rules of the speech game that takes place in police interrogations. People involved in interrogations are more or less aware of the rules, even if seldom bound to make them explicit.

Moderating Alisa's statement regarding Medicine, Ilona potentially acts to save the interlocutors' faces. Simultaneously she sees to it that communication continues smoothly on a focused issue (i.e. the applicant's view of her Soviet education in a Swedish context).

Mitigation as a means of sustaining a cooperative atmosphere and simultaneously exercising discoursal control, attempting to keep the client relevant and 'on topic' is a well known phenomenon, described, for instance, in a study of interaction between counsellors and their clients in a family planning project (Candlin and Lucas 1986).

Somewhat modifying the illocutionary force of Alisa's statement, the interpreter is in a sense teaming up with the applicant, which implies a potential face-threat to her professional self, if it is understood as advocacy – by definition a violation of interpreters' official norms. Ilona's post-interview comment to the observer can partly be explained as a face-preserving action.

2.3 Communicative 'repair' and changes of 'footing'

Returning to the police officer's last long utterance cited above (1:23–27), where he initiates a negotiation of the meaning of *skola om sig* ("retrain (oneself)") (1:23), we may note that he re-uses the formulation given by Ilona and not the one given by Alisa (naturally enough, as he does not speak or understand Russian). In the literature on social interaction, partial repetition of prior talk is assumed to occur in particular sequence-types. Among these are "other-initiated repair" (Schegloff, Jefferson and Sacks 1977), speaker's disagreement with prior speaker's self-deprecations (Pomerantz 1984:83–4), and the activity of arguing (Goodwin and Goodwin 1987). All these findings might add to the explanation of why Ilona, in the situation discussed here, takes on a personal responsibility; she aligns herself as 'responder', providing a direct response and thus relates to her utterance as both 'animator', 'author' and 'principal'.

On the local level, Ilona's action (i.e. the one that made her angry with herself) is thus tied to changes of 'footing'. This means, among other things, that more than one person must be involved; that something is happening in and by interaction. In this connection Peter's final addition, "can we clear this up. (.) just a little." (1:27) should be particularly noted. A certain change in how he relates to his interlocutors is displayed here. The recording reveals that a change of 'footing' is contextually cued by voice characteristics. More precisely, if the first part of the officer's utterance could well be understood as relating to Ilona as recipient–'reporter' (i.e. *Alisa* is the one referred to in his "you mean" etc.), then the end of it, conveyed in a somewhat lower tone, gives rather the impression that the interpreter is addressed directly and expected to respond not by repeating but by providing a new initiative. Potentially she is included in the pronoun of address ('we') when the officer says "can we clear this up" (1:27).

Understood like this, the officer projects upon Ilona a 'responder's' listenership in relation to what she hears. Ilona, in turn, aligns with such a position, addressing in her subsequent utterance not the applicant but the officer. The officer additionally supports this change in Ilona's 'footing' by implicitly drawing attention to the time limits to the encounter in question, set by the public institution, when he finally says, in an even quieter voice, "just a little." (in 1:27).

The above excerpt illustrates a dilemma which lay people in institutional encounters sometimes have to face. It showed an instance where a lay person, Alisa, had difficulties in expressing herself on a particular issue initiated by a police officer. She needed to answer him, and she started to do so without being sure what, really, she wanted to say. This in itself constitutes a certain threat to the interpreter-mediated interaction order. It seems to touch the heart of a classic dilemma faced by interpreters. Highly plausibly, Alisa's feeling of having picked an unfortunate formulation, saying *mne nado pereuchitsja* ("I have to retrain myself"), spread to Ilona, and her use of the expressions *pereuchitsja* and *skola om sig* ("retrain (oneself)"). One should note, however, that this becomes manifest *only* when Peter brings up the meaning of the expression as the focused topic in conversation. This constitutes an additional threat to the interactional order. The fact that Peter ascribed to Ilona a 'responder's' role, and that she aligned to it (1:23–27) meant that she changed her relationship to the expression. Where Ilona had once related to *skola om sig* ("retrain (oneself)") as an 'animator' of another's words, she is later ascribed and/or takes on the role of someone *more* responsible for the words used. This is where self-blame, a result of participants' joint activity, becomes a means by which the standard interaction order is re-established.

3. "SAY WHAT HE SAYS NOW."

The key factor in the structure of social encounters, in Goffman's view, is the maintenance of a mutually established definition of the situation, a definition which has to be expressed, and this expression has to be sustained in the face of a multitude of potential disruptions (Goffman 1990:246). A situated system of activity and the organization in which this system is sustained, Goffman argues, provide individuals with that one of their roles that will be given principal weight on this occasion. But even while the local scene establishes what individuals will mainly be, many of their other affiliations will simultaneously be given little bits of credit. It is right here, in manifestations of *role distance* – through justifying actions as not quite 'seriously meant' in the current activity – that each individual's personal style is to be found (Goffman 1961:152) (cf. Chapter 5:1.1.1).

The following example illustrates how an interpreter's occasional distancing from the 'normative role' of interpreter serves as a way to manipulate the interaction order. The instance where this happens involves a communicative phenomenon Goffman (1967) identifies as *face-work*, i.e. the action taken by a person to make whatever he is doing consistent with face. 'Face-work', in his definition, serves to counteract communicative incidents – that is, events whose effective symbolic implications threaten face. 'Face-work' is performed to counteract the risk of hurting others' feelings with disrespectful behaviour and consequent losses in self-respect. To a large extent, interlocutors' measures to maintain face dictate the overall progression of talk (Goffman 1967:12).

As will be demonstrated in the second example, interpreter-mediated conversations may involve various types of 'face-work' simultaneously, which all at some level constitute challenges to the interpreter's work on sustaining a shared definition of the situation, and a shared understanding of the interaction order. The example consists of a longer sequence, drawn from a consultation at a local Swedish health clinic. In order to make the analysis easier to follow, it will be presented in seven shorter stretches of talk.

A young Russian-speaking man has an appointment for a medical check-up. He meets Nina, a young nurse. The interpreter is Inna, a native Russian woman in her forties. The passages cited occur when the visit has just started and the patient, Pavel has expressed a wish to be tested for venereal diseases (as it turns out, his most urgent motive to turn up at the clinic is to get an HIV infection test). Nina asks him if he has any physical complaints. Pavel is somewhat hesitant, and Nina lists some possible symptoms of venereal infections. Pavel re-starts while Inna is still speaking, relapses into silence and then starts anew:

(2) (G31:3)

1 Pavel: м::: во- (.) вроде . . . н- нет. ну так- (.) ((blowing sound))
            m::: k- (.) kind of . . . n- no. but so- (.)

2   вроде нет, ну иногда что-то вот- сейчас . . .
            kind of no, but sometimes something like- now . . .

3   ((swallows)) ну, я- я не знаю, что-то так сразу не
                                    well, I- I don't know, the thing is all at once

4   объяснишь, врод- вообще-то нет. нет,
            you can't explain it, kind of- on the whole well no. no,

5   ⎡   не:::j. inte.
    ⎢   *no::: . not.*
    ⎣ Inna: нä:::e, jag tror inte att e::: de:::
            no::::, I don't think that er::: tha:::t

6 Pavel: ну::: ((blowing sound)) иногда:::
            bu:::t.   someti::::mes

7 Inna: det är svårt att förklara på en gång.
            it's difficult to explain all at once.

Pavel's lengthy answer (2:1–5) to the nurse's question as to whether he has any physical symptoms could have been succinctly expressed by a simple "no". This is actually how he himself sums it up, finally

concluding, in Swedish, *ne:::j. inte.* ("no:::. not.") (2:5). This might
have been comprehensible to Nina, even without Inna's rendition.
However the interpreter, according to her professional obligation,
hears and recapitulates more than a simple "no". Inna's version
reflects some of the hesitation in the patient's long, fragmented
utterance ("no::::, I don't think that er::: that . . .") (2:5). Pavel fills in
with a new attempt (2:6), which, however, soon fades away. All the
same, the interpreter latches on where he falls silent.

In monolingual spoken interaction, the patient's activity would
rather strongly indicate that he wishes to hand over the turn. In
an interpreter-mediated conversation, the 'contextualization cues'
here identified seem to lose some of their significance. Partly this
is simply due to the specific pre-defined interaction order – that
every second turn at talk belongs to the interpreter. By necessity,
the current speaker every now and then has to relinquish the turn
– whether or not he has got to the point.

Inna in the next turn revoices Pavel's excusatory comment on
his fragmented speech from a moment ago: "all at once you can't
explain it" (in 2:4) which comes back as: "it's difficult to explain all
at once" (in 2:7). This time Inna speaks less hesitantly than before,
though far from rapidly and self-confidently. The patient's communicative behaviour does not really invite a 'reporter's' listenership. It
is as if he is thinking aloud, conveying only preliminary formulations, as if awaiting the interpreter's ratification, or hints about how
to continue.

To the nurse, what Inna says about explaining (in 2:7) leaves
room for alternative understandings on two important points. For
one thing, Nina may get the impression that Pavel wishes to keep
the initiative, or she may think that he would rather see her take
over. Another ambiguity concerns participation framework. In the
transcript, the statement in question can easily be localized as first
uttered by the patient. Yet Nina, who knows no Russian, might
perceive either Inna or Pavel as its originator. Who, actually, thinks
that it is difficult to express these things all at once – the patient or
the interpreter? Nina's verbal behaviour does not tell us much about
her current understanding of the exchange:

(2) (G31:3)
8 ⌈Nina   mhm
  │   *mhm*
  ⌊Pavel: нет иногда вот что-то ((blows)) (.) ((swallows))
           no sometimes something like

9   ⌈   я не знаю, я так- такие- я так- такие-
                I don't know, I sort of- like- I sort of- like-
     ⌊ Inna: °не стесняйся°
                °*don't be embarrassed*°

10   Pavel: это можно говорить как будь-то я вот . . . ((blows))
                you might say it's as if I am like . . .

Nina's *mhm* (2:8) invites the patient to go on talking, but having
started Pavel once more gets stuck. He again provides more blowing sounds than words. While Pavel is continuing with "I don't
know," etc. (2:9), Inna simultaneously makes a quiet remark: "don't
be embarrassed". To us, this little encouragement reveals a split
focus in the interpreter's listenership. The interpreter is here taking
a stand primarily as 'responder', as she subsequently can be seen
as the 'principal' of an utterance (2:9). By recognizing the patient's
embarrassment, Inna tries to encourage him, 'off-the-record', as it
were, to go on speaking. A person who lacks knowledge in Russian,
however, has alternative ways of understanding what is happening.

To the nurse it is not clear whether Inna is concentrating on
memorizing and transferring what is said (which is what she generally expects from interpreters) or whether the interpreter is taking
command of the interview herself. Even if ignorant about exactly *what*
they are dealing with, Nina can see and hear Pavel and Inna tuning
in with each other in some kind of exchange. And while Nina continuously gets further support for possible assumptions about being
side-stepped, Pavel is, as before, hesitant about how to continue.

(2) (G31:3)

11   Inna: да.
             yes.

12   Pavel: как е:::
             how er:::

13   Inna: да,
             yes,

14   Pavel: потому что я не могу только- ((laugh)) как
             e::: because I can't just-   *how*

15 ⌈   сказать это а::::::: ((laugh))
         er::: shall I put it a:::::
   ⌊ Inna: mm. frågar om::: det går att prata sådär
                     mm. asks if::: it's possible to talk that

16   öppet, för att det är svårt att förklara, berätta.
          openly, because it's difficult to explain, to tell.

17   Nina: mm,
             mm,

Inna is, of course, aware of Russian being incomprehensible to Nina.
She knows that if the nurse is to be involved in what is bothering
the patient just now then none but herself can enable this to happen. Hence, Inna tells the nurse what the patient is doing, referring
again to difficulties in talking openly. This, in actual fact, also summarizes what Pavel has said in his extended turn, but if Nina had
expected to hear about symptoms of venereal diseases she is bound
to be disappointed. Is the interpreter hiding something from her?
As interaction continues, she is again made to wait.

(2) (G31:3)

18	Pavel	а::: ну короче- во- короче- вот так вот значит
		a::: well to be short- so- to be short- sort of like that is
19		попи́саешь, да?
		you go for a pee, okay?
20	Inna:	mm,
		mm,
21	Pavel:	вот:::
		sort o:::
22	Inna:	mm,
		mm,
23	Pavel:	е::: и::: (.) ну как сказать? попи́саешь. ((laugh))
		e::: and::: (.) well how shall I put it? you go for a pee.
24	Inna:	да, да.
		yes, yes.
25	Pavel:	((laugh)) потом значит- е (.) да действительно
		then that is- er (.) yes it's really
26		тру- ((laugh)) так просто не выразишься. ((laugh))
		dif- not so easy to express yourself.
27	Inna:	нормально.
		okay.

To my mind, this stretch of talk could be described as the patient's
searching for a careful or tactful way of introducing his medical
problem. With or without *his* intention, these efforts, which are
including little, if anything, on the medical issue, are interpreted by
Inna within a frame of meta-talk, the content of which she has interpreted for the nurse twice already. Moreover, being an expert on
how to express oneself, Inna apparently sees herself in a position to
urge the patient to go on talking: *mm* (2:20), *mm* (2:22), *da, da.* ("yes,
yes.") (2:24). Her back-channelling, confirming that she understands
what he says, becomes gradually louder. Pavel continuously tries, but

is coming up mainly with embarrassed laughter and no additional substance to what he has said already. Finally, Inna interprets what he says as a request for her expert opinion and ratifies what he is, or says, as *normal'no*. "okay." (2:27).

It can thus be seen that the interpreter evaluates Pavel's talk, rather than just concentrating on memorizing it. Nina may have little or no idea about the content of the Russian exchange, but she indeed gets an impression of its interactional significance(s).

Pavel, if he was to reflect upon it, would probably have no doubts about his and the interpreter's collaboration being obvious and at the same time obscure to the nurse. Yet, Nina's possible disapproval of this would not necessarily occur to him. Actually, one could presume that Pavel's way of talking is partly due to the fact that he (rightly) presumes the nurse to have no knowledge of Russian whatsoever. In contrast, Inna's knowledge of Russian makes her, in this situation, a potential ally.

From what follows, it is obvious that the nurse is not at all supportive of this alliance, despite the fact that Inna may very well perceive herself to be serving Nina's goals when she tries to help the patient to get rid of his tension and embarrassment. As we have observed, however, the interpreter simultaneously gets involved in a way which neither from the nurse's, nor from the patient's, nor indeed from her own point of view, is altogether satisfactory.

(2) (G31:3–4)

28	Pavel:	потом значит вот я,
		then that is sort of I,
29	Nina:	m-
		m-
30	Pavel:	допустим вот на-ночь.
		let's say sort of at bedtime.
31	Inna:	mhm,
		mhm,

32 ⎡ Nina: vill du- vill du bryta av och säga vad han säger nu.
             would you- would you break off and say what he says now.
  ⎣ Pavel: нет я всё ((hawks))
                                        no I [will say] everything

The nurse finally expresses her disapproval of this situation in which the interpreter must appear to be going beyond her authority, and the patient to be addressing the wrong person. She makes a small attempt to enter the conversation (2:29), but lets Pavel continue. After another pair of turns involving the patient and the interpreter, however, Nina comes in more energetically: "would you- would you break off and say what he says now." (2:32).

It is worth noting that throughout this whole encounter (nearly one hour long) Nina seldom starts talking until the preceding speaker relinquishes his or her turn, and, as a rule, she immediately withdraws when someone competes with her for the floor. The patient, on the other hand, seldom drops the turn at talk before someone else (normally the interpreter) is well on her way to taking it over. Overlapping talk does not seem to disturb him in the same way as it appears to annoy Nina.

In social interaction, overlapping speech can be assigned diverse meanings, partly on culturally specific grounds. The significance people conventionally attribute to the phenomenon can, according to Tannen (1984), be of two diametrically opposing kinds. In some contexts it counts as pushy, domineering behaviour, while in others it is seen as a means of displaying positive involvement. If Nina has a tendency to understand overlapping speech as antagonistic conduct, Pavel, it seems, does not.

Analysing how Nina joins the conversation in 2:32, I can note that she, for once, does not interrupt herself, regardless of the fact that another person starts to talk simultaneously. This could be taken as evidence for a change in how she, at this moment, understands the situation. The immediate function of her contribution (2:32) is not to add to the ongoing talk. It is to comment on, and take charge of the situation; to show disapproval of the current interaction order, of being out of touch with what the others are doing. At this point she ascribes a 'responder's' role to Inna, i.e. she expects her *not* to memorize what she says at the moment but to join with her in an exchange which momentarily disconnects Pavel as a conversational partner.

The young man, in turn, does not accept the role of a bystander or non-addressee. Nina's meta-communicative request is overlapped by his assurance: "no I [will say] everything" (2:32).

From the interpreter's point of view, the interlocutors' contradicting expectations create a dilemma. To Nina the patient is currently the ratified speaker in the interviewing activity (regardless of the fact that he actually falls silent at the moment Nina starts talking) where she is the ultimate addressee, forced to wait for his message to be conveyed.

From Pavel's point of view the nurse is indeed the addressee in the health-care interviewing context, but at the moment he is in the midst of making his point. Both interlocutors count on the interpreter to succeed them as speaker. Each of them counts on her attentive listening and responding to *their* respective initiative, excluding, for the moment, the other party from talk. Inna goes on not by translating, but by asking for repetition:

(2) (G31:4)

33   Inna: va?
              what?
34 ⌈Nina   vill du bryta av nu och ta och säga vad han har sagt nu
    | *would you break off now and just say what he has said now*
    |Pavel: короче на-ночь попи́саешь,
    ⌊   *in short you go for a pee at bedtime,*
35   Nina: till mig.
              to me.
36   Pavel: на-ночь попи́саешь,
              you go for a pee at bedtime,

The interpreter's abrupt *va?* ("what?") (2:33), is equally accessible to all persons present, and it is succeeded by another instance of double discourse. We may note (in 2:34) that Nina repeats almost exactly what she just said, except that she uses the perfect tense (i.e. "has said" instead of "says"). This indicates a new slight change of event frames from the nurse's point of view. To her, the interviewing activity is momentarily at a standstill. Requesting the interpreter to recollect the patient's words, she again ascribes to her the role of addressed 'responder' vis-à-vis Nina's own utterance.

The young patient, in turn, goes on making his point within the health-care interviewing frame, saying "in short you go for a pee at bedtime" (2:34), repeated again in (2:36). Thus he attributes to Inna a 'reporter's' role. This means that Inna is once more ascribed two different recipient's roles by Nina and Pavel. They both invite the interpreter to take the next turn, succeeding them on a floor where they, however, presuppose different focuses, with each of their invitations implying for Inna a different projected speaker's alignment towards her next utterance. Nina's latest comments, however – indicating that she perceives the interpreter's behaviour as norm breaking, and the current frame of interaction as being in the process of change – provide Inna with an opportunity to display 'role distance'.

She responds in Swedish, that is, directly to Nina, giving an off-the-record account to justify her occasional actions as not quite 'seriously meant'. Her 'private' exchange with the patient did not really belong to 'serious talk' (the 'real' interpreter-mediated health-care interview).

(2) (G31:4)
37 Inna: det är inte en hel mening än.
         it's not a whole sentence yet.
38 Nina: nä.
         no.
39 Inna: mhm
         mhm
40 Pavel: значит на-ночь пописаешь, идёшь ложиться, е (.)
         that is you go for a pee at bedtime, you go to bed er (.)
41   вот.
         like.

Stating "it's not a whole sentence yet." (2:37), the interpreter enters the conversation at the point where she has been selected (by both parties, in fact) as next speaker. Putting herself, and thereby the interaction order, into focus is a resource for meeting primary parties' contradictory demands. In referring to grammatical rules, Inna partly de-personifies the ultimate responsibility behind her own talk and partly passes responsibility to the patient, indicating that he has not yet succeeded in providing what she needs to go on with 'serious' talk – a full sentence. Nina confirms the insufficiency, saying *nä.* ("no.") (2:38) (in this context meaning 'that's correct', i.e. confirming the negation in the preceding statement) and simultaneously acknowledges current talk as an instance of 'role distance'. Inna confirms with "mhm" (2:39), and the meta-talk exchange between her and the nurse is immediately closed.

Pavel takes the opportunity and comes back with his familiar formulation. This offers Inna a chance to align again as 'reporter', and subsequently as 'animator' of a primary interlocutor's words, and the interaction order reconforms to the standard pattern.

In interpreter-mediated interaction, the space for negotiation of how 'talking' is to be organized is fairly restricted, which is why the interpreter may have a principal interest in preventing 'talking' from becoming a focused issue. Looking closely, we have seen that, in this encounter both primary parties, partly overlapping, have tried to topicalize 'talking'. Both parties thereby initiated negotiation of the frames for the current communicative activity. The exchange between the patient and the interpreter went on for a while. The nurse's initiative, however, led to an immediate close of the meta-talk. The interpreter used it as an opportunity both to reassure the nurse that she (Inna) shared her understanding of the situation and to give the reason why it might appear that she did not. To perform 'role distance' and still sustain a shared definition of the situation one needs the support of the 'role others'.

3.1 Mutually opposing expectations on the role of interpreter

Thus far, the argument about the interpreter's measures to sustain a single definition of the situation concerns events at a turn-by-turn level. These measures and their local manifestations can be further explained by reference to socio-cultural factors inherent in the situation at a more global level – the type of encounter, the constellation of people and their respective social roles, interactional goals and mutual relations. Performing in the role of interpreter, Inna may simultaneously be seen by her interlocutors as a holder of other social identities, which may have coloured her performance and thereby also the substance and the progression of discourse.

It is evident that the primary interlocutors' various presuppositions about the role of interpreter constituted a challenge to Inna's role performance in the encounter quoted above. What shines through in the transcriptions is confirmed in the interviews made immediately after the recordings. The patient and the nurse were separately asked to comment on how they had experienced the encounter, how they evaluated the contact with their respective counterpart and how they perceived the interpreter. Apparently, their frames of references were quite different.

Nina spontaneously expressed surprise over the openness displayed by the young man. Most often, she said, "they [the patients] do not seem to feel that they can discuss just anything, and therefore it takes a long time before they come to the point; to what really bothers them".[2] Asked if she thought this had something to do with the fact that talk goes via an interpreter, the nurse replied that it had rather to do with the individuals in question. Her impression today was that the young man had been truly worried and therefore had decided beforehand to try and be as open as possible.

The nurse took the post-interview as an opportunity to declare her view on interpreter-mediated conversations generally, and this largely reflected the official normative perspective. It could be mentioned that only the day before she had been attending a meeting where hospital staff colleagues, interpreters and interpreter-service administrators had been discussing problems with using interpreters. In other words, Nina had recently heard a lot of thoughts about this matter and had perhaps formulated some herself. Besides, such discussions were not uncommon to her. Since the great majority of patients coming to the clinic were people with little or no knowledge of Swedish, the staff members knew a lot about what the presence (or absence) of interpreters meant for their daily work.

When speaking about her own expectations regarding the role performance of interpreters, the nurse criticized unqualified persons who do not stick to the official Code of Conduct. The majority of interpreters were qualified, she said. Yet some lack education; perhaps not so much in vocabulary knowledge, she guessed, as concerning professional ethics. And then she mentioned what she understood as three important points in the Ethical Code (cf. Chapter 3:3.1). Interpreters should not "themselves interfere (with their own opinions) in the conversation"; should "speak in the I-form" (i.e. not *about* the primary parties); and "all the time translate everything verbatim". As it appeared to her in retrospect, Inna's interpretation had been satisfactory on these points. The actual micro-level breaches of these rules, discovered in the above analysis, apparently did not colour her lasting impression of the encounter (at least not the one she wished to convey to me).

Pavel, asked about his impressions of the encounter, also started by speaking in general. He did not, however, say anything that suggested reference to the Code of Conduct the nurse mentioned. His ideas of what could be expected and evaluated in an interpreter's work departed quite substantially from Nina's. The interpreter, he said, is "a very important mediator, in particular these very experienced interpreters. They do not just formally translate, but, how to put it, understand perhaps better than myself sometimes what I want to say. [...] When he [sic] sees a particular person, he can predict what he will say. Perhaps he would sometimes not have to be waiting, listening, because everything is clear anyhow." In short, Pavel evaluated the interpreter's competence in terms of familiarity with people and ability to empathize and to express people's wishes. As the patient understood it, an interpreter "decides for himself how to do the interpreting, but it must be less interesting to just formally translate, without considering emotions and such".[3]

Pavel did not, it seems, share Nina's view of interpreters as first and foremost having *restricted* rights and responsibilities in interaction. Rather he perceived these actors as having *special*, unique rights and responsibilities. He remarked on the fact that Nina paid almost no attention to the interpreter during the encounter. This was something he had found a bit odd. However, he immediately modified his statement with light laughter, indicating that this was not meant as a critique.[4]

According to Nina, some patients tend to hand over to interpreters responsibility for things that go beyond their authority. And when this happens, it will be difficult for the interpreters to avoid meeting their expectations. Nina had found a tendency for patients to count on the interpreters as their friends and advocates, especially those who discuss their problems with the interpreters in the waiting room before meeting the nurse or her colleagues. This was something she essentially disapproved of and found to be disturbing for her communication with the patients.

3.2 Dimensions of 'face-work' in interpreter-mediated interaction

Vagueness in interaction can be a means to find out about others' frames of reference, basic values, and so forth. Frankness and explicitness are a lot riskier, in the sense that one may cross the boundaries of tact and appropriateness (as understood by others), and as a consequence lose self-respect and hurt interlocutors' feelings. Talking vaguely can thus be a way of doing what Goffman (1967) calls 'face-work'. Evidently, interpreter-mediated interaction provides particular conditions for the performance of this communicative behaviour.

One might identify three different respects in which 'face-work' could be actualized. In the present situation, these were all simultaneously in operation. Firstly, a primary interlocutor – the patient – displays a wish to save face. This places an expectation upon the interpreter to convey this wish while speaking on his behalf. Secondly, the interpreter has her own face to save as a professional. In other words, she must see to it that the primary parties' confidence in her as translator and coordinator is not jeopardized. And thirdly, interpreters' social identities (in addition to the role of interpreter), if brought to the fore, may call for yet another type of 'face-work'.

To Inna it is obvious that Pavel is very embarrassed. He has brought up a topic concerning a delicate and intimate matter, without really knowing how to talk about it or what to say. He is now in a foreign environment, meeting unknown people in an unfamiliar situation. In addition, he talks about intimate male issues, observed by three women, all of whom are attentively listening (for various reasons) to what he has to say. Inna undoubtedly realizes that the patient's way of speaking conveys a wish to preserve face.

Compared to Pavel, Inna is an expert on Swedish discourse in general and health-care discourse in particular, and more specifically, on what is usually or legitimately talked about in Swedish consulting rooms. In this capacity, she has a certain authority, in the eyes of Pavel, to confirm whether or not he expresses himself appropriately. Inna's "don't be embarrassed" (2:9) strengthens an image of her as a person to whom the patient may say anything. Encouraged by this, Pavel might presuppose substantial support from Inna, for example that she would be careful about expressing correctly what he mentions as "going for a pee", a formulation which he might himself take to be a bit out of place. Throughout the sequence, he provides laughter, probably intended partly as a way of modifying this somewhat awkward expression. This seems to have a reciprocal impact on the interpreter's 'footing', and consequently on the organization of the interaction.

There is a relatively good, although limited, chance of the nurse seeing that Pavel is very embarrassed and is searching for words. It may even be clear to her that this is precisely what Pavel and Inna are discussing. However, she apparently does not approve of being largely excluded from the ongoing activity. Given that she is aware of Pavel's distress, she may either be insensitive to it or deliberately want to counteract it. From the perspective of a clinician, or a person used to frank discussion of sex, talk on the present topic is nothing to feel shame at. If this is what she wishes to communicate, she needs the assistance of Inna. In any case, Nina sees herself as having a legitimate right to claim the interpreter's services right away. In this situation, the interpreter also has her own face to save. Performing 'role distance', Inna simultaneously performs 'face-work' in response to Nina's admonition to cover up for not yet having translated fully.

Moreover, even if the nurse, as she claims, sees the interpreter mainly as a tool for communication, Inna may identify with the patient as, for instance, a woman, an educated person, a mother, an immigrant and a fellow countrywoman. In the passages cited above, the interpreter gradually takes on a neutral attitude to the matter talked about (which in this case coincides more with the nurse's position), but early in the interview – when the issue of possible symptoms of sexual diseases had just been brought up and Nina started to talk in a matter-of-fact manner about them – Inna's stumbling and hesitating talk revealed a certain embarrassment. In all probability she, as well as the patient, had not been exposed to information on sexual matters in school or any other public setting with mixed sexes in her former home country. Inna's and the young man's shared awareness of having a feeling of shame in common may in fact add to a mutual unease.

These facts would indicate that Inna indeed is understood not only as interpreter, but also in (activity) roles such as those mentioned above. Potentially, then, she also has the face of these roles to save. Inna's awkwardness, connected to the fact that she can see these different faces as threatened, must be counted as a contributing reason why she gets involved in exchanges with the nurse and the patient separately. No doubt 'face-work' may obstruct an interpreter's concentration and active listening. In other words, the demand for face preservation must be counted as a factor adding considerably to the complexity of the interpreter's task.

The more the patient himself repeated his own words, the less his interrupted and fragmented utterances seemed to count as ready and valid contributions to focused interaction. His talk consisted to quite a large extent of interrupted onsets, hedges, and other typical features of spontaneous speech. Even if Inna had been listening very actively in order to memorize Pavel's exact words, she would certainly have realized that this is practically impossible. In addition to these cognitive constraints, and perhaps more importantly, there are certain social constraints involved in repeating others' false starts, blowing sounds and searching for words.

4. "IT'LL ALL BE HUNKY-DORY"

The last two examples in this chapter, (3) and (4), will show – perhaps even more obviously than the preceding ones – how circumstances tied to the overarching activity type, and its associated activity roles, are indeed intimately and reciprocally connected to the distribution of responsibility between the participants, including the interpreter, for the progression and the substance of interaction. The discussion will focus on the relation between interpreter's role performance and primary interlocutors' expectations as regards team members' communicative competence.

The extracts are from an encounter at a health-clinic. The first one, Example (3), is from the later part of it while Example (4) is taken from closer to the start. The encounter is of the same kind as the one in Example (2), i.e. standard medical check-ups, offered to immigrants and refugees. The nurse, Nelly, meets a family, consisting of the seven-year-old child Clara, her newborn sister, their mother, Marta, father, Felix, and a grandmother, Galia, all recently arrived in Sweden from the USSR.

The number of people taking part in the encounter and their mutual status relations has an evident impact on expectations vis-à-vis the interpreter's, Inna's rights and obligations. Moreover, the mere appearance of a little child may constitute a challenge to the sustaining of participants' common understanding of the current situation and the situationally relevant communicative behaviour.

In Example (3) the first sequence of talk begins where Agnes, the assistant nurse, has entered the room, and the encounter continues with a new kind of activity, the taking of blood tests. In order to make the procedure run smoothly Agnes proposes to start with the little girl. The nurse decides in line with Agnes's idea ("we'll take Clara first"), which Inna relays as a gently-spoken proposal, with Clara as the explicit addressee. Before the child says anything, Marta complies on her daughter's behalf.

(3) (G34:39)
1 Marta: да.
            yes.
2 Nelly: då ska vi se. ska du få sitta här. ((rises, points))
            then let us see. you may sit here.
3 ⌈Inna: садись там. (.) и я с тобой сяду.
            sit there. (.) and I will sit with you.
  ⌊Nelly: i den bruna stolen. och mamma kommer
                            in the brown chair. and mummy comes here
4 ⌈   med här också.
            with you as well.
  ⌊Marta: да.
            yes.

The nurse accepts Marta's "yes" (3:1) as an answer without Clara's compliance. She instructs the little girl where to sit. We may note that this is accomplished by starting with including herself in a common "we" ("then let us see.") (3:2), and by addressing Clara explicitly plus

her mother indirectly "you will sit here" (3:2) "in the brown chair.
and mummy comes here with you as well." (3:3–4). Inna, in turn,
addresses the child in a soft voice, using the imperfective verb aspect
in Russian (conventionally the more polite one), aligning as 'animator'
and 'author' of what could be taken as Nelly's words "sit there",
and adds, on her own behalf, "and I will sit with you." (3:3).

Soon afterwards, Clara, sitting on the brown chair, silently starts
to cry. This calls for increased attention to her on the part of those
gathered next to her, Marta, Nelly, Agnes and Inna. Moreover, a
general change of tone can be heard, adapted to the ears of a distressed child. When Agnes, holding Clara's arm, starts to look for the
vein in which to insert the needle, her voice conveys friendliness
and consolation.

(3) (G34:39)

24	Agnes:	men man ska inte börja gråta i förväg för det är inte
		but there's no need to start crying beforehand because it isn't
25		någe farligt.
		anything dangerous.
26	Inna:	ты знаешь что тебе говорит тётя.
		you know what the lady says to you.
27		не плачь заранее потому что не знаешь,
		don't cry in advance because you don't know,
28		больно это или нет
		if it hurts or not.
	Marta:	((light laughter))

Comparing Agnes' words of comfort with Inna's subsequent rendition, it is particularly interesting to note the interpreter's introduction: "you know what the lady says to you" (3:26), explicitly pointing out "the lady" as the origin of what she is about to say and Clara as
her ultimate addressee. Thus Inna lays out for Clara the participation
framework as seen from the girl's perspective, i.e. she explains that
talk is directed to her, and she is expected to respond adequately
(e.g. stop crying).

Translating Nelly's subsequent question she does the same, explicitly mentioning the nurse as its ultimate source. This also implies
that she appoints herself to the position of the girl's interlocutor.

(3) (G34:39)

29	Nelly:	har du tagit blodprover nån gång Clara?
		have you ever taken any blood-tests Clara?
30	Inna:	Клара, а раньше тебе делали уколы когда-
		Clara, and have you ever had an injection before

31		нибудь тётя спрашивает тебя. Нелли.
		the lady asks you. Nelly.
32	Marta:	делали тебе уколы?
		have you had an injection?
		(.)
33	Clara:	не помню.
		I don't remember.
34	Inna:	jag kommer inte ihåg. ((light laughter))
		I don't remember.

The above excerpt includes one of the few instances where the child utters anything during the whole encounter. On the rare occasions when she is explicitly addressed by a staff member, her mother, as a rule, answers in her place. When she nods for yes or no, or responds by speaking, as in the present case, her involvement is likewise intimately connected to how her mother relates to the utterance addressed to the child.

The nurse's question (in 3:29) is first translated by Inna. Then Marta comes in with a new "translation": "have you had an injection?" (3:32), and after some hesitation the girl answers quietly: "I don't remember" (3:33). The adults' joint efforts have directed Clara's attention to something new, something outside the present upsetting situation. She stops crying and shares for a moment the interactional focus of the encounter. The instance is a neat illustration of how the distribution of speaker–hearer roles in conversation is an outcome of interlocutors' collaboration in and through the process of interaction.

Perhaps not surprisingly, Inna does not translate Marta's "have you had an injection?" (3:32). Indeed, it is a partial repetition of her "own" words. Inna keeps quiet and awaits Clara's answer with the others. For her to take, at this point, the stipulated interpreter's second turn at talk might have meant counteracting Nelly's and Marta's efforts to elicit an utterance from Clara and distracting her attention from what was frightening her. It is obvious that the mother's revoicing of the question was designed to ratify Clara in the role of addressed 'responder'.

Nelly goes on talking softly to the child in order to prevent her feeling miserable. At the same time, Agnes puts a dab of some kind of cream on the girl's right arm.

(3) (G34:39)

35	Nelly:	näe. du ska se. det är inte **alls** sådär farligt
		*no. you'll see. it isn't at **all** that dangerous*
36		som man tror,
		as one thinks,

37	Inna:	да. ну это совсем не опасно как ты думаешь.
		yes. well this isn't at all dangerous as you think.
38	Nelly:	och så när man bedövar med den här salvan då känns
		and then when you numb it with this cream you can
39		det nästan ingenting.
		hardly feel a thing.
40	Inna:	и знаешь что. когда они тебе уже помазали этим
		and you know what. when they have smeared you with this
41		кремом. когда они будут тебе помазать. тогда
		cream. when they smear you. then
42		совсем ничего не чувствуется.
		you don't feel anything at all.

The assistant's decisiveness and quickness in movements is accompanied by Nelly's careful assurances and Inna's concerned renditions of them. When the critical moment, the pricking, comes near, Agnes also does some persuasive talking.

(3) (G34:39)

43	Agnes:	då gör vi såhär att du sitter ända här högst upp på-
		this is what we do you come and sit right back on-
44		på stolen. i hörnet här. här. här. då kommer det här och
		on the chair. in the corner here. here. here. then
	Inna:	да и сделаем так что-
		yes and we'll do it like this that-
	Agnes:	gå jättefint.
		it'll all be hunky-dory.
45	Inna:	так немножко повыше на стуле.
		that's it a little higher on the chair.
	Nelly:	om du håller mamma i andra handen ska vi se då.
		if you hold mummy by the other hand let's see then.
46		kan du flytta dig litegrand.
		could you move a bit.

Monitoring this activity of taking blood-tests, the nurse addresses Clara and indirectly her mother: "if you hold mummy by the other hand let's see then" (3:45). The interpreter is here proposed first and foremost the listenership of 'reporter'. As Nelly continues, however, there is a change in 'footing' within the same utterance. Her addition, "could you move a bit", is by gaze and gestures marked as expecting an addressed 'responder's' reaction from Inna, and indeed she does act from such a position, by word and deed, declaring (in Swedish) her movement and moving a little to the side. Subsequently, she takes a stance from the same position when reacting to Clara's bursting into silent sobbing.

(3) (G34:39)

47   Inna: jag kan sit- jag kan vara här. (.) да. Клара. знаешь
             I can sit- I can be here. (.) yes. Clara. you know
48   сколько я уже ребят видела. как делали. и я
             how many children I have seen already. who've had it done. and I
49   не видела ни одного что- (.) знаешь что. были
             haven't seen a single one that:- (.) you know what. there have been
50   такие. плакали как ты. а потом они так
             those. who cried like you. and afterwards they were so
51   удивились что всё прошло. они так говорят. это
             surprised that it was all over. this is what they say. is
52   уже всё:::? потом им дали красивые картинки, и
             that all:::? then they were given lovely pictures, and
     Marta: (xx xx) ((speaks silently near to the child))
53   Inna: они побежали радостные. (.) да.
             they run away happy. (.) yes.
     Marta: (xx xx) ((speaks silently near to the child))

The last sequence of talk in Example (3) covers the few seconds when a needle goes into the vein of little Clara. As is visible from the transcript, Inna's utterance does not correspond to anything said by a primary party. Instead she provides her own story about other children coming to the clinic and experiencing the same blood-test situation as her young compatriot is now doing.

To me, observing this situation, it is clear that the interpreter did not have any intention of relating with a reporter's listenership to Marta's silent words, which are overlapped and indistinguishable in the recording. Speaking to Clara, Inna does not display any attentiveness either to Nelly and Agnes as listeners or to Marta as speaker.

It is impossible to tell whether or not anyone present (apart from the researcher) pays attention to the interpreter's behaviour at this particular moment as a case where she drops her normal ambition of memorizing and conveying others' talk; that is, in principle, as a cast of norm-breaking.

4.1 Children in interpreter-mediated interaction

Example (3) could serve to illustrate the reciprocal dependency between interpreters' role performance and the environment in terms of constellation of people and their respective verbal and

non-verbal activities and social relations. We just observed that the
loosening of the frames for the focused gathering-for-talk situation
coincides with Inna's behaviour being less strict in relation to the
normative role of interpreter. Where the excerpt started people had
begun to move from where they were sitting around a table. Some
walked, in accordance with the nurse's suggestion, towards the chair
set aside for blood-tests. Others moved in the same direction but
stayed close to a window where they ultimately formed a separate
group. The child took her assigned place, holding her mother's
hand. Marta squatted by her daughter's side. Inna placed herself
close to the girl on the opposite side of the chair. I stayed where
I was, at a table in the background.

Quite a lot of verbal activity from this relocation procedure can
be heard on the tape. It is hard to distinguish what exactly people
talk about, but in the situation it was clear that Inna talked, and
did so on her own behalf rather than in the name of others. Galia
and Felix, staying by the window, continued to talk in the background, to each other and to the baby. It was evident to me that
none of the primary participants at this point directed talk to Inna so
as to get in touch with another person. The others' communicative
behaviour rather supported and presupposed her as an 'ordinary'
co-interlocutor responding on her own behalf and listening only on
her own account. Primary parties' moving about in the room seems
to be a circumstance which enables occasional redefinitions of the
interpreter-mediated talk as system of activity, and, consequently,
allows the interpreter momentarily to distance herself from her
occupational role.

Most people have their own experiences of being 'pricked' by
nurses and doctors in their childhood. Few would claim they had
a say in the matter. Another point to be made in connection with
the above sequence concerns small children's highly flexible status
as co-interlocutors. A child can abruptly be transformed/transform
her- or himself from a person talked and listened to, into an object
talked about and vice versa. When someone is unskilled in the art
of following or maintaining the common focus of interaction (or
expected to be so), this seems to happen regularly. In the above-
analysed part of the encounter this means that the person who
speaks least appears to be the one who exercises the greatest influence on the interpreter's role performance. Even if Inna remains
principally 'the interpreter', occasionally (when Inna and Clara
attend to each other) she simultaneously distances herself from this

role and comes across rather in the role of 'kind lady', comprehensible first and foremost by the child.

In general, where Clara was talked to or about, Inna's talk was designed to gain the child's attention and keep it on a common focus of discourse; to make her feel involved as co-interlocutor. It could be noted that her way of addressing the child differs from the approach favoured by the nursing staff. For instance, Agnes was indirect, using the impersonal referent *man* ("you", "one") when she told the child not to start crying beforehand (3:24), while Inna was more direct "don't cry in advance" (3:27). Partly, this may be due to cultural differences in what is considered appropriate to request from a child, in general, and in the presence of its parents. Partly, the discrepancies are due to the various relations Clara has established with the two ladies – Agnes and Inna – in the situation. What Agnes conveyed through non-vocal activity repelled rather than attracted the little girl. Moreover, the possibility of Agnes getting in touch with the child through talk presupposed Inna's assistance. Inna, in turn, had worked on establishing contact with Clara ever since Nelly decided that the girl should be the one to begin the test. Simultaneously with the interpreter being loyal to the representatives of the institution and their plans for the encounter, she also acted as Clara's ally. Indeed the coordinating aspect of her work was foregrounded before the translating one. And, no doubt, she achieved more sharedness and closeness with Clara than the assistant nurse did.

Of course, the fact that Agnes was to be understood by a seven-year-old person had a great impact on Inna's role performance. She adapted and extended prescribed standards in order to involve the child. The interpreter's efforts were designed to console and comfort Clara, as well as to make her comply with the plans of the nursing staff.

5. "ABOUT FOUR YEARS AGO?"

Example (4) topicalizes some specific features of interpreter-mediated interaction involving more than two primary interlocutors, occasionally all engaged in the communicative exchange. We may observe how the interpreter works at sustaining the definition of the situation partly by protecting one team-member's current position as ratified interviewee. Moreover, amusement is used as a resource to create a shared focus. The example, which will be presented in three short excerpts, starts when Nelly is in the middle of interviewing the oldest member of the family, Galia. The nurse follows a standard routine, filling in a sheet of questions, and so far she has noted the old woman's present health problems. When Nelly moves on to previous causes of medical treatment, Marta reminds her mother-in-law about an operation, and Galia recalls the incision on her gall-bladder. Nelly follows up:

(4) (G34:11)

→ 1   Nelly: när var det ungefär?
                    when was this roughly?

   2   Inna: когда это было?
                    when was this?

   3   Galia: °а когда это у меня было?
                    °*and when was it I had this?*

   4   года четыре тому назад?°
                    about four years ago?°

   5 ⌈Marta: °н::: два два года по-моему.°
     | °*n::: two. two years I think.*°
     |Felix: °(когда это было?)°
     ⌊   °(*when was this?*)°

   6   Galia: °нет четыре.°
                    °*no four.*°

   7   Felix: °нет три года.°
                    °*no three years.*°

   8 ⌈Galia: °так что. ведь четыре?°
     | °*what then. probably four?*°
     |Marta: °два или три. три года назад.°
     ⌊   °*two or three. three years ago.*°

   9 ⌈Felix: °три года назад.°
     | °*three years ago.*°
     |Inna: когда **три** года назад?
     ⌊   *when?* **three** *years ago?*

  10 ⌈Galia: сейч-
     | *now-*
     ⌊Felix: примерно три года.
                   about three years ago.

When Inna has repeated, in Russian, Nelly's question "when was this?" (4:2), Galia repeats it a second time, "and when was it I had this?", and suggests an answer: "about four years ago?" (4:4). This turns out to be the beginning of a negotiation.

Galia addresses her daughter-in-law (who is at her side), speaking with her voice lowered and with a questioning intonation, thus underlining by vocal and non-vocal means that this utterance is not yet intended to be counted as the answer. She wants it first to be sanctioned. Marta, however, comes up with a counter-suggestion: "n ::: two. two years I think." (4:5). At this point Felix engages in what is already an internal discussion among the Russian-speaking visitors.

Galia persists in her first bid and there follow another two rounds of negotiation during which the correct year for the operation is being established. The family members display engagement with the issue, partly overlapping each other's talk. Then Inna comes in, repeating again Nelly's question "when?", and expands with a suggestion corresponding to the young couple's opinion "three years ago?" (4:9). One may note that Inna has now twice disambiguated Nelly's question in a way which implies a slight up-grading of the level of specification. If Nelly's original request signalled a tolerance towards inexactness, the family may have got the impression that quite an accurate response is expected.

As it seems, Galia thinks the answer Felix once more has confirmed as correct – "about three years ago" (4:10) – is unsatisfactory. She continues on the same issue, counting from the current year:

(4) (G34:11)

11 ⌈Galia: сейчас восемьдесят девятого,
           now it's eighty-nine,
    Inna: dom räknar.
                       they're counting.
    Marta: восемьдесят шестой год.
                       in eighty-six.
   ⌊Nelly: ja
                       yes

12 ⌈Inna: °räknar åren.° åttinio,
                       °count the years.° eighty-nine,
   ⌊Nelly: ungefär då. som-
                       roughly then that-

While Galia and her family continue talking, partly in overlap, the interpreter and the nurse simultaneously establish a separate exchange. By informing Nelly about what is happening "they're counting." (4:11), the interpreter satisfies the nurse's possible wish for insight both into what the family is talking about and why their talk is not immediately translated; thus Inna wards off, as it were, a potential competing claim of attention from Nelly, a potential reason for the nurse to lack confidence in her as interpreter and a potential threat of an even more substantial split of the interactional focus.

The exchange in Swedish runs in parallel without competing with the ongoing Russian talk until Inna markedly raises her voice in mid-utterance. She translates a year just mentioned by Galia. The change in loudness corresponds to the interpreter's change of 'footing' "°count the years.° eighty-nine," (4:12).

Being acquainted with what the visitors' talk is about, Nelly reminds the group that she does not need an exact figure: "roughly then. that- " (4:12). This could be heard as a contribution envisioning a reason from either Galia or her spokesperson (potentially including Inna). That is, Nelly asks whoever knows approximately to please provide the required information.

Yet one function of Inna's marked changed volume in repeating the date given by Galia is of course to make Nelly see that she, the interpreter, is not in a position to convey what Nelly asks for. From her perspective, information on the current issue has to come from Galia, the one who is interviewed. This does not necessarily mean that Galia herself claims that her own word is the most valid one.

(4) (G34:11)
```
13  Galia:    a?
              what?
14 ⌈Marta:   нет. восемь- даже два года назад.
   |          no. eighty- even two years ago.
   ⌊Galia:                        восемьдесят четвёртого,
                                  in eighty-four,
15 ⌈         по-моему операция была.
   |          I think the operation was.
   ⌊Marta:   нет.
              no.
16 ⌈Felix:   нет. примерно три года.
   |          no. about three years.
   |Inna:          mellan fyra, tre och två
   |                between four, three and two
   ⌊Nelly:   ((laugh))
   ⌈Inna:    ((laugh)) ska dom enas.
   |                they are coming to an agreement.
17 |Felix/Marta:  (xx xx) ((laugh))
   |Galia:                   забыла ((laugh))
   |                         forgot
→  ⌊Inna:                        когда?
                                 when?
```

Marta apparently hears her mother-in-law's "what?" (4:13) as a new request for her opinion. And indeed, Galia tries again to get support (4:15) and Marta again disconfirms (in 4:15) as does her husband (in 4:16). Inna subsequently once more describes – this time in further detail – what the family is doing (in 4:16). Her talk functions to inform Nelly of the substance of their talk at the same time as she brings the negotiators' attention to the fact that the nurse and herself are waiting for them to get ready to continue.

If Inna a moment ago spoke quietly, she now talks in a loud voice, with some cheerful expressiveness. The interpreter's amused account of the family members' talk initiates convergence around a common focus of interaction. Inna's rendition is met by Nelly's laughter, and subsequently joint laughter is released among the adults of the group. Thus, the enjoyment indeed creates a sharedness in interaction.

The extent to which people share a common motive for their respective laughter is of course hard to tell. Galia's subsequent utterance would perhaps imply that she assumes her forgetfulness to be, at least partly, what has provoked the mirth. However, her comment, "forgot" (4:18), is overlapped by Inna's quick new initiative. The interpreter profits from the moment of shared focus to raw attention back to Nelly's initial question "when", and thereby initiates a re-establishment of regular frames for the medical interview.

5.1 Co-authored statements and overlapping talk

Throughout the present interview, the visiting family every now and again cooperates in providing answers to questions that are more or less explicitly directed at various individual members. On the whole, all of the Russian-speaking adults are quite talkative. This means a rather high incidence of discourse activities that are parallel to the one which the interpreter understands herself primarily to be set to coordinate. The interpreter has a central role in the establishment and re-establishment of exchanges between the nurse and the family member she (initially Nina) has assigned in the role of interviewee. Inna, on the basis of her unique position, in and by her flexibility of 'footing', can direct and redirect primary parties to attend to a focus in common, or to divergent issues; to ignore as well as to consider each other as interlocutors. Once again, it is evident that there is an inherent coordinating function in the role of interpreter which can be more or less foregrounded.

Multi-party talk potentially increases the occurrence of side-activities, including verbal ones, given that the situation is socially and culturally defined in a way which allows for this. In the present case, this means that utterances now and then are voiced without necessarily being intended for all to hear and understand. Thus, an interpreter's potential power to relegate and include primary parties' contributions as meant off-the-record and on-the-record respectively may increase with the number of participants. The function is inherent in the typical role of interpreter in face-to-face interaction, but not in the normative role. The norm, as stipulated in Ethical Codes, does not advocate any verbal activity which excludes one or other of the co-present interlocutors. In practice however, these situations do indeed occur.

6. CONCLUSION – CHALLENGES AND COUNTERMEASURES

Normally, only interpreters have immediate access to everything said and insight into the communicative orderliness of an interpreter-mediated encounter. Due to interpreters' unique middle position in interaction, they normally can – and will – take measures to support the establishment of a shared focus and to counter anything identified as a threat to the interaction order. Two kinds of locally occurring circumstances seem to be inherently challenging. One is the situation where primary interlocutors display competing expectations towards the interpreter's alignment, and another is the situation where competing activities – conversational and otherwise – occur.

Sometimes the demands laid upon interpreters by the shared professional Codex are hard to match with primary interlocutors' plans and goals. These demands may be taken to be more or less valid by the primary parties. The officially codified ideas of the role of interpreter are culturally bound.

Occasionally, institutional standards and lay persons' views of what talk should be about, and/or how it should be organized, are difficult to fit together. Moreover, since interlocutors are 'multi-role performers', interpreters embrace a range of social statuses and identities which may also be locally mobilized when 'interpreter' is the current dominant one. For instance, co-actors' shared social identity in terms of national origin, gender, age etc., what Erickson and Shultz (1982:17) term *co-membership*, may become relevant in interaction.

These other identities may promote an interlocutor's understanding of the situation which he or she shares only with the interpreter.

6.1 Competing views and competing activities

In interpreter-mediated encounters, the interaction order may be challenged by primary interlocutors' negotiations of what is being said and meant, as is the case in both Excerpt (1) and (2). Talk about talk means that an issue is touched upon which, in a sense, 'belongs' to the interpreter. When a primary party topicalizes the substance of talk, the ultimate responsibility for the words spoken may become unclear, and, moreover, the interpreter's know-how is indirectly questioned. In my experience, interpreters tend to simply ward away meta-talk, rather than feeding it into the conversation, with the aim of achieving talk which more obviously and concretely connects to the official, institutionally defined issues. In such cases, work on sustaining a common definition of the situation is thus accomplished at the price of imprecision in translations.

In instances where the physical frames of event are altered – for instance, where interlocutors move about in the room, or make use of artefacts, thus integrating new frames of activity in a pervasive way – the participation framework of talk, perhaps not surprisingly, is altered as well. Example (3), where a blood-test was done on little Clara, illustrates this.

Example (3) and (4) demonstrated that multi-party encounters potentially increase the incidence of simultaneously occurring activities, including verbal ones (different 'floors'). Such instances will of necessity provoke measures for interactional coordination. In Example (4) we could see that the interpreter switched between taking co-actors' respective perspectives and adopting a bystander's perspective from which she commented upon current interaction, and this was part of how the regular interaction order was re-established, and a shared focus of interaction ultimately was achieved.

When primary parties do not share a common understanding of how responsibility for the progression and the substance of talk is – or should be – distributed, the interpreter's professional ability is put to the test. At times, primary parties – for instance, small children – may be simply unwilling to communicate on the institutionally given conditions.

In this connection it is worth noting the comments of two paedi-atric practitioners interviewed during my fieldwork in hospitals. They strongly disapproved of what they perceived as interpreters' tendency to engage very actively in convincing children to comply with the requests of nursing staff, for instance, to take a vaccina-tion. The practitioners' negative attitude partly stemmed from their lack of control in the encounter, and partly from their impression of the interpreters as being too authoritarian. In situations where they primarily had wished to establish a rapport and make the child feel comfortable, over-ambitious interpreters had ruined this, they claimed, by taking as their first duty to see to it that the explicitly mentioned goal of the encounter was reached as fast as possible, sometimes without any communicative exchange whatsoever, let alone a negotiated consensus between the child and the doctor.

The more diverse the respective parties' ideas are, the greater the challenge for the interpreter as coordinator. Occasionally, as was demonstrated in all of the above examples, to sustain a single definition of the situation, interpreters sometimes tend to direct the interlocutors' focus on themselves, and to their function in the role of interpreter; to resort to acting from the position of *non-person*,[5] whose contributions to interaction by definition are meant to be 'off-the-record', but who nevertheless has an impact, not necessar-ily on the substance but certainly on the progression of talk.

When primary parties talk in overlap, interpreters' competence in translating and coordinating is put to the test. The ability to manage the communicative event is needed. Roy (1993), exploring an interpreter-mediated exchange involving American English and American Sign Language, summarizes her observations of situations where speech occurred in overlap, in terms of the interpreter's four options. (The author presupposes the typical role performance to imply interpretation of everything said in the preceding turn, at every second turn at talk.)

1. The interpreter can stop one or both speakers and, in that way, halt the turn of one speaker, allowing the other speaker to continue.
2. The interpreter can momentarily ignore one speaker's overlapping talk, hold in memory the segment of talk from that speaker, continue interpreting the other speaker, and then produce the 'held' talk immediately following the end of the other speaker's turn.

3. The interpreter can ignore the overlapping talk completely.
4. The interpreter can momentarily ignore the overlapping talk, and upon finishing the interpretation of one speaker, offer a turn to the other primary speaker, or indicate in some way that a turn was attempted (Roy 1993:350).

In the empirical data I have studied, it can indeed be seen (as in the above excerpts) that interpreters, in cases of overlapping talk, normally are in the position to select one speaker before another, and occasionally, to direct the interlocutors' attention to themselves, and their need for space to talk. Sometimes, however, it is hard to talk at all of 'options' for the interpreter. In an interview study I carried out among community interpreters (Wadensjö 1987), some informants, when speaking about what they found most difficult in their job, mentioned cases where it had been hard to provide delayed interpretation of utterances occurring in overlap, and hard to offer the turn at talk to the party whose contribution had not yet been translated for the reason that the primary interlocutors had simply ignored them, as well as their respective counterpart. Some of the interpreters meant that they at times did not have a chance to even try to halt the flow of speech where necessary.

One interpreter recalled an extreme case where a woman whose child had been taken care of by the authorities visited a social welfare bureau and was supposed to be informed of the measures taken. The interpreter complained that he had had no chance at all to prepare for the commission, and that it had left him with considerable frustration and the question: Is this really what you are supposed to do as interpreter? People shouted at each other, via the interpreter, but without leaving him any space to speak, until the social secretary ordered him to stay with the woman and calm her down while she went away to fetch some colleagues. He felt sorry for the mother, so he did try to comfort her, but at the same time he felt it to be unfair that he thus became associated with the authorities that had put her in this despairing mood.

My personal reflection in this connection would be to urge interpreters to prepare for encounters including conflict; to also anticipate the possibility of stepping aside and waiting, or even walking out, if the conditions to perform the work one is hired for do not seem to materialize. As an interpreter one also needs to learn how to support the establishment of communicative interaction between quarrelling antagonists, and how to perform as an interpreter without denying the parties their right to be (and their responsibility for being) angry with one another.

With training, interpreters can gain greater insight into the dynamics of conversational participation framework, and flexibility in shifting from one participation status to another in relation to what is heard and said. With training, interpreters can learn to utilize these shifts in the coordination of primary interlocutors' conversations. An ability to keep in mind various production and reception formats – to look through them analytically and to keep them apart – is essential in the performance of interpreters.

What interpreters on duty say is responsive to the primary interlocutors' immediately prior talk. In an interpreter-mediated conversation, the progression and the substance of talk, the distribution of responsibility for this among co-interlocutors, and what, as a result of interaction, becomes mutual and shared understanding – all will to some extent depend on the interpreter's words and deeds. And this is of course true regardless of how the individual interpreter may cope with his or her task; whether the interpreting is perceived as successful, adequate, poorly done, and so forth. The interpreter's power – and responsibility – stems from the position in between.

Nevertheless, fluctuations of participation framework necessarily result from *participants' joint activity*. In a similar way, the development of misunderstandings depends on interlocutors' collaboration (cf. Bremer *et al.* 1996). The general tendency in interaction to attribute guilt to someone in particular, especially when misunderstandings are discovered or feared, is due to the limited perspective of individual actors in the here-and-now situation. In a detailed analysis it is possible to discover the complexities of connections between interlocutors' contributions (cf. Linell 1995). This will be explored in greater detail in Chapter 8, problematizing the nature of shared understanding and its opposite, miscommunication.

NOTES

1. For further discussion on communicative genres and the potentials of this analytical tool in research on speaking practices, see e.g. Bergmann and Luckmann (1995).
2. Quotations translated from post-interview made in Swedish.
3. Quotations translated from post-interview made in Russian.

4. As a side-point one could mention that when asked if there are, in his opinion, things that interpreters generally ought to, and/or ought not to do, the patient followed a chain of association very different from the one Nina had taken. He spoke of the possible duties interpreters may have in reporting to something corresponding to the Soviet KGB. However, he argued, in Sweden, a person who gets sacked (which would be the expected consequence of not collaborating with the secret police) can always get other employment.
5. cf. Goffman (1990:141–65) and Chapter 4:1.4.

EIGHT

Communication and miscommunication

Die laxere Praxis in der Kunst geht davon aus daß sich das Verstehen von selbst ergiebt [. . .] Der Grund dieser Ansicht ist also die Identität der Sprache und der Combinationsweise in Redenden und Hörenden. [. . .] Die strengere Praxis geht davon aus daß sich das Mißverstehen von selbst ergiebt und daß Verstehen auf jeden Punkt muß gewollt und gesucht werden (Friedrich Schleiermacher [1819] 1959:86).[1]

One likes to think that the interpreter's professional skill should guarantee the avoidance of misunderstanding. Accordingly, primary interlocutors, when experiencing problems with understanding, naturally seek guidance and support from the interpreter. And if the interpreter's efforts do not compensate for a felt lack of understanding, people may attribute this lack to a failure on the part of the interpreter. But who is to blame if, for instance, a social worker and his client misunderstand one another? Am I, as interpreter? Do I translate 'to the best of my ability', if I suspect misunderstanding between the primary parties without pointing this out to them? What if my efforts to prevent misunderstanding clarifies for one of the parties and obscures for the other? To what extent, or in what sense, is others' shared understanding the responsibility of the interpreter?

1. PROBLEMATIZING 'UNDERSTANDING'

The present chapter aims to elaborate further on the question of the interpreter's rights and responsibilities by problematizing 'understanding' in conversation, and its opposite – miscommunication. To underline the dialogical[2] theoretical framework presupposed, 'miscommunication' is preferred to 'misunderstanding'. *Miscommunication* within a particular communicative exchange is taken as *lack of fit between the sense aimed at by one interlocutor, and what is displayed by another as the sense made of the current message.*

Having, as a rule, immediate access to what is said by all others present, my capacity as interpreter to foresee and see through how people make sense of interaction is unique. Seeing a need for suppressing or counteracting miscommunication interpreters tend to act in order to do this, sometimes at the expense of exactness in translation. Detailed analyses of discourse data should make it possible to detect the interactional conditions for the occurrence of this kind of activity, and its intended and unintended consequences.

1.1 Understanding – a public, cooperative activity

If understanding in dialogue involves mutuality and reciprocity,[3] so does misunderstanding. Understanding, whether failed or accomplished in and by interaction, is at some level a shared social activity (cf. Bremer *et al.* 1996). When there is understanding between interlocutors it means that their communication is characterized by sharedness and mutuality. Miscommunication implies a *lack* of shared and mutual understanding between people who are in the process of interacting, identified by at least one interlocutor.

It takes a minimal amount of sharedness for an encounter to be established and sustained as such. When interaction is established – and since communication takes for granted a certain degree of reciprocity – interlocutors most of the time do experience a certain mutual understanding. Ordinarily, it takes quite strong indications before a recipient understands others' talk as not making any sense whatsoever.

Even where interlocutors hold a hostile or suspicious attitude towards one another, an exchange of talk is impossible without a minimal amount of mutuality, at least concerning the current interaction order. Learning to be an interlocutor involves acquiring the means to mark mutual understanding, or to make up for actual and suspected miscommunication. Schegloff, Jefferson and Sacks (1977), in their pioneering paper on 'the organization of repair in conversation', showed in detail how competent communicators in an ordinary conversation make use of such means, rather than letting interaction collapse.

As interlocutors we have a number of ways to routinely check the existence of intersubjectivity between us. Instances where we make use of such routines reveal our experience or our fear of lack of fit between understandings. This implies that possible and actual sources of miscommunication can appear as factors *promoting* communication.

1.1.1 Understanding – protecting one's own world view

To interact in a conversation means to step out (at least at some level) of one's own frame of mind into that of others. Interlocutors' failure or unwillingness to take the other's perspective – and to acknowledge the possible existence of divergent opinions or attitudes – challenges reciprocity and mutuality, and ultimately results in miscommunication. Either this is compensated for, or the conversation ceases to exist. Connor-Linton (1995) argues that some and perhaps much misconception, at one level of meaning, is used in itself as a means to communicate meanings of social identity, of inclusion and exclusion. He analyses the exchange that took place in a 'spacebridge' meeting, a talkshow that was broadcast live between the USSR and the US (with on-line simultaneous Russian–English, English–Russian interpreting). This was at the beginning of the 1980s and the audience, two groups of 'ordinary' people placed in two television studios, one in each country, were supposed to interact with one another. The author identifies numerous instances of what he, following Gumperz (1982a, 1982b), terms 'crosstalk' – cross-cultural miscommunication. Agreeing on the basic goals of an exchange, but rejecting some of the premises given by the counterpart, interlocutors can protect and argue for their own identity and world view (Connor-Linton 1995:321) (cf. also Gumperz 1992). For instance, persons in the US audience raised questions like: "We would protest wildly if the state treated a person like Sakharov the way you do. Why don't you let people move freely in and out of the town of Gorky?" A couple of people in the Soviet audience responded, but took the questions as concerning their personal opinion of Gorky (today renamed Nizhny Novgorod) or of the Nobel Prize winner Sakharov. In their answers "we" and "you" were ascribed to the people currently sitting in the two television studios. Thus, they did not agree to the "we" = the people of the US, and the "you" = the Soviet state or the people of the USSR, presupposed by the question.

It is worth paying attention to the fact that the interaction analysed by Connor-Linton involved mediating parties. Apart from the interpreters there were two show-hosts, one in each studio, neither of whom displayed any problem with understanding their respective studio guests. On the contrary, they were explicitly making sense of the interaction by summarizing and linking together speakers' contributions, seeing to it that communication went on.

1.1.2 Understanding – incomplete and responsive in nature

One perhaps likes to think that good interpreting should guarantee full understanding. As an interpreter I may experience full understanding of others' talk, and give the primary interlocutors a similar sense of completeness. Yet complete understanding cannot be found except in a complete world. From a more global perspective, understanding is by necessity *partial and fragmentary* (Rommetveit 1985). An utterance never has one meaning in and of itself. As Bakhtin (1979) argues in his essay on speech genres, its meaning is never closed, and it can therefore always be understood and interpreted beyond any given interpretation (Bakhtin 1979:263–4). A communicative exchange can be seen as consisting of practical problem-solving routines in situated action. Interlocutors engage in achieving *sufficient understanding of current communicative activity*, that is, an understanding that makes it meaningful for participants to proceed with the shared activity.

If individuals in conversation generally speak without particularly reflecting on talk as such, it is not unlikely that interpreters develop a certain ability to do this. The simple fact that they occasionally are searching for words to match given formulations indicates one type of reflection on talk. Moreover, primary participants involved in interpreter-mediated talk may find reason – and time – to reflect upon what they are saying and how. The conditions for reflection on one's own talk differ, of course. For instance, when utterances are short and one speaker spontaneously and rapidly succeeds another, this demands a different kind of involvement than, say, an exchange which consists mainly of one party's rehearsed, monologically performed information.

Again, from a more global perspective, to reflect upon one's own speech while talking is not always within reach, neither for interpreters nor for primary interlocutors. And when it is, it can be done only partly. Bakhtin explains this by referring to speakers' basic need to receive others' responses in order to understand their own talk. Even when I am speaking to myself, my understanding of a particular utterance is partly shaped by imagining others' responsive understanding (Bakhtin 1979:290).

Given that understanding is *responsive in character*, interpreters' utterances in interaction display different aspects of their understanding of the primary interlocutors' talk. Interpreting is, if you wish, *answering* (in Bakhtin's sense) from the culturally and socially defined role of interpreter.

1.2 Miscommunication events

Regardless of people's preparedness and ability to take others' viewpoints while communicating, an unconscious bias is constitutive for social interaction. As a speaker, I cannot reflect on all the contextual conditions, preconditions, connections, etc., which a particular utterance depends on. Leaving things partly unexplained is in itself a precondition for communication with others. Interlocutors have to rely on each other's sincerity in communicating what they seem to communicate; on each other's preparedness to respond adequately. The mere fact that people interact in conversation implies the existence of a *contract* concerning the common activity, to use a central notion in Rommetveit's (1974) social psychology.

In his book *On Message Structure*, Rommetveit (1974) suggests that explorers of the socio-psychological foundation of intersubjectivity should look at what happens when the foundation appears to break down. The orderliness of social processes is likely to become most visible, he argues, when the expected order is at stake. The process of creating shared understanding would thus come most to the fore in instances where interlocutors are actively seeking it but have apparent trouble in achieving it (Rommetveit 1974:52).

A number of features of discourse may indicate that interlocutors sense miscommunication. According to Linell (1995) these can be identified as *miscommunication events*, which implies a diagnosis related to *indicators in the discourse itself*. Miscommunication is sensed, identified and/or dealt with at instances of:

repairs, or at least repair initiations, such as clarification requests;
(meta-)comments, related to understanding problems;
negotiations of meaning, incongruent threads of discourse;
non-interlocking utterances, incoherence and hitches in dialogue,
    salient silences within topics, i.e. lack of uptake;
vocal or non-vocal signs of uncertainty, irritation, uncomfortableness (Linell 1995:188).

Using 'miscommunication event' as an analytical unit, this chapter will shed light on how factors combine in problems of understanding; on the complexity of their genesis and development. They may also be used to pinpoint possible causes contributing to the appearance of miscommunication in a concrete situation.

As Linell points out, the dialogic nature of miscommunication events revealed through close reading of transcripts and repeated listening to tapes may never be immediately visible to interlocutors-in-action. Speakers tend to relate interlocutors' displayed understanding to their own self-perceived intent and, in cases of misfit, perhaps blame the other for misunderstandings but do not see their own part in them (Linell 1995:207). Acting in the role of interpreter, one probably has a better opportunity than as a primary interlocutor to see that (and perhaps why) others talk on different discourse trajectories without noticing this themselves. Regardless of level of professional skill and experience, however, one does not share the position of a detached analyst. Interpreters on duty are at the same time both distanced from and involved in interaction.

1.2.1 Analysing miscommunication

In the analyses below I will make a general division between 'trouble sources' tied to the *local*, turn-by-turn organization of talk, and *global* 'trouble sources', which would refer to the different interlocutors' respective views, beliefs and attitudes in relation to subject matter, to the encounter and to one another (cf. Chapter 5:3.3 above, on different notions of context).

Bremer (1996) suggests for analyses of understanding problems in intercultural encounters (dialogues involving two individuals, a minority worker and a majority interviewer, communicating in a language which one of them was learning and the other commanded as a native) a distinction between lack of shared background assumptions on the one hand, and individuals' linguistic competence on the other (Bremer 1996:37). This would partly correspond to my 'global' and 'local' levels. Yet, when looking for triggers, reasons and supporting factors for understanding problems in encounters involving more than two participants, there is reason to further distinguish, at the local level, between those tied to *linguistic* factors (understanding based on words spoken, in relation to linguistic, prosodic and phonetic standards in a given language), and 'trouble sources' tied to the local *coordination* of communicative efforts (understanding

based on words spoken, in relation to agency and addressivity conveyed – verbally or non-verbally – when speaking).

In order to sort out levels where possible 'trouble sources' may
occur in interpreter-mediated encounters, this chapter will analytically distinguish, on the 'global' level, between factors tied, on the
one hand, to participants' expectations and knowledge concerning
the institutional encounter in which talk occurs (patient–doctor consultation, police-interrogation, etc.) and, on the other, assumptions
and beliefs as regards *interpreter-mediated conversation*.

'Local' factors	'Global' factors
'Local' 'linguistic' problems	Discrepant views of institutions
'Local' coordination problems	Discrepant views of interpreters

In interpreter-mediated conversation, the communicative links where
shared understanding and/or miscommunication may be identified go not just between the primary interlocutors, but also – and
simultaneously – between each of these and the interpreter (as separate dyads) and between the three as a triadic group.

In conclusion to this first section, I will use a fellow interpreter's on-
the-spot account of an assignment to more concretely demonstrate
– from the perspective of an interpreter on duty – how the analyses
count on the presence of diverse levels of understanding.

1.3 Ingrid's story: on various levels of understanding

Ingrid works as an interpreter with Russian-speaking refugees in
Denmark. Once she had an assignment at a camp for refugees where
a social worker met a family of four, a husband and wife with two
small children. They were newcomers in the country and at the
camp. Introducing himself and his family, the husband mentioned
their origin as being Armenian. One of the first things he pointed
out was that Armenians are Christians, and Ingrid quotes his statement: *vveli christianstvo usche v 301 godu do nashej ery* ("Christianity
was already introduced [by the Armenians] in the year 301 BC.")
The last part, "before Christ" (in Russian: *do nashej ery*, lit. "before
our era"), Ingrid says she deliberately left out. (It is impossible to
tell, however, whether she wilfully decided to interpret as she did, or
if she interpreted automatically, as it were, but, on second thoughts,
wanted to explain the omission.) After the encounter, she told the

social worker that she had left out this part of the man's remark and explained why.

Taking Ingrid's point of view, and analysing her explanation (as she retold it to me), I have sorted out some important dimensions of understanding present in interpreter-mediated interaction.

Ingrid understood the man's utterance to be a comical contradiction, and she was afraid that translating it as such would make it difficult for her to keep a straight face, knowing herself – and also the social worker, a woman of her own age – to be easily provoked to laughter. Hence, there was the risk of making the man feel ridiculed, not only in front of two foreign women, but also in front of his wife and children. A 'close' translation, she felt, would have involved a danger of damaging the authority of someone who was trying to present himself as the knowledgeable head of the family, while, at the same time, his talk put him in precisely the opposite light. Of course, this is partly what made the situation comic.

In sum, one dimension of Ingrid's understanding is triggered by what the man said, as a *decontextualized utterance*, another by the way *the speaker* presented himself as an *individual and as a team member* (e.g. as a member, of a family, of an ethnic group). A third dimension of her understanding is formed by the way she interprets the needs and expectations of *other persons* present; by her understanding of others' understanding.

Ingrid's interpreting in this situation thus seems to have been concentrated on the second and third dimensions. She understood the refugee's utterance, including the added "before Christ", to be meant, first and foremost, as an expression of his and his family's belonging in the new country. Emphasizing the Armenians' Christian faith, the man defines himself as part of a certain religious and cultural sphere; as being not Muslim, even if Armenia is geographically placed in an area of Islamic countries. Anticipating possible xenophobic feelings towards people of other religion, colour, way of dressing and talking etc., he presents himself and his family by focusing on an obvious similarity between Armenia and the host country.

Ingrid told me this story because she wished to question the relevance of interpreters' obligation always to translate everything said by primary parties. She remembered this as one of the few cases when she had deliberately restrained from translating part of an original. After the encounter she brought the social worker's attention to this particular utterance precisely because she felt a need to legitimate her violation of the basic interpreters' rule – not to omit anything. When Ingrid confessed the omission, however, the social worker did not immediately see what difference the last words would have made. More precisely, her inclination to see any humorous aspect in the statement which Ingrid had only partly translated was practically non-existent. Eventually she did see the funny side, but she also said that she would probably have paid no attention to it in the encounter. Meeting the family, she had been totally occupied thinking about accommodation, childcare and other practical matters. Moreover, she meant that to her, having no religious inclination of her own, the information about Armenians being Christians seemed to have no relevance whatsoever.

The example shows that interpreters on duty (as well as researchers exploring interpreter-mediated interaction) must be aware of and count on the currency of frames of reference for understanding which are only partly shared between the persons interacting. The institutional frame is valid at some level, at least for the professional party. Lay people involved may simultaneously orientate themselves according to different understandings of the situation and its participants. Finally, the interpreter-mediated mode of communication provides an additional frame of reference, imposing its own rationalities as regards possible interpretations of words, utterances, persons and situations.

2. "WE MISUNDERSTOOD EACH OTHER . . ."

Following the interactionist line of thought, all actors in any conversation have interpretative work to do. The presence of an interpreter does not liberate the primary interlocutors from actively seeking understanding and taking the perspective(s) of their interlocutor(s). Understanding in interpreter-mediated encounters derives from at least three persons' (more or less) joint efforts. But people normally develop routines to control intersubjectivity in direct, monolingual interaction, routines which are partly suspended in interpreter-mediated conversations. The primary parties' ability to read markers of miscommunication, and thereby to control interaction, is of necessity limited. The involvement of an interpreter can substantiate the primary parties' impression of sharedness in understanding also at points where there is little reason for this. It is part of the interpreter's 'contract', to use Rommetveit's business metaphor, to take over some of the primary parties' work of understanding one another.

Because of its specific character, comprising at once two dialogues within one triadic conversation, the interpreter-mediated conversation provides unique scope for exploring the evolution of shared understanding and of miscommunication. In the following excerpts I will centre on how interpreters work on overcoming problems of understanding when these are sensed or identified.

Taking the point of view of interpreters, I will explore what kinds of miscommunication they – the interpreters – take responsibility for counteracting, and how. Apart from the questions of *what* causes of comprehension problems can be identified, *if* and *how* these are dealt with, the analysis will also be guided by the question *who* experiences lack of shared understanding, and *with whom* does he or she share this experience.

The first three sets of excerpts were recorded at the immigration department of a local police station, and the latter two at a healthcare clinic and a childcare clinic. In the first short sequence of talk the two primary interlocutors both fear misunderstanding. One of them even mentions explicitly his experience of mutual misunderstanding. Looking closer at discourse one individual's mishearing of a certain gloss and/or another's mispronunciation of it can be identified as 'locally' occurring 'trouble sources'. Other 'locally' manifesting 'trouble sources' would be the interpreter's missing vocabulary, and/or that, in her talk, Russian linguistic conventions interfere with Swedish, and/or that a primary party lacks sensitivity for her markers of turn-taking. At a 'global' level of discourse, these instances would indicate that interlocutors' insufficient language proficiency could count as 'trouble sources'. Another 'globally' present 'trouble source' is the participants' differing views of the interpreter's responsibility for the content of talk and for the distribution of turns at talk.

All excerpts show how the interpreter sees to it that the primary parties are, at one level, on the same track and that communication proceeds. The primary interlocutors' respective experience of lack of shared understanding is handled in somewhat different ways. The problem identified with the layperson is dealt with in common interaction, while the professional's experience of misunderstanding is dealt with 'off-the-record'.

In the first excerpt, Anton has his first interview as an applicant for residence permit in Sweden (cf. Chapter 6:4). Peter, a police officer takes care of his case, and Ilona interprets between them. We come in where the officer brings up the issue of housing. His inquiries concern how the applicant's and his family's needs are being met.

(1) (G21:11–12)

1 Peter: mm. ((draws breath)) em . . . (2) jo. rent praktiskt? din
         mm   em . . . (2s.) well. just a practical? question. your

2   mamma? hur stor- lägenhet? har hon eller . . . hur hon nu
         mother? how big- flat? does she have or . . . however she now

3   bor. och. hur många personer. bor det. **där**?
         *lives. and. how many persons. live **there**?*

   Ilona: чисто . . .
                                              just a . . .

4   практический вопрос. ((draws breath))
         practical question

5   какая. у вашей мамы. квартира? размеры её.
         what. is your mother's. flat like? its dimensions.

→ 6 Anton: как квар- сейчас?
           what the fla- now?

   Ilona: сколько человек живёт там и . . .
               how many people live there and . . .

           (.)

→ 7 Anton: вот мы сейчас четверо живём. площадь какая?
           well there . . . are four of us living there now. what size
           [lit. area]?

   Ilona: just nu bor vi . . . fyra
                                        at the moment four of us

→ 8   stycken. yt-   yt- menar du ytan?
           are living. ar-   ar- do you mean the area?

→   Anton: площадь какая?
               what area?

           (0.05)

9 Ilona: lägenhetens?
         of the flat?
           (0.05)

→ 10 Peter: utan? lägenhet. (.) näe. i lägenheten menar jag.
           without? flat. (.) no. in the flat I mean.

11 Ilona: hm?
   Peter: ((clears throat))

12   i lägenheten menar jag. (.) ja du- vi missförstod
         in the flat I mean.   (.)   yes you- we misunderstood

13   varandra. jag vill veta hur stor lägenheten
         each other. I want to know how big the flat

14		är. hur många personer som bor **där**.
		*is. how many people are living **there**.*
→ 15	Ilona:	мм, я хочу узнать е::: какая ... размеры. ((swallows))
		mhm, I want to know eh::: what ... the dimensions.
→ 16	Anton:	размеры?
		the dimensions?
→ 17	Ilona:	квартиры и сколько человек вы живёте-
		of the flat. and how many people of you live-

The applicant, it seems (in 1:6, 1:7 and 1:8), has problems with understanding the officer's question concerning housing. It is clear that a description of the mother's flat is needed, but exactly what kind of description? Its size? He has problems with the term *razmery* ("dimensions") (as we may clearly note later, in line 16). This is a non-standard word in Russian when speaking about flats, and it seems to puzzle more than it clarifies. Anton provides an alternative, namely *ploshchad'* ("area"), which is the term conventionally used in Russian when talking about the size of apartments in terms of square metres (and also the measure used by Soviet citizens when they made claims for housing, all state owned, to the authorities). The applicant seemingly fears a lack of shared understanding, so he seeks to clarify, asking repeatedly *ploshchad' kakaja?* ("what size?") (1:7, 1:8). It is as if he expects the interpreter's confirmation, that he indeed has understood correctly that the officer is asking for the size of the flat. But he speaks while Ilona is in the process of translating. What is probably not clear to the applicant is that she tries to make the police officer answer his request. The fact that the applicant and the interpreter have differing preconceptions concerning the distribution of turns at talk, and of the role of interpreter in the local management of talk, is in itself a possible 'trouble source'. It influences communication between the interpreter and the applicant, between the interpreter and the officer, and between all participants in the encounter as a whole.

Checking back while Ilona is talking, Anton contributes to splitting the interpreter's attention. When she translates *ploshchad' kakaja?* (here: "what size?" lit. "area what?"), starting with the term *ytan* ("area"): "ar- ar- do you mean the area?" this indicates that the Russian version interferes with her Swedish one. The police officer stays silent, and Ilona specifies: "of the flat?" (1:8–9). To ask about the size of a flat in this way in Swedish is quite unusual to say the least, which must add to the officer's difficulties in grasping at once what the interpreter means to say. (A more conventional way to ask back in Swedish would be something like: *Menar du hur många kvadrat meter?* "Do you mean how many square metres?") Another problem in the interpreter's formulation is her pronunciation of the word *ytan* ("the area"). The officer hears this as *utan* ("without") (1:10). Most people who have learned Swedish as adults, not least those with a Slavonic language background, pronounce the Swedish *y*-sound with a noticeable accent. (It is a combination of the sounds of 'e' and 'u' in English.) People who are not used to listening to non-natives' talk can sometimes have trouble in comprehending words containing the '*y*'-sound.

In this case, as we note, the officer identifies mutual misunderstanding, and repeats his own question (1:10). His lack of shared understanding, however, is not forwarded to the applicant. Ilona leaves the officer's comment on misunderstanding (which also accounts for why he repeats himself) off the record, and forwards only his remarks on housing.

The applicant subsequently decides, without having had any confirmation, that square metres is the kind of description the officer wants, and gives such an account which Ilona translates. The police officer inserts in the midst of this his conclusion: "that is, a two-room flat", indicating what kind of information he needs. However, by the time the interpreter has finished translating for the other party, who in parallel continues with his project of giving the measurements of each room in the mother's flat in terms of square metres, the comment has already missed its relevance. Peter regardless of the answer continues with *his* project, and introduces a new topic without any further comments.

In the above case, the interpreter is able and willing to support shared understanding that is sufficient for the interview to continue on the topic of housing, but that excludes shared understanding of the officer's lack of shared understanding. Elaborating on the rationality of this behaviour I could point at the following contextual facts.

The applicant's question "what size?" was only one of his many markers of uncertainty and hesitation during the encounter in question. By various means he displayed readiness to offer more, or more detailed information on the subject matter, and simultaneously a general fear of miscommunication. The interpreter had reason to interpret him as a person who needed guidance and confirmation. Often – not only during the particular time when the extract above was recorded – he shifted to the edge of his chair and leaned forward to the officer at the other side of the desk. He realized that much was at stake and knew that his and his family's future life depended on how he handled the situation. He frequently puts the tag "you see?" at the end of his answers and comments. (A 'trouble source' at the 'global' level, as it were, is thus his implicitly not taking mutual understanding for granted.)

Providing a vague, open ending ("and e:::") (1:6) (indicating that she does not know what exactly the officer needs to know about the flat), the interpreter had prompted the applicant to ask back in the official's address. It just so happened that counteracting miscommunication at one end, Ilona introduced a new 'trouble source', which is a primary factor behind the miscommunication identified by the officer.

The officer's explicit comment on misunderstanding (1:12–13) was immediately followed by a repetition of what information he needed, that is, the question concerning housing. Concentrating on the agenda-type of questions, and leaving out the comment on miscommunication, the interpreter made the dialogue continue according to institutional routines. Avoiding being explicit on (mis)understanding, she kept away from giving a possible reason to doubt her own competence.

Besides, the main 'trouble source' triggering miscommunication between the interpreter and Peter (1:8, 1:10) is of necessity hard for Ilona to explain, since it involves the problematic 'y'-sound.

It is in the nature of the interpreter-mediated encounter that only one person – the interpreter – is in practice able to let (mis)understanding become a common issue. The fact that she or he sometimes avoids this may fit perfectly into participants' expectations. Police officers' questioning techniques when interviewing clients, let alone when interrogating suspects, presuppose a certain lack of shared understanding. Police officers who suspect that the person they are interrogating is trying to withhold information will attempt to outwit him or her. Their goal would be to make this person reveal relevant information without being able to see through why it is needed. In other words, police officers' questioning is based on a certain shared understanding about intentions, previous information, presuppositions and so forth, but it also presupposes the existence of differing understandings. Furthermore, it presupposes the questioning party's control of the situation. The fact that the present interpreter deals 'on-the-record' with problems of understanding indicated by the layperson, and 'off-the-record' with those indicated by the officer, fits with these presuppositions. Ilona was, consciously or not, promoting and occasionally reinforcing a prototypical asymmetric pattern between officer and layperson, rather than empowering the weaker party. Asymmetry in interaction can in itself be identified as a 'trouble source' of a 'global' kind.

In the following two excerpts, drawn from later in the same interview it will be all the more clear that shared understanding is not a goal that is mutually sought between Anton and Peter. As has already been indicated in the above excerpt, a significant 'trouble source' at the 'global' level of discourse is the primary parties' differing views as regards what topics are relevant to the exchange.

3. "HAVE BEEN DIVORCED"

We are coming to the end of the interview when Peter, the police officer, takes out a sheet of paper from an old file on his desk. He has obtained some information about Anton beforehand, from the applicant's uncle who is living in Sweden. Anton takes the sole mention of this person's name as a request to provide information about who he is, when he was born and where he lives. The applicant may have presumed that the fact that he has kin in Sweden would improve the family's chances of staying in the country.

The officer, however, has a completely different project of discourse in mind. He mentions the uncle as the provider of the information he currently takes from a "questionnaire for referee". Using this name for the document he cites is one way by which the officer presents himself as commissioner of the immigration authorities, and marks the current interview as a case subject to treatment in accordance with general, official rules.

Only much later, however, the officer gets the information he was fishing for, namely whether the applicant is currently formally married, and, if so, when this marriage took place. As we know, immigration authorities are interested in finding out about marital status, including whether marriages are genuine, and questions raised in certain types of interviews may have the overt or hidden intention of clarifying such circumstances.

In order to get spontaneous and truthful answers, interrogating personnel learn to use different questioning strategies. One common strategy is to quote statements concerning the matter from persons known but not present. Citing from the document in front of him what the referee states about the applicant, the officer invites Anton to provide a first-hand version of the same issue. He expects him – it is implied – to explain, confirm or disconfirm the statement. As I have discussed elsewhere (Wadensjö 1997), however, in the interpreter-mediated conversation this technique of inquiry can appear to be disabled.

(2) (G21:20)

1 Peter: denne man din morbror han skriver nämligen att du är
this man your uncle he writes you see that you are

2 skild från din fru. skild står det.
divorced from your wife. divorced it says

Anton: ((clears throat))

3 Ilona: eh::: и этот человек, сказал что ((swallows)) вы
er::: and this man, said that   you are/were

4 разведены е::: с женой.
divorced er::: from your wife.

5 Anton: мы- мы **были** в разводе.
we- we were/have been divorced (lit.:in divorce).

6 Ilona: ja vi har **varit** skilda
yes we have been divorced.
(0.05)

→ 7 Anton: мы **были** в разводе.
we were/have been divorced.

8 Ilona: vi har **varit** skilda.
we have been divorced.

→ 9 Peter: har **varit** skilda. men . . . numera? vilket förhållande
have been divorced. but . . . nowadays? what relation

10 råder just nu?
is prevailing right now?

11 Ilona: а сейчас какие у вас отношения?
but now what relations do you have?

12 Anton: (.) с кем?
(.) with whom?

13 Ilona: med vem?
with whom?

14 Peter: (.) med din fru.
(.) with your wife.

15 Ilona: с вашей женой,
with your wife,

16 Anton: ну, хорошие, самые нормальные.
well, fine, the most normal ones.

17 Ilona: ja de e . . . trevliga dom bästa förhållanden.
well, it's . . . nice, the best relations.

18	Peter:	mm. frågan är int- har ni **varit** formellt **gifta** och hu-
		*mm. the question is no- have you **been** formally **married** and ho-*
19		hur är **det** förhållandet just nu?
		*how is **that** relation right now?*

When Ilona translates Peter's quote: "this man your uncle he writes you see that you are *divorced* from your wife. *divorced* it says" (2:1–2), Anton comments briefly: "we- we *were* divorced" (2:5). The officer does not immediately respond to this answer, and Anton repeats it anew. The short silence together with the repetition marks Anton's identification of miscommunication. Communicative misfit is apparently noticable to the officer too. Having heard the same answer twice, Peter initiates a repair "*were* divorced. but ... nowadays? what relation is prevailing right now?" (2:9–10). Latching onto the word "were" in the preceding utterance, the officer uses a technique of inquiry which could be called 'format tying' (Goodwin & Goodwin 1987). Since it is an interpreter-mediated conversation, however, potentially *two* individuals may identify as the person the word of which is cited – the primary speaker and the interpreter.

The second, interpreted, version of the officer's question – "but now what relations do you have?" (2:11) – suppresses possible miscommunication as far as its addressivity is concerned. Simultaneously, the applicant is kept uninformed about the officer's comprehension problem and is not reached by his request for clarification as regards the intended meaning of "*were* divorced".

Moreover, in one sense, Ilona's simplified version (2:11) of the officer's question *adds* a certain ambiguity to discourse. Peter's formulation "*were* divorced. but ... nowadays? what relation is prevailing right now?" (2:9–10) is quite vague as it is (I here identify yet another questioning strategy – not to be too explicit in order to elicit spontaneous answers), and without the contrast between the first response part – "*were* divorced" – and the second follow-up part the question becomes even more vague. In addition, where the officer says "relation" (in the singular), Ilona says "relations" (in the plural). This possibly supports Anton's associations towards his everyday experiences of family life, rather than in the direction of his formal marital status.

Peter continues his project of finding out the facts about the divorce. Even if it seems clear that the applicant and his wife are at present lawfully married, the officer still needs to know more about the formal side of the changes in Anton's civil status. Several minutes later they are still on the same topic.

(2) (G21:20–21)

46	Peter:	ha. hu- hur går det **där** till rent formellt? alltså först så
		*see. ho- how do **such** things happen in formal terms? that is first*
47		**skiljer** man sig formellt. har ni **gift** er **igen**? (.)
		*you **divorce** formally. did you then **marry again** (.)*
48		formellt.
		formally.
49	Ilona:	а . . . каким образом это произошло? вначале вы
		but . . . what way did this happen? in the beginning you
50		развелись официально, а потом поженились ещё
		got divorced officially, and then you got married once
51		раз официально.
		more officially.
52	Anton:	её отец приехал к нам в гости. он нас позорил.
		her father came to visit us. he made us quarrel/put shame upon us.
53	⌈	понимаете? ((light laughter))
		you see?
	⌊ Ilona:	hennes- eh::: hennes pappa kom till- och
		her- er::: her dad came to- and
54		hälsade **på** oss och han eh::: han gjorde allt för att eh:::
		visited us and er::: he made everything to er:::
55		((swallows)) det blev bråk mellan oss,
		there was trouble between us,
56	Anton:	а потом мы сошлись. через два года.
		and then we- got together. after two years.
57	Ilona:	och senare, efter två år. blev- vi blev sams igen.
		and later, after two years. became- we made it up.
→ 58	Peter:	ha, 1987, när din morbror skrev det där så. var ni alltså
		see, 1987, when your uncle wrote that so. were you actually
59	⌈	officiellt skilda. **när** gifte ni er sen igen. officiellt.
		*officially divorced. **when** did you marry again then. officially.*
	⌊ Ilona:	знач-
		actu-

Prior to the sequence quoted above, the applicant has told about the
day when he and his wife made it up again, about his son's welcom-
ing him back into the family and other details of his marital life. For
quite some time, Anton takes the officer's question to concern his
personal experience of getting divorced and then remarried again.
He continually reports on how it happened that he and his wife separated, projecting the responsibility for this onto "her father" (2:52).

The officer after some time extracts from what he has heard the
information that the uncle's statement about a divorce was correct
(2:58). This is something he can enter into the report. From here

he can go on to ask about when the applicant got married again. Details of Anton's family life, however, are not registered at all.

The 'trouble sources' identified 'locally' have a parallel on the 'global' level of discourse, without which it is hard to explain the miscommunication event analysed above. It is evident that the applicant and the police officer understand differently the current situation, including what is relevant to talk about in it. Interestingly enough, both parties manage to find support for their respective understandings in what they hear from the interpreter.

It is not unlikely that Anton is aware of the immigration authorities' interest precisely in circumstances concerning marriage and divorce. Subsequently it comes out that the couple remarried just before they left the USSR. To Anton, it might be unclear whether this information is putting him and his wife in a less favourable position as applicants. Perhaps this is why he keeps stressing the fact that they were living together when they were formally divorced. When the officer focuses on the formal side of Anton's marriage, the applicant tries to focus on questions concerning his and his wife's life together as a married couple. His persistence in talking about this has a background in Soviet life, where many divorced couples were forced to live together whether or not they wished to, due to the great lack of housing in many regions. The applicant's story was designed to communicate the fact that he and his wife, in spite of the divorce, had been living together because they wanted to stay as a family.

The officer can see that he and the applicant do not share the same background knowledge, but this does not make him – as the person in charge of the encounter – take measures to clear up differences between their ways of thinking and acting. This is simply not the kind of understanding he works at achieving. The encounter is organized around a standard set of questions, to which he needs to report answers. Those of the applicant's answers that do not fit in are virtually ignored by the officer.

As described in the literature (e.g. Cedersund and Säljö 1993, Sarangi and Slembrouck 1996), the institutional interactional format generally assigns a dominant position to the representative of the organization. This also means that the serving officer gets the best opportunities to voice his or her perspective. A difference between interpreter-mediated and 'ordinary' encounters which this example points to is that in routine cases, where lay and professional perspectives clash, the two different views may still be maintained even if they are communicated (and even if one interlocutor – the interpreter – understands them to be clashing) whereas in a direct dialogue such a discrepancy would ultimately lead to some kind of clarification or to communicative breakdown.

4. "ME OR US?"

Police interrogations are organized around the composition of a police report. In principle, the police officer asks questions and selects relevant parts of the interviewee's answers for inclusion in the report. In the Swedish context, this kind of encounter has a concluding phase which is by definition focused on possible mis-communication. The interviewee is asked to confirm, not confirm or to amend what is stated about him or her, hence the checking routine has a two-fold social implication. On the one hand, the inter-rogated person is given the chance to dismiss something mistakenly noted. On the other hand, by confirming the report as correct the interviewee becomes bound by it in an additional way; he or she is made ultimately responsible for its content.

Police officers may arrange this checking-the-report routine in various ways. Some use a tape-recorder and every now and then dictate the draft text of the report. They thus only record orally a text that is afterwards printed out by another person. In other cases, police officers themselves write down the report during the interroga-tion proper.

The routine of checking the report implies an additional oppor-tunity to trace miscommunication that would otherwise perhaps be hard to discern in discourse. This holds true for its actual readers, as well as for researchers of miscommunication events. Had it not been for the report, the particular miscommunication to be analysed here would scarcely have been realized either by the participants or by me. But while actors taking part in the encounter had no chance to check again how words and utterances actually came out, analysts of transcribed discourse may localize distinctive 'trouble sources'. In the present encounter, a main 'trouble source' 'locally' manifesting itself, is the layperson's reduced opportunity to see what the police officer's question is designed to elicit. It coincides with the existence of what may be termed a 'global' 'trouble source', namely participants' differing understandings of implicit norms of how to address one another; what pronoun to use in order to mark respect and sincerity.

In interpreter-mediated conversations, the written or the not-yet-written (dictated) reports constitute originals to be relayed after the completed interview. The officer reads his or her notes aloud, or plays the tape in sections, and the interpreter works consecutively as before during the encounter. Alternatively, the interpreter reads and translates directly from what is written (so-called 'sight translation'). In the sequence quoted below, this is what happens.

The interview takes place at the immigration department of a local police station, and it concerns prolongation of a temporary residence permit in Sweden. We come in where the final checking-up phase has just begun. Alex is a Russian-speaking young man who recently married a Swedish woman and moved to live with her in Sweden. The police officer, Pia, has been typing up the report while interviewing. Iza, an interpreter often engaged at this particular police station, is translating it aloud into Russian when the applicant suddenly interrupts:

(3) (G26:12)		
123	Alex:	а это- извиняюсь. это что, в множественном?
		but this- excuse me. what is this, in the plural?
124		числе там написано. ((light laughter))
		written there.
125	Iza:	что здесь написано. **de** har inte rest runt i regionen
		what is written here. **they** *did not travel round in the region*
126		i sommar. e::: **они** не разре- не разъезжались по- e:::
		*this summer. er::: **they** did not tra- travel round in- e:::*
127		в области летом.
		in the area during summer.
→ 128	Alex:	я понимаю но она задала вопросы **мне** или
		*I understand but did she put the questions to **me** or*
→ 129		**нам**? я:::
		us? I:::
	Iza:	e::: har du ställt frågan beträffande **mig** eller
		*e::: did you ask the question concerning **me** or*
130		beträffande **oss**?
		*concerning **us**?*

The applicant focuses on a possible mistake in the report (3:123–124). The interpreter reacts to this first by summarizing (in Russian) how she has understood the applicant's question: "what is written here" (3:125). Then she reanimates the relevant sequence in the Swedish text, and provides a new Russian version of it. Emphasizing the personal pronouns *de* ("they") (in Swedish) and *oni* ("they") (in Russian) (3:125–126), Iza confirms that the report indeed involves plural references. Alex, slightly irritated, reformulates his question: "I understand but did she put the questions to *me* or *us*? I ..." (3:128–129).

The interpreter directs the issue towards the officer "e::: did you ask the question concerning *me* or concerning *us*?" (3:129–130). At this point the reading-of-the-protocol procedure has temporarily stopped. A three-party exchange starts, concerning how, in actual fact, the interviewer's preceding questions should have been understood.

Shared understanding between the primary interlocutors is achieved at one level – understanding concerning the fact that some kind of miscommunication had taken place in the past interview. But despite the fact that the primary interlocutors mention and deal with the main 'trouble source', the interpreter seems to be unable, or unwilling, to resolve the shared problem of understanding. This should tell us something about the strength of certain social conventions, including those regarding the use of pronouns of address and the habit of treating languages (here: Russian) as wilful and demanding subjects. This particular interpreter apparently experiences a strong 'taboo' against addressing some of her Russian-speaking clients using *ty*, the informal mode of address. The present case shows some unintended consequences of this reluctance. In Swedish, the *tu*-form is the conventionalized, widely used form. In Russian it is conventionally used between friends, and could, if used between non-acquainted adults, be understood as a marker of disrespect. Conversely, the Swedish *vous*-form would in many cases mark exaggerated respect or even be taken as irony.

After a short silence, the officer replies to the applicant's question concerning "me or us":

(3) (G26:12)

131	Pia:	e::: (0.05) ja i allmänhet tror jag att jag fråg- när jag
		e::: *yes in general I think that I as- when I*
→ 132		fråga **ni** så menar jag ... alltså både **du** och din fru.
		*ask **you** then I mean ... that is both **you** and your wife.*
→ 133	Iza:	но если я спрашиваю вас то я нормально e:::
		but if I ask you then I normally er::: have
→ 134		имею в виду вас обоих. значит вас вместе. вас и-
		you both in mind. that is you together. you and- and
135		с женой.
		[your] wife.
136	Alex:	да я это понимаю но тогда я тоже знаю что она
		yes I understand this but then I also know that she is

137   сейчас тоже пройдёт е::: ((telephone rings))
      also soon going to er:::
138   интервью. ((telephone rings)) так что ((Pia lifts the
      be interviewed.   *so that's*
139   receiver)) я думал это касается меня, всё.
      I thought it concerns me, all [this].

The officer decontextualizes, as it were, the two pronouns *du* ("you" in the singular) and *ni* ("you" in the plural) and emphasizes the distinction between them prosodically (3:132). Iza's translation of the officer's explanation does not at all contain the distinction between *ni* and *du* (3:133–134). This can partly be explained by the fact that the officer's way of making the distinction in Swedish is at present not available to the interpreter in Russian. In the current talk *vy* ("you" in pl.) is already established as a pronoun which may refer to the applicant alone. To sort out the difference between *du* and *ni*, the interpreter would have needed to explain, using more or other words than those she applies (for instance, she could mention the troublesome Swedish glosses (i.e. in Swedish) when speaking in Russian).

As it appears in the transcript (3:136–139) – and this was confirmed in the post-interview – the applicant at this point got the impression that the officer's questions had all been meant to be about him and his wife, while he had thought they normally had concerned himself alone. In the interview, however, this topic was closed when the interpreter explained to the officer that one must say *vy* in Russian, in order to avoid being impolite; this protects, as it were, the position of someone who knows the 'secrets' of both sides. The officer in reply dismissed further discussion of the issue, referring to the limited time. In other words she, in turn, protects the position of a person in charge of the encounter.

The sequence again reminds us of the fact that some cases of miscommunication are due to interlocutors' (including interpreters') need to protect their own views of themselves and the world.

In the following section I will be tracing how the divergent understandings of the referential meanings of the different forms of 'you' could develop and survive through the whole exchange. It will be seen that the interlocutors' differing views were actually strengthened at an instance where a miscommunication event triggered by a similar 'trouble source' occurred, that is the Russian '*vy*' and the Swedish '*ni*' were used to refer to *various* entities (to an individual and to a couple) without the interlocutors noticing this.

The encounter has been going on for a while when the officer brings up a new topic – activities during the past summer:

(3) (G26:7)

1 Pia: har ni gjort nånting? speciellt i sommar? (0.02)
          did you do something? special this summer?
2 ┌   rest eller?
   │   *travelled or?*
   │Iza: вы не занимались чем-то::: (.) интересным?
   │   *you didn't do anything::: (.) interesting?*
3   летом.
          this summer.
4 Alex: нет. ничем.
          no. nothing.
5 ┌Iza: nej. ingenting.
   │   *no. nothing.*
   │Pia: ni har- ni har int rest runt här i området?
   │   *you did- didn't travel round here in the region?*
   └Iza: путешествовали
                                            travelled round
6   (.) вокруг по району?
          (.) in the region?
7 Alex: нет. я был только в городе.
          no. I was only in town.
8 Iza: nej. jag har varit bara i sta'n.
          no. I have only been in town.

When Pia asks about summer activities she uses *ni* ("you" in plural form) (3:1) as a pronoun of address. This is relayed as *vy* ("you" in plural form) (3:2). Alex's answer, including a non-emphasized "I" (3:7) suggests that he understands this *vy* to refer only to himself.

Nevertheless, the police officer understands the Swedish version of Alex's answer, also including a (non-emphasized) *jag* ("I") (3:8), to refer to the young couple. To judge from the written report, this is how Pia heard, or, if you wish, misheard it. She may also have assumed that Iza mistakenly used the "wrong" pronoun. As we may note in the immediately surrounding context, her own distinction between *ni* and *du* is something she takes for granted. After a moment of typing, the officer brings up another new topic:

(3) (G26:7)

9 Pia: m. har **du** några släktingar eller vänner som bor i sta'n
          *m. do **you** have any relatives or friends who live in town*
10   som du kände **innan** du flyttade hit?
          *whom you knew **before** you moved here?*

11   Iza: у вас имеются или родные или друзья с
           do you have either relatives or friends with
12   которыми вы были знакомы **до** того, когда вы
           *whom you were acquainted **before**, when you*
13   переселились сюда?
           moved here?

Pia's emphasis on *du* ("you" in sg.) indicates that she wishes to mark a contrast to the *ni* ("you" in pl.) in the preceding question. The new question concerns his life before he was married, while they so far (from the officer's perspective) had been talking about the life of the couple. But at the moment there is no corresponding need to mark contrast in the Russian version. Iza can go on using the conventional *vy* ("you" in pl.) when addressing Alex, and the applicant's understanding of the question is sufficient to make him continue providing the requested information.

From the interrogator's point of view, her own understanding of *du* and *ni* respectively is further consolidated when she shortly afterwards takes up the standard question in these settings: "What plans do you (in pl.) have for the future?" Alex accounts in quite some detail for his own plans, to learn Swedish and to look for a job, again taking the question as referring to himself alone. Pia listens and takes notes, but when the applicant has concluded: "At least they are the most immediate plans" and then stays silent, Pia looks up from her desk and asks:

(3)(G26:8)
37   Pia: nå din **fru** då?
           *but your **wife** then?*
38   Iza: и ваша жена?
           *and your **wife**?*
           (0.04)
→ 39 Pia: nå'ra speciella planer. för det här gäller ju främst **dej**,
           *any special plans. because this concerns **you** first and foremost,*
→ 40 Iza: это касается конечно в первую очередь вас,
           this concerns of course first and foremost you [vous-form],
41   (.) но планы вашей жены.
           (.) but the plans of your wife.
42   Alex: aha,
           oh,
           (0.02)
43   Iza: jaså?
           oh?

When the officer says "but your *wife* then? any special plans.
because this concerns *you* first and foremost," (3:37, 3:39) it should
be understood that the applicant's answers ought to have concerned
his wife too. The officer has thus identified a lack of shared understanding. But Alex remains under the illusion – as he will up to the
moment when the record is read aloud for him – that her inquiry
mainly concerns himself alone; that this question about his wife
was an addition. Alex's "oh," (3:42), denotes that he has understood and is preparing to provide more information.

Feedback tokens such as these are ordinarily seldom, if ever,
translated, but here Iza matches Alex's *aha*, ("oh,") with a *jaså?*
("oh?") (3:43). If the officer had paid attention, this could have made
her alive to the applicant's hesitation. It could also possibly have
served as an account of why the expected information was still
missing. Iza's marking of surprise on behalf of the applicant can
be understood as the interpreter's handling of the current miscommunication. But the means she uses to do this are very subtle,
particularly in comparison with the measures she had taken immediately before to protect face-needs between the applicant, the officer
and herself.

Iza indeed translated the officer's reproach "but your *wife* then?
(0.04) any special plans. because this concerns *you* first and foremost," (3:37, 39), but the interpreter's version of it was somewhat
softened: "this concerns of course first and foremost you (in pl.), (.)
but the plans of your wife") (3:40–41). And if 'this' in Pia's statement referred to what Alex (via Iza) has already said, and what the
officer had written down, the reversed word order and the inserted
polite "of course" made 'this' in Iza's version come out to mean
something like "this interview" or "this encounter". Alex was thereby
reassured that what he had said so far (elaborating on his own
activities and plans) indeed had answered the officer's requests.

In conclusion, I would argue that the interpreter's preoccupation
with protecting face (including her own) and with protecting the
'given' meaning of particular words (*du/ni* – "you") (thus applying
a narrow 'talk-as-text' approach) causes her to miss an opportunity to resolve quite a simple instance of miscommunication. The
'locally' occurring 'trouble source' was dealt with more than once,
but the measures taken did not promote the primary interlocutors'
shared understanding of its nature. In the encounter, the plural
form of "you" (in Russian *vy*, in Swedish *ni*) had been used to refer
simultaneously to two distinct entities, without the participants'
noticing this. This insight was perhaps beyond the understanding

also of the interpreter on duty. Perhaps not surprisingly, both parties' lasting impression of the interview was coloured by irritation and mistrust. Afterwards, the officer complained to me about the interpreter's way of doing her job, and the applicant uttered a certain discontent with the officer for being unnecessarily vague.

5. "YOU MENTIONED PARASITES"

The present section explores a miscommunication event identified in a meeting recorded at a health-care clinic. The interpreter identifies miscommunication and localizes a specific 'trouble source' – the ambiguity of the word 'parasite'. This is brought into common focus. Going stepwise through the transcriptions, we may observe how miscommunication is jointly created and jointly counteracted, and how the interpreter's measures to handle it have both intended and unintended effects. Other 'trouble sources' will be identified along the way. One is connected to the 'local' ambiguity of laughter, another to the ambiguity of overlapping talk. This, in turn, connects to interlocutors' reduced opportunities to mark topic shift and topic closure, and to read these kind of discourse markers, in interpreter-mediated interaction.

Extract (4) is from an encounter where a patient, Pavel, meets Nina, a nurse, and Inna interprets between them. It is a standard check-up visit offered by local health-care authorities to newly-arrived immigrants and refugees (the same people and place as in Excerpt (2) in Chapter 7 above). In order to prepare a report for a follow-up encounter with a doctor, Nina has asked Pavel about present and previous medical care needs. The interview follows the ordinary routine and she now begins to introduce the next phase – talk about tests, and test-taking. But Nina's information on this issue is to come only after a longer stretch of talk, characterized by lack of shared understanding.

(4) (G31:17)

1   Nina: °okej° (0.02) jag berättar om dom prover vi tar idag.
           °okay°   I'll tell [you] about the tests we're doing today.
2   det du ska lämna, ((clears throat)) och det du får resultat
           what you'll be providing   and which you'll get the results
3   på nästa gång.
           from next time.
4   Inna: я расскажу о::: этих анализах которые мы
           I'll tell [you] about . . . this tests that we're

```
 5 ⌈          сегодня возьмём.
   |          doing today.
   |Pavel:    mm.
   ⌊          mm
 6 ⌈Inna:     которые вы с- ((snuffles lightly))
   |          that you'll be pr-
   ⌊Nina:           dels- ингår det då avföringsprover både för
                    so this partly- includes stooltests both for
 7 ⌈          bakteriell och parasitologisk analys. då,
   |          bacterial and parasitological analysis. then,
   ⌊Inna:          анализ кала, это е::: мы узнаём если
                   stooltest, that is er::: we'll get to know whether
 8            есть бактерии и::: va sa du nästa? jag hörde inte.
              there are any bacteria a:::nd what did you say next? I didn't
              hear.
 9            och ... е:::
              and ... er:::
→ 10 ⌈Nina:  bakteriell och parasitologisk analys.
    |         bacterial and parasitological analysis.
→   ⌊Inna:   bak-                      aha. и тоже если есть
              bac-                      aha. and also if there are any
 11           паразиты.
              parasites.
→ 12 Pavel:  вы про паразиты, ((laughs)) это- извините.
              you mentioned parasites,        this is- excuse me.
```

The transcription shows that there is a discoursal split connected in some way to the mention of "parasites". The local history of this term starts in the nurse's "bacterial and parasitological analysis" (4:7), repeated (in 4:10), after Inna's request (in 4:8). The interpreter is alive to the fact that this special language terminology might be difficult for patients to comprehend and translates into layman's language ("we'll get to know whether here are any bacteria a:::nd" (4:7–8) "and also if there are parasites" 4:10–11). Pavel subsequently latches on to this gloss when he starts talking "you mentioned parasites. this is- excuse me." (4:12). At this point, the interpreter identifies and acts to suppress miscommunication. Interpreting the patient's repetition of the gloss 'parasites' as a repair initiation, she specifies what it means.

```
(4) (G31:17–18)
13 Inna:   паразиты это::: глисты и разные-
           parasites that's::: worms and different-
14 Pavel:  aha:::
           o:::h
```

15 Inna: паразиты. называется. да.
             parasites. is the name for it. yes.
16 Pavel: а. ну да. да ещё изв- да. я забыл что-то у меня-
             ah.. well yes. yes what more sorr- yes. I forgot something I've got-
17 ⌈Inna: för att parasiter på ryska, det betyder att människor
  | *because parasites in Russian, it means that people*
  |
  ⌊Pavel: ((clears throat))
18 Inna: som . . . arbetar inte.
             who . . . don't work.
             (.)
19 ⌈Nina: ja ja att e::: a ja. men **dom** hittar vi väl knappast häri
  | *(.) yes yes that er::: oh yes. but we'll hardly find **those** in here.*
  |
  ⌊Inna: ((laughs)) så därför . . .
                                                    that's why . . .
20 ⌈Nina: ((laughs))
  ⌊Inna: ((laughs)) но здесь мы их не найдём. ((laughs))
             but we won't find those here.
21 Pavel: мм да. да извин-
             mm. yes. yes sorry-

Understanding Pavel's repeating of the word 'parasite' as an allu-
sion to the Soviet notion of 'parasitism' – a crime for which a person
could be brought to trial – Inna is again prepared to bridge a gap
not only between Swedish and Russian, but also between special
medical language and laypeople's talk. The patient's mention of the
word in this way confirms her interpreting of him as someone in need
of clarification of medical terms. Inna also conveys this message to
the nurse (4:17–18).

This miscommunication event indicated the existence of a
'trouble source' of 'global' character – the interpreter's tendency
to underestimate the patient's ability to understand (which is
sometimes considered patronizing). Here this combines with the
'local' manifestation of another 'global' 'trouble source' inherent
in interpreter-mediated conversations as systems of activity – the
non-standard regulation of the turn-taking order. Markers of topic
shift, or attempts at topic closure, such as Pavel's "you mentioned
parasites" (4:12) and "a. well yes" (4:16), are regularly efficient in
monolingual conversations, but in interpreter-mediated talk there
seem to be obstacles.

Through Inna's interpreting, the language- and culture-specific
ambiguity of 'parasites' is becoming a focused issue in the conversation. Explaining to Nina what 'parasites' associates with in Russian
(in 4:17–18), Inna also provides an account for what had made the

patient laugh before (4:19). The nurse contributes on the topic: "(.)
yes yes that er::: oh yes. but we'll hardly find *those* in here" (4:19)
and Inna and the nurse burst into light laughter. Nina continues
jokingly, using the verbal ambiguity when describing what 'parasites'
stands for in the medical context. In other words, she takes a shared
responsibility for counteracting the miscommunication which Inna
has just identified. As can be seen at the end of next transcription,
however, neither Inna's nor Nina's clarification appears to be what
Pavel had anticipated.

(4) (G31:18)

21   Nina: parasiterna som kan leva i **tarmen** och inte
               *the parasites which can live in your **intestines** and do*

22   arbetar utan suger ut det dom behöver ifrån din tarm
               not work but suck what they need from your intestines

23   ⌈   istället
               instead.

      ⌊ Inna: ну есть паразиты тоже которые живут в
               well there are parasites also which live in the

24   кишечнике и не работают и только
               bowels and do not work and just suck

25   ⌈   всё хорошего сосут.
               all the good [things].

      ⌊ Pavel: да вы извините. наверно я **такой** боязливый что
               *yes [would] you excuse [me]. I'm probably **such** a coward that*

26   ⌈   вы такого не встречали. е- ну ладно.
               you've never met anyone like [me]. e- well okay.

      ⌊ Inna: ursäkta mig, jag är kanske
                                            excuse me, perhaps I'm such a

27   jätterädd av mig, så du har aldrig stött på sån.
               scared one that you've never come across like me.

28   Pavel: но вы сказали паразиты значит. ((laughs)) и я
               but you said parasites then.   and I

29   вспомнил. мне что-то стало ((laughs))
               remembered. I've got something

30   Inna: nä, nä du har sagt parasiter, eller jag.
               no, no you said parasites, or I [did].

31   ⌈ Pavel: мне вот эти последние чуть две недели,
               I've had these last almost two weeks,

      ⌊ Inna: ni-
                                           ni-

32   Pavel: вот здесь вот чешется. ((laughs))
               see here see it's been itching.

Comparing instances of laughing in the three excerpts I noted that while the two ladies were laughing, the patient was not, and vice versa. They apparently had different things in mind. This becomes evident when the patient again uses the term 'parasites' (in 4:28). At this point, other grounds for his laughter and displayed tension become visible to Inna. More precisely, she sees his mentioning of this word as a way to connect to preceding talk, and thereby legitimate the introduction of an adjacent topic (which, in actual fact, had little to do with the current one). Pavel was making another request for advice from the nurse, whom he had been talking to for some twenty minutes already, and was apparently anticipating that she would perhaps deny him more attention. He realized that, from the perspective of the nurse, the talk-on-care-needs phase of the encounter was over, when he remembered the itching that had been bothering him.

The ambiguity of laughter must be identified as a 'local' 'trouble source'. As Adelswärd (1989) shows, laughter is an activity pregnant with distinctive and somewhat contradictory features. It is regularly triggered by something considered funny, and has a strongly inviting character, but neither the first nor the second condition is vital. In dialogue, Adelswärd argues, individuals often laugh alone, and not always at funny things. This is due to another function of this means of communication, namely to modify verbal expressions or attitudes and assist interlocutors in handling ambiguities and tension (Adelswärd 1989:107). The interpreter first identifies the patient's laughter (in 4:12) to be of this character, and works on converting it into shared laughter (4:20). As we noted, it became shared only between herself and the nurse. When Pavel again laughs alone (4:28–29), Inna acts differently.

Had it not been for the interpreter's perception of his first mention of 'parasites' as a request for specification of word meaning, the discourse would perhaps never have been diverted into the side-track just quoted. As we may note, however, Inna's first (mis-)interpretation of the patient's use of 'parasites' was supported, as it were, by Pavel. He displayed acceptance, with *aha:::* ("o:::h") (4:14) in a rising, open-ended intonation, as if expressing surprise and interest, when Inna explained (in 4:13) the ambiguous meaning of 'parasites'. The interpreter's subsequent confirmation – "parasites is the name for it. yes." (4:15) – indicates that she indeed thinks that she had interpreted him correctly. In retrospect, however, and in the longer sequence of talk, I would rather interpret this "o:::h" (4:14) as Pavel 'doing being surprised', in order to protect face-needs. (This reading is supported by information from the post-interview, where Pavel turned out to be a very well-educated person.) The patient refrained from engaging in the ongoing discussion on semantics. Instead, he waited for a chance to bring up his additional ailment.

Seen from another perspective, had it not been for this miscommunication event – the 'time-out' from the interview proper that it created and the playfulness that was added to the atmosphere – the patient would perhaps not have had the time to overcome his embarrassment and come out with what he wanted to say.

In interpreter-mediated (as opposed to monolingual) interaction, the individual interlocutor's reduced ability to efficiently mark in discourse such activities as topic shift, and also his or her reduced ability to read this kind of marker in the others' talk, suggests itself as a 'globally' present 'trouble source', which is actualized 'locally'. Similarly, in interpreter-mediated encounters, as well as in monolingual ones, individuals' indirectness may constitute a 'local' 'trouble source'. Seen from another perspective, however, in interpreter-mediated interaction, the primary parties' reduced ability to be indirect – for instance, in order to avoid being impolite – may constitute a 'global' 'trouble source'.

6. "HOW IS THIS LOOKED UPON?"

In the fifth and last extract in this chapter miscommunication between the primary parties is nipped in the bud, as it were. A close analysis of transcribed discourse reveals that the parties approach the current topic from quite different angles, and yet, after a short while, they share a similar view on the subject matter.

Maria, a Russian-speaking mother visits a local child welfare clinic with her baby. The nurse, Nancy, has invited her. Maria gave birth three months ago, and has met the nurse at the centre a number of times before. There has not always been an interpreter to assist them. Maria and Nancy both have a basic command of English. For this particular encounter, however, the municipal service bureau has provided an interpreter, Ivana. To profit from the opportunity of being assisted by an interpreter, the mother has prepared a list of issues beforehand. One of these, concerning a vaccination scar, has just been quite extensively discussed (cf. Chapter 9 below). The next one concerns a different area – feeding. We come in when Maria, with the little baby on her lap, looks at a piece of paper in her hand.

(5) (G42:17)

1 Maria: а вот в магазинах я вижу много питания, всякие
            and well in shops I see a lot of foods, different

2   банки, всякое (.) е::: вообще в принципе как это
            tins, different . . . er::: on the whole, in principal how is this

→ 3   считается. хорошо? или лучше готовить что-то
            looked upon? good? or is it better to prepare something

4   самим?
            by yourself?

5 Ivana: när jag är ute och handlar så ser jag många såna här
            when I am out shopping then I see many such tins of

6   barnmatsburkar, och då vill jag gärna veta
            food for children, and then I would like to know

   Nancy: ja
                               yes

7 Ivana: va de **e** för nånting. om de e **bra** för barnet eller om
            *what this **is** actually. if it is **good** for the child or if*

   Nancy: mm   a just de
            mm   yeah exactly

8 Ivana: man helst ska satsa på egen eeh barnmats . . . (tillagning)
            one should rather go in for one's own er children's food . . .
            (preparation)

   Nancy: aa   till och börja med
                                       yeah   to start with

9   när vi ger- så vill vi helst att man ska börja med
            when we give- then we preferably want people to start with

10   grönsaker till exempel pota::tis, majs, morot, och
            vegetables for instance pota::toes, sweetcorn, carrots, and

11   pota::tis behöver man ju inte köpa på burk, så det kan
            pota::toes you don't need to buy in a tin, so you might as

12   man ju koka.
            well cook it.

13 Ivana: eh::: так сказать при переходе на нормальное
            er::: so to speak in the changeover to normal

14   питание мы идём- исходим из принципа
            food we go- take the principle of gradualness

15   постепенности и рекомендуем начать с
            as a point of departure and recommend to start with

16   картошки варёной, кукурузы во-вообще овощей.
            boiled potatoes, sweetcorn on- on the whole vegetables.

17		а картошку вам зачем в ма- вот в магазине
		and potatoes, why should you buy [them] in a- in a shop
18		покупать. вы можете сами готовить. варить.
		you can prepare [them] yourself. boil.
	Maria:	естественно то есть-
		naturally that is-
19		то есть в принципе **лучше**, когда это не
		*that is in principle it's **better**, when it's not*
20		консервировано? наверно.
		in tins? probably.
21	Ivana:	så i princip så är det alltså bättre
		so in principle that is it is better
22		att tillverka egen mat och s- s- skippa den konserverade.
		to prepare one's own food and s- s- skip the tinned one.
	Nancy:	allafall jaa i allafall
		any case yes in any case
23		med pota:::tis och- såna som går **enkelt** för dej. å **göra**
		*with pota:::toes and- such like which is **easy** for you to **make***
24		men det kan va jobbigt kanske stå å **koka** morot e:: majs
		*but it may be hard perhaps to stand and **boil** carrots e::*
25		å hacka och greja. **då** kan man köpa dom här burkarna.
		*sweetcorn and chop and do them. **then** you can buy these tins.*

Maria's question whether it is in principle better to prepare your own fresh babyfood than to buy tinned food (5:1–4) presupposes two things: the nurse's expertise on the two types of food, and that it is meaningful to claim something general about the quality of tinned food for small children. In her translation, Ivana specifies the question to concern what is good "for the child" (5:7). Nancy's response in turn does not express any firm attitude, either negative or positive, about tinned food in general. The mother subsequently formulates her inquiry as a yes/no question (in 5:18–20), still expecting to hear the nurse's opinion regarding tinned food for babies, or perhaps the official view of the child welfare institution.

Nancy, however, ignores this aspect of the question. She starts to talk about what is considered good babyfood, but to her the comparison between tinned or freshly-made food is simply not relevant to the issue. Instead she (in 5:24–27) engages in expressing her view of what would be good from a practical and an economic point of view, for the feeding parent. This is part of her standard repertoire as a child-care adviser. Childcare institutions of this kind have an official task in the Swedish welfare system to inform, among other things, about proper nutrition. The nurse is prepared to provide a certain amount of information, which does not include warnings against tinned food produced specifically for small children and broadly sold in all Swedish grocer's shops. Rather she anticipates what to her might be the standard problems of the mother-cook.

Talk from here moves on to concern refrigeration of baby-meal portions and their preparation, and at this point tinned food is already established as something just as good for the child as freshly-made food. This was not something brought up in the post-interview, and we will never know whether Maria was really convinced that there is no reason to question the nurse's neglecting of possible differences in quality. From the recording it is only clear that the issue ceases to be a relevant topic after the short sequence presented above.

Shared understanding and knowledge thus appears to have been achieved. It should be noted, however, that it is the perspective of the health-care provider that is made common. Ivana is well acquainted with the regular routines of child welfare centres. In her version of Nancy's advice, the use of a certain vocabulary emphasizes the nurse's role as someone possessing the valid knowledge. For instance: "in the changeover to normal food we go- take the principle of gradualness as a point of departure and recommend to start with" etc. (5:13–18).

This perhaps answered perfectly well to Maria's expectations of how experts should behave. In the process of talking, the mother was more prepared to take Nancy's perspective than Nancy was to adapt to Maria's point of view. This is of course understandable for several reasons, not least because Maria – as a mother of a new-born baby and as a newcomer to Sweden, unacquainted with Swedish welfare provision – is the one who seeks advice.

In institutional encounters, in contrast to 'ordinary conversations', there are one or more predefined goals. These do not perforce include shared understanding among the persons involved. As a rule, the professional party has an expert's authority to collect and evaluate certain information about the layperson. Sometimes the expert will also inform the lay party about institutional routines, including his or her task and authority in the current situation. The layperson, on the other hand, has the predefined duty or opportunity to provide situationally relevant information about him- or herself. This would imply that a certain task-orientation is mutually preferential.

A person in charge of handling a specific task – an expert – by definition enjoys the privilege of defining what constitutes task-relevant talk. A client or interviewee meeting the expert has the more restricted power of a subordinate party, that of answering or avoiding answering questions and asking for advice on issues which, if considered relevant by the professional party, will be a topic dealt with in interaction.

Arguably, the attaining of sharedness would be naturally sought in health-care interviews and child-care consultations. Clinicians have a professional ambition to influence the future behaviour of the visitors on the one hand, and, on the other, patients and parents as a rule, so it is expected, attend to and comply with what medical experts say. This would then suppose that both parties in these kinds of settings would make sure that there is some kind of convergence between them, and hence, that they would tend to check for mutual understanding. Studies of medical interviews show that this is a greatly idealized picture (e.g. Cicourel 1983, Aronsson *et al.* 1995). Indeed, it is acknowledged as a problem in medical practice, not least when people with culturally and ethnically different backgrounds meet (e.g. Sachs 1983, Prince 1986, Erickson and Rittenberg 1987), that patients and doctors may not have reached an adequate amount of shared understanding, even if they may have exchanged a considerable amount of what each of them in their own way regarded as task-relevant talk. This is the situation in which interpreters appear.

7. RESOURCE FOR COMMUNICATION AND SOURCE OF MISCOMMUNICATION

The present chapter has identified a number of triggers and contributing factors – 'trouble sources' – behind miscommunication in interpreter-mediated interaction. 'Locally' manifesting causes of comprehension problems have been seen to combine with 'trouble sources' at a more 'global' level of discourse. The distinction between 'local' and 'global' is, of necessity, arbitrary and dependent on the situation and its many levels of contexts. 'Trouble sources' on the whole 'belong' to the situation, and not vice versa, i.e. the existence of a factor identified at some point as a 'trouble source' does not always lead to events where someone experiences lack of shared understanding.

In the analyses above, we identified 'locally' operating 'trouble sources' such as: missing vocabulary, mishearing, mispronunciation, interference between languages, interfering communicative activities, ambiguous participation framework, ambiguous use of particular words, obscure substance of talk, ambiguity of laughter and other non-verbal discourse activities and of discourse markers. These are all of a kind that, in principle, could have been found in any exchange. The fact that we can identify them as factors suppressing shared understanding cannot be explained, however, without paying attention to the character of the situations in which they occurred in real life. These were institutional, interpreter-mediated encounters. The exchanges between professionals and lay people investigated above would simply not have taken place had it not been for the interpreters, but being a resource for communication, the interpreter-mediated mode of communication may occasionally, by invoking its own standards, cause miscommunication between its interlocutors.

7.1 'Trouble sources' in interpreter-mediated interaction

Shared and mutual understanding by necessity concerns not all, but certain aspects of interaction, for instance, a topic, a participant's emotional status, a participant's role as a team member or goals and needs of individuals and groups. Lack of shared understanding may, moreover, be experienced by one interlocutor at the same time as others present in the same encounter see no such lack. Differing views of the surrounding world, including the current exchange, can pass quite unnoticed. Equally, they can occasionally constitute a 'trouble source' of a 'global' kind. In any encounter, interlocutors' preparedness to expect the unexpected and willingness to acknowledge the existence of different attitudes and opinions ideally promotes sharedness of understanding, while the opposite would suppress it.

In encounters between people with various language backgrounds – perhaps more than in exchanges between people who share their first language – the achievement of shared and mutual understanding is bound to be obstructed at times by interlocutors' varying proficiency in the currently used language. Lack of sharedness as regards vocabulary, intonational patterns and implicit norms of interacting – for instance, various understanding of the significance of overlap – could here constitute 'trouble sources' of a 'global' kind.

In encounters between experts and laypersons, more than in conversations between equals, sharedness of understanding can be hindered by, for instance, the interlocutors' unevenly distributed insight into the subject matter, and their various ideas of what should count as relevant to the current talk. It comes as no surprise that a layperson's and a professional's perspectives sometimes clash, and this could reinforce (rather than resolve) interlocutors' mistrust or fear of miscommunication, which, in turn, will tend to promote miscommunication rather than shared understanding.

Looking for miscommunication events where the interpreter necessarily plays the most active role, I have pointed to instances of 'literal' translation (interpreters' 'talk-as-text' bias) which gave primary interlocutors problems of understanding. Interpreters' excessive willingness to explain for one of the parties, thus taking over the responsibility of the other party, may also turn out to be a 'trouble source' obstructing sharedness between the primary interlocutors.

At some point or other, however, the actual miscommunication events analysed above all relate to some specific properties of interpreter-mediated conversations; with their characteristic interaction format. Insofar as these properties are non-standard in relation to direct, monolingual conversation these features constitute 'trouble sources' inherent in the interpreter-mediated mode of communication:

- the non-standard turn-taking and the fragmentation of discourse,
- the non-standard back-channelling,
- the non-standard dependence on a mediator's understanding, or, seen from the point of view of the person in the middle,
- the non-standard position of understanding on others' behalf and of understanding others' (mis)understanding.

7.2 Turn-taking and the fragmentation of discourse

As considered in Chapter 7 above, the interpreter-mediated encounter implies a specific turn-taking order which is dependent on the interpreter's local management of interaction. It is principally presupposed that interpreters take every second turn at talk. Their capacity for memorizing, the participants' style of communication etc., put limits upon the space that can be made available each time primary interlocutors wish to talk. To get across what they want to communicate, they need to stop talking every now and then, to let the interpreter translate. At times, when complex messages are split into small pieces, and each piece is translated as a decontextualized whole, participants in conversation (including the interpreter) may draw premature conclusions about the points a speaker wishes to make. This was seen in Example (4), in the medical interview, where the patient (Pavel) hesitantly tried to introduce a new topic. The *fragmentation* of discourse can thus – even if designed to promote shared understanding – potentially also contribute to miscommunication. Story-telling is perhaps another discourse activity which the necessary fragmentation of interpreter-mediated talk would make more difficult. The interruptions may make primary interlocutors' lose the thread.

The fragmentation and the non-standard turn-taking provide the interlocutors with a specific opportunity for structuring interaction. A participant (say, an interviewer) who has a well defined, strategic goal can easily find opportunities to control the next turn by orientating or reorientating discourse towards what he or she considers the relevant topic. In other words, with each new contribution on the part of the interpreter, he or she potentially gets a new chance to assume control of the interaction. For this purpose primary interlocutors may sometimes utilize the 'pauses' – when the interlocutor talks in the unknown language – to reflect upon how to act next.

Ordinarily, in direct monolingual conversation between adults, manipulating topic control involves a certain face-threat. In interpreter-mediated conversation, primary interlocutors who overlap and interrupt the interpreter do not expose themselves quite as much to the danger of being perceived as intruders as they would do with the same behaviour in direct interaction. They do not even have to await a micro-pause or a non-verbal sign from the interpreter showing who is selected to be the next speaker, but may select themselves and regard the interpreter as a non-person, i.e., someone whose participation in conversation may be ignored (Goffman 1990:150, cf. Chapter 4:1.4).

Finally, when an encounter aims towards a documentation of the exchange itself – which is regularly the case in institutional encounters – the interviewer first and foremost needs to ensure that some kind of exchange does indeed come about. To get something written in a police report or in a medical record, the interrogating officer or the interviewing nurse or practitioner must get the interviewee to utter something. It would hardly be surprising to find that interpreters have generally incorporated the idea of making people talk into their view of their professional mission. This attitude dovetails neatly with the needs of interviewers.

7.3 Non-standard back-channelling

In interaction, feedback activity has an auxiliary function in that it helps interlocutors to organize their turn-taking. It also helps in the control of mutual understanding; speakers interpret listeners' understanding, and listeners confirm by back-channelling that communication may continue. One of the 'trouble sources' characteristic of interpreter-mediated interaction is that mutual feedback between the primary parties is delayed and often non-existent.

Comparing primary interlocutors' 'originals' with interpreters' 'renditions' as 'texts', a number of studies have shown that feedback parts of utterances tend to be reduced or omitted (cf. Jönsson 1990, Englund Dimitrova 1991, 1997 and Linell *et al.* 1992). And comparing monolingual institutional dialogues documented in the literature with interpreter-mediated encounters (to judge from those we have studied in the Linköping corpuses), the amount of feedback and other mutual checking of shared understanding is also strikingly less compared to 'ordinary' exchanges between people interacting.

Primary interlocutors may of course observe each other and identify some behaviour as back-channelling. Yet the less transparent their talk is to one another, the more dependent they are upon the interpreter to understand whether they are following each other or not. Someone who is collecting pieces of information from their counterpart according to a certain, institutional routine is arguably less dependent on the counterpart's feedback than someone who is supposed to provide information, in particular if this person is unfamiliar with what is counted by the institution as relevant.

The fact that primary interlocutors' back-channelling behaviour seldom, if ever, appears to be message content is probably also a reason why interpreters practically never translate it. When it happens, the interpreter's version tends to communicate something other than just confirmation that communication may continue. There was an illustration of this in Example (3) above, when Iza translated "oh," with "oh?".

In one of my health-care recordings (G35), there is an interesting case of sudden change in back-channelling behaviour. When the physical examination was about to begin and people were moving around in the room without saying anything – in other words, when the frames of the encounter as situated activity was partly slackened – the interpreter slipped in a comment of her work (in

Russian): "it is hard to translate when all three of you understand Russian" (G35:7). She knew that the Swedish doctor understood Russian. The practitioner admitted this, in Russian, and this came as a total surprise to the patient. The doctor then explained that she understood a lot without the interpreter's assistance, but that she had difficulty speaking Russian herself. Before this was revealed, the practitioner had given frequent verbal feedback, but exclusively when the interpreter was talking. After this short three-party exchange in Russian, she started to accompany also the patient's talk with frequent *mhm*-s. This illustrates the connection between feedback behaviour and knowledge about what is mutual as regards shared understanding.

7.4 Interpreting others' (mis)understanding

As was emphasized in the introduction to this chapter, whatever is accomplished or fails in communication is a *collective* activity. Nevertheless, the interpreter has a strategic and potentially powerful position whenever on duty in conversation. An interpreter's very presence is a precondition for the primary interlocutors' exchange, a resource for the attaining of shared understanding and for suppressing and counteracting instances of miscommunication. Interpreters in themselves constitute a guarantee against communicative breakdown. Merely by offering translations they communicate the existence – at some level – of understanding. Their activity can encourage primary interlocutors to go on talking without worrying about occasional miscommunication between each other even when there could, in fact, be causes for concern.

It partly lies in the nature of interpreter-mediated conversation that the primary interlocutors have reduced insight into what is shared and mutual in the communicative exchange. Nevertheless, interpreters can treat problems of understanding in various ways. Either they deal with them as something that should be made a commonly shared topic, or as something 'belonging' only to themselves. In the latter case, the interpreter would try to work out the problems of understanding as if outside the exchange proper. This attitude follows from an interpreter's view of the primary parties' exchange as solely concerning some particular 'subject matter', and that this matter excludes talk on problems of comprehension.

The orientation among interpreters is, in general, not unlike that of 'ordinary' interlocutors in the sense that they work on creating understanding-for-all-practical-purposes. The current interpreter's view of what constitutes sufficient understanding is therefore crucial to whether, and how, he or she handles instances of miscommunication in a given interpreter-mediated encounter. For practical reasons interpreters may find it best to smooth over problems of understanding, without letting it show that they ever existed, let alone topicalizing them or their possible causes. In this way, the official agenda is maintained, and no extra time is spent on questions which are not foreseen in the institutional routines (at least not among those known to the interpreter).

The analyses above principally showed three different ways of handling miscommunication events while performing in the role of interpreter. Interpreters sometimes make interlocutors' lack of shared and mutual understanding a focused issue. Sometimes, however, miscommunication remains an off-the-record matter between the interpreter and the primary interlocutor in relation to whom comprehension problems have been identified. Sometimes, interpreters handle the feeling that miscommunication has occurred by keeping it to themselves. In so doing, they sometimes contribute to the evolution or the sustaining of divergent discourse trajectories, and protect, as it were, the primary interlocutors' differing world views.

NOTES

1. There is a less rigorous practice of this art which is based on the assumption that understanding occurs as a matter of course: [. . .] In short, the less rigorous practice is based on the fact that the speaker and hearer share a common language and a common way of formulating thoughts. [. . .] There is a more rigorous practice of the art of interpretation that is based on the assumption that misunderstanding occurs as a matter of course, and so understanding must be willed and sought at every point (Schleiermacher 1986:109–10).
2. On 'monologism' and 'dialogism', see Chapter 2:4.
3. Definitions of sharedness, mutuality, reciprocity, intersubjectivity and other related concepts are discussed at length by Graumann (1995) and Linell (1995).

NINE

When I *say what* you *mean*

«Чужая речь» – это *речь в речи, высказывание в высказывании* но
в то же время это и *речь о речи, высказывание о высказывании*
(Voloshinov 1930:113).[1]

Isabella works as a community interpreter in a small Swedish town,
where she arrived as an immigrant from Chile some fifteen years
ago. She told me once about an experience at work which had
affected her most unpleasantly. It was when she was appointed to
interpret in a situation where a Spanish-speaking man was to be
notified about the authorities' decision concerning his residence
in Sweden; more precisely, he would be informed that he was to
be deported and sent back to his country of origin. Isabella accompanied a police officer to the place where the man lived to assist
as interpreter. She recollected their meeting in something like the
following words (translated from Swedish):

> "We have decided not to give you permission to stay in Sweden",
> says the police officer. I translate: "We have decided not to give you
> permission to stay in Sweden". The man rushes up to me and shouts
> in anger and despair: "And me, I always thought you were my
> friend!"

What made Isabella take this situation so much to heart was that
she had become associated with the police officer in a way she had
not quite expected, and which was against her intention and will.
This story is only one of the many I have heard through the years,
about sometimes dramatic, sometimes awkward, sometimes funny
incidents due to miscommunication as regards the interpreter's share
in the substance of current talk.

The present chapter will further explore the distribution of responsibility in interpreter-mediated interaction, and the complexity
of the role of interpreter, by problematizing the notion of interpreter

neutrality, investigating how – in interpreters' conveying of others' speech – the interpreter's self is distinguished from others' selves and by focusing on interpreters' use of direct speech, compared to preceding speakers' mode of speaking.

1. PROBLEMATIZING 'NEUTRALITY'

Taking the perspective of the civil servant, Isabella in the above example understood herself to be translating neutrally. She saw the police officer as someone just doing his duty. In Isabella's view, he had played no part in the decision about the man's deportation (any more than she had herself). He was just executing the order given by his employers, commissioners of the immigration authorities. Seeing the reaction of the Spanish-speaking man, however, she realized that her (as well as the officer's) behaviour, from *his* point of view, was read as partial – against him and in the favour of them.

Neutrality, detachment and impartiality are key notions in the professional ethics of interpreters (Colin and Morris 1996, Berk-Seligson 1990:227–38). But what do these notions mean in practice? Many interpreters I have met have expressed trouble with understanding, preparing for, and describing impartiality in their everyday work.

The principle of impartiality involves, on the one hand, a duty to relate neutrally to people and what they say, that is, to convey a neutral – meaning *no* – attitude of one's own to both of the parties and their goals in interaction. Here neutrality refers to the character of the *relations* in which the interpreter gets involved. On the other hand, when referring to the interpreter's *behaviour*, the notion of 'neutral' may also be understood to mean *formal* or *strict*. To my mind, this confusion of references for 'neutrality' might explain some of the difficulties interpreters may experience in living up to the principle of impartiality. Just like any single word the gloss 'neutrality' is associated with particular, conventional *meanings* ('znacheniya') but has no *sense* ('smysl') in and by itself (Bakhtin 1979, cf. Chapter 2:4.1).

In his essay on speech genres, Bakhtin problematizes the concept of neutrality and claims that neutrality of style presupposes similarity between the addressee and the speaker, including a unity of their expectations and viewpoints (Bakhtin 1979:294/1986a:98).

Indeed, the issue of neutrality is actualized in the practice of interpreters first and foremost when expectations among those present, in terms of communicative style, topic choice and perspectives on topics, are markedly diverse. For instance, if one of the parties acts in a strict and formal style, and the other party is emotional, this party may understand what the interpreter says as biased and in favour of the strict and formal interlocutor. If the emotional party suspects an alliance between the two others, a resemblance in their communicative styles may strengthen this impression. Isabella's story about her translation of the police officer's notice could perhaps serve as an illustration of precisely this. When a civil servant speaks with a minimal amount of expressiveness to a layperson who is upset, the interpreter's minimal amount of expressiveness may mislead the distressed person to confuse the distribution of responsibility. How then can interpreters avoid being seen as the ultimate source of talk? How do interpreters mark distinction between their own and others' self?

1.1 The relevance of exploring direct and reported speech

Going through professional rules and regulations for legal interpreting in a range of countries, Colin and Morris (1996) find it to be a firmly established standard in legal processes that interpreters render the primary interlocutors' speech in direct and not reported speech (e.g. "I left at eight ..." and not "he says that he left at eight ..."). Interpreters on duty are supposed to talk in the first person singular ("I-form") (Colin and Morris 1996:146). The same principle of direct-speech-interpreting is also recommended for medical and other public service settings (González *et al.* 1991:28–9). To avoid misunderstandings related to the referent of this 'I', interpreters' guidelines suggest a standard solution, namely to inform the participants about this working principle beforehand, and, if necessary, remind them during the process of interpreting. Reminders, it is expected, prevent primary interlocutors from talking to their counterparts indirectly ("tell him that ..." etc.). Addressing only the other counterpart directly, they, in turn, prevent the interpreters from introducing their own initiatives, opinions and attitudes. In practice, interpreters sometimes use neither direct nor indirect speech, but use the passive voice (e.g. "the house was left at eight ...").

In her book on court interpreting, Berk-Seligson (1990), drawing upon the works of Pomerantz (1978), Atkinson and Drew (1979) and others, investigates the implications involved in interpreters' use of active and passive grammatical forms. Berk-Seligson observes that their use of these forms occasionally differs from preceding speakers' use, and concludes that interpreters must be unconsciously aware that the passive voice distances agents from actions and that the active voice links the two. She identifies interpreters' feelings of antipathy or sympathy for specific actors as underlying causes behind their choice of verb voice (active/passive); that they use the active verb form in order to highlight the responsibility of certain participants, and the passive verb form to diminish the responsibility of others, or depersonify responsibility and attribute blame to, for instance, unhappy circumstances (Berk-Seligson 1990:97–118). Berk-Seligson also sees interpreters' use of the passive as a way to avoid misunderstanding – by defendants in particular – of the interpreters' level of responsibility for what they are saying on behalf of attorneys and judges. She finds it particularly common that interpreters avoid the subject pronouns 'I' and 'you' when interpreting judges' speech to defendants, and especially during the declaration of the sentence (Berk-Seligson 1990:115).

The present chapter will investigate interpreters' use of direct speech, comparing their talk with primary interlocutors' corresponding talk. Focusing on personal pronouns and direct discourse, the analyses will explore the connection between the interpreters' way of performing and their need to indicate the limits of their own responsibility for what they say, to mark the distinction between self and other, to present themselves as impartial and as talking on behalf of others.

Explorations of speakers' involvement in (and responsibility for) what they utter normally take as a point of departure the basic grammatical model distinguishing between first, second and third person singular and plural forms. This model is sufficient for describing relations between syntactic constituents, such as subject pronoun and verb, but clearly insufficient when it comes to accounting for a range of features of speakers' responsibility as speakers.

Scholars within different fields have advanced other models to describe and explore what is called – again in linguistic terms – 'reported speech', 'direct speech', 'direct discourse' or 'direct quotation'. At the beginning of the century debates on this issue were generated by literary theorists, and concerned how the speaker (narrator or novelist) relates to the person(s) whose speech they report. During recent decades speakers' use of others' words has been an issue within sociolinguistics and psycholinguistics. Some researchers have concentrated on the relationship between reporting speakers and their audience, in contrast to others who have focused on the relationship between the individual speaker and their talk – the quotations. The following three subsections will highlight similarities and differences in these approaches.

1.1.1 The work of 'quotations'

Clark and Gerrig (1990), investigating 'quotations', emphasize that these as communicative activities are necessarily selective. Quotations do not exhibit all features of the originals, and they are always dependent on the person who does the quoting and the context in which the quoting takes place. Moreover, quotations, they argue, can be classified as "demonstrations", which in turn allocates them to a class of "nonserious actions" which additionally includes practising, playing, acting and pretending (Clark and Gerrig 1990:766).

Clark and Gerrig investigate quotations as the quoting person's device, and provide a wide sample of illustrations of how an individual by use of a citation may mark a certain distance to what he or she is saying. Their project is to find and map all possible (universal?) functions of 'quotations'. Their project is 'linguistic' in the sense that they explore sequences of texts in which they have identified lexical entities as constituting types of 'quotations'. In other words, the authors basically take an outside, general perspective to classify typical speaker's actions. This makes their reference to Goffman somewhat misleading. To explain the use of the concept of "nonserious action" they refer to Goffman's writings on *keys* and *keyings* (Goffman 1974:40–81). These concepts are used by Goffman in a genuinely interactionistic analytical framework and, as I take it, his aim is not to map types of verbal actions, but rather to investigate the organization of social order, taking into consideration the points of view of those whose interaction is being explored (cf. Chapter 5:1).

Understood within a dialogic paradigm, Goffman's model implies that any action may be meant seriously by the actor, and, simultaneously, be understood to be meant nonseriously by an observer of this action, or vice versa. Take, for instance, 'asking for the time'. You may intend to be seriously wanting to know the time, while your interlocutor understands your asking to be meant to distract her attention from something or someone else. Your 'asking for the time' may be assumed to be intended *only* to get the other's attention, and the *answer* to the question to be of virtually no interest to you. When characterizing an action as being of a certain kind we necessarily invoke a particular perspective, and, simultaneously, exclude other perspectives.

How actions are perceived in practice will depend partly on how actors 'key' them while performing, and partly on how efficient these 'keyings' are perceived by different members of the audience (depending, in turn, on the respective actor's expectations and background knowledge, connected to place, time, overall type of activity, etc., as discussed in Chapter 8 above).

1.1.2 Literary theory and social psychology: Telling or showing

Londen (1989:61ff.) describes the rights and responsibilities of the narrator, being a reporter of others' speech, as a recurrent issue of discussion in literary theory and praxis during the twentieth century (not least at the beginning of the century). The 'subjective' narrator – the one who is *telling*, accounting for, commenting on and generalizing from others' words and deeds – is often set in opposition to the 'objective' narrator, who dramatizes scenes, *showing,* as it were, utterances, conversations and other verbal activities as they would appear to the characters involved in the story. The concepts go back to an older distinction between *diegesis* (telling) and *mimesis* (showing), used in literary theory to describe two basically different narrator positions. 'Diegesis', on the one hand, would signify the case where the narrator assimilates into his own discourse the voices of the others about whom the story is told, reporting their speech *in indirect form.* 'Mimesis', on the other hand, would stand for a diametrically different rhetorical style, namely the case where the narrator systematically dramatizes others' utterances, presents (or re-presents) them as if they were spoken by these others, that is, in *direct discourse.* The result would be a drama, or a dramatic monologue.

Bergmann (1987/1993) discusses in his sociological study *Klatsch* ("Gossip") 'the quote' as a communicative form characteristic of gossip. Exploring its communicative functions in interaction, he finds that quotations are efficient means used by gossip-producers to maintain their audiences' attention (Bergmann 1987:149–66). In her book *Talking voices*, Tannen (1989) demonstrates how speakers, by framing accounts of another's words in the form of dialogue, add a dramatic touch to them. She shows how this makes the accounts an engaging and effective means of focusing the attention of the participants (Tannen 1989:98–133).

1.1.3 Goffman's concept of 'figure' – marking self and other

Goffman (1974, 1981) discusses the issue of individuals' involvement in talk, and responsibility for its substance and progression, when developing his model of 'participation framework' (outlined above in Chapter 5:1). Introducing the concept of *figure* he examines a speaker's means of *representing* him- or herself in talk, i.e. the individual's opportunities in interaction for involving him- or herself and simultaneously displaying a certain self-reflection, a certain distance from his or her own words. In the earlier essay, Goffman (1974) discussed 'figure' as one of four basic terms to describe aspects of an individual's possible engagement in ordinary talk. The others in the typology were *strategist, principal* and *animator* (Goffman 1974:523). In the later modification of this model, Goffman (1981) distinguishes more clearly between *author, principal* and *animator*, on the one hand, as aspects of self, and *figure*, on the other, as a *speaker's communicative means of marking a distinction between self and other*. He particularly attends to the question of how speakers use the notion of 'I'.

> As speakers we represent ourselves through the offices of a personal pronoun, typically "I", and it is thus a *figure* – a figure in a statement – that serves as the agent, a protagonist in a *described* scene, a "character" in an anecdote, someone, after all, who belongs to the world that is spoken about, not the world in which the speaking occurs (Goffman 1981:147).

When individuals animate a character in their speech this implies that they distance themselves from their selves. And just as actors on stage will be perceived as actors *staging* a make-believe character, and not as *being* this character, the individual animating a 'figure' (including him- or herself) displays a relative distance (and a relative proximity) to what she or he is saying. A 'figure' refers to another – to someone else, or to oneself as talked about – in a somewhat objectified way.[2]

By different prosodic, semantic and syntactical means, for instance the pronoun 'I', a speaker may point out an actor from which current talk should be understood as originating. The voiced person – the 'figure' – is made distanced from the currently speaking self, and, at the same time, involved in the here-and-now situation. In and by the act of singling out the currently speaking 'I' from the other or others, including using 'I' for 'oneself in the here-and-now situation', a speaker marks both a personal involvement and a certain distance.

1.2 'Displaying' and 'replaying' what others mean to say

Interpreters on duty in face-to-face interaction are comparable with the narrator in a novel in one respect – they are reporters of others' speech. And just as literary theorists argue for the novel, and socio-linguists have observed in discourse studies, the pragmatic effects of interpreters' use of direct and indirect speech respectively seem to differ significantly.

In a written text or a spoken monologue, a narrator may, by 'showing' or 'telling' others' speech, give voice to a range of novel characters and present these characters' points of view, but the text remains, at one level of meaning, the narrator's. Novel characters are unable to perform, feel or think independently. The narrator alone creates what, as a rule, is the *only version* of a certain story and is therefore, as it were, the absolute ruler of the text. This makes it possible to apply a formalist approach when exploring the narrator's reporting of others' speech. Various cases of reporting can relatively easily be classified in relation to independent grammatical units and stylistic properties.

The interpreter-mediated interaction, in contrast, which basically is constituted as *two versions* of the same talk, involves living people. The interpreter is dependent on these actual others for her or his reporting of others' (i.e. their) speech, just as these others are dependent on the interpreter for their participation in interaction. The narrator's version is, of necessity, the result of joint efforts.

Like interlocutors in any type of human interaction, participants in interpreter-mediated conversations are dependent on their ability to take co-actors' perspectives to foresee where the conversation is heading. Even in institutional settings this is not completely fixed in advance. Talk achieves a certain meaning in context, a meaning which is the basis for subsequent sense-making in interaction. To language workers, such as interpreters, much talk might indeed appear predictable, since language use is to a great extent routinized and conventionalized, even if speech conventions, of course, may be modified or simply not recognized by participants in a conversation.

Exploring how interpreters relate as narrators of others' speech, I will apply concepts that take into account the relation between interpreters' and primary interlocutors' talk. Linguistically defined criteria (syntax, grammatical form, etc.) can be used to identify differences and similarities between 'original' utterances and the corresponding second interpreters' versions (cf. Chapter 6). To characterize interpreters' reporting of others' speech as such, however, it takes an analytical model of a more flexible kind. I will contrast *relaying by displaying* (representing), with *relaying by replaying* (re-presenting) others' talk. This analytical tool is again partly derived from Goffman (1974).

These two ways of relaying should be seen as endpoints in a continuum. The single interpreter's performance depends on his or her proficiency and on the constraints and possibilities inherent in the situation; on the primary interlocutors' reactions and confirmations and on the interpreter's need to mark distinctions between self and other. 'Relaying by displaying' implies, for instance, to speak with a minimal amount of expressiveness also when the original speaker has been talking animatedly, aggressively, sarcastically, hesitantly, and so forth. The interpreter's minimal amount of expressiveness, or, if you like, strictness of style, is then one of the key ways in which he or she conveys an impression of him- or herself as a person using others' words.

'Relaying by replaying', in contrast, implies an effort to re-present the expressiveness of the preceding talk; more of a serious staging of the other's role, as it were. In Goffman's terms, the interpreter would then "live the part of" the primary interlocutor(s), or be "replaying" (Goffman 1974:504). In 'relaying by replaying', interpreters will try to imitate the other's semantic, syntactic, phonetic and paralinguistic communicative features, including voice characteristics and performative style, and rely upon other means to mark the necessary distinctions between self and other, for instance, emphasis, modulation of voice, gaze direction, and so forth (cf. Lang's (1976) observations from a court in New Guinea, Chapter 4:2.2 above).

The communicative events selected for analyses in this chapter involve some instances where the interpreter's need to mark the distinction between the currently speaking self and the meaning other is particularly stressed. In some cases this is due to a complexity created when primary interlocutors in their talk use direct speech to voice non-present protagonists. Other analyses will show cases where the interpreters' emphasized need to distinguish between self and other(s) is connected to their wish to take initiatives and speak on their own behalf as coordinators of current interaction. Doing this, interpreters may try to hide their coordinating function in talk, anticipating that this could be perceived to be obtrusive behaviour. Three excerpts are drawn from encounters at a local police station, and three from recordings made in health-care settings. All sequences involve one person's short account of another's words in the form of dialogue.

In the first excerpt, the interpreter represents a verbal exchange from a moment ago, between herself and a primary party. In the following four extracts, a primary interlocutor gives voice to 'figures' that belong to a past event. The last excerpt, finally, illustrates how the interpreter can make herself 'visible' as the ultimate source of background information which she provides in the midst of rendering speech on the primary interlocutor's behalf.

2. "SHE SAYS: NO, I'M REFERRING TO CARS"

The first extract is drawn from a hearing at the immigration department of a local police station. It illustrates the interpreter's voicing of exchanges between herself and the two primary parties. To counteract misunderstanding and simultaneously avoid topicalizing mistranslation, the interpreter initiates side-exchanges with the primary parties. What each party says in these exchanges is 'displayed' in the respective other language as messages fitting first and foremost with the interpreter's communicative projects (namely, promoting mutual and shared understanding of the subject matter, presenting herself as a confident, accurate and unobtrusive interpreter, and that of 'displaying' the responsibility for the content of preceding talk as shared between the members of the encounter. Evidently, the interpreter's communicative goals could in this case not have been accomplished with a 'relaying by replaying' approach.

The encounter concerns an application for prolongation of a residence permit. We come in as the police officer (Pia) is busy typing. Her method of collecting information is to first take notes with a pen, and then, after a whole complex of questions and answers, to type them up into the report. This creates instances of participants' silence. In one of these pauses the interpreter (Iza) addresses the applicant (**Alla**). In the interview the latter had mentioned that her husband takes casual jobs polishing cars for a sales firm. The interpreter, who has realized that she mistakenly on several occasions had translated the Russian word *mashiny* ("cars/machines") as *maskiner* ("machines") in Swedish, now draws the officer's attention to this mistake, by first engaging the applicant – the ultimate source of the erroneously interpreted word – in a separate exchange.

(1) (G27:6–7)

1	Iza:	чтобы не возникло недоразумения, вы сказали
		so that there won't be a misunderstanding, you said
2		машины ((Pia stops typing)) вы имели в виду
		"mashiny" *did you mean*
3		машины? или **авто**машины?
		*machines or **auto**cars?*
4	Alla:	**авто**машины? автомобили.
		***auto**cars? automobiles.*
5	Iza:	mm::: hon har sagt **maskiner**, och då ställde jag
		*mm::: she has said **machines**, and then I put the*
6		frågan eftersom det **kan** tydas på två olika sätt. om hon
		*question since it **can** be interpreted in two different ways. if she*
→ 7		åsyftade maskiner eller bilar. hon säger: nej, jag
		was referring to machines or cars. she says: no, I'm
8		åsyftar **bilar**.
		*referring to **cars**.*
		(0.1)
9	Pia	vad var det för sammanhang?
		in what connection was this?
10	Iza	e::: mm i samband med makens arbete. för maskin det
		e::: mm in connection with the husband's job. because machine
11		är vad **vi** säger. men på ryska säger man alltså
		*this is what **we** say. but in Russian one thus says*
12		автомашина och det betyder på svenska bil.
		"avtomashina" and this means in Swedish car.
13	Pia	mm?
		mm?
14	Iza	så hon åsyftade bilar.
		so she was referring to cars.
15	Pia	så det var fråga om att polera bilar?
		so polishing cars, that was the matter?
16	Iza	значит он полирует автомашины?
		that is he polishes autocars?
17	Alla	ну да,
		well yes,

The staged dialogue between the interpreter and the applicant (1:5–8) is designed as an account in Swedish for the exchange they just had in Russian. Iza tells the police officer what she just asked, and why. When saying "no, I'm referring to *cars*" (1:7–8), the "I" refers to Alla. If we compare the immediately preceding talk – the applicant's two-word utterance – this involves a request for clarification ("autocars?") and a correction ("automobiles.") (1:4). Iza, however, interprets this as a confirmation of her own statement. Iza's main aim, one may assume, was to counteract current miscommunication, something she was uniquely in the position to do. Her subordinated aims were to legitimate her own behaviour as correct, to reduce her own burden of responsibility for the current misunderstanding and to highlight the applicant's share in it. It was designed to protect her own prestige and authority. The use of passive voice when arguing that *mashiny* "*can* be interpreted in two different ways" (1:6) simultaneously serves to depersonify responsibility for the interpreting, to ascribe this to the ambiguity of the word in itself.

Looking further through the transcription, we may note that the officer's first request for clarification "in what connection was this?" (1:9), indicates that she has problems seeing the point of the interpreter's effort at all. Iza answers directly, linking the preceding interview context with the present translation problem: "e::: mm in connection with the husband's job. because machine this is what **we** say. but in Russian one thus says 'avtomashina' and this means in Swedish car" (1:11–12). It could be mentioned that the applicant who, in contrast to the interpreter, is a native speaker of Russian has frequently used the term *mashiny* for cars, and the archaic gloss *avtomashiny* ("autocars") only once (1:4) (when she repeated it from Iza's question). This interpreter thus goes to quite some lengths to legitimate her erroneous translating of *mashiny* as "machines". In the next couple of turns she ascribes responsibility for her clarifying initiative also to the police officer. Pia's next request "so polishing cars, that was the matter?" (1:15) is translated into Russian as "that is he polishes autocars?". In essence, this is the interpreter's first question (1:1–3) reformulated. Comparing the later request and Iza's subsequent version of it, I note that she 'displays' it not as being about current talk, but as concerning the husband's occupation, using the term she herself just introduced: "that is, he polishes autocars?" (1:16). In other words, Iza forwards to the applicant that *the officer* had problems understanding Alla's first account, where she had spoken about her husband polishing '*mashiny*'.

2.1 Sticking to the letter, or . . . ?

An interview immediately after the encounter indicated that this particular instance had indeed made the interpreter ponder on the question of guilt. Iza spontaneously draws attention to the sequence cited above as a concrete example of a typical interpreter's dilemma. What rights and/or duties does she have to take initiatives of her own in interaction? In her view, she had in this case performed in accordance with the interpreters' Code of Ethics, since she had seen "an immediate danger" (of miscommunication?).

> It took some time before I understood if she meant the one or the other [CW: that she meant cars and not machines]. It was not unambiguous. Then one does not know. Should one interfere? Should one not intervene? But when I see that there is an immediate danger . . . Yes, then I do so. And I do *not* believe that it can be seen as a deviation from the ethical rules.

> [. . .] Of course, I can let it lead to an explosion between the parties: "For goodness' sake, what do you *mean*?!" "For goodness' sake, what do *you* mean?!" According to the ethical rules I should stick absolutely to the letter. So if I start to translate *mashiny* ("cars/machines") with *maskiner* ("machines") then I have to continue. But I realized that it was actually wrong. And then I intervened.

Iza goes on, explaining in this connection, her understanding of rules of ethics and what they are good for.

> [. . .] Ethical rules, they must be something concerned with something humanitarian. Whereas this I considered as something definitely and absolutely a technical matter. Which did *not* have anything to do with . . . emotions and . . . ; did not concern anything human. But it- it was a question of concepts. Something like as if you look into a dictionary. If you have two different explanations of one and the same gloss, then, if you *know* the language, then you will choose the *right* synonym. *If* it is a synonym. It needn't be so. And if you do *not* have the right feeling, then you will automatically pick the incorrect word. Then it will turn out wrong.[3]

Interpreters may perhaps recognize themselves in Iza's talk-as-text model of thinking with claims like "I should stick absolutely to the letter" or "if you *know* the language, then you will choose the *right* synonym". The analyses should have made it clear, however, that thinking of meaning as property of words ('texts') has limited relevance when it comes to understanding and explaining the distribution of responsibility and communicative resources in real-life, interpreter-mediated interaction.

3. "AND THEY SAY THAT . . ."

The second excerpt illustrates that an interpreter's efforts to 'relay by replaying' may invoke specific difficulties for a primary party in the process of telling a story. 'Relaying by replaying' demands a profound proficiency in vocabulary, syntax, standard intonation and, not least, it requires the interpreter's sense of timing. The interpreter in this exchange performs a simultaneous mode of interpreting which occasionally disturbed more than it promoted an exchange between the primary interlocutors. Speaking in a loud voice, she silences the speaking applicant in the middle of utterances. From time to time she obstructs her own listening. Occasionally, the interpreter is indeed able to 'replay' word by word the applicant's account; however, the account as such becomes fragmented by her style of interpreting.

Excerpt (2) is also drawn from an encounter in the immigration department at a local police station. A Russian-speaking woman is being interviewed about an application for her grandmother and mother to come and stay with her and her family in Sweden. In her view, a strong argument for their resettlement is the current ethnic tension in the part of the former Soviet Union where her relatives live, and where they belong to an ethnic minority. A related reason is the lack of food in this area, and their difficulties in getting it. As we come in, the officer has asked the interpreter (Irina) to read the report she has just finished typing, and the applicant (Anna) asks for permission to add something. She wants to make sure that the urgency she sees in her relatives' need to leave the USSR gets across to the officer and to the Swedish immigration authorities.

(2) (P10:19)

```
1  Anna:   бабушка- бабушка может ходить. она раньше
           grandma- my grandmother can walk. before she
2          ходила всегда в магазин.
           always went to the shop.
   Irina:  min mor-              min mor hon kan gå. tidigare hon
           my mother-           my mother she can walk. before she
3          har alltid gått
           has always went
   Anna:            она всегда вела хозяйство.
                    she has always done the housekeeping.
```

4   Irina: **alltid** har hon e::: brytt sig om hushåll.
              always she has e::: cared about housekeeping.

5   Anna: но последний раз, её выбросили из оч- из
              but the last time, they threw her out of the que- of
     Irina: men sista gången,
                                              but the last time,

6   Anna: очереди. она стояла.
              the queue. she queued.
     Irina: dom har kastat ut henne från (.) kö.
                        they have thrown her out of (.) queue.

7   när hon stog där.
              when she was standing there.

8   Anna: е:: и сказали что:::
              e:: and they said tha:::t
     Irina: å dom har sagt till henne att
                              and they have said to her that

9   Anna: что:::
              tha:::t

10   Irina: att
              that

11   Anna: **своим** мяса не хватает.
              *there is not enough meat for our **own** [people].*

12   Irina: att till våra **egna** (.) är inte det med kött tillräckligt.
              *that to our **own** [people] (.) there is not meat enough.*
              (0.5)

13   Anna: и никто не заступился за неё.
              and nobody stood up for her.
     Irina: och   de e ingen som försvarade
                        and   *there is none who defended*

14   henne.
              her.

15   Anna: она еле пришла домой, потому что была вся в
              she could hardly walk home, because she was black and blue all
     Irina: å sen gick hon-
                                         and then she went-

16   Anna: синяках.
              over.

17   Irina: sen gick hon ju hem, eftersom-
              then she went home didn't she, since-
     Anna: старый- то есть старый человек,
                              an old- that is an old person,

18   Irina: eftersom hon var full med blå:::märken. hon är ju en
              since she was black and blue::::: all over. she is isn't she an

19   gammal gammal människa.
              old old person.

Using a simultaneous mode of interpreting may in itself be a main means by which the interpreter keys her talk as originating in other's speech. Speaking closely behind the applicant is to guarantee, as it were, that every single word spoken by the other is translated. It is perhaps also to remind the speaker that the interpreter's official task is to translate everything said and do nothing but translate. Each time the interpreter in this excerpt starts to talk she comes in energetically and loudly. This implies that she gets the floor and the applicant stops talking. Now and then short periods of silence occur (as between line 8 and 9).

Starting to translate after having heard just one or a few words, Irina constantly competes with the applicant for the floor. Being unwilling to leave it, the applicant raises her voice. Irina occasionally 'replays' words of the applicant, as if they had been emphasized as particularly important to the content of talk. For instance, the stress on "always" (2:4) and the non-standard emphasis on "that" (2:8, 2:10) seems to result from the parties' struggling for the floor.

Being insensitive to the importance of timing, the interpreter ends up restricting quite severely the primary interlocutors' communicative space and, simultaneously, as a result, obstructing her own work. She misses key information, for instance, Irina says "mother" instead of "grandmother" (2:2). To compensate for this, as it were, she performs an exaggerated imitation of the applicant's performative style. The applicant's description of her grandmother's difficulty in walking home after having been thrown out of the meat-queue ("she could hardly walk home, because she was black and blue all over") (2:15) has its correspondence in an interpreter's version presented in fragments: "and then she went- then she went home didn't she, since- since she was black and blue:::: all over" (2:15, 2:17, 2:18). Irina's version involves a *ju*, a device marking something like 'it is understood', by which speakers may attribute responsibility to listeners for creating coherence out of current talk. The same device is used in the interpreter's subsequent: "she is isn't she an old old person" (2:18–19). The information corresponds to the applicant's mention of her grandmother being old "an old- that is an old person" (2:17). Anna's repetition of "old", however, is rather to make sure that the interpreter hears what she says, since she talks with her in overlap, than to particularly emphasize the grandmother's old age, as it came out in the second version. Irina's effort to 'relay by replaying' is made at the expense of interactional order. In organizational terms, what Schegloff (1996:97) phrases 'transition spaces', are no less parts of interaction than talk itself.[4]

3.1 Staying closely behind – unintended consequences

My first-hand impression of the interlocutors being 'out of tune' was confirmed in the interview with the applicant. She had felt the interpreter to be inferring in a disturbing way. The interpreter's fragmented speech comes out as an imitation, which to a bilingual (Russian–Swedish) audience could appear close to parody. To understand something as parody presupposes knowledge about a specific or typical original, however, and this is something the recipient officer hardly had.

The interpreter used a similar way of speaking Swedish (with a strong accent and with non-standard prosodic emphasis) in all encounters where I recorded her, and the police officer, who often worked with this particular interpreter, was used to this. In the interview afterwards she told me that she understood Irina's way of interpreting to be the normal one; that she got from Irina what she expected from an interpreter.

Concludingly it could be noted that the officer provided little (if any) direct feedback. This made Irina all the more responsible for organizing interaction. The interpreter's version is perhaps not altogether comprehensible to the officer, but it is the only version she can work with. All the more remarkable then that, during the whole encounter, there are no initiatives on the part of the police officer to make the applicant (or the interpreter) clarify something said.

4. "CAN YOU ASK HIM TO COMMENT"

The third excerpt in this chapter illustrates that the interpreter's task of managing the interaction order occasionally may counteract their ability and/or willingness to 'relay by replaying'. The semantic complexity of the primary parties' talk would have constituted quite a challenge to any interpreter trying to 'relay by replaying'. The present interpreter basically relays by 'displaying' throughout the sequence explored. This implies that the second version, for better or worse, comes out as simplified in many respects. Interpreters sometimes opt for 'relaying by displaying' to avoid overtaxing their cognitive, translatory and coordinative abilities. Furthermore,

different performative styles are evidently not equally suitable to
interpreters' 'replaying'. Being imitated by an interpreter in face-
to-face interaction, some styles appear to be more vulnerable to
the interpreter's evaluation. The second version may change, as it
were, the interactional significance of the first one, when the two
are contrasted with one another. This seems to depend partly on the
convergence between the current speaker's style and the typical[5]
interpreter's style (understood as being formal and strict), and partly
on the degree of similarity or diversity the interpreter understands
between the primary interlocutors' expectations and viewpoints.
This, in turn, would depend on the social identities (and loyalties)
that are activated in interaction.

Excerpt (3) is drawn from an encounter at the immigration
department of a local police station. The actors are the police officer
(Peter), in whose office the encounter takes place, the applicant for
a residence permit in Sweden (Anton), and the interpreter (Ilona).
(Other parts of this meeting were explored in Chapter 6, Examples
(7) and (8) and in Chapter 8, (1) and (2).) Comparing what the police
officer says and what Ilona voices in his name as regards their
respective animation of 'figures', we may observe some significant
discrepancies.

Fairly close to the end of the talk, which all in all was about an
hour long, the officer comes back to Anton's relation to Germany.
Is the visitor a German citizen? If not, has he applied for German
citizenship? What Anton has said so far on the matter does not
satisfy Peter. He leafs through the file in front of him and takes out
a letter, simultaneously explaining why he is returning to this issue,
already extensively discussed. As it appears, the applicant's statements do not entirely fit with the information received beforehand
by the immigration authorities.

(3) (G21:25)

1   Peter: mm. då- då- jag måste återkomma till detta med Sovjet.
             mm. then- then- I have to return to this matter of the USSR.

2   ⌈   det här är-
             this is-
    ⌊ Ilona: я хочу ещё раз вернуться об этом ...
             I want to return about this once again ...

3   Peter: Tyskland. förlåt. °jag är lite trött idag.° detta är ett- ett
             Germany. sorry. °I'm a bit tired today.° this is a- a

4   brev från svenska ambassaden i Moskva till
             letter from the Swedish embassy in Moscow to the

5		Invandrarverket. såhär står det: denna man har
		Immigration Board. it says this: this man has
6		förklarat sig införstådd med och beredd att **om**
		declared himself to be in agreement with and prepared if
7		erforderligt resa- att om **erforderligt** resa till
		*necessary to travel- if **necessary** to travel to*
8		Tyskland i avvaktan på beslut om uppehålls- och
		Germany while awaiting a decision about residence- and
9		arbetstillstånd, e::: det normala e att man får inte söka
		work permits. er::: normally you're not allowed to apply for
10		tillstånd i Sverige utan man ska ordna det (xx)
		a permit in Sweden but you're supposed to arrange this (xx)
11	Ilona:	mhm.
		mhm.
12	Peter:	och ibland alltså så blir dom tjuriga på Invandrarverket
		and sometimes then they happen to get grumpy at the Immigration
13		och säger: åk utanför Sverige så ska vi se vad vi kan
		Board and say: go outside Sweden and we'll see what we can
14		göra. ungefär.
		do. something like that.
15	Ilona:	mhm.
		mhm.
16	Peter:	och då- då- en del människor som- dom vill inte åka
		and then- then- some people who- they don't want to go
17		till sitt **hemland** utan dom åker nån annanstans å bor
		*to their **home country** but they go somewhere else and stay*
18		på hotell,
		at a hotel,
19	Ilona:	mhm
		mhm
20	Peter:	eller nånting sånt där. det är bakgrunden. kan du be att
		or something like this. that's the background. can you ask
21		han kommenterar.
		him to comment.
→ 22	Ilona:	mhm. я хочу, ещё раз вернуться к этому письму
		mhm. I want to return once again to this letter
23		из шведского посольства в Москве. в
		from the Swedish embassy in Moscow. to
24		иммиграционное бюро здесь. вы сказали. что вы
		the immigration office here. you said. that you
25		понимаете и согласны на то чтобы е- если
		understand and agree to i- if
26		нужно выехать в Германию, в то время когда
		necessary travel to Germany, while

27		решение о вашем- о возможности вашей
		the decision about your- about the possibility of your
28		остаться жить бу- будет решаться.
		staying to live is- is decided.
29	Anton:	я- тут было так сказано. если Швеция не нам
		I- there it was put like this. if Sweden don't let us
30		оставит, если не к матери не оставит, тогда вы-
		stay, if [it] don't let me stay with [my] mother, then I
31		буду **вынужден** выехать в Германию.
		*for- I'll be **forced** to travel to Germany.*
32		понимаете? потому что …
		you understand? because …

When the above stretch of talk was recorded, the interpreter marked herself as speaker not of her own, but the officer's words, by speaking rather monotonously and by looking at nobody (just straight in front of herself). The distance from her own speech is further emphasized by the strictness of style. The officer animates a dialogue, involving various 'figures'. Ilona simplifies this, animating just one 'figure' – the officer. In this way she avoids 'replaying' his irritation, hesitation and so forth; she avoids conveying involvement, and, simultaneously, a risk of being understood as sharing the officer's irritation, and thereby as being partial.

Ilona's summary in Russian is short. Its shortness is perhaps partly due to the organization of interaction; to the fact that Anton comes in with a comment (which the officer had requested (3:20–21)) before Ilona has said anything about the attitude of the Immigration Board to applications sent from within Sweden. But it could probably also be explained by the complexity of the officer's statement, in terms of implied fluctuations in 'participation framework', including the various 'figures' animated.

Three actors are explicitly marked as distanced from the police officer's displayed self. Firstly, he talks about himself ("I") when re-introducing the issue of the applicant's connection to Germany (3:1) and when excusing himself for being distracted (3:3). Secondly, he animates the voice of the Swedish embassy in Moscow (3:5–9), and, thirdly, the Immigration Board ("we") (3:13–14). Furthermore, when he finally says: "can you ask him to comment" (3:20–21), the "him" refers to the applicant, and consequently the "you" must refer to the interpreter. In other words, the applicant comes to belong to those Peter speaks *about*, while Ilona is cast as the one spoken *to*.

Investigating the officer's speech in detail, I further noted a mixture of performative styles, from one utterance to another, and even within utterances. Along with the introduction of a new 'figure' goes a shift of vocabulary, gesture and also voice characteristics. His hesitation at the beginning is followed by an explanation for being hesitant – "I'm a bit tired today" (3:3). He reads the letter from the Swedish embassy, written in formal, bureaucratic language, in a tone which differs quite considerably from his subsequent speech, his own 'interpretation', as it were, from officialese into everyday-life, informal language. He uses the non-standard, somewhat disrespectful expression *tjuriga* ("grumpy") (3:12) when speaking about 'them' at the Immigration Board, and, accounting for what is sometimes done by people who have not applied for a residence permit in their country of origin. Indirectly, Peter is in this way telling how Anton could act if the Immigration Board refuses to handle his application, which is delivered in Sweden, and not, as it normally should be, processed before the immigrant enters the country (3:9–14). At this moment, the officer waves the letter lightly in the direction of Ilona, to whom he also directs almost all of his attention. This possibly strengthens the impression that some of the officer's talk is intended only for the interpreter.

4.1 Strictness and simplification

As opposed to the officer's mixed style, the performative style of Ilona could thus be characterized as consistent and quite strict throughout. In her version, the only 'figure' animated is "I" – the officer, and it is understood that the past and the present are seen and spoken about from his present point of view. What is said in the letter from the Swedish embassy is conveyed as if authored here and now by the officer. The applicant is not spoken about in the third person form, as the officer did by quoting the letter – "this man" (3:5) –, or by talking directly to the interpreter – "can you ask him to comment" (3:20–21). Ilona consistently addresses Anton by using "you", which implies that she gives voice to the officer in a way that conveys unfailing attention directed to the applicant. Ilona in this way radically reduces the need to mark distinctions between various 'figures' and, simultaneously, to mark distinctions between self and other.

The interpreter's behaviour above all serves the purpose of keeping interaction focused around the issue of Anton's citizenship. In this context, Ilona might have experienced the officer's private-style comment about his employers – the immigration authorities (3:12–14) – as superfluous or even counterproductive. The question of Anton's connection to Germany had indeed already been extensively discussed, a fact which evidently contributed to a slight irritation in the officer's voice. Possibly, the interpreter counts on this aspect of his talk to be heard and seen by the applicant even without her conveying it. Whether or not this is the case, the strictness of her style of talking marks a certain contrast to the preceding speaker's style(s). Moreover, to 'replay' Russian officialese corresponding to the Swedish in the letter would have demanded the interpreter's oral fluency in this written genre. This would have constituted quite a challenging task. The fast switch between the written language style and the spoken language slang would have made 'relaying by replaying' even more difficult. 'Relaying by displaying' here fits better the interpreter's level of language proficiency. 'Displaying' the officer's request she evidently promotes continued focused interaction, but simultaneously, as we saw, she misses an opportunity to highlight the primary interlocutors' lack of sharedness concerning what is mutually understood as regards the correct way to apply for a residence permit in Sweden. The background information about how applications are usually handled by the Immigration Board was, in this encounter, not mentioned again.

5. "SHE GOES: YES"

The fourth excerpt highlights embarrassment in institutional interpreter-mediated interaction and the inherent resistance to this emotional aspect of talk being 'relayed by replaying'. In this excerpt the interpreter avoids being identified as embarrassed herself when she animates an embarrassed patient's talk, by doing this in quite a strict and formal manner. In this way she also avoids being understood as parodying. The patient's talk is dramatized through his animation of 'figures' from a past event. The interpreter's style becomes more formal partly through her 'displaying' this dialogue in the form of an account where only the patient talking in the here-and-now situation figures. Hence, 'replaying by displaying' helps organize interaction and promote focusing on a medical issue (HIV testing) as the main one.

Excerpt (4) is drawn from an encounter (quoted also in Chapters 7 (Ex.2) and 8 (Ex.4)), where the patient, a young Russian-speaking man (Pavel) has an appointment with a nurse (Nina) at a local clinic. The transcription begins when Pavel has started to introduce what appears to be the main reason why he has turned up at the clinic. Firstly, he speaks in general terms about the increased risk of getting an HIV infection in his former home country. Secondly, he approaches his personal problem and his fears, which are connected to a particular event in the past.

(4) (G31:8)

1 Pavel: и я боюсь в общем из-за одного, что . . . одна
         and I'm afraid on the whole because of one thing, that . . . one
2   девушка там . . . я с ней значит полгода не
         girl there . . . she and I that is for half a year we hadn't
3   встречался. вот. а потом опять встретился.
         seen each other. like. and then I saw [her] again.
4 Inna: jag är lite rädd. e::: de e . . . funnits en flicka som jag
         I am a bit afraid. er::: there . . . was a girl I
5   träffade.
         used to see.
6 Pavel: а потом чего-то просто так вот просто так
         and then something it's just like that just like this
7   спросил,
         I asked
8 Inna: och efter ett halvår har jag inte träffat henne
         and after half a year I didn't see her
9 Pavel: mm . . .
         mm . . .
10 Inna: träff-
         see-
11 Pavel: я как раз- ну я так спросил, утром значит. и . . .
         it was just that I- well I asked like this, in the morning that is.
10   а, ты с иностранцами не была, там случайно, за
         and . . . well, you haven't been with foreigners, by any chance,
11   это полгода? вот . . . ну я был уверен что: нет.
         in the last half year? so . . . well I was convinced that: no.
12   а она значит: ((laughs)) да. один раз была значит.
         but she goes that is: yes. once she had been that is.
         ((laughs))

→ 13   Inna: och jag ... när vi var tillsammans så frågade jag henne
              and I ... when we were together then I asked her
   14   på morgonen om hon har varit ihop med någon
              in the morning if she had been with a
   15   utlänning och e ... å det hade hon. för att e ...
              foreigner and er ... and she had. because er ...
   16   Pavel: да
              yes
   17   Inna: jag träffade henne inte under ett halvår och ...
              I didn't see her for half a year and ...

In Pavel's mini-account two 'figures' are voiced from a scene taking place in the patient's former home country – a girl and Pavel himself. In Inna's translation, there is one 'figure' – "I", which animates the patient in the present situation, telling a story *about* what he and his former girlfriend said on some particular occasion.

Inna thus goes for a 'relaying by displaying' approach. Firstly, this reduces her need to memorize in detail the exact word order of his fragmented and stumbling speech, what seems like quite a demanding task, cognitively. Another aspect worth mentioning concerns interactional face-work. The persons quoted in Excerpt (4) differ quite considerably in emotional expressiveness. Pavel's frequent use of words like *no* ("but"), *vot* ("so/like") and *znachit* ("that is"), plus his embarrassed tone of voice, underlined by unilateral laughter, furnish his utterance with an overall sense of embarrassment, hesitation and caution. In contrast, the nurse (whose talk is not seen in the above sequence) and Inna both adopt a style of speaking which is rather matter-of-fact, considerate, strict, or, if you wish, neutral, in relation to the current topic, a style which answers to expectations normally projected upon interpreters.

5.1 Strictness to counteract embarrassment

It is not hard to realize that if the interpreter had tried to 'replay' the patient, she would have run the risk of appearing to ridicule or parody him in front of the nurse. This does not imply that her attitude towards embarrassment necessarily is negative, or that she thinks the nurse thinks negatively of it. It is rather that this performative style is not suitable to be 'replayed' in this situation. For one thing, awkwardness and shame do not belong to the typical style of interpreter. Furthermore, there may be social constraints in a situation against mimicking embarrassment.

In view of the communicative goal the interpreter has identified with the patient, she has a certain interest in conveying clearly his message promoting this goal – his reason to ask for a HIV test. To reassure this coming through, Inna corrects her first interpretation of the patient's "for half a year we hadn't seen each other" (4:2–3). She had mistakenly used the adverb "after": "and after half a year I didn't see her" (4:8). Coming back a second time she translates the same clause as "I didn't see her for half a year" (4:17). The 'relaying by displaying' approach here fits the interpreter's level of proficiency and the overall institutional goal of time efficiency.

Goffman (1971) in his book *Relations in Public* argues that an individual's embarrassment blocks the situated social organization of face-to-face interaction. It seems to undermine the very foundations of mutually coordinated activity (Goffman 1971:97–112). Inspired by Goffman, and drawing on findings from his own investigations of doctor-patient interactions, Heath (1988) has observed that one aspect of the threat to interactional organization posed by embarrassment is that it renders the individual conscious of his or her own action and his or her involvement in interaction with others (Heath 1988:155).

Every now and then, when talking with fellow interpreters, I have discussed the question of how to translate emotions. Some interpreters complain that emotions are lost in interpretation. For instance, they may understand clients to be talking animatedly about injustice, pain, prosecution and other horrors, but their versions of the stories seem to come out in a desiccated fashion, and the officials' subsequent chilly reaction makes the interpreter feel that the clients doubt the faithfulness of their interpretation. Applying an interactionistic view, one may consider the officials' cool and remote attitude as in itself constituting a condition which promotes a strict and formal style of interpreting when addressing the officials. Moreover, different kinds of emotion involve various kinds of complexity. Embarrassment, as I would argue, is inherently resistant to being 'relayed by replaying'.

6. "WHAT IS THIS? THEY SAY: IT'S OKAY"

The last two excerpts illustrate cases in which the interpreter (Ivana) was closer to 'relaying by replaying' than any of the other interpreters in the preceding cases. This is partly explained by her proficiency, in terms of vocabulary in Russian and Swedish, in speed, translation fluency and, not least, in her sense of timing. Partly it was due to the fact that, in both instances, the interpreter's need to mark the distinction between speaking self and meaning other is considerably diminished given the fact that the primary parties largely share expectations and viewpoints concerning common interaction and the interpreter's part in it.

In Excerpt (5) the interpreter gives voice to several 'figures' which have just been staged in a primary interlocutor's talk, more precisely an "I" and the protagonists of this "I" in past events. In other words, she goes for 'relaying by replaying'. Clearly, the interpreter counts on the audience's ability to distinguish between the speaking self and the meaning others and the conditions for this, as it seems, are created in interaction.

The excerpt is drawn from an encounter at a small neighbourhood child-care clinic (the same as in Excerpt 5, Chapter 8). A young Russian-speaking woman (**Maria**) mother of a baby girl, meets with a paediatric nurse (**Nancy**). They know each other from before and have, not without difficulty, communicated in English on other occasions. For the present encounter they have decided to use an interpreter (**Ivana**). The analysed sequence mostly consists of the mother's talk, but also of frequent feedback from the actively listening nurse. The professional party's involvement, as it appears, substantially helps the interpreter to structure interaction, including her own participation in it.

We come in when Maria has just brought up the problem of "the infection" which she sees on her daughter's leg. The nurse tries to explain that it is not actually an infection, but "an abscess". Maria appears to find this information unsettling. What is it, actually, that has annoyed the baby more or less from birth?

(5) (G42:13–14)

```
 1  Maria:    да то есть буквально- и мы (в начале у неё)
                yes that is literally- and we- (in the beginning she had)
 2            приходила- мне это очень беспокоит. я всё
                [I] came- this worries me a lot. I came
 3 ⎡Ivana:                                      mm
   ⎣Maria:    время приходила к врачу: что это? они
                all the time to the doctor: what is this? they
 4            говорят: всё хорошо, всё хорошо . . . а я же видела.
                say: everything's okay, everything's okay . . . but I still saw.
```


5 что-то такое.
something like this.

Ivana: mhm,   mm och jag har varit,
                  mhm,   *mm and I have been,*

6 väldigt orolig hela tiden, jag har, frågat läkaren eller . . .
very worried all the time, I have, been asking the doctor or . . .

Nancy: aa

→ 7 Ivana: eh . . . sjuksköterskorna **hela** tiden: va- va kan de
*eh . . . the nurses **all** the time: what- what can be*

8 bero på?
the reason?

Nancy: aa
weell

→ Ivana: a de e okej, de e okej. de e inget att oroa sig för.
well it's okay, it's okay. this is nothing to worry about.

9 Nancy: mm mm   jaa
        mm mm   *yes*

Maria: то есть- а это?
                   that is- but this?

10 Nancy: de va-   problemet-
        that was-   *the problem-*

Maria: вообще **бывает**. вот **что** это такое.
*does this **occur/happen** at all. so **what** is it.*

11 потому что я . . .
because I . . .

Ivana: men eh . . . det **händer** alltså . . . och vad **är** det
*but er . . . it **happens** that is . . . and what **is** it*

12 egentligen? vad kan det bero på.
actually? what is the reason.

Nancy: ja de-
                   yes it-

Maria's mini-story is told as a dialogue between two 'figures' – "I", Maria and "they", the doctors. Talking to Nancy (and Ivana) at the centre, she paints a picture of past encounters with nursing staff members, where she "all the time" has been asking: "what is this?" (5:3), while they have answered: "everything's okay, everything's okay . . ." (5:4). This might be also how she interprets the nurse's answer in the present encounter. In that case, the protagonists she quotes from the past potentially also include Nancy.

Ivana mimics Maria's staged characters, using semantic means similar to those utilized by the original speaker. She gives voice to an "I", signifying Maria in interaction at past occasions with members of medical staff, including, possibly, the immediate past. She quotes the mother in the dialogue: "what can be the reason?" and "the doctor or the nurses" (5:6–7): "well it's okay, it's okay. this is nothing to worry about." (5:9).

To convey Maria's message more clearly, Ivana provides two versions of the latter quotation, one which is linguistically 'closer' to the original, and another which is more explanatory. In this, her relaying acquires more of a 'display' character. Ivana's displayed analysis of the situation is, however, voiced from the perspective of the 'figures' staged in the mother's talk. It answers directly to the way in which Maria introduced her story – "this worries me a lot" (5:2). The mother's narration ends in a question which in view of the described past dialogues could be read as quite a critical comment. She has still not received an answer to the question "does this *happen* at all. so *what* is it." (5:10). Is her daughter's problem with her leg really what normally happens to babies? What, actually, is the nurse's expert opinion? This is the direction in which Ivana interprets, and how Nancy subsequently responds to the mother's request. The intensively and quite extensively discussed issue is settled after some more rounds of talk, and then dropped.

6.1 Building upon the participants' involvement

The exchange cited in Extract (5) in reality took 28 seconds. It contains a mini-story conveying worry, accumulated over numerous encounters with medical institutions. Worry as a dominating emotional expression colours the interpreter's contributions as well. This relative closeness between Maria's and the interpreter's talk is clearly supported by the nurse's displayed involvement. Nancy shows strong interest and eagerness to take part of the mother's thoughts. Interestingly, the 'tightness' of discourse has a correspondence in the physical space created between the participants of the encounter. When Maria sat down in the middle of Nancy's small office, the nurse immediately brought her own chair from behind her desk and placed herself very close, so that she could reach the baby on the mother's lap, and the baby could easily be moved to her own. Maria, in turn, displays an anxiousness to share her worries with Nancy; to hear what the nurse has to say on the current matter.

The relaxed and intimate atmosphere between the women is probably also favourable for the interpreter's 'relaying by replaying' style. The interlocutors exchange a lot of smiles and laughter. Their

meeting, about 30 minutes long, takes place in a spirit of consensus and shared enthusiasm. The nurse and the mother had been
acquainted for quite some time and had met in several situations
similar to the present one. Hence, a certain sameness of expectations and viewpoints between them may be assumed.

The two primary interlocutors' talk is often overlapping, and
overlaps with the interpreter's utterances are frequent. Largely
thanks to the interpreter's speed and timing, however, the parallel
discourse promotes rather than obstructs interaction. Turns are exchanged with high frequency. Another factor which deserves some
attention in this connection is that the object of conversation – the
baby – is present for all to see. The situations which Maria recalled
from the past were similar to the present one and concerned the
same issue, namely the problem with the baby's leg. Ivana thus had
the opportunity to direct talk to the child when speaking about the
child, as Maria did. Ivana, moreover, shared Maria's experience of
being the mother of a small child and having met health-care personnel in this role. These are all factors which speak in favour of
this particular interpreter here 'relaying by replaying' the role of
the worried mother. Apparently, some conditions facilitating and
promoting interpreters' 'relaying by replaying' are established in
the process of face-to-face interaction.

7. "WOULD YOU ALLOW ME TO ADD?"

The following excerpt involves a long stretch of uninterrupted,
professional-language-style talk. The speaker is not the professional
party, however, but the layperson. His communicative style differs considerably from the young mother's in the above example.
Nevertheless, the encounter as a whole involves a feature which
again seems to promote the interpreter's performing 'relaying by
replaying', namely a clear similarity in expectations and viewpoints
between the primary interlocutors. The encounter takes place in
a doctor's surgery. The interpreter is the same as in the preceding
excerpt, i.e. Ivana. She had special training in medical interpreting,
which explains additionally why, to her, both the vocabulary and
the style of speaking are fairly easy to mimic. Nevertheless, at one
point 'relaying by replaying' is not the approach that could best
serve her communicative project, namely to provide contextual facts

in order to promote shared knowledge between the parties on a specific subject matter.

It is a routine medical check-up where a Russian-speaking couple with a small child meet a general practitioner. The wife mentions her troubles with her heart and lungs. The doctor (Dan) follows up by inquiring about what kind of medicines she uses. The woman mentions a few types of medication and takes out a little box from her bag. She shows it to the interpreter (Ivana) who takes it and reads from the label. The practitioner goes on: "Are these the *only* ones you take?" The husband mentions another sort, and this is where Extract (6) begins. The **man** (**Maxim**) inserts quietly:

(6) (G32:9–10)

1	Maxim:	позвольте мне добавить?
		would you allow me to add?
2	Ivana:	får jag lägga till?
		would you allow me to add?
3	Dan:	javisst,
		sure,
4	Ivana:	пожалуйста.
		you are welcome.
	Maxim:	мм. е::: положение это у неё::: достаточно
		mhm. er::: this condition of hers er::: is quite
5		серьёзное. потому как е::: е::: вплоть до того
		serious. because of how er::: er::: up to the point
6		что . . . е::: она вынуждена была сменить работу.
		that . . . er::: she was forced to change her job.
7		будучи педагогом. и перейти на более лёгкую. и
		being a teacher. and move to a more easy one. and
8		речь постоянно стояло об инвалидности более
		there was constant talk of disability of the more
9		тяжёлой группы. только нежелание связываться с
		severe type. only unwillingness to get in contact with
10		бюрократической машиной советской медицины,
		the bureaucratic machine of the Soviet medical system,
11		не довели мы это до конца.
		kept us from carrying this through.

[. . .]

27		потому что сейчас она задыхается-
		because now she's short of breath-
	Ivana:	с::: стоп. не успеваю.
		s:::stop. I can't manage.
28	Maxim:	ага.
		oh.

→ 29 Ivana: ПОТОМ. сейчас скажете. jo. jag skulle alltså lägga till
                     afterwards. soon you can speak. well. that is I would like to add
30   följande. att hennes situation är mycket allvarlig och det
                     the following. that her situation is very serious and this
31   kan jag bedöma e::: korrekt. alltså hon måste- hon
                     I can judge er::: correctly. that is she has to- she
32   känner sig så pass dålig att hon måste till och med byta
                     feels bad to such an extent that she even had to change
33   jobb, hon är egentligen pedagog, men hon sku- måste
                     her job, actually she is a teacher, but she was- that is had to
34   alltså byta till ett lättare jobb. och det var dessutom tal
                     change to an easier job. and moreover there were discussions
35   om **invaliditet**. e::: °här måste jag förklara att i Sovjet
                     *about **disability**. er::: °here I have to explain that in the*
36 ⌈   så är det flera grader av **invaliditet**, det vill säga ett
                     *USSR there are several degrees of **disability**, that is a*
  ⌊Dan: *mm*
                           mm
37 Ivana: slags förtidspensionering, då man får ett- ersättning
                     kind of disability pension, when you get a- compensation
38   från staten och slipper då vissa svårare jobb.° alltså det
                     from the state and are let off from more difficult jobs.° that is
39   var tal om hennes **invaliditet**. alltså hon skulle
                     *there were discussions about her **disability**. that is she was about*
40   invalidiseras. inte behöva . . . arbeta men det- det enda
                     to be disabled not have to . . . to work but the- the only thing
41   som stoppade oss den här gången det- det är den
                     that stopped us this time it- it is the
42 ⌈   sovjetiska byråkratin den byråkratiska . . . ((breath)) ja.
                     Soviet bureaucracy. the bureaucratic . . .   *yes.*
  ⌊Dan: mm
                           mm
43 Ivana: apparaten då.
                     the machine then.
[. . .]
58 Dan: mm, visst, jorå . . .
                     mm. sure, well yes . . .
59 Maxim: и:::
                     a:::nd
60 Dan: visst, kommer vi ordna.
                     sure, we'll arrange [this].

Characteristic of Maxim's talk is a professional matter-of-factness, which means that Ivana had no problem with fitting in a strict and formal style of interpreting. The "I" introduced by Maxim refers to himself, talking from his position here-and-now. He speaks from this same position through quite an extensive turn at talk (in reality it was a monologue one minute and 32 seconds long, most of which is left out here). The 'figure' animated in the Russian doctor's talk is only "I", meaning himself in the present situation. He tells his and his wife's story about past times, his expert opinion as doctor (and husband) about her present state and his hope that she will get adequate help in the future.

Maxim's consistency of performative style probably supports Ivana's memorizing. The particular significance of his style becomes quite clear in view of how the encounter in question started. The general practitioner opened it by asking the man about his profession, and subsequently it was established that the two could speak as one doctor to another. Maxim thus speaks not only as a husband *for* his wife, but also, simultaneously, *about* his wife, who is sitting by his side, in a relatively 'objectified' way, as a practitioner speaking to a colleague about a case. Underlining his identity as medical expert, Maxim appeals to his co-actor's professional loyalty – to their *co-membership* (Erickson and Shultz 1982:17). The fact that the interlocutors are seen as having an identity in common – their medical profession – considerably downplays the interpreter's need to mark distinctions between self and other; to mark her own speaking as speech on another's behalf, in order to avoid being understood as partial.

7.1 The work of sameness and contrast

Ivana repeats Maxim's story in the name of an "I", talking from the perspective of the Russian man. Apart from conveying this in great detail, however, Ivana, at one point, inserts a piece of background information; a translator's note, as it were, to the immediately preceding interpretation. Her way of marking this as stemming from herself, and not from the Russian man, is by creating a contrast in the process of vocalizing, through shifts in pitch and the rhythmic repetition of a key gloss. She communicates a separateness between the "I" in this note, and the "I" that current talk belongs to, by lowering her voice when saying: "here I have to explain that in the USSR there are several degrees of *disability*, that is a kind of disability pension, when you get a- compensation from the state and are let off from more difficult jobs" (6:35–38), and then continuing in the same voice pitch as before. Ivana's return to words which originate in the other's utterance is additionally marked through her repetition of and emphasis on the word "disability". The first and last instances where this word is uttered frame the inserted comment.

The simultaneous change of gaze direction is another means to mark the shift of relation between figuring selves. When talking from her own point of view (6:35–38), Ivana looks up from her notes, and directs attention to the doctor. Notetaking helps Ivana to 'replay' Maxim's close to written-language-standard expert-talk.' Probably this would not have been sufficient, however, if she had not been well acquainted, through experience and training, with health care expert style and vocabulary.

8. THE ANALYSING ASPECT OF REPORTED SPEECH

Interpreters on duty in face-to-face interaction may occasionally feel a need to be explicit about the fact that what they say stems not from themselves, but from someone else. Primary parties may, more or less occasionally, simply find it unnatural to address their counterpart directly when they assume that this person (but not the interpreter) is incapable of understanding what they say. In practice, despite interpreters informing and reminding them about the direct-discourse principle of professional interpreting some primary interlocutors may persist in addressing the *interpreter* directly, and mentioning the other as 'she' or 'he'.

I have found significant differences between people's accounts of how they talk through interpreters, and the ways they actually do it in real-life interpreter-mediated encounters. People who claim that they consistently talk directly to their foreign-language counterparts in practice occasionally address the interpreter directly and speak about the other interlocutor. The simple fact that interpreters are *present* in interaction, and responsibility which ultimately lies with another person can be attributed to them, sometimes creates the main difficulty in the task of interpreting. Conversely, for primary interlocutors communicating with the assistance of an interpreter, a major pitfall may be their inability to distinguish the limits of the interpreter's responsibility for what she or he utters, and to distinguish the other party's responsibility for the interpreter's talk. The analytical model suggested in this chapter helps link thoughts of these aspects of interpreter-mediated interaction with how they may be worked out in practice.

8.1 Interpreting – analytical transmission of another's speech

The model outlined at the beginning of this chapter basically distinguishes between two ways for interpreters to cope with the task of reporting others' speech. The relationship between the original version of a certain instance of talk and the interpreter's second version of it can be classified as 'relaying by replaying' and 'relaying by displaying'. The two styles of relaying can be seen as endpoints in a continuum. In practice they are, moreover, used interchangeably. Sorting out situational reasons why the one approach could be preferred to the other I started by identifying the interpreter's need to mark the distinction between the currently speaking self and the meaning other. Related to this is the interpreter's need to every now and then position him- or herself as impartial and neutral in interaction. Both these needs, in certain situations, clash with a 'relaying by replaying' approach and demand more 'relaying by displaying'.

Interpreters' ways of marking limited responsibility for what they utter – by semantic means, vocal pitch, gaze and body positioning – become part of their personal style of performing. Their need to mark limited responsibility is partly also a question of personality. It is a question of being more or less confident with the relative proximity and non-involvement implied in the role of interpreter.

Voloshinov (1930) brings forward reported speech as an issue to focus on when investigating overall tendencies of language development. Discussing the history of forms of utterances, he observes that so-called 'quasi-direct' or 'free indirect discourse' is regarded by some authors as a matter of grammar and by others as a question of style. Voloshinov's point is that the borderline between grammar and style is fluid; while some forms of utterances are undergoing grammaticization, others are undergoing degrammaticization. Divorcing grammar and stylistics as two separate aspects of language, one misses the linguistic essence of indirect discourse, namely the *analytical* transmission of another's speech (Voloshinov 1986:126–8). In other words, the very act of reporting others' speech also involves analysing it.

The inherent commenting aspect of reporting others' speech complicates the interpreter's need to mark distinction between self and other. Paradoxically enough, an extra effort to relay by 'replaying' the primary party's utterance, imitating his or her rhetorical style, manner of speaking, prosody, and so forth, may occasionally direct attention not to the primary interlocutor's message, but to the interpreter, or rather, to how he or she relates to these utterances, provided on others' behalf. Interpreters' mimicking may, in certain circumstances, be taken as a critical evaluation of preceding talk. Thus, despite – and because of – the similarities between the two versions, the 'replaying' may serve to focus attention on the inevitable difference between the first and the second one.

This brings to mind what Berk-Seligson (1990) notes in her experimental study concerning the impact of interpreters on mock jurors' evaluations of witnesses. She observes that when the persons acting as jurors heard an interpreter mimicking paralinguistic Spanish utterances in equivalent paralinguistic English form, they clearly found this behaviour to be comical (Berk-Seligson 1990:193). In the Linköping data, one encounter (G32:4), recorded in a meeting at a hospital, involves an instance where the interpreter repeats a single back-channelling *mhm*, imitating the preceding speaker's prosody. The primary interlocutors reacted with surprise and amusement. Suddenly, both *mhm*-s stood out as separate contributions to discourse. Both findings illustrate, firstly that solely by being followed by a second version, the 'specific weight', as it were, of a first version may change, secondly that interpreting potentially involves properties of parody.

8.2 'Relaying by replaying' – possibilities and limitations

The present chapter has demonstrated a range of possibilities and limitations inherent in the role of interpreter in face-to-face interaction. It has shown how these are created partly in and by the situation, by its participants and their activities. The interpreters themselves, as well as their co-actors, set limits on their actions and create new possibilities. A conclusion to be drawn from this would be that a whole range of aspects relevant to interpreting do not lend themselves to description without a talk-as-activity frame of reference. The analyses suggest a wide definition of talk, including not only 'talk-as-text', and not only talk as verbal activity, but also talk as a combination of verbal and non-verbal activities. This wider definition has both practical and theoretical implications.

The above analyses have explained how 'relaying by replaying' and 'relaying by displaying' serve various functions in interaction, and how these functions are dependent on the immediate communicative context. Interpreters routinely shift between more of a 'relaying by replaying' and more of a 'relaying by displaying' approach in order to achieve three basic goals in the role of interpreter, namely to promote primary interlocutors' continued focused interaction, their illusion of mutual and shared involvement in an activity in common and their (at some level) shared and mutual understanding.

The analyses suggest some 'new' features to look at when developing methods by which quality in interpreting could be measured. For instance, the interpreter's ability to modulate the voice, to consciously use gaze and body positioning for interactional purposes and the interpreter's sense of what Erickson and Schultz (1982:72) explain with the Greek term *kairos* – the right time, the *now* whose time has come. There is no doubt that interpreters' ability to utilize adequate transitional moments in interaction is essential for the overall social organization of interaction.

The analyses also demonstrate the importance of realizing, as an interpreter, one's own level of proficiency and the limitations this has in a given interpretation situation; the importance of being strong enough to risk the disclosure of one's own weaknesses.

NOTES

1. "'Reported speech' is *speech within speech, utterance within utterance,* and at the same time also *speech about speech, utterance about utterance*" (Voloshinov 1986:115). Italics, etc. normalized in accordance with original.

2. An exotic illustration: People speaking in the traditional Stockholm slang clearly mark this relative distance by using *en annan* ("another") when talking about themselves, that is, where the standard Swedish would be *jag* and the standard English would be "I".

3. Quotation translated from interview carried out in Swedish.

4. See Apfelbaum (in press) for a discussion of the applicability of Schegloff's analytical model in relation to interpreter-mediated interaction. She scrutinizes encounters where a German-speaking technical specialist instructs two French-speaking technicians with the assistance of an interpreter, and focuses on the pattern of turnconstruction and turnallocation. Her observation suggests that 'transition space' is an analytical unit which indeed could be used to shed light on the specific nature of interpreter-mediated interaction.

5. Referring to *typical role* (cf. Chapter 5:2.1).

TEN

Bridging gaps and sustaining differences

Но с ответственностью связана и вина (Bakhtin [1919] 1979:7).[1]

In this book I have presented interpreter-mediated interaction as an everyday practice in public institutions, and as an object of scholarly inquiry. The book addresses on the one hand practitioners – such as police officers, doctors, nurses and interpreters – i.e. people involved in this kind of interaction as professionals. On the other hand it is written for students and researchers within Law, Medicine, Translation studies, Sociology, Anthropology, Pragmatics, Communication, and other fields where interpreter-mediated interaction constitutes a relevant field of study. The exploration of triadic encounters has generated knowledge relevant to mediated face-to-face communication in general, and to interpreter-mediated situations in particular.

The book takes up research issues which are new to the empirical field of interpreting. I present an analytical framework that explores both translation as an aspect of interpreting and the dynamics of interpreter-mediated interaction. A *monological* model of language and mind treats interpreting as a transfer of messages from one linguistic system to another, and interpreters as 'channels', which are temporarily hosting primary speakers' messages in their brains. This can be contrasted with a *dialogical* model of language and mind, which treats interpreting as interaction between participants in a social event. A dialogic – or interactionistic – conceptualization of interpreting allows the exploration of various communicative activities, their nature and their mutual interdependence in social interaction.

The book moreover demonstrated that interpreter-mediated interaction offers rich opportunities for exploring various communicative means, for instance, those interlocutors deploy to mark the distinction between self and other.

275

1. TRANSLATING IN INTERPRETING – IN A DIALOGICAL FRAME

Traditionally, interpreting has basically been treated as spoken translation, as equivalent to written translation. Research on interpreting has been focused on establishing correspondence between orally provided 'source texts' and 'target texts'. To investigate interpreting as interaction as I have done implies an extensive modification of this approach.

Exploring authentic interpreter-mediated discourse data, I start in Chapter 6 by examining interpreters' talk within a narrower talk-as-text paradigm. Interpreting is here identified as constituted by two main activities – translating and coordinating. The chapter presents two fairly simple, mutually compatible taxonomies of 'close' and 'divergent' 'renditions', contrasted with 'explicit' and 'implicit' 'coordinating moves'. Interpreting involves simultaneously focusing on the semantic and pragmatic content of discourse, and, at the same time, paying attention to its social organization. Furthermore, it is necessary to find an adequate balance of attention between these aspects. Treating interpreters' utterances as kinds of 'texts' one can explore how this is accomplished, distinguishing between speakers' 'text orientation' and 'interactional orientation'.

Investigating interpreters' utterances as kinds of 'texts', it might be tempting to view 'renditions' as an outcome of a comparatively passive action ("just translating"), with 'non-renditions' being the result of more active intervention. Yet, interpreters' impact upon the substance and the progression of a conversation is accomplished merely by their presence; by their providing translations every now and then ('implicit' coordination). In addition to this, interpreters sometimes explicitly initiate changes in the interaction order ('explicit' coordination). 'Passivity' is therefore a misleading notion in this connection. Active involvement is part and parcel of all interpreting – intra-lingual as well as inter-lingual. Hence, interpreters must maintain a minimum level of attentive listening and a state of preparation for active interpreting in order to carry out their job.

1.1 Rationalities of translation

A translator works with a theoretical model of two languages – source language and target language – and the relation between these two. The activity of translation demands that two separate linguistic entities are recognized and a gap between them is sustained. If interpreting is treated as equivalent to translation, the languages currently used by those requiring the intervention of an interpreter are consequently treated as separate linguistic domains. Moreover, the identities of those participating in the situation where interpretation occurs are each linked only to one of these domains. One person equals one language. The theory of translation invokes a certain 'linguistic absolutism' (cf. Gilroy 1987, Ch. 2, on 'ethnic absolutism'). Interpreting as translation gives exclusive emphasis to individuals' linguistic belonging. This hides or backgrounds their affiliations to all other social categories, such as those related to gender, class, age, professional status, and so forth. Moreover, interpreting as translation emphasizes one specific linguistic belonging and hides or backgrounds people's various associations with different languages; people's use of language(s) across linguistic borders.

For instance, the lay people occurring in this book all spoke Russian. Treating interpreting as translation I foreground their identity as Russian-speaking persons. In reality, two of them were equally fluent in two languages – Russian and the majority languages of the Soviet republics from which they respectively originated. In the context of the USSR, these languages were both minority languages. Many people associating with these minorities grew up as 'natives' not in one language, but in a combination of two languages. This is what happens to many young people today, growing up in and among a language minority and a majority speaking another language.

If interpreting is regarded as interaction, it becomes possible to investigate both the implications of 'linguistic absolutism' and the way it is established, maintained and neutralized as a feature of interpreter-mediated talk. In one encounter, for example, there was a sudden change in the flow of interaction when the interpreter mentioned to the Russian-speaking patient that the Swedish-speaking doctor understood Russian. (She had immigrated some twenty years ago from an Eastern European country.) From that moment on, the practitioner gave frequent feedback directly to the patient, and the patient looked straight at her when talking, instead of at the interpreter.

Interpreting as interaction makes it possible to identify non-linguistic features which link people together, and also non-linguistic differences between people – differences in world views – which make shared understanding between them difficult to achieve despite the interpreter's bridging of the language gap.

1.2 Interpreters, service and control

Most representatives of public institutions have a dual function of both service and control. In health care, the professionals' service function is normally prominent and the control function backgrounded. In legal encounters, the control function is perhaps the more obvious one. A significant difference, however, between medical and legal settings lies in the role of long-term control coming from written records. A talk between a patient and a doctor and an interrogation at a police station are both designed to be occasions where the professional elicits information from the layperson. The professional subsequently produces a document which is based on the interaction itself. These documents address a non-present audience. The officials are held responsible for their reports, and these become part of the files of the institution. In addition, for reports written by a servant of the law the interviewed person may also be held legally responsible. Such documents have legal status and may be used in litigation.

Interpreters too have a dual function of service and control. This is not necessarily recognized, however, by the actual institution. The law may acknowledge that an individual has spoken in a foreign language, and that he or she is quoted in the language of the legal setting, but in practical terms the interviewee's talk and the interpreter's version of this talk are taken as identical. Furthermore, the versions are seen as independent units, belonging to various individuals and to separate languages. In this way, the monological view of language and mind allows the use of second versions as legally binding first-hand records. In monologistic theory, the individual speaker alone 'determines' the meaning of what he or she is saying. In addition, speaking is understood to consist largely of individuals' brains processing units of languages, and these units (words, morphemes, etc.) are seen as 'meaningful' in and by themselves.

Yet no 'source text' can be exactly replicated in a 'target text'. This view of translations and translatability is now generally accepted, even by many lawyers. Nevertheless, the law has to personalize, as it were, the meaning of each utterance, and does this in accordance with monologistic assumptions. Legal systems presuppose the existence of a 'true' speaker's intention, and a 'true' word meaning, inherent in each word and utterance. Interpreters are supposed to transfer this intended meaning into another language. Lawyers, in contrast, have the court's mandate to sort out and reveal possible 'hidden' speakers' meanings. The dominating view of interpreters in legal settings is that of disembodied containers of others' messages. Interpreters as speakers are basically thought of as individuals processing information in their brains, which are furnished with two language systems, instead of the ordinary one.

There are challenges to this idealized view of legal interpreting, for instance, by Barsky (1994) and Morris (1993, 1995). In previous work I have also criticized the transfer model of interpreting and brought attention to the coordinating aspect inherent in interpreter-mediated discourse (Wadensjö 1992) (cf. also Roy 1989, 1993). This book further elaborates the distribution of knowledge and responsibility among speakers, and the interdependencies between speakers and between communicative activities in interpreter-mediated interaction.

1.3 Participation framework – modes of listening and speaking

The choices interpreters make in interaction as speakers and listeners make a significant difference to the progression and the substance of common discourse. Dealing with interpreting within a talk-as-activity, dialogical theoretical frame allows for exploration of the work accomplished by interpreters' shifting in interaction between various modes of listening and speaking.

The implications of dialogism are numerous. For instance, it implies that the meaning of what is said is settled in and by interaction between individuals. Moreover, the interactionally established meanings depend partly on how interlocutors make sense of particular words, gestures, and other 'contextualization cues', partly on how they understand each other's listenership and speakership, and partly how they understand each other's needs, interests and current understanding.

Qian (1994), suggesting a communicative approach to interpreting, identifies a specific quality in professional interpreters' listening. Their ability to "suppress instincts or impulses to interact with the participants of a communication event", according to him, constitutes their professional mode of listening (Qian 1994:218). This statement appears to be founded on a static view of human communication. It is as if Qian presupposes similarity and stableness in primary inter-locutors' communicative behaviour and, furthermore, sameness and mutuality in their understanding of interpreters' behaviour.

Yet interlocutors in face-to-face interaction, including interpreters, are normally flexible in modes of listening and speaking. Explorations of discourse data, transcribed in detail, make it possible to show how interpreters utilize the possibility of emphasizing various modes, in order to present themselves as more or less responsible for the content and the progression of current interaction. The role of inter-preter is performed through these actors' effective displaying, in interaction, of aspects of their listening and speaking selves. Hence, the role of interpreter is established and sustained interactionally.

1.4 Joint achievement of understanding – of facts and alignments

It goes without saying that interpreter-mediated interaction involves a certain lack of shared understanding. Interpreters are present to bridge a gap between parties who are unable or unwilling to understand each other directly. Hence, interpreters are by defini-tion placed in a position of promoting the primary interlocutors' mutual understanding. Chapter 8 explored levels of understanding in interpreter-mediated encounters. It distinguished between parti-cipants' understanding of various aspects of interaction – the con-tent of words and phrases used, the progression of interaction, the responsibility of various agents for the content and the progression of talk. Additionally, participants' understanding may concern the significance of current focused interaction for a specific factual task or for the development of a certain social relation.

The analyses concentrated on instances where interlocutors occa-sionally indicated lack of shared understanding by mentioning it explicitly. This, however, did not necessarily mean that misunder-standing became a focused issue in the triadic talk. Interpreters' counteracting of miscommunication was found to be typically for the benefit of sustaining a goal-orientated communicative exchange between the primary interlocutors.

In practice, interpreters adapt their performance to their under-standing of others' needs. At some points, shared understanding between the primary parties is not identified as a current need, even if one of them has indicated lack of shared understanding. Just as other participants in interaction do, interpreters may sometimes give priority to promoting a certain factual understanding at the expense of social rapport, and vice versa.

The analyses presented here examined the way interpreters handled lack of shared understanding between the primary parties. This issue is worth further exploration. When the officials indicated miscommunication this tended to be dealt with off-the-record. Laypersons' communication of lack of shared understanding was more frequently made a shared issue. Furthermore, many identified miscommunication events were treated by the interpreters as tasks for themselves alone to solve. The non-intended consequence of this was that the communicative contact between the primary interlocutors was severed, more or less temporarily. Being in settings where they appear to be experts on language and culture, interpreters run the risk of depriving the primary parties, especially the laypersons, of power and responsibility.

Paediatricians in particular (but also other caregivers I have talked to) have sometimes expressed frustration about difficulties in establishing rapport with their patients when talking through a third party. They feel some interpreters get too involved and take over too much in encounters with children. In such cases, the exchange of factual information may be sufficient for a particular treatment, but the practitioners' rapport with the child is judged to be compromised. One surgeon told me about a case where also the factual point of his question was lost completely because of the interpreter's wish to "help" the child and to "please" the doctor. He had asked a young boy, whose head had been injured by a bomb, if he remembered what the bomb looked like. The interpreter forwarded the question, but not the boy's immediate response, nor the following long discussion between herself, the boy and his mother. The interpreter came back to the surgeon only when she had some information about the bomb, which not necessarily the boy had provided. Hence, it remained unclear what the boy actually remembered about the event, and whether he at all was able to recapitulate it. Some practitioners pointed out that the same kind of problem occurs in monolingual encounters, when a parent talks for a child and the doctors' preference is for the child to speak directly. Any mediating person may be taken as inhibiting communicative contact between two individuals rather than promoting it, when they appoint themselves as the primary participant and spokesperson for others.

1.5 Institutional and lay rationalities

The dialogical perspective treats all participants in a communicative event as doing interpretative work. In making sense people bring all kinds of rationalities to interaction. A key question is to what extent lay perspectives are allowed to become visible in institutional talk. From a wide variety of studies of monolingual institutional encounters one can conclude that this depends on the ability and willingness of the representative of the organization to take the time to see the layperson's perspectives. It is also found to depend largely on how the clients (patients, applicants, etc.) master what have become the bureaucratically acceptable and expected modes of communication. The literature also shows that the institutional interactional format assigns a dominant position to the institutional party, and that they normally have more extensive opportunities to voice their perspective (e.g. Cedersund and Säljö 1993, Sarangi and Slembrouck 1996, Gunnarsson et al. 1997). Cicourel (e.g. 1981) demonstrates how the asymmetry between professionals and lay people determines the social organization of exchanges between them. Exploring doctor–patient interviews, he shows how the practitioner generally controls the structure and the content of interviews. The patients request little information, and, as a consequence, do not always provide the practitioner with the most appropriate information. This limits the extent to which practitioners may be able to provide patients with the information they require.

In interpreter-mediated encounters, the official party has to delegate a certain control to the assisting interpreter. In some cases the client assigns to the interpreter the responsibility for requesting appropriate information. The present data indicates that interpreters normally reinforce rather than downplay the dominance of an institutional perspective. An actual interpreter's understanding of the current institutional party's view, however, does not always coincide with the actual professional's understanding.

Evidently, the presence of an interpreter can have a significant impact on encounters where a layperson lacks the interest, motivation or apparent inclination to talk to the professional, even though the professional tries to initiate communication. For instance, a suspect meeting a police officer or a child meeting a doctor may prefer to keep quiet. But interpreters need others to talk. To maintain a 'middle ground' position, the interpreter depends on the primary interlocutors' verbal interaction. Interpreters depend on a relative proximity and a relative distance between the primary participants. Two persons must be willing, at some level of meaning, to engage in a joint activity, and to be assisted (and partly monitored) by a third – the interpreter. Paradoxically, they must simultaneously lack the ability or willingness to speak directly with one another. Without these conditions being mutually established and sustained, there is no scope for an individual to perform in the typical role of interpreter. In order to keep this activity system intact, however, interpreters occasionally take initiatives which are counter to their own principles. They sometimes speak directly to a primary party and this helps to reorganize the current interaction order into a standard interpreter-mediated one.

A role holder's attachment to a normative role is normally visible in the measures they take to sustain and keep intact the system of activity of which the role forms part. Interpreters participating in institutional encounters, such as health-care interviews and police interrogations, seemingly are ascribed and take on responsibility for sustaining *two* systems of activity simultaneously. An institutional encounter as system of activity is related as means to ends to the interpreter-mediated encounter as system of activity. Occasionally, individuals' presuppositions and expectations related to the one clash with those connected to the other. The analysed discourse data show that the interpreters gave high priority to keep interactional focus on a given, institutionally relevant issue, sometimes at the cost of exactness in translation, or – in interactional terms – sometimes assisting the institutional party to voice his or her perspective, and, simultaneously, not assisting the layperson to voice his or hers. It remains to be investigated how these tendencies are influenced by interpreters' proficiencies in various areas, by primary interlocutors' attitudes and knowledge, by various institutional routines, settings, and so forth.

1.6 Problematizing neutrality

By prosodic, semantic, gestural and other verbal and non-verbal means, interpreters mark distinctions between what they say on their own behalf and what they voice on others' account. Chapter 9 presented an analytical model which distinguishes between *relaying by displaying* and *relaying by replaying* – two modes of reporting others' speech which interpreters may apply in face-to-face interaction.

Depending on the circumstances, interpreters tend to emphasize one mode or the other. The three basic demands normally posed on interpreters are all of central importance in this connection: Interpreters need to make themselves understood by the current listeners, to present themselves as trustworthy witnesses of the preceding speakers, and to present themselves as impartial.

Since neutrality is a relational notion, a certain reporting of others' speech may stand out as partial or not, depending on the speech it is compared to. Hence, when two primary interlocutors differ substantially in communicative style and one – for instance, the official party – talks in a formal and strict way while the layperson is upset or angry, the interpreter who keeps to a formal and strict mode of interacting may be understood as biased in favour of the official party. Interpreters' fear of being confronted with this inherent dilemma was demonstrated in Isabella's story introducing Chapter 9, where she recollects being associated with the police against her intention.

Conversely, primary parties are dependent on the interpreter's involvement in interaction to be able to contribute in their own right to a certain communicative atmosphere. For instance, I interviewed a midwife and a pregnant woman after one of their regular encounters, and they both claimed that the interpreter's formal style had made it hard for them to talk and laugh as they had done before, when assisted by another interpreter. The midwife reported that she and the mother had started enthusiastically, but that the interpreter's style had made them lose interest in communicating. They had read his dry and formal tone of voice as displaying a lack of interest.

In their book *The Counsellor as Gatekeeper*, Erickson and Schultz (1982) examined the temporal complementarity between speaking and listening behaviour in face-to-face institutional encounters. They observe that rhythmic regularity, for example, nods, body positioning and prosodic pattern of speech, more than the substance of talk, made the participants (students meeting with students' counsellors) perceive each other as "being *with*" one another. In contrast, while jointly performing in "interactional arrhythmia", they were revealing themselves as not sharing an adequate interpretative framework (Erickson and Schultz 1982:143). The regularity in time and timing plays an essential, constitutive role in the social organization of interaction. This was touched upon in this book (Chapter 9), but it remains to be further explored in the context of interpreter-mediated encounters.

2. INTERPRETERS AND PROFESSIONALISM – A CONCLUSION

It is commonly considered highly desirable – and even necessary for a successful performance – that interpreters should be strongly attached to the prescribed norms of their role. Yet, as Goffman remarks (1961:86), there may be a middle-class bias in a conception of role attachment coming from the learned professions. In discussions among interpreters at training sessions and in other public settings, I have often heard experienced interpreters argue (and I have occasionally argued myself) that sticking to the official ethical norm "just translate and translate everything said" is indisputably the best way to perform as an interpreter. Those who allowed themselves to question this notion of professionalism in public were often newcomers or people who were for other reasons more loosely tied to the profession of interpreter. In fact, loyalty to colleagues might sometimes explain why the interpreter's typical self-image concerns 'the interpreter as translator', which simultaneously often amounts to a condemnation of 'the interpreter as mediator'. The uncompromising defence of the 'just translating' model should perhaps be understood as the interpreters voicing the credo of an occupational group. As is the case with other so-called liberal professions, the individual practitioner is responsible before her or his colleagues. The single member either belongs to the association of professionals and accepts its norms, or is excluded and will be grouped among the non-serious performers or the amateurs. Yet, when experienced interpreters account for concrete instances of interpreting (as can be seen from investigations of actual interpreting in face-to-face interaction), it is obvious that they are well aware of the fact that interpreting involves a complexity of activities. 'Just translating' as a description of reality applies to just one dimension, seen from the specific monological, talk-as-text perspective.

'Just translate and translate everything' is probably the most useful shorthand explanation of the interpreter's task to primary interlocutors and to newcomers to the profession, but how useful is it for the defining and the development of interpreters' professionalism? Or *how* is it useful for the defining of interpreters' professionalism? Arguments about 'just translating' must partly be understood as the interpreters' way of keeping apart professional and personal life, i.e. making a distinction between professional and lay identities, rights and responsibilities. 'Just translating and translate everything' as rules of thumb allows for a certain detaching of responsibility as a fellow human being from acts in the professional life; that is, it serves as a justification for acting as a *non-person*.

A main practical implication of this book is that explorations of authentic, transcribed interpreter-mediated interaction is a way to provide insights into the task of interpreting, knowledge which to my mind is necessary in order to accomplish professionalism in the field. In my view, it is essential to make candidate interpreters subject official professional standards to testing and criticism. Difficult distinctions between 'right' and 'wrong' should not be denied but should be foregrounded in interpreter training. Detecting and exploring dilemmas in concrete everyday practice is a way to gain knowledge about them and thus prepare to overcome them. To achieve more than interpreters' paying lip service to official Codes of Conduct, a thorough understanding of professional rules and recommendations is needed; of what they imply in theory and in actual interpreter-mediated interaction.

2.1 Evaluating professionalism

In programmes for interpreter training, and when evaluating the actual work of interpreters, there is naturally a need for criteria defining professionalism. A distinction could be made primarily between two sets of criteria. One set of criteria for inclusion among professionals concerns interpreters' ability to make a living by their work. Related to this is their association with a group of colleagues. A different set of criteria concerns the whole issue of evaluating (the degree of) interpreters' professional skill.

Thinking of interpreting basically as a kind of translating opens up for exploration, for instance, the interpreter's language proficiency in terms of vocabulary, syntax, grammar and other 'linguistic' matters. Applying a talk-as-text model, one self-evident criterion of professionalism would concern to what extent translations are exact. As has been extensively demonstrated in this book, however, this model of thinking also introduces certain dilemmas, insofar as it provides no space for handling the dialogical character of interaction. Consequently, it does not attend to the normal unpredictability of human conversation, and it gives no room for evaluating its social organization.

Perceiving translating as *one* aspect of interpreters' performance, co-existing with a coordinating or mediating aspect, implies that interpreters' professionalism must also be evaluated in relation to norms for social interaction. Other criteria by which proficiency in interpreting could be evaluated should concern their ability to attend simultaneously to various key details in discourse, and the interpreters' flexibility in positioning themselves as speakers and hearers; their ability to perform communicative activities on others' behalf and simultaneously distinguish what they contribute on their own account.

Following Erickson and Schultz (1982:76), we could argue that it is the sequential organization of communicative behaviour in real time (*chronos* time) that enables conversationalists to engage in fluent discourse and to regard one another as interactionally competent. If interpreters manage to match their communicative activities right on time (*kairos* time), this would, reasonably, facilitate the participants' finding of a common communicative rhythm. One criterion of professionalism could concern interpreters' sense of timing. This could be evaluated, for instance, in terms of their ability to synchronize with the other speakers' rhythm. Interpreters' ability to set a slower or a quicker pace of interaction could be evaluated as well.

Shackman (1984) writes about the (UK) community interpreter that "she is responsible for enabling the professional and client, with very different backgrounds and perceptions and in an unequal relationship of power and knowledge, to communicate to their mutual satisfaction" (Shackman 1984:18). Such a policy would presuppose, however, the primary interlocutors' willingness to negotiate communicative goals between themselves, and/or the interpreters' willingness and competence to mediate between participants whose needs, goals and worldviews clash. Ideas of satisfaction, as well as views of efficiency, adequacy and normality are culturally bound. As some of the present analyses showed, interpreters sometimes keep to themselves any disparities in primary interlocutors' understandings, perhaps to guarantee "mutual satisfaction" between them. Non-intended consequences of this interpreting strategy may be seen later, however, in the development of the factual exchange, or of the social relation.

In practice, there are no absolute and unambiguous criteria for defining a mode of interpreting which would be 'good' across the board. Different activity-types with different goal structures, as well as the different concerns, needs, desires and commitments of primary parties, imply various demands on the interpreters. One criterion of professionalism could involve the interpreter's emphatic competence, for instance, their ability to handle situations involving embarrassment. Some situations put strong demands on the interpreter's ability to make people feel at ease when communicating; on their ability to enable others to communicate sincerely (without hiding possible animosity), seriously, or jokingly.

Interpreters sometimes find that they have to protect the parties from getting embarrassed or puzzled by foreign conventions concerning, for instance, the degree of formality in addressing one another. Occasionally, interpreters find it best to avoid challenging conventions regarding the appropriateness of bringing up what are conceived of as taboo topics, such as money, sex, drinking and religion. They deliberately smooth down cultural differences for the purpose of promoting people to go on communicating, i.e. avoiding communicative breakdown. Such protective initiatives, however, may imply that the parties are kept ignorant about each other's conventions, and the culturally appropriate reactions to them.

2.2 A look ahead

Apart from situated encounters, such as those explored in this book, other contacts between interpreters and their users may also have key importance for how interpreting is actually performed. Naturally, when interpreters are fully informed before starting an assignment this facilitates more focused preparation. For example, it makes a difference if I am told in advance about the diagnosis in a health-care case, and about the charges against someone in a criminal case. The way in which interpreters are informed cannot guarantee, however, a symmetrical distribution of knowledge and power between the primary parties. In informing the interpreter before the start of an assignment, primary interlocutors may reveal grey areas of uncertainty as regards expectations vis-à-vis the interpreter. For instance, patients who inform the interpreter in advance about their ailments may assume that the interpreter will explain their – i.e. the patients' – symptoms to the doctor. In informing the interpreter about their views and suspicions, police officers may implement a subconscious frame of reference which promotes some and blocks other understandings of what suspects or witnesses say. This may in turn obstruct the interpreter's ability to see things from the layperson's perspective (see Wadensjö 1997).

It goes without saying that comparative studies of interpreter-mediated conversations in various settings and with various constellations of people would yield additional knowledge concerning the generality or typicality of phenomena such as those identified in this book. Yet not all lend themselves very easily to quantification. The role of interpreter needs further exploration in broadly-conceived, quantitative and qualitative investigations. Detailed discourse studies should provide more information of how social and cultural gaps are bridged, sustained or dissolved. Analyses of authentic discourse could also reveal facts concerning the interdependence between the social organization of activities and interpreters' remembering and immediate recall of primary interlocutors' talk. Combining linguistic and ethnological methods one could further explore issues of social and cultural identity. These could concern, for instance, in what contexts and how identities such as Russian, migrant, expert, Muslim, teenager, non-English-speaking woman are made relevant, or how they lose relevance for participants in a social encounter.

Interpreters may feel a duality in loyalties, being associated with a minority group, and having relatively more access to the majority society than others associated with this group. Dual loyalties may, moreover, spring from the complex mixture of foreground and background in interpreters' interactional practices. Ethnographic investigations of the everyday work of interpreters would give ideas about their role in a societal perspective. Explorations of individual interpreters' professional history and investigations of interpreters' networks would indicate the role of interpreters in the process of integration or segregation of members of minority groups in the public life of a majority society. One way of exploring this is to see how this is made an issue within the professional groups with which interpreters work. What factors and personal categories do participants invoke to explain problems and conflicts – and to solve them? What factors coincide with institutions' negative or positive evaluations of interpreters?

In addition, facts are needed about how interpreter training correlates with style of interpreting. What preparation is offered for interpreters working in, for instance, health-care settings? Which ideas of human communication in health-care settings does the education invoke? How can it be improved? How is the organization of activities in these settings influenced by the dynamics of triadic, interpreter-mediated talk? What personal qualities – in interpreters and in therapists – need to be trained for mental health interpreting?

The analyses presented here indicate that primary interlocutors have a lot to gain from preparing themselves specifically for the particularities and peculiarities of interpreter-mediated interaction. Above all, it is worth giving consideration to the social and cultural bias communicated in one's own style and manner of interaction. Being prepared, one can take advantage of this specific mode of communication, rather than let oneself be disturbed by it.

NOTE

1. But answerability entails guilt, or liability to blame (Bakhtin [1919, 1990:1]). *Otvetstvennost'*, the gloss used by Bakhtin, is conventionally translated as responsibility. The English translator's choice of an alternative term, "answerability", brings the reader's attention to the connection between answering-responding and responsibility, a connection visible also in the Swedish word for responsibility, *ansvar*.

Bibliography

Adelswärd, V. (1988) *Styles of Success – On Impression Management as Colaborative Action in Job Interviews* (Dissertation, Linköping Studies in Arts and Sciences 23). Linköping: Department of Communication Studies.

Adelswärd, V. (1989) Laughter and Dialogue. *Nordic Journal of Linguistics*, 12, 107–36.

Agar, M. H. (1985) Institutional Discourse. *Text*, 5, 147–68.

Anderson, R. & W. Bruce (1976) Perspectives on the Role of Interpreter, in R. Brislin (ed.), *Translation: Applications and Research*. New York: Gardner Press.

Apfelbaum, B. (in press) Instruktionsdiskurse mit Dolmetscher-beteiligung. Aspekte der Turnkonstruktion und Turnzuweisung, in A. Brock & M. Hartung (eds), *Neure Entwicklungen in der Gesprächsforschung* (Vorträge der 3. Arbeitstagung des Pragmatischen Kolloquiums, Freiburg 1997). Tübingen: Narr.

Apfelbaum, B. & C. Wadensjö (1997) How Does a VERBMOBIL Affect Conversation? Discourse Analysis and Machine-Supported Translatory Interaction, in C. Hauenschild & S. Heizmann (eds), *Machine Translation and Translation Theory*. Amsterdam: Mouton de Gruyter, 93–122.

Aronsson, K. (1991) Facework and Control in Multy-Party Talk: A Paediatric Case Study, in I. Marková & K. Foppa (eds), *Asymmetries in Dialogue*. Hemel Hempstead: Harvester Wheatsheaf, 49–74.

Aronsson, K., U. Sätterlund Larsson & R. Säljö (1995) Clinical Diagnosis and the Joint Construction of a Medical Voice, in I. Marková & R. Farr (eds), *Representations of Health, Illness and Handicap*. Chur: Harwood Academic Publishers, 131–44.

Atkinson, M. J. & P. Drew (1979) *Order in Court: The Organisation of Verbal Behaviour in Judicial Settings*. London: Macmillan.

AUSIT (1992) *Invisible Interpreters and Transparent Translators*. Australian Institute of Interpreters and Translators, Victoria: AUSIT.

Austin, J. (1962) *How To Do Things with Words*. Oxford: Oxford University Press.

Bailey, F. G. (1969) *Stratagems and Spoils: A Social Anthropology of Politics*. Oxford: Blackwell.

Baker, M. (1992) *In Other Words – a Coursebook on Translation*. London/New York: Routledge.

Bakhtin, M. M. (1979) *Estetika Slovesnogo Tvorchestva*. Moscow: Isskusstvo.

Bakhtin, M. M. (1981) *The Dialogic Imagination: Four Essays by M. M. Bakhtin*, M. Holquist (ed.), (transl. by C. Emerson and M. Holquist). Austin: University of Texas Press.

Bakhtin, M. M. (1984) *Problems of Dostoevsky's Poetics*, C. Emerson (ed.), (introd. by W. C. Booth, transl. by C. Emerson). Minneapolis/London: Minnesota University Press.

Bakhtin, M. M. (1986a) *Speech Genres and Other Late Essays*. C. Emerson and M. Holquist (eds), (transl. by V. W. McGee). Austin: University of Texas Press.

Bakhtin, M. M. (1986b) K filosofii postupka, in *Filosofia i sociologia nauki i techniki* (Ezjegodnik ("yearbook") 1984–1985). Moscow: Nauka.

Bakhtin, M. M. (1990) *Art and Answerability*, Holquist, M. & V. Liapunov (eds), (transl. and notes by V. Liapunov). Austin: University of Texas Press.

Barik, H. (1972) Interpreters Talk a Lot among Other Things. *Babel*, 18, 3–10.

Barsky, R. F. (1994) *Constructing the Productive Other: Discourse Theory and the Convention Refugee Hearing*. Amsterdam/Philadelphia: John Benjamins.

Bateson, G. (1972) *Steps to an Ecology of Mind*. New York: Ballantine.

Bergmann, J. R. (1987) *Klatsch, Zur Sozialform der diskreten Indiskretion*. Berlin: de Gruyter.

Bergmann, J. R. (1990) On the Local Sensitivity of Conversation, in I. Marková & K. Foppa (eds), *The Dynamics of Dialogue*. Hemel Hempstead: Harvester.

Bergmann, J. R. (1993) *Discreet Indiscretions*. New York: de Gruyter.

Bergmann, J. R. & T. Luckmann (1995) Reconstructive Genres of Everyday Communication, in U. Quasthoff (ed.), *Aspects of Oral Communication*. Berlin: de Gruyter, 289–304.

Berk-Seligson, S. (1990) *The Bilingual Courtroom: Court Interpreters in the Judicial Process*. Chicago: The University of Chicago Press.

Blomqvist, A. (1996) *Food and Fashion: Water Management and Collective Action among Irrigation Farmers and Textile Industrialists in South India* (Dissertation, Linköping Studies in Arts and Science 148). Linköping: Department of Water and Environmental Studies.

Bremer, K. (1996) Causes of Understanding Problems, in K. Bremer, C. Roberts, M.-T. Vasseur, M. Simonot & P. Broeder (eds), *Achieving Understanding: Discourse in Intercultural Encounters*, Language in Social Life Series. London/New York: Longman, 37–65.

Bremer, K., C. Roberts, M.-T. Vasseur, M. Simonot & P. Broeder (1996) *Achieving Understanding: Discourse in Intercultural Encounters*, Language in Social Life Series. London/New York: Longman.

Brown, P. & S. C. Levinson (1978) *Politeness: Some Universals in Language Usage*. Cambridge: Cambridge University Press.

Candlin, C. N. & J. Lucas (1986) Interpretations and Explanations in Discourse: Modes of 'Advising' in Family Planning, in T. Ensink, A. van Essen and T. van der Geest (eds), *Discourse Analysis and Public Life, Papers of the Groningen Conference on Medical and Political Discourse.* Dordrecht: Foris Publication, 13–38.

Carr, S., E. R. Roberts, A. Dufour and D. Steyn (eds) (1997) *The Critical Link: Interpreters in the Community. Papers from the 1st International Conference on Interpreting in Legal, Health, and Social Service Settings, Geneva Park, Canada, June 1–4, 1995.* Amsterdam/Philadelphia: John Benjamins.

Cedersund, E. (1992) *Talk, Text and Institutional Order: A Study of Communication in Social Welfare Bureaucracies* (Linköping Studies in Arts and Science 78). Linköping: Department of Communication Studies.

Cedersund, E. & R. Säljö (1993) Bureaucratic Discourse, Conversational Space and the Concept of Voice. *Semiotica*, 97, 79–101.

Cicourel, A. V. (1981) Language and Medicine, in C. A. Ferguson and S. B. Heath (eds), *Language in the USA*. Cambridge: Cambridge University Press, 407–29.

Cicourel, A. V. (1983) Hearing Is Not Believing: Language and the Structure of Belief in Medical Communication, in S. Fisher and A. D. Todd (eds), *The Social Organization of Doctor–Patient Communication*. Washington, D.C.: Center for Applied Linguistics, 222–38.

Cicourel, A. V. (1992) The Interpenetration of Communicative Contexts: Examples from Medical Encounters, in A. Duranti & C. Goodwin (eds), *Rethinking Context – Language as an Interactive Phenomenon*. Cambridge: Cambridge University Press, 291–310.

Clark, H. H. & R. J. Gerrig (1990) Quotations as Demonstrations. *Language*, 66:4, 764–807.

Colin, J. & R. Morris (1996) *Interpreters and the Legal Process.* Winchester: Westerside Press.

Connor-Linton, J. (1995) The Role of Lexical Variation in Crosstalk: Pronominal Reference Choices in a Soviet-American Spacebridge. *Journal of Pragmatics*, 23, 301–24.

Crapanzano, V. (1980) *Tuhami. Portrait of a Moroccan.* Chicago and London: The University of Chicago Press.

Delisle, J. & J. Woodsworth (eds) (1995) *Translators through History.* Amsterdam/Philadelphia: John Benjamins/UNESCO Publishing.

Downing, B. & K. Helms Tillery (1992) *Professional Training for Community Interpreters: A Report on Models of Interpreter Training and the Value of Training.* Minneapolis: Center for Urban and Regional Affairs, University of Minnesota.

Downing, B. & L. Swabey (1992) *A Multilingual Model for Training Health Care Interpreters.* Paper presented at National Conference on Health and Mental Health of Soviet Refugees, held in Chicago, Illinois, USA, 10–12 December 1991.

Drew, P. & J. Heritage (1992) Analysing Talk at Work: An Introduction, in P. Drew & J. Heritage (eds), *Talk at Work: Interaction in Institutional Settings* (Studies in Interactional Sociolinguistics 8). Cambridge: Cambridge University Press.

Dunnigan, T. & B. Downing (1995) Legal Interpreting on Trial: A Case Study, in M. Morris (ed.), *Translation and the Law* (American Translators Association Scholarly Monograph Series VIII) Amsterdam/Philadelphia: John Benjamins, 93–113.

Duranti, A. (1986) The Audience as Co-author: An Introduction. *Text*, 6:3, 239–47.

Duranti, A. & C. Goodwin (eds) (1992) *Rethinking Context: Language as an Interactive Phenomenon* (Studies in Social and Cultural Foundations of Language 11). Cambridge: Cambridge University Press.

Edelsky, C. (1981) Who's Got the Floor? *Language in Society*, 10, 382–421.

Edmondson, W. J. (1986) Cognition, Conversing and Interpreting, in J. House & S. Blum-Kulka (eds), *Interlingual and Intercultural Communication*. Tübingen: Gunter Narr, 129–38.

Edwards, A. B. (1995) *The Practice of Court Interpreting*. Amsterdam/Philadelphia: John Benjamins.

Ekvall, R. B. (1960) *Faithful Echo*. New Haven, CT: College and University Press.

Englund Dimitrova, B. (1991) När två samtalar genom en tredje. Interaktion och icke-verbal kommunikation i medicinska möten med tolk. *Rapporter om tvåspråkighet, No. 7*. Stockholm: Centre for Research on Bilingualism, Stockholm University.

Englund Dimitrova, B. (1997) Degree of Interpreter Responsibility in the Interaction Process in Community Interpreting, in S. E. Carr, R. Roberts, A. Dufour & D. Steyn (eds), *The Critical Link: Interpreters in the Community*. Amsterdam/Philadelphia: John Benjamins, 147–64.

Erickson, F. (1982) Money Tree, Lasagna Bush, Salt and Pepper: Social Construction of Topical Cohesion in a Conversation Among Italian-Americans, in D. Tannen (ed.), *Analysing Discourse: Text and Talk*. (Georgetown University Round Table on Languages and Linguistics, 1981). Washington, D.C.: Georgetown University Press.

Erickson, F. & W. Rittenberg (1987) Topic Control and Person Control: A Thorny Problem for Foreign Physicians in Interaction with American Patients. *Discourse Processes – A Multidisciplinary Journal*, 10:4, 401–15.

Erickson, F. & J. Shultz (1982) *The Counselor as a Gatekeeper: Social Interaction in Interviews*. New York: Academic Press.

Falck, S. (1987) *Rett tolk? – En undersokelse av tolker, språk, rettssikkerhetsproblemer og rollekonflikter innen politi og domstoler*. Institutt for kriminolgi og strafferett, Universitetet i Oslo, Oslo: Universitetsforlaget.

Fenton, S. (1997) The Role of the Interpreter in the Adversarial Courtroom, in S. E. Carr, R. Roberts, A. Dufour & D. Steyn (eds), *The Critical Link: Interpreters in the Community*. Amsterdam/Philadelphia: John Benjamins, 29–34.

Foucault, M. (1971) *L'Ordre du discours*. Paris: Gallimard.

Frishberg, N. (1986) (2nd edn. 1987) *Interpreting: An Introduction*. Rockville, MD: RID Inc.

Garfinkel, H. (1967) What is Ethnomethodology?, in H. Garfinkel (ed.), *Studies in Ethnomethodology*. Englewood Cliffs, NJ: Prentice-Hall, 1–34.

Gentile, A., U. Ozolins & M. Vasilakakos (1996) *Liaison Interpreting: A Handbook*. Victoria: Melbourne University Press.

Giddens, A. (1981) *A Contemporary Critique of Historical Materialism* (Power, Property and the State Vol. 1). Basingstoke: Macmillan.

Gile, D. (1990) Scientific Research versus Personal Theories in the Investigation of Interpretation, in L. Gran & Ch. Taylor (eds), *Aspects of Applied and Experimental Research on Conference Interpretation*. Udine: Campanotto, 28–41.

Gile, D. (1995) (guest editor) Special issue "Interpreting Research". *Target*, 7:1.

Giles, H., A. Mulac, J. Bradac & P. Johnson (1986) Speech Accommodation Theory: The First Decade and Beyond, in M. L. McLaughlin (ed.), *Communication Yearbook* (Vol. 10). Beverley Hills, CA: Sage, 13–48.

Gilroy, P. (1987) *There Ain't No Black in the Union Jack*. London: Hutchinson.

Goffman, E. (1961) *Encounters: Two Studies in the Sociology of Interaction*. Indianapolis/New York: The Bobbs-Merrill Company.

Goffmann, E. (1967) On Face-Work: An Analysis of Ritual Elements in Social Interaction, reprinted from *Psychiatry: Journal for the Study of Interpersonal Processes*, 18:3 (1955), 213–31, in *Interactional Ritual, Essays on Face-to-Face Behaviour*. New York: Pantheon Books.

Goffmann, E. (1971) *Relations in Public Microstudies of the Public Order*. Harmondsworth: Penguin.

Goffmann, E. (1974) *Frame Analysis. An Essay on the Organization of Experience*. Cambridge, MA: Harvard University Press.

Goffmann, E. (1981) *Forms of Talk*. Philadelphia: University of Pennsylvania Press.

Goffmann, E. (1990 [1959]) *The Presentation of Self in Everyday Life*. Harmondsworth: Penguin.

González, R. D., V. F. Vásques & H. Mikkelson (1991) *Fundamentals of Court Interpretation: Theory, Policy and Practice* (University of Arizona Summer Institute for Court Interpretation Series). Durham, NC: Carolina Academic Press.

Goodwin, C. & A. Duranti (1992) Rethinking Context: An Introduction, in A. Duranti & C. Goodwin (eds), *Rethinking Context: Language as an Interactive Phenomenon* (Studies in Social and Cultural Foundations of Language 11). Cambridge: Cambridge University Press, 1–42.

Goodwin, C. & M. H. Goodwin (1987) Children's Arguing, in S. U. Philips, S. Steele & C. Tanz (eds), *Language, Gender and Sex in a Comparative Perspective*. New York: Cambridge University Press.

Goodwin, C. & M. H. Goodwin (1990) Interstitial Argument, in A. D. Grimshaw (ed.), *Conflict Talk: Sociolinguistic Investigations of Arguments in Conversation*. Cambridge: Cambridge University Press.

Goodwin, C. & M. H. Goodwin (1992) Context, Activity and Participation, in P. Auer & A. di Luzo (eds), *The Contextualization of Language*. Amsterdam: John Benjamins.

Graumann, C. F. (1995) Commonality, Mutuality, Reciprocity: A Conceptual Introduction, in I. Marková, C. F. Graumann & K. Foppa (eds), *Mutualities in Dialogue*. Cambridge: Cambridge University Press, 1–24.

Gulliver, P. H. (1979) *Disputes and Negotiations. A Cross-Cultural Perspective*. New York: Academic Press.

Gumperz, J. J. (1982a) *Discourse Strategies*. Cambridge: Cambridge University Press.

Gumperz, J. J. (1982b) *Language and Social Identity*. Cambridge: Cambridge University Press.

Gumperz, J. J. (1992) Contextualization and Understanding, in A. Duranti & C. Goodwin (eds), *Rethinking Context: Language as an Interactive Phenomenon* (Studies in Social and Cultural Foundations of Language 11). Cambridge: Cambridge University Press, 229–52.

Gunnarsson, B.-L., P. Linell & B. Nordberg (eds) (1997) *The Construction of Professional Discourse* (Language in Social Life Series). London/New York: Longman.

Harris, B. (1981) Observations on a Cause Célèbre: Court Interpreting at the Lischka Trial, in R. P. Roberts (ed.), *L'Interprétation auprès des tribunaux*. Colloque, Ottawa, 10–11 avril 1980.

Harris, B. (1990) Norms in Interpretation. *Target*, 2:1, 115–19.

Harris, B. (1992a) (1st version 1977) The Importance of Natural Translation, *Working Papers on Bilingualism 12*, Ottawa: University of Ottawa, 96–114.

Harris, B. (1992b) Natural Translation: A Reply to Hans P. Krings. *Target*, 4:1, 97–103.

Harris, B. (1994) *A Taxonomic Survey of Professional Interpreting, Part 1*. Draft for the International Conference on Interpreting, Turku, 25–26 August 1994.

Harris, B. & B. Sherwood (1978) Translating as an Innate Skill, in D. Gerver & H. W. Sinaiko (eds), *Language Interpretation and Communication*. New York/London: Plenum Press.

Hatim, B. & I. Mason (1990) *Discourse and the Translator* (Language in Social Life Series). London/New York: Longman.

Haviland, J. B. (1986) 'Con Buenos Chiles': Talk, Target and Teasing in Zinacantán. *Text*, 6:3, 249–82.

Heath, C. (1988) Embarrassment and Interactional Organization, in P. Drew & A. Wootton (eds), *Erving Goffman – Exploring the Interaction Order*. Cambridge: Polity Press, 136–60.

Herbert, J. (1952) *The Interpreter's Handbook: How to Become a Conference Interpreter*. Geneva: Librairie de l'Université.

Holmes, J. S. (1988) *Translated! Papers on Literary Translation and Translation Studies*. Amsterdam: Rodopi.

Holquist, M. (1990) *Dialogism: Bakhtin and His World*. London: Routledge.

Holz-Mänttäri, J. (1984) *Translatorisches Handeln. Theorie und Methode.* Helsinki: Annales Academiae Scientiarum Fennicae B 226.

Holz-Mänttäri, J. (1988) Translation und das biologisch-soziale Gefüge „Mensch", *Translationstheorie – Grundlagen und Standorte,* Justa Holz-Mänttäri (ed.), *Studia Translatologica,* series A, Vol. 1. Tampere, Finland: Instituts für Übersetzen und Dolmetschen Universität.

Hymes, D. H. (1962) The Ethnography of Speaking, in T. Gladwin & W. C. Sturtevant (eds), *Anthropology and Human Behaviour.* Washington, D.C.: Anthropological Society of America.

Hymes, D. H. (1964) *Language in Culture and Society – A Reader in Linguistics and Anthropology.* New York, Evanston and London: Harper & Row.

Hymes, D. H. (1972) On Communicative Competence, in J. B. Pride & J. Holmes (eds), *Sociolinguistics: Selected Readings.* Harmondsworth: Penguin.

Jansen, P. (forthcoming) The Role of the Interpreter in Dutch Courtroom Interaction and the Impact of the Situation on Translational Norms, in P. Jansen & A. Robyns (eds), *Translation and the Manipulation of Discourse: Selected Papers of the CERA Research Seminar in Translation Studies, 1992–1993.* Leuven: Katholieke Universiteit Leuven, Publications of the CERA Chair for Translation, Communication and Cultures.

Jefferson, G. (1973) A Case of Precision Timing in Ordinary Conversation: Overlapped Tag-positioned Address Terms in Closing Sequences. *Semiotica,* 9, 47–96.

Johnson-Laird, P. (1983) *Mental Models – Towards a Cognitive Science of Language, Inference, and Consciousness.* Cambridge: Cambridge University Press.

de Jongh, M. Elena (1992) *An Introduction to Court Interpreting: Theory and Practice.* Lanham, MD: University Press of America.

Jönsson, L. (1990) Förmedlade samtal: Om återkoppling i tolkade rättegångar, in U. Nettelbladt & G. Håkansson (eds), *Samtal och undervisning. Studier till Lennart Gustavssons minne* (Linköping Studies in Arts and Science 60). Linköping: Department of Communication Studies, 71–86.

Kalina, S. (1992) Discourse Processing and Interpreting Strategies: An Approach to the Teaching of Interpreting, in C. Dollerup & A. Loddegard (eds), *Teaching Translation and Interpreting: Training, Talent and Experience.* Amsterdam: John Benjamins, 251–7.

Kammarkollegiet (Legal, Financial and Administrative Services Agency) (1996) *God tolksed – Vägledning för auktoriserade tolkar* (Guidance for Good Practice for Certified Interpreters). Stockholm: Kammarkollegiet & C. E. Fritzes AB.

Kasanji, L. (1995) *Let's Talk – Guideline for Government Agencies Hiring Interpreters.* Te Tari Taiwhenna: Ethnic Affairs Service, Department of Internal Affairs, Auckland, New Zealand.

Kaufert, J. M. & W. W. Koolage (1984) Role Conflict among Culture Brokers: The Experience of Native Canadian Medical Interpreters. *Social Science Medicine,* 18:3, 283–6.

Kaufert, J. M., P. Leyland Kaufert, J. D. O'Neil and W. W. Koolage (1985) Advocacy, Media and Native Medical Interpreters, in R. Paine (ed.), *Advocacy and Anthropology*. Institute of Social and Economic Research, Memorial University of Newfoundland. Toronto: University of Toronto Press, 98–115.

Keith, H. A. (1984) Liaison Interpreting: An Exercise in Linguistic Interaction, in W. Wilss & G. Thome (eds), *Die Theorie des Übersetzens und ihr Aufschlußwert für die Übersetzungs- und Dolmetschdidaktik – Translation Theory and its Implementation in the Teaching of Translating and Interpreting*. (Akten de Internationalen Kolloquiums der AILA). Tübingen: Gunter Narr, 308–17.

Knapp, K. & A. Knapp-Potthoff (1985) Sprachmittlertätigkeit in der interkulturellen Kommunikation, in J. Rehbein (ed.), *Interkulturelle Kommunikation*. Tübingen: Gunter Narr, 450–63.

Knapp-Potthoff, A. & K. Knapp (1986) Interweaving Two Discourses – The Difficult Task of the Non-Professional Interpreter, in J. House & S. Blum-Kulka (eds), *Interlingual and Intercultural Communication*. Tübingen: Gunter Narr, 151–68.

Knapp-Potthoff, A. & K. Knapp (1987) The Man (or Woman) in the Middle: Discoursal Aspects of Non-Professional Interpreting, in K. Knapp, W. Enninger & A. Knapp-Potthoff (eds), *Analyzing Intercultural Communication*. Berlin: Mouton de Gruyter, 181–211.

Kohn, K. & S. Kalina (1996) The Strategic Dimension of Interpreting. *Meta*, 41:1, 118–38.

Krings, H. P. (1986) *Was in den Köpfen von Übersetzern vorgeht: Eine empirische Untersuchung zur Struktur des Übersetzungsprozesses an fortgeschrittenen Französischlernern* (Tübinger Beiträge zur Linguistik 291). Tübingen: Narr.

Kulick, D. (1982) Interpretation and Discourse, in *Om tolkning, Praktisk lingvistik* 7, Lund: Institutionen för lingvistik, Lunds universitet, 5–45.

Lang, R. (1976) Interpreters in Local Courts in Papua New Guinea, in W. M. O'Barr & J. F. O'Barr (eds), *Language and Politics*. The Hague/ Paris: Mouton.

Lang, R. (1978) Behavioral Aspects of Liaison Interpreters in Papua New Guinea: Some Preliminary Observations, in D. Gerver & H. W. Sinaico (eds), *Language Interpretation and Communication*. New York and London: Plenum, 231–44.

Laster K. & V. Taylor (1994) *Interpreters and the Legal System*. Leichhardt, NSW, Australia: The Federation Press.

Lederer, M. (1994) *La traduction aujourd'hui*. Paris: Hachette.

Levinson, S. C. (1988) Putting Linguistics on a Proper Footing: Explorations in Goffman's Concepts of Participation, in P. Drew & A. Wooton (eds), *Erving Goffman: Exploring the Interaction Order*. Oxford: Polity Press, 161–227.

Linell, P. (1982) *The Written Language Bias in Linguistics* (Studies in Communication 2). Linköping: Department of Communication Studies.

Linell, P. (1988) The Impact of Literacy on the Conception of Language: The Case of Linguistics, in R. Säljö (ed.), *The Written World: Studies in Literate Thought and Action.* Berlin/Heidelberg: Springer Verlag, 41–58.

Linell, P. (1995) Troubles with Mutualities: Towards a Dialogical Theory of Misunderstanding and Miscommunication, in I. Marková, C. F. Graumann & K. Foppa (eds), *Mutualities in Dialogue.* Cambridge: Cambridge University Press, 176–213.

Linell, P. (1996) Approaching Dialogue – On Monological and Dialogical Models of Talk and Interaction, *Working Papers from the Department of Communication Studies 1996:7.* Linköping: Department of Communication Studies.

Linell, P., C. Wadensjö & L. Jönsson (1992) Establishing Communicative Contact through a Dialogue Interpreter, in A. Grindsted & J. Wagner (eds), *Communication for Specific Purposes – Fachsprachliche Kommunikation.* Tübingen: Gunter Narr, 125–42.

Linton, R. (1936 [1964]) *The Study of Man* (Student's Edn) (The Century Social Science Series). New York: Appleton-Century.

Londen, Anne-Marie (1989) Litterärt talspråk, studier i Runar Schildts berättarteknik med särskild hänsyn till dialogen, in L. Huldén (ed.), *Humanistiska avhandlingar 3.* Helsingfors: Svenska litteratursällskapet i Finland.

Lotman, Ju. M. (1992) *Kul'tura i vzryv (Progress).* Moscow: Grozis, Progress Publishers.

Marková, I. & K. Foppa (eds) (1990) *The Dynamics of Dialogue.* Hemel Hempstead: Harvester Wheatsheaf.

Marková, Ivana, C. F. Graumann & K. Foppa (eds) (1995) *Mutualities in Dialogue.* Cambridge: Cambridge University Press.

Mason, I. (1990) The Interpreter as Listener: An Observation of Response in the Oral Mode of Translating, in G. McGregor & R. S. White (eds), *Reception and Response – Hearer Creativity and the Analysis of Spoken and Written Texts.* London and New York: Routledge, 145–59.

Mikkelson, H. (1996) *The Professionalisation of Community Interpreting.* Paper presented at the 1996 ATA (American Translators Association) conference 'The Professionalisation of Community Interpreting'.

Morris, M. *et al.* (eds) (1995) *Translation and the Law* (American Translators Association Scholarly Monograph Series VIII). Amsterdam/Philadelphia: John Benjamins.

Morris, R. (1993) *Images of the Interpreter: A Study of Language-Switching in the Legal Process.* PhD Thesis, Department of Law, Lancaster University.

Morris, R. (1995) The Moral Dilemmas of Court Interpreting. *The Translator,* 1:1, 25–46.

Morson, G. & C. Emerson (1989) Introduction, in G. Morson & C. Emerson (eds), *Rethinking Bakhtin.* Evanston, IL: Northwestern corp.

Moser-Mercer, B. (1991) Research Committee Paradigms Gained, or the Art of Productive Disagreement. *AIIC Bulletin,* XIX:2, 11–15.

Müller, F. (1989) Translation in Bilingual Conversation: Pragmatic Aspects of Translatory Interaction. *Journal of Pragmatics*, 13, 713–39. North-Holland.

Nida, E. (1964) *Toward a Science of Translating*. Leiden: E.J. Brill.

Nida, E. (1976) A Framework for the Analysis and the Evaluation of Theories of Translation, in R. W. Brislin (ed.), *Translation: Applications and Research*. New York: Gardner Press.

Nida, E. (1977) Translating Means Communicating: A Sociolinguistic Theory of Translation, in M. Saville-Troike (ed.), *Georgetown University Round Table on Languages and Linguistics 1977*. Washington, D.C.: Georgetown University Press.

Niska, H. (1991) A New Breed of Interpreter for Immigrants, Community Interpreting in Sweden, in C. Picken (ed.), *Institute of Translation and Interpreting, ITI Conference 28/4/90. Proceedings*. London: Aslib (The Association for Information Management), 94–104.

Oakley, A. & S. Houd (1990) *Helpers in Childbirth: Midwifery Today*. New York: Hemisphere Publishing Corporation.

O'Barr, W. M. & B. K. Atkins (1980) 'Women's Language' or 'Powerless Language'?, in S. McConnell-Ginet, R. Borker and N. Furman (eds), *Women and Language in Literature and Society*. New York: Praeger.

Ochs, E. (1979) Transcription as Theory, in E. Ochs & Bambi B. Schieffelin (eds), *Developmental Pragmatics*. New York: Academic Press.

Paine, R. (ed.) (1971) *Patrons and Brokers in the East Arctic*. Institute of Social and Economic Research, Memorial University of Newfoundland. Toronto: University of Toronto Press.

Parsons, T. (1968) Professions, in D. L. Sills (ed.), *International Encyclopedia of the Social Sciences*, No. 12. New York: The Free Press.

Phillips, H. P. (1960) Problems of Translation and Meaning in the Field Work. *Human Organization*, 18, 184–92.

Plimer, D. & C. N. Candlin (1996) *Language Services for Non-English-Speaking-Background Women*. Canberra: Bureau of Immigration, Multicultural and Population Research (BIR), Australian Goverment Publishing Service.

Pomerantz, A. (1978) Attribution of Responsibility: Blaming. *Sociology*, 12, 115–21.

Pomerantz, A. (1984) Agreeing and Disagreeing with Assessments: Some Features of Preferred/Dispreferred Turn Shapes, in J. M. Atkinson & J. Heritage (eds), *Structures of Social Action*. Cambridge: Cambridge University Press.

Prince, C. (1986) *Hablado con el doctor: Communication Problems between Doctors and their Spanish-Speaking Patients*. Dissertation, University Microfilms International, Stanford University, CA.

Qian, H. (1994) Looking at Interpreting from a Communicative Perspective, *Babel*, 40:4, 214–21.

Rabin, Ch. (1958) The Linguistics of Translation, in *Aspects of Translation*. London: Secker and Warburg for The Communication Research Centre, University College London, 123–45.

Reddy, M. (1979) The Conduit Metaphor: A Case of Frame Conflict in our Language about Language, in A. Ortony (ed.), *Metaphor and Thought*. Cambridge: Cambridge University Press, 284–324.

Reiß, K. & H. J. Vermeer (1984) *Grundlegung einer allgemeiner Translations-theorie*. Tübingen: Niemeyer.

Roberts, R. P. (ed.) (1981) *L'Interpretation auprès des Tribunaux – Actes du minicolloque tenu les 10 et 11 avril 1980 à l'Université d'Ottawa* (Cahiers de traductologie No. 3). Ottawa: University of Ottawa Press.

Rommetveit, R. (1974) *On Message Structure – A Framework for the Study of Language and Communication*. London: Wiley Interscience.

Rommetveit, R. (1985) Language Acquisition as Increasing Linguistic Struc-turing of Experience and Symbolic Behaviour Control, in J. Wertsch (ed.), *Culture, Communication and Cognition: Vygotskian Perspectives*. Cambridge: Cambridge University Press, 183–204.

Rommetveit, R. (1992) Outlines of a Dialogically Based Social-Cognitive Approach to Human Cognition and Communication, in A. Heen Wold (ed.), *The Dialogical Alternative: Towards a Theory of Language and Mind*. Oslo: Scandinavian University Press, 19–44.

Roy, C. B. (1989) *A Sociolinguistic Analysis of the Interpreter's Role in the Turn Exchanges of an Interpreted Event*. Dissertation, Georgetown University, Washington D.C.

Roy, C. B. (1993) A Sociolinguistic Analysis of the Interpreter's Role in Simultaneous Talk in Interpreted Interaction. *Multilingua*, 12:4, 341–63.

Sachs, L. (1983) *Evil Eye or Bacteria: Turkish Migrant Women and Swedish Health Care* (Stockholm Studies in Social Anthropology, 12). Stockholm: Department of Social Anthropology, University of Stockholm.

Sacks, H., E. A. Schegloff & G. Jefferson (1974) A Simplest Systematics for the Organization of Turn-taking for Conversation, *Language*, 50, 696–736.

Säljö, R. (1988) The Written World: Introduction, in R. Säljö (ed.), *The Written World – Studies in Literate Thought and Action*. Berlin/Heidelberg: Springer-Verlag, 1–10.

Sanders, M. (1992) Training for Community Interpreters, in C. Picken (ed.), *ITI Conference 6 Proceedings*. London: Aslib, 45–50.

Sarangi, S. & S. Slembrouck (1996) *Language, Bureaucracy & Social Control* (Real Language Series). London/New York: Longman.

Schegloff, E. A. (1996) Turn Organization: One Intersection of Grammar and Interaction, E. Ochs, E. A. Schegloff & S. Thompson (eds), *Interaction and Grammar*. Cambridge: Cambridge University Press, 52–133.

Schegloff, E. A., G. Jefferson & H. Sacks (1977) The Preference for Self-Correction in the Organization of Repair in Conversation. *Language*, 53, 361–82.

Schjoldager, A. (1994) Interpreting Research and the 'Manipulation School' of Translation Studies. *Hermes, Journal of Linguistics*, 12, Århus, 65–89.

Schleiermacher, Fr. D. E. [1805–1833] (1959) *Hermeneutik, Nach den Handschriften*, H. Kimmerle, (new ed. and introd.) (Abhandlungen der

Heidelberger Akademie der Wissenschaften). Heidelberg, Carl Winter Universitätsverlag.

Schleiermacher, Fr. D. E. (1977, [1986]) *Hermeneutics: The Handwritten Manuscripts*, H. Kimmerle (ed.) (transl. by J. Duke & J. Forstman). American Academy of Religion, Scholar Press Reprint 1986.

Schmidt, P. (1964) *Statist auf diplomatischer Bühne*. Frankfurt am Main: Athenäum.

Schweda Nicholson N. (1994) Community Interpreter Training in the United States and the United Kingdom: An Overview of Selected Initiatives. *Hermes, Journal of Linguistics*, 12, Århus, 127–39.

Searle, J. (1969) *Speech Acts*. London: Cambridge University Press.

Seleskovitch, D. (1977) Why Interpreting is not Tantamount to Translating Languages. *The Incorporated Linguist*, 16:2, 27–33.

Seleskovitch, D. (1978) *Interpreting for International Conferences*. Washington, D.C.: Pen and Booth.

Seleskovitch, D. & M. Ledrere (1984) *Interpréter pour traduire*. Paris: Didier Erudition.

Shackman, J. (1984) *The Right to be Understood: A Handbook on Working with, Employing and Training Community Interpreters*. Cambridge: Cambridge National Extension College.

Silverman, D. (1993) *Interpreting Qualitative Data: Methods for Analysing Talk, Text and Interaction*. London/Thousand Oaks/New Delhi: Sage.

Simmel, G. (1964) *The Sociology of Georg Simmel* (transl. from German, ed. and with an introduction by K. H. Wolff). New York: Free Press.

Snell-Hornby, M. (1988) *Translation Studies: An Integrated Approach*, Amsterdam/ Philadelphia: John Benjamins.

Snell-Hornby, M. (1991) Translation Studies – Art, Science or Utopia?, in K. M. van Leuven-Zwart & T. Naaijkens (eds), *Translation Studies: The State of the Art. Proceedings of the First James Holmes Symposium on Translation Studies*. Amsterdam: Rodopi, 13–23.

Solomou, C. (1993) Training of Professionals in a Multicultural Environment: The Victorian, Australia, Perspective, in C. Picken (ed.), *XIII FIT World Congress Proceedings*. London: Aslib.

Tannen, D. (1984) *Conversational Style. Analysing Talk Among Friends*. Norwood, NJ: Ablex Publishing Company.

Tannen, D. (1989) *Talking Voices: Repetition, Dialogue, and Imagery in Conversational Discourse* (Studies in Interactional Sociolinguistics 6). New York: Cambridge University Press.

Tebble, H. (1992) A Discourse Model for Dialogue Interpreting, in *AUSIT Proceedings of the First Practitioners' Seminar*. Canberra: Australian Institute of Interpreters and Translators Inc. National Office.

The Law Society of New South Wales (1996) *Lawyers, Interpreters, Translators: Lawyers Working with Interpreters & Translators in a Legal Environment*. Sydney: The Law Foundation of New South Wales, Australia.

Toury, G. (1980) *In Search of a Theory of Translation*. Tel-Aviv: Porter Institute.

Toury. G. (1995) *Descriptive Translation Studies – and Beyond.* Amsterdam/ Philadelphia: John Benjamins.

Vermeer, H. J. (1988) From Cicero to Modern Times – Rhetorics and Translation. *Translationstheorie – Grundlagen und Standorte,* Justa Holz-Mänttäri (ed.), *Studia Translatologica,* series A, vol. 1. Tampere, Finland: Instituts für Übersetzen und Dolmetschen Universität, 93–128.

Voloshinov, V. N. (1930 [1929]) *Marksizm i filosofija jazyka – Osnovnye problemy sotsiologicheskogo metoda v nauke o jazyke (Marxism and the Philosophy of Language – The Basic Questions concerning Sociologic Method within the Science of Language).* Leningrad; reprinted in the Netherlands 1972 by Koninklijke Drukkerij C. C. Callenbach n.v., Nijkerk.

Voloshinov, V. N. (1986, 1973 [1929]) *Marxism and the Philosophy of Language* (transl. by L. Matejka and I. R. Titunik). Cambridge, MA: Harvard University Press.

Wadensjö, C. (1987) Kontakt genom tolk. *Working Papers 1987:10.* Linköping: Department of Communication Studies.

Wadensjö, C. (1992) *Interpreting as Interaction: On Dialogue Interpreting in Immigration Hearings and Medical Encounters.* (Dissertation, Linköping Studies in Arts and Science, 83). Linköping: Department of Communication Studies.

Wadensjö, C. (1996) *The Bilingual Courtroom: Court Interpreters in the Judicial Process* (Berk-Seligson) and *Fundamentals of Court Interpretation: Theory, Policy and Practice* (González, Vásques & Mikkelson). Review article in *The Translator – Studies in Intercultural Communication,* 2:1, 104–9.

Wadensjö, C. (1997) Recycled Information as a Questioning Strategy: Pitfalls in Interpreter-Mediated Talk, in S. E. Carr, R. Roberts, A. Dufour and D. Steyn (eds), *The Critical Link: Interpreters in the Community.* Amsterdam/ Philadelphia: John Benjamins, 35–54.

Wertsch, J. (1991) *Voices of the Mind.* Cambridge, Mass.: Harvard University Press.

Wilss, W. (1981) Handlungstheoretische Aspekte des Übersetzungsprozesses, in W. Pöckl (ed.), *Europäische Mehrsprächigkeit: Festschrift zum 70. Geburtstag von Mario Wandruszka.* Tübingen: Niemeyer, 455–68.

Wodak, R. (1996) *Disorders of Discourse.* London/New York: Longman.

Index

Author Index

18203676R00185

Printed in Great Britain
by Amazon